I0831553

The Papers of Howard Washington Thurman

Volume 2

The Papers of Howard Washington Thurman

VOLUME 2

Christian, Who Calls Me Christian?
April 1936–August 1943

Senior Editor	Walter Earl Fluker
Managing Editor	Kai Jackson Issa
Associate Editors	Quinton H. Dixie, Peter Eisenstadt, Catherine Tumber
Advisory Editor	Alton B. Pollard III
Senior Advisory Editor	Luther E. Smith, Jr.

The University of South Carolina Press

Published by the University of South Carolina Press
Columbia, South Carolina 29208

www.sc.edu/uscpress

Manufactured in the United States of America

21 20 19 18 17 16 15 14 13 12   10 9 8 7 6 5 4 3 2

Library of Congress Cataloging-in-Publication Data

Thurman, Howard, 1900–1981.
The papers of Howard Washington Thurman / senior editor Walter Earl Fluker ; associate editor Catherine Tumber ... [et al.].
p. cm.
Includes bibliographical references and index.
ISBN 978-1-57003-804-4 (cloth : alk. paper)
1. Baptists—Doctrines. 2. Theology. 3. Thurman, Howard, 1900–1981—Correspondance. I. Fluker, Walter E., 1951– II. Tumber, Catherine. III. Title.
BX6495.T53A25 2009
280'.4092—dc22
[B]

2008052256

Vol. 2 ISBN: 978-1-61117-043-6

This volume would have not been possible without the generous financial and material support of the following contributors:

The Lilly Endowment Inc.
The Louisville Institute
The Henry Luce Foundation
The Pew Charitable Trusts
The National Historical Publications and Records Commission
The National Endowment for the Humanities

NHPRC
DOCUMENTING DEMOCRACY
National Historical Publications and Records Commission

Contents

Illustrations

Preface and Acknowledgments

"What then is the significance of Jesus? He places before the world an impelling dream, growing out of a fundamental interpretation of the meaning of life—human life—all life; a methodology by which that dream might be translated into living power—in a living community; he points out a dynamic available to men by which they may stand in the universe, and also a power by which they may be able to work out a wide series of anticipations of the new community without inner defilement and without self destruction."

Howard Thurman, "The Significance of Jesus VI,"
16 September 1937

The central underlying message of all of Thurman's writings, public addresses, and personal ruminations is the creation of "the new community" or, as he often called it, "a friendly world underneath friendly skies." The theme of citizenship for Thurman was at once the connective tissue that rendered concrete this glorious vision of community. Volume 2 of the Howard Washington Thurman Papers, titled *Christian, Who Calls Me Christian?* is a product of the collaboration of many institutions, organizations, and individuals who have made financial contributions, sacrifices, and offered support in making this "wide series of anticipations of the new community" possible. Since its inception the Thurman Papers Project has attracted financial support from a variety of sources. With its startup support and subsequent grants, the Lilly Endowment, Inc., has contributed the largest percentage of this support. Special thanks to Craig Dykstra, vice president of religion, and the Reverend Jean Smith, religion program officer, who rescued the work of the project when it appeared that our dream for this multivolume series would not come to pass. James Lewis of the Louisville Institute for the Study of Protestantism and American Culture deserves special recognition. In the fall of 1994, I received a grant from the Louisville Institute supporting a sabbatical leave to work exclusively on the project, and since the spring of 2005, I have been the recipient of a grant for the present work on the volumes. The Henry Luce Foundation, under the leadership of Michael Gilligan and with the assistance of program officer Lynn Szwaja, provided assistance for the period from 1998 to 2000 and most recently has funded both the editorial and public education components of our work for 2009–2011. During our early development we received a three-year grant from the Pew Charitable Trusts under the directorship of Joel Carpenter, and the grant was subsequently renewed. The National Historical Publications and Records Commission (NHPRC) awarded the project consecutive annual grants for the years 1994 to the present. Our NHPRC program officer, Timothy Connelly, has been a loyal supporter and adviser in every way. I am honored that in 2009 and 2010 the project received National Endowment for the Humanities (NEH) funding under its We the People initiative supporting projects that help advance knowledge of the principles that define America. Special thanks to Lydia Medici, our NEH program officer in the Division of Research, and Peter Scott our NEH grants administrator, for their support, encouragement, and enthusiasm for our work. Olive Thurman Wong, to whom this volume is dedicated, and her son, Anton Wong, have continued to provide counsel and much-needed spiritual support for the project. Olive represents what her father called "a fruitful tree by a well of water, whose branches hang over the fence." Her ardent prayers and clarity of vision are viable and consistent resources that refresh our memory and call us back to our purpose when our raison d'être and goals seem unclear and unrealizable. Thank you, Olive.

The project has had two institutional homes, which also served as Thurman's undergraduate and graduate alma maters. From 1991 through June 1998, the Thurman Papers Project was sponsored by Colgate Rochester Divinity School/Bexley Hall/Crozer Theological Seminary in Rochester, New York. This early period provided a rich historical heritage as a backdrop for our beginnings. Having access to the archives of the American Baptist Historical Society, a Howard Thurman Listening Room, and one of the largest theological libraries at the time, which held Thurman's official seminary transcripts, records, and other pertinent historical materials, made Colgate Rochester Divinity School an ideal setting for the first phase of our work.

From 1998 to 2010, the project was housed at Morehouse College, a fitting institutional home because, as with Rochester Theological Seminary, Thurman is one of Morehouse's most illustrious alumni. Morehouse established one of the first Howard Thurman listening rooms and has named one of its buildings in Thurman's honor. The remains of Thurman and his wife, Sue Bailey Thurman, are interred within the Howard Thurman International Memorial outside of the Martin Luther King Jr. International Chapel on the Morehouse campus.

Throughout our twelve-year tenure at Morehouse, the college continued to commit numerous resources to the project through in-kind support. The college generously provided office space for the Thurman Papers Project free of charge and committed its development and human resources offices to the project's needs. My special thanks to President Robert M. Franklin, former president Walter E. Massey, Willis B. Sheftall, John Williams, Philip Howard, Toni Mosley, Lawrence Edward Carter Sr., and Otis Moss Jr. for their support and faith in the dream of common ground that has inspired generations of Morehouse men and will continue through the ongoing education, research, publication, and training that this project has helped produce. While at Morehouse I offered an annual seminar on the religious thinking of Howard Thurman and a core leadership studies class on spirituality, ethics, and leadership for which the project provided resources and instruction. My recent publication, *Ethical Leadership: The Quest for Character, Civility and Community* (2008) utilizes Thurman and King as critical resources for the development of leaders for the twenty-first century.

In 2000–2001 Morehouse College granted me part-time leave to teach courses and to conduct research at Harvard Divinity School and the Center for Public Leadership at the John F. Kennedy School of Government. Special thanks are extended to Professor David Gergen at the Center for Public Leadership, where Thurman's insights provided a critical resource for my work on ethical leadership. To Preston Williams, whose invitation to come to the Divinity School and to the wonderful students whose genuine interest in Thurman made my stay all the more exciting and enriching, I extend my heartfelt thanks. In 2004–5 I was fortunate to serve as a visiting scholar at Princeton Theological Seminary, where I conducted research and editorial review of this volume. My special thanks to professors Peter J. Paris and Albert Raboteau, members of the project's advisory board, who provided occasional opportunities to meet and discuss my research and editing for this volume. From 2003 to 2006, I served as visiting scholar at the Columbia Theological Seminary in Decatur, Georgia. The seminary generously provided office space, library privileges, and a wonderful staff that made our many and sometimes seemingly impossible tasks possible. Special thanks to former president Laura S. Mendenhall; D. Cameron Murchison, dean of faculty and executive vice president; Tim Browning; Robert Thomson; Randall Tyndall; and Kim LeVert.

In the summer of 2010, during the production of this volume, the project moved again to Boston University School of Theology, upon my appointment to the university as the Martin Luther King, Jr. Professor of Ethical Leadership. Our present home is most appropriate, for Howard Thurman served as dean of Marsh Chapel at the university from 1953 to 1965, the first African American to occupy such a position at a major university. The project has always shared a special relationship to the Special Collections at Boston University, renamed in 2003 the Howard Gottlieb Archival Research Center to honor its founder. The late Howard Gottlieb and his entire staff provided assistance and granted access and authority to catalog the bulk of the then-yet-unorganized papers.

Vita Paladino, the present director of the Gottlieb Center, has been a fountain of inspiration and support. The late George Makechnie, founder of the Howard Thurman Center at Boston University and close friend to the Thurman family, was an advocate for our work within the university and beyond, always demanding that we not forget the dream of community. Kenneth Elmore, dean of students, and Katherine Kennedy, the present director of the Thurman Center, deserve mention for the excellent work on diversity and student programming that marks the life of the center. Our new home at the School of Theology owes a great debt to the generous hospitality and graciousness of spirit embodied in Dean Mary Elizabeth Moore, the faculty, the staff, and the students who are a part of a long and cherished tradition of producing prophetic leaders for the church and the world.

I am honored to acknowledge our editorial staff. Since 2003 managing editor Kai Jackson Issa has not only provided the bulk of the editorial work on the volumes but has managed the day-to-day operations of the project with astounding success. Kai recently published an award-winning children's book, *Howard Thurman's Great Hope*, and is presently writing a book on Sue Bailey Thurman. Project assistants Paula Birth and Jamison Collier have tirelessly assisted Kai and me with the operations of the project in too many ways to name. Associate editors Peter Eisenstadt and Quinton Dixie, who have been with the project since Rochester, have exhibited outstanding grace and acumen in the difficult task of determining selections and fit for the documents that make up this volume and that best tell the story of Howard Thurman during these years. Moreover their consummate professionalism and quest for historical accuracy have given a sense of coherence and intellectual sophistication that astute readers will appreciate and admire in their recent publication *Visions of a Better World: Howard Thurman's Pilgrimage to India and the Origins of African American Nonviolence*. Without the patience and dedication of these fine historians, the present volume would not have been possible.

Clarissa Myrick-Harris was responsible for preparing a large share of the correspondence in the volume and continues in her role as a consulting editor. Alma Jean Billingslea was responsible for much of the editorial work on Sue Bailey Thurman. Laura-Eve Moss lent her incredible expertise in documentary editing to the production of this volume. Luther Smith, my longtime colleague and friend, continues to serve as senior advisory editor of the volumes. Luther's seminal work, *Howard Thurman: The Mystic as Prophet*, remains the authoritative text on Thurman's thought.

Scores of individuals, institutions, and organizations contributed to this volume through granting permission to publish documents for which they held legal rights. Individuals include Bernice Mays Perkins, niece of Benjamin Elijah

Mays; Mrs. Allan A. Hunter; Nancy Kester-Neale; Earl P. Matthews; Sharon Watson Fluker; Peter J. Muste; Kenji Murase; and Audra Zellner. The institutions and organizations that have assisted us in obtaining permissions include the Moorland-Spingarn Research Center of Howard University; the A. Philip Randolph Institute; the Association for the Study of African American Life and History; the Smith College Archives; the YMCA of America; *Christian Century*; the Student Christian Movement of Canada; the United Methodist Church; the Urban League of Springfield, Illinois; Simon & Schuster; the National Baptist Convention; Pendle Hill; Eden Theological Seminary; the Mary McLeod Bethune Foundation; Colby Sawyer College; the University of Chicago Press; Harold Ober Associates; Florida Memorial University; Case Western Reserve University; Fellowship Farm; Fellowship of Reconciliation; and Garrett-Evangelical Theological Seminary.

A host of others have made invaluable contributions along the way. Much of the early work on volume 2 is a product of the research and editorial acumen of Catherine Tumber, the first associate editor of the project, who anchored our work in Rochester. Catherine and I also coedited a commercial trade volume, *A Strange Freedom: The Best of Howard Thurman on Religious Experience and Public Life*, published in July 1998. Martin E. Marty, renowned historian of American religion, wrote the foreword.

Mentors and friends such as Clayborne Carson, James Earl Massey, Edward Kaplan, Dwight Hopkins, James H. Cone, Tavis Smiley, Barbara Holmes, and Cornel West at various stages of the development of the project found ways to encourage our work. Others who have worked with project over time include Alton Pollard and Michael Joseph Brown. I deeply appreciate all of the dedication and hard work of our research associates Tami Groves and Michelle Meggs for their careful and scrupulous pursuit of excellence and eye for detail. I extend special thanks to my former core staff at the Leadership Center at Morehouse College, who created the space and opportunity for my work with the project: Melvinia Turner King, Geri Oladuwa, LaKetha Hudson, Carter Savage, and Samantha Stewart.

Finally, I would like to thank my family. My wife, Sharon Watson Fluker, and our two sons, Clinton Rahman and Hampton Sterling, whose love and support make it possible to pursue my dreams.

Walter Earl Fluker, Senior Editor

List of Abbreviations

The following abbreviations describe original documents, and the acronyms describe the locations of documents or are organizations.

Collections and Repositories

BTP-GEU — Bailey-Thurman Family Papers, Emory University Special Collections, Atlanta
DAF-GAS — Deceased Alumni Files, Spelman College, Atlanta
MWJ-DHU-MS — Howard University Archives, Mooreland-Spingarn Research Center, Washington, D.C.
HTC-MBU — Howard Thurman Collection, Boston University, Boston
HTPP — Howard Thurman Papers Project, Boston University School of Theology, Boston
JLH-GAU — John and Lugenia Hope Collection, Woodruff Library, Atlanta University Center, Atlanta
RB-NN-SC — Ralph Bunche Papers, Schomburg Center for Research on Black Culture, New York Public Library, New York
RJ-PHC — Rufus Jones Collection, Haverford College, Haverford, Pennsylvania
LAF-OO — Student Leadership Alumni Files, Oberlin College, Oberlin, Ohio
WEBD-MU — W. E. B. Du Bois Collection, University of Massachusetts, Amherst

Abbreviations Used in Source Notes

Format

A Autograph (manuscript in author's hand)
H Handwritten (manuscript in hand other than author's)
P Printed
T Typed

Type

At Audio tape
D Document
Fm Form
L Letter or memo
Ph Photo
W Wire or telegram

Version

c Copy (carbon)
d Draft
f Fragment

Signature

I Initialed
S Signed
Sr Signed with representation of author

Howard Thurman in a casual moment. Courtesy of the Thurman Family and Arleigh Prelow/Howard Thurman Film Project.

Biographical Essay

> Among the many gifts of the spirit I was bringing back with me was the "feel" of a moment of vision standing in Khyber Pass looking down into Afghanistan as the slow camel train ambled by en route to India[1]—it was there that I knew a way must be found to answer the persistent query of the Indian students about Christianity and the color bar.[2]

Howard Thurman remembered his vision of community at the Khyber Pass as a crucial personal impetus and a source of sustained vision for his subsequent career. In many ways his experience at Khyber Pass was a distillation of the complex questions of race, religion, and culture that he faced on his historic "Pilgrimage of Friendship" to India, Burma, and Ceylon from October 1935 through March 1936. The pilgrimage was critical for Thurman, because it provided him with concrete instances, in a global setting, that forced him to come to terms with his own commitment to the Christian faith in light of the problem of racial inequality and oppression in the United States. This introspection propelled him to experiment further with his developing sense of the power of religious experience to create human community among diverse ethnicities, religions, and cultures.

Thurman remained forever haunted by his encounter with a Ceylonese lawyer he met early on in the pilgrimage, who told him that given the monumental crimes and hypocrisy of American Christianity toward dark-skinned peoples, any black man who came to Asia preaching Christianity was "either a fool or a dupe." In some ways Thurman spent the rest of his career providing a full answer to this charge. His first response was to make a critical distinction between Christianity and "the religion of Jesus," placing himself firmly in the position of the latter. As he wrote in 1937, his ministry was an exploration of "the problems that arise in the experience of people who attempt to be Christian in a society that is essentially un-Christian."[3] Such a radical reenvisioning required placing one's life, and the relation of one's life to the broader society, under the strictest divine scrutiny. Thurman would grow more assertive in his contention that most people who professed to be Christians were nothing of the sort and had long since made their peace with evil, tolerating it in their daily lives, their communities, and their governments. In "Christian, Who Calls Me Christian?" a talk delivered before a large and rapt audience at Miami University in Oxford, Ohio, at the end of 1937, Thurman set out a message he imparted again and again during these years: followers of the religion of Jesus were those who were willing to exercise to the limit of their "power, moral suasion upon men in the interest of the redemption of themselves and of society," and who could "against the darkness of the age . . . see the illumined finger of God guiding [them] in the way that [they] should go" ("Christian, Who Calls Me Christian," published in the present volume). The rest were mere pretenders, of whom it might be asked, "Christian, who calls me Christian?" Thurman set a stern standard, one that required a radical transformation of American society, a refashioning of Christianity, and a critical examination of his relation to both. It was one he explored with himself and with others through the remainder of his life.

This second volume of *The Papers of Howard Washington Thurman* spans the spring of 1936, upon his return to the United States from India and South Asia, through to the fall of 1943, just before he begins to contemplate his participation in what would become one of the nation's boldest religious experiments yet—the formation of an interracial, interfaith church. Throughout these years the interrelated themes of personal religious experience, the critical engagement with the theocentric "religion of Jesus" (as opposed to Christocentric "religion about Jesus"), and its implications for social and political reform are prominent concerns in the deepening of his theological perspective, pastoral ministry, and prophetic witness. These cannot be separated from Thurman's personal quest for spiritual fulfillment and the attendant restlessness that he experienced upon his return to Howard University from the Indian pilgrimage. This period marks a change in his teaching and ministry and highlights a deeper issue for Thurman's unfolding vision of diversity and inclusiveness that reached beyond traditional conceptions of the church and democratic culture.

THURMAN'S THEOLOGICAL CONTEXT: AMERICAN RELIGIOUS LIBERALISM, MYSTICISM, AND THE BLACK CHURCH TRADITION

In 1981, in one of the first significant works of scholarship on Thurman, Luther E. Smith identified Thurman's intellectual sources within the stream of American religious liberalism.[4] A number of dissertations, essays, and books have followed Smith's influential work in viewing Thurman as a product of early-twentieth-century Protestant modernism, with its emphasis on historical interpretation of sacred text, critical attitudes toward traditional dogma, and engagement with social reform.[5]

Thurman's embrace of modernism was very much of his own fashioning. Alton Pollard observes that though Thurman embraced the modernistic claims of the liberal school, he took exception to its fascination with the inherent notions of progress and positivism and, with a few exceptions, its slighting of the question of race as a determinant in theological and ethical discourse and practice.[6] Gary Dorrien identifies Thurman as a proponent of a "black social gospel" that placed emphasis on institution building and social justice preaching rather than purely academic concerns. To Thurman and his peers in the movement (individuals such as Benjamin Mays, William Stuart Nelson, and Mordecai Wyatt Johnson), Dorrien writes, "the social gospel movement had barely begun; what was needed was an American Christianity that took seriously its own best preaching and ethics on behalf of equal opportunity, racial integration and peace. . . . The most promising religious thinker among them, Thurman, gave up his academic career to launch a model ministry of inclusion. He called American Christianity to its best religious vision and in several ways exemplified it."[7]

The perspective offered here and in subsequent volumes provides a fuller depiction of Thurman's intellectual life and his practical concerns surrounding the institutional arrangements that conspired against equality and the dignity of the individual. Thurman's theological and ethical method is pragmatist in orientation, building on his early readings of John Dewey and William James. His essentialist rendering of self, God, and history, however, becomes problematic when tested against postmodernist readings.[8] For Thurman, God is at work in the complex processes of history and human agency. The human project, therefore, is the quest for meaning, understanding, and purpose in the midst of tragic existence—and it is this human quest that marks the primal center of innocence and becoming. The character of the moral struggle for Thurman is shaped by the frustration experienced when the ends one seeks to fulfill are limited by ambiguity, contingency, difference, and internal or external constraints. Frustration, *moral angst*, is always tied to private and personal outreach; but when private and personal ends are extended beyond self, the moral struggle ensues. For Thurman there is no escape from the vicissitudes of history and the moral struggle that must be worked out in public life.[9]

A key that helps us to gain access to Thurman's approach is the African American genius of appropriation and improvisation of mood, which is closely related to what Theophus Smith calls "conjuring culture," the imaginative art of taking that which is at hand, that which experience gives us, and refashioning it into creative tools. It is a type of "spiritual bricolage," the process of inclusion, exclusion, and reconfiguration of experience through an internal locus that seeks vindication and fulfillment in public interaction and citizenship rights.[10] Unlike many of his correspondents who appear in this volume, such as John Nevin Sayre, Edgar S. Brightman, A. J. Muste, and other proponents of American theological liberalism, Thurman's theological vision is forged on the borderlands between American liberal theology, mystical experience, and the black Christian tradition of protest, racial uplift, and social advancement of the race.

This alchemy of traditions, especially his usages of mystical religious experience, allowed Thurman to create an "autonomous third zone" where cultures could meet and interact. This feat of "straddling" diverse worlds may be Thurman's most distinctive contribution to American theological discourse as will be illustrated in this and subsequent volumes.[11]

A consistent theme in Thurman's theological construction is the primacy of the individual's religious experience and the mystical distinction between the "inner" and "outer." Thurman defined religious experience, most basically, as "the conscious and direct exposure of the individual to God."[12] He viewed this encounter as a cooperative affair and asserted that "religious experience in its profoundest dimension is the finding of man by God and the finding of God by man."[13] Thurman also believed that religious experience involved a volitional element, by which the self actively and consciously participates.[14] Through these encounters an individual experiences the love of God, which becomes the basis for each person's relating to others. As Thurman concluded, what a person learns through "his religious experience he must define in community."[15] At stake for Thurman in his construal of agency was how the deep issues of the inner life might be translated into effective and transformative action in the world. The resolution of this tension between "the inner life and world-mindedness," as he later called it, had vast implications for traditional ways of understanding the nature and role of the church.[16] As early as 1927, in his published writings and correspondence to his mentor, Mordecai Wyatt Johnson, Thurman struggled with the need to reconcile his personal need for spiritual nourishment with the overwhelming structural issues of society in which he was engaged:

> I believe with all my heart that our task is two-fold—seek how we may release to the full our greatest spiritual powers that there may be such a grand swell of spiritual energy that existing systems will be upset from sheer dynamic—and make whatever temporary adjustments as may prove helpful in relieving intolerable situations until there is genuine uprooting. . . .
>
> The second thing that is giving me much thought is the question of church membership. This may be a very premature judgment but it is a fact of my thinking and reflection just now: There seems to be something about joining a church which deprives the individual of the keen obligation to be exercised increasingly about being Christian. Those in my church who seem so to be are those who apparently have transcended the church. Perhaps Jesus was wisest when he rested his case with the "contagious spirit" rather than a scheme or plan of salvation.[17]

After his sabbatical with Rufus Jones in 1929, where he studied mystical traditions ranging from St. Francis of Assisi to Meister Eckhart to Madame Guyon, this quest for inner harmony and the larger quest for social justice became driving subjects of concern in his intellectual and pastoral pursuits.[18] The correspondence, lectures, and writings made available in this volume demonstrate a deeper intellectual inquiry than previously evinced by Thurman and reflect a personal search for what Jones called "the conjunct life," a personal devotion to the religious meaning and authenticity and the concomitant need for social transformation.[19]

Although Thurman was not a religious thinker whose output is characterized by sharp changes of direction or dramatic shifts—there is instead a constant focus on a few themes that deepens over time—the years covered in this volume form a distinct phase in his thought and ministry. This was an intensely political time, at home and abroad.

As the period covered in this volume opens, it is dominated by the economic dislocations of the Depression, the widespread sense that capitalism was failing, and the resultant turning to alternatives, primarily socialism or communism, that seemed to hold out the promise of greater stability and social equality. And the final years of this volume are enveloped by World War II and its countless ramifications for Thurman and almost everyone he knew. The impact of these national and international events filtered in myriad ways into Thurman's thinking and speaking.

For all that, the events of the time, even in the 1930s and 1940s, generally remained a backdrop to Thurman's religious thinking, forming an essential context without being the direct object of his discourse. It is often not easy to be specific about his political commitments, which he spoke about infrequently. Still there is much evidence of his sympathy for moderate socialism, of the sort advocated by the Socialist Party led by Norman Thomas, and he had a genuine interest in many currents of progressive economic thinking. If there is one central tenet to his social thinking, it was his unflinching commitment to pacifism, the belief that violence in any form was illegitimate and that nonviolence was a constructive method of radical social change. Thurman's commitment to pacifism was surely tested by the events of the late 1930s and early 1940s, though in the end, in many ways, it was only strengthened.

One of the common threads that unites many of Thurman's writings during this period is his continuing effort to come to terms with the legacy and meaning of his time in India and South Asia; and of course with his general political views came his own political situation and the situation of black people in America. In his politics as in his religious thinking, Thurman eschewed abstractions, and he viewed the world from the vantage point of his own situation (and insisted that everyone else also start from their own perspective and extrapolate outward). As he wrote a correspondent in 1937, "my point of interest is religion interpreted against the background of my own life and the life of my group in America. I am very much interested in some of the problems that arise in the experience of people who attempt to be Christian in a society that is essentially un-Christian."[20] Thurman was cautiously optimistic about the prospects for an improvement in the status of American blacks. Jim Crow remained a daily reality for him and for millions of others; outrages continued to make headlines, and Thurman had no illusions about the size and scope of the obstacles that stood in the way of black equality. Still, like many black intellectuals of the time, he looked at the task with a guarded hope. When Thurman, in February 1936, just before the scope of this volume opens, was asked by Mahatma Gandhi, in their famous meeting, "Is the prejudice against colour growing or dying out?" his response was mixed. "It is difficult to say because in one place things look much improved, whilst in another the outlook is still dark." He pointed to a new positive attitude he felt among college students, including southern whites, demanding an end to the racial status quo of their elders. However, he added, "the economic question is acute everywhere, and in many of the industrial centres in Middle West the prejudice against the Negro shows itself in its ugliest form."[21] But on the whole Thurman was encouraged by the trends he saw at home, where racial injustice was increasingly at the center of the agenda of Christian and progressive organizations, labor unions, and even some politicians, and he was convinced that, with enough prodding, Americans could be convinced to live up to the democratic ideals they sometimes so glibly professed.

The most basic requirement for democracy was real citizenship, and for Thurman, speaking in 1940 in a talk titled "A 'Native Son' Speaks," the fundamental reality of American life was "that generally speaking the Negro is not a citizen. He is several steps removed from active participation in those social, economic, political arrangements by which our common body politic is controlled."

Citizenship for Thurman was always more about responsibilities than privileges, and the deepest tragedy of the exclusion of blacks from citizenship was that "when responsibility is withdrawn from the individual or not permitted him, then democracy is imperiled. . . . Responsibility, a free initiative, the sense of the future, these are the things that make for civic character, that make real citizens. These are denied the Negro." Citizenship for Thurman was a religious as well as a civic quality. He had already argued in his 1935 article "Good News for the Underprivileged" that the essential quality of the religion of Jesus was that it was created in a conquered province harshly ruled by their Roman overlords and was a religion created by and for colonized and oppressed noncitizens.[22] And that without real citizenship, without full membership in the "common body politic," individuals will always find partial and achingly incomplete the answers religion has to offer.

But one of the lessons Thurman learned from Gandhi and his time in India was that citizenship would have to be wrested from those who refuse its extension and that, of necessity, this would have to be outside regular politics. Thurman's distinctive religious thought of this time can be found in many of the letters and writings; probably the two most important are "The Significance of Jesus" (1937) and "Mysticism and Social Change" (1939). They were published obscurely at the time and are being reprinted for the first time in the current volume. "The Significance of Jesus," six lectures delivered in Ontario in September 1937 for the Student Christian Movement of Canada, marks a refinement in Thurman's religious and theological evolution. It was his longest and most sustained literary effort to date—his first book-length exposition of his religious ideas. Although drawing on his earlier work, it is very much a work of its time in its emphasis on economic inequality, condemnation of private property, and on small dedicated groups of like-minded persons committed to nonviolent social transformation. These ideas are developed further in "Mysticism and Social Change," four lectures delivered at Eden Seminary in St. Louis in 1939, in which the mystic's experience of total, absolute, and undifferentiated unity becomes the model for a social and political world that would tolerate no artificial distinctions or barriers between peoples, ethnicities, or nations. At stake for Thurman is the inherent worth of the individual, which is affirmed in religious experience, and its significant implications for the freedom and equality of the individual within democratic society. In later works this theme becomes even more prominent and focused. In the final lecture, Thurman borrows from Jones's notion of "affirmation mystics," those "who are concerned with working out in a social frame of reference the realism of their mystic experience."[23] However, Thurman places the obligations of affirmation mystics to seek social justice in a socialist context that is in keeping with his other writings on social justice in the late 1930s. People face a "life and death struggle for bare security" in large part because "a few persons have possession of the means of production and are in a position to control for their own interests and the perpetuation of their kind, while denying personhood for the rest of humanity."[24]

There were also more practical results, for both Howard and Sue Bailey Thurman, of their time in India and South Asia. Both tried to find some way to extend the experience for themselves and others. The time in Asia had been called by the World Student Christian Federation a "pilgrimage of friendship," and the Thurmans made friends with people from all walks of life, in the hope that their time in India might help initiate an enduring process of cultural exchange. Talks about sending black students and teachers to Asia started when the Thurmans were still there. Thurman himself was very interested in returning, writing P. O. Phillip, on the faculty of Union Christian College in Alwaye (the only Christian college in India founded by native rather than Western Christian denominations), that "I shall get a sabbatical leave in two or three years, and it might be possible for me to consider spending part of it there as a guest lecturer." However, this did not happen, nor did Thurman's plans for his friend and protégé, Melvin Watson, to go to Alwaye.[25]

But if the press of Thurman's schedule in the end interfered with his plans to establish an ongoing connection to India, Sue Bailey Thurman soon made this her project, and in the years between her return from India and the outbreak of World War II in 1939, she put much of her plentiful energy into raising money to send black female students to India. This work was largely accomplished by Sue as the creator and chief fund-raiser for the Juliette Derricotte Memorial Scholarship Fund, named after the abundantly talented YWCA national secretary and college administrator who in 1928 traveled to India as a delegate to the International Student Christian Conference and who died in a traffic accident in 1931 after being refused admittance to a nearby white hospital. She had been a close friend of both the Thurmans (Howard delivered her eulogy), who were not yet married at the time of her death.[26] Sue Bailey Thurman thought that there was an urgent need for better and enhanced knowledge between Indians and African Americans, in part because of the deliberate distortions and stereotyping in the Indian press, which reduced the few American blacks that received any press attention, such as Joe Louis, to comic figures. She felt this treatment was deliberate, an effort to treat persons of color with maximum disrespect, and wrote a few months after her return to the United States that American Negroes and Indians alike were victims "of the most careful, astute, invidious systems of modern propaganda that modern imperialism has yet perfected." Despite this, the hunger of Indian students for authentic knowledge of American blacks was great, and she wrote that through South Asia, students "wanted to know every possible thing relating to the Negro's life and experience in the New World." In all, "it is a sincere belief, held by many in India, that furthering the intercourse of the ancient racial culture of Negroes and Indians will yield increasing benefits, through their mutual respect and esteem."[27]

Shortly after she returned to the United States, Mrs. Thurman started to give a series of lectures/recitals/exhibits titled "The Beauties of Indian Civilization."[28] She would mount the stage in a sari (sometimes accompanied by her sari-clad daughter, Olive). Sue would relate her impressions of India, play some Indian songs and music on native instruments, and display some of the artifacts she had collected, including hand carvings in exotic woods, ivory, and ebony, exquisite rugs and tapestries, along with her greatest treasure, a swatch of cloth handwoven by Gandhi.[29] By May 1937 she had raised enough money to send the first two recipients, Marion Benfield Martin from Howard University and Anna Brown from Oberlin College, to study in India, with Martin being the recipient

Thurman with Howard University students. Courtesy of the Thurman Family and Arleigh Prelow/Howard Thurman Film Project.

of funding for a full academic year of study. By the following year she had given more than thirty lectures from Tulsa to Boston and raised enough to send two more students. Margaret Bush and Elizabeth McCree were the scholarship recipients in 1939.[30] If the outbreak of World War II brought the scholarship program to a close—Misses Bush and McCree had some exciting stories to tell of navigating naval minefields in Singapore harbor in early 1940—Sue Bailey Thurman was proud to have developed one of the very first study abroad programs for African Americans.[31]

The Capstone of Negro Education: Thurman's Years at Howard University

A review of Thurman's journey to this period of transition is important because in many ways Howard University had afforded him the unique opportunity to test his earlier ideas in the context of one of the most creative experiments in American education. When Mordecai Wyatt Johnson became the first African American president of Howard University in 1926, among the first things he did was to invite Thurman to join the Department of Religion.[32] This did not happen, for a number of reasons, until the fall of 1932. But long before he came to Washington, Thurman had been eager to join the faculty at Howard. Among the reasons for leaving Morehouse and Spelman colleges was his deteriorating relationship with Spelman's president, Florence Read, and his interest in a change of scene after the death of his first wife, Katie Kelley Thurman. Few black academics of the era would have resisted a call to Howard. Howard was more visible, cosmopolitan, and wealthier than all the other black schools, and the only true university. Its unique status was a product of Howard's position as the only black institution of higher education chartered by and supported by the federal government. Johnson proved to be a very able administrator and displayed great talent as a fund-raiser. During his thirty-four years as college president, the annual congressional appropriation increased from $218,000 in 1926 to $7.1 million in 1960, in addition to substantial federal support for building and capital expenditures.[33]

There was another reason why Thurman was no doubt eager to go to Howard, beyond the prospect of a slightly higher salary, which was a mere $3,500 when he was hired in 1932.[34] He would be joining a faculty that had probably the greatest concentration of leading African American intellectuals at any one institution of higher learning at any time before or since. This was a reflection of both the prestige and financial clout of Howard and the lack of options for talented black academics, who through the end of World War II were unable to obtain positions at mainstream universities. Indeed when Thurman became dean of chapel and professor of spiritual resources and disciplines at Boston University in 1953, he was among the first prominent black academics to obtain a permanent academic position outside the network of black colleges.

For all these reasons, Howard University was able to attract the cream of the crop of that era's black intellectual talent, from the social sciences (political scientist Ralph Bunche, sociologist E. Franklin Frazier, and economist Abram Harris Jr.), philosopher Alain Locke, poet Sterling Brown, historian Rayford Logan, and biologist Earnest E. Just, physician Charles Drew, and in the law school Charles Houston, the architect of the NAACP legal strategy that culminated in the 1954 U.S. Supreme Court decision in *Brown* v. *Board of Education*.[35]

While Thurman shared in the general intellectual excitement at Howard and benefitted from the proximity of great scholars, the School of Religion he joined was the ugly duckling among the attractive swans of Howard's graduate programs. And this was so despite the fact that, since its founding in 1867, almost all of the presidents of Howard University had been ministers (including Johnson). Of all the professional schools at Howard, the School of Religion was the one with the least prestige, the least secure funding, and least distinguished faculty—in all, Howard's "poor cousin," in the words of historian Rayford Logan.[36] Indeed it was only in 1932, the year Thurman arrived, that the former theological department had been upgraded to a formal School of Religion with ambitious plans for its improvement, among them a more distinguished faculty, higher entrance requirements for students, and a better physical plant.

The Immaculate Conception in "Living Madonna in Art" series, Rankin Chapel, Howard University, 1939. Courtesy of the Moorland-Spingarn Research Center, Howard University Archives.

The School of Religion was in many ways apart from the rest of the university, housed in the mid-1930s in "a dilapidated old frame house, in need of paint, across the street from the main campus."[37] It was separate in other ways as well. It was the only part of the university that did not receive financial support from the federal government because of its overt religious purpose as a school for ministerial training. Presbyterians and Congregationalists had somewhat acrimoniously vied to supply funding for the Theological Department, with the Congregationalists (via the Congregationalist American Missionary Association) coming out on top.[38] But the funding stream, which was never that large, was beginning to dry up by the 1920s, and the theological department was unable to attract substantial amounts of private funding.[39] In part because of the School of Religion's inability to receive federal funding, salaries were lower there compared to positions elsewhere in the university.[40] The program limped along with small classes, only twenty-seven students in 1934 and fifty-eight graduates between 1927 and 1935.[41]

Despite these many obstacles, there was a concerted effort to improve the School of Religion in the 1930s. Bringing Thurman on board in 1932 was part of

Johnson's plans. The chief architect of the transformation was Benjamin Elijah Mays, who became dean of the School of Religion in 1934. Among his reasons for accepting the position at Howard, Mays "felt the challenge to make the School of Religion outstanding, to lift it, if possible, from its stepchild role to a place of respectability in the institution."[42] Mays had some success in his quest. By 1936 all enrolled students in the School of Religion were college graduates, ending undergraduate enrollment in the graduate school, and in 1939 the Howard University School of Religion was formally accredited by the American Association of Theological Schools.[43] That same year the School of Religion moved into more commodious quarters at the former Carnegie Library on campus and acquired thirty-nine thousand volumes from the library of the former Auburn Theological Seminary in New York State.

Thurman was a key part of the effort to revive the School of Religion. In his autobiography James Farmer describes the shock that many students, accustomed to a more traditional theology, experienced on arriving at Howard. Many left, and some of those who stayed did so while fervently praying for the lost souls of their instructors.[44] The newly named "School of Religion" reflected an ongoing effort, at Howard and elsewhere in schools of Christian higher education in the 1930s, away from an identification with Christian theology to a more nondenominational and interreligious curriculum.[45] The courses Thurman taught at Howard reflected the range of his religious interests. Although one of Thurman's titles at Howard was professor of Christian theology, he rarely, if ever, taught a course specifically on Christian theology. (In 1939 he proposed to Johnson that his title be changed to professor of the history and philosophy of religion, a change that evidently was never made.)[46] Among the courses Thurman taught with some regularity during his years at Howard (the records are incomplete) are Introduction to the Study of Religion (taught six times), The History of Religions (four), Introduction to the Psychology of Religion (three), and Modern Trends in World Religions (four). He also frequently offered a class on the History of Mysticism (five) and sometimes offered a special seminar on Meister Eckhart and Rufus Jones (two).[47]

Thurman was, by all accounts, a remarkable teacher. He used his class sessions not to expound or lecture but to push his students to get in touch with their deepest thoughts and to get to the roots of their own religious commitments. And he encouraged his students to approach social questions from the basis of their own private religious experience. His student James Farmer offers a memorable portrait of Thurman as a teacher at Howard in the late 1930s:

> When this extraordinary man walked into social ethics class, a silence born of awe reigned. It always seemed as if we had dragged him away from private meditation. He would look over the heads of those in class, into space, for

what seemed minutes. Then he would open up, in his slow, laborious manner, with a provocative thesis, such as "When you young preachers fulminate about what you should do in any given situation, remember one thing: we are what we do—in spite of reservations."

He would wait for a response. My hand was usually up first with a question: "Dr. Thurman, are you saying that if a soldier kills the enemy, he is a murderer, or at least a killer? Or if one accepts an assigned status of inferiority—let us say, sits in the balcony of a Jim Crow theater—he *is* inferior?"

Thurman would say, "Ah," and recognize one of the several hands now held aloft.

We would leave the class with no answers, but many intriguing questions that had not occurred to us before. It was Thurman's belief that answers must come from within, from the bit of God in each of us.[48]

Thurman's public speaking skills were even more important in his other main responsibility at Howard, conducting and supervising services at Rankin Chapel. In October 1932 he was appointed chairman of the University-Wide Committee on Religious Life, with responsibilities for the weekly worship at the chapel and what Mordecai Wyatt Johnson called the "the general supervision of the religious life of the University Community."[49] In April 1936, while he was returning from India, Thurman was named dean of chapel. This position was a recent innovation in academic life, getting its start only in 1928, when both Princeton and the University of Chicago appointed deans of chapel. Thurman was a good friend of the University of Chicago's dean of chapel, Charles W. Gilkey, who like Thurman was a prominent exponent of Protestant modernism. Thurman's familiarity with Gilkey's deanship at Chicago may have inspired an effort to create a similar institution at Howard.[50]

The precise responsibilities of the dean of chapel were left somewhat open by Johnson and depended on a charismatic figure such as Thurman to take a full measure of the possibilities the position offered. Writing to Johnson in 1937, he argued that "we must realize that we are pioneering in this field and there are no precedents established" and further noted that at Princeton and the University of Chicago "the functional significance of the job is very loosely defined."[51] For Thurman part of the attraction of the position was that it enabled him to develop a connection to the university as a whole, free of the aegis of the School of Religion. As he wrote to Johnson in 1939, "there are certain very definite limitations placed upon my work psychologically if at every point it must be identified with the School of Religion. After all, the School of Religion is one of the nine colleges of the University and my work as Dean of the Chapel involves increasingly all of the aspects of the total University life." Thurman wanted his role as dean of chapel to be separate from the School of Religion (and the

Performers in "Living Madonna in Art" series, Rankin Chapel, Howard University, 1939. Courtesy of the Thurman Family and Arleigh Prelow/Howard Thurman Film Project.

perception of conventional religiosity), and at the same time he wanted to assert his equal status with Howard's other deans, including the dean of the School of Religion.[52]

The position of dean of chapel was an effort to give more visibility to the university chaplaincy at a time when it was undergoing rapid change at Howard and elsewhere. By 1920 mandatory chapel attendance, more or less universal at most colleges at the turn of the twentieth century, was under serious attack, a persistent bone of contention between student groups and college administrators. By 1940 mandatory chapel service had been abolished at Yale, the University of

Chicago, Brown, Dartmouth, and other prominent institutions, and the practice was soon retained at only a minority of colleges.[53] Black colleges, most of them small and many of them relying on denominational funding, tended to lag behind white colleges in the elimination of compulsory chapel. Howard was the most prominent exception:[54] compulsory chapel had been abolished there in 1922, following student protests, under the administration of the school's last white president, J. Stanley Durkee.[55]

When mandatory chapel services ended at Howard, as in other colleges, attendance at chapel plummeted. Benjamin Mays in 1940 observed that the services at Howard "are among the best to be found anywhere in the country"; they had superb music and were well planned and relatively short (no more than ninety minutes). He estimated that about 500 people attended service on the average Sunday, and less than half of those were students from Howard, the remainder being faculty and people from the community; no more than 15 percent of the approximately 1,800 students at Howard regularly attended services.[56]

Within the constraints of the position at the chapel, Thurman was very successful in achieving his goal of innovative services that appealed to a variety of audiences. The careful attention to the worship services at Howard is one of the areas where Thurman's experimentation with religious experience joined his critique of Protestant modernism to the deep call to mystical encounter. Thurman had long felt constrained by traditional Protestant religious services, with their didacticism fostering the illusion that the heart of religion could be reached through intellectual discussion rather than a more direct personal religious experience. Immediately upon his return to the United States, he started to offer alternative forms of worship alongside more conventional services. Thurman tried to incorporate elements from South Asian religions, especially Hinduism, into some of his worship services. These new features included meditation and aspects of the arts and dance, such as dramatic presentations of T. S. Eliot's *Murder in the Cathedral* or readings from Kahlil Gibran's *The Prophet*.[57] These and related services used art and dance as a way of stimulating spiritual sentiments and reflections across usual divides. Another series of services consisted of Thurman reading selections from the Bible to a low organ accompaniment, ending with the congregation sitting in silence for five minutes of meditation.

Thurman was also very interested in seeing whether the aesthetic dimension of worship could provide a spiritual unity among diverse perspectives and backgrounds that was more influential than religious, racial, and cultural divisions. In his "Living Madonna," Thurman, with the help of students, re-created tableaus of representations of the Madonna and Child by famous Renaissance and Baroque artists such as Raphael and Andrea del Sarto, accompanied by settings of the "Ave Maria." This became a feature of the Christmas season at

The Madonna Enthroned in "Living Madonna in Art" Series, Rankin Chapel, Howard University, 1939. Courtesy of the Moorland-Spingarn Research Center Howard University Archives.

Rankin Chapel for Thurman's remaining years at Howard. In his most daring and controversial effort at expanding the meaning of worship services, he introduced modern dance. In the 1930s and 1940s, modern dance often dealt with mythological and religious imagery, and Thurman and the dancer constructed a program around the themes "Praise—Thanksgiving—Contrition—Faith." While Thurman's announcement of the dance service raised both eyebrows and prurient comments—Thurman insisted the dancer cover her leotard with a flowing robe—the service was evidently a success. He wrote later that the dancer, a white Roman Catholic, created a performance that "was as if a wall was removed and we became one people, feeling one thing. It was magnificent."[58]

These efforts in creating new forms of worship provided Thurman with evidence "that a way could be found to unite people of great ideological and religious diversity through experiences which were even more compelling than the concepts that separated and divided." Although he allowed "that the environment was somewhat controlled and to that extent artificial," nonetheless, "the faith in the creative possibilities of such experience could not be devalued."[59] For

Thurman creating a new, inclusive type of religious service involved far more than just inviting people of different religious and racial backgrounds; rather it involved a radical rethinking and reconceptualizing of the meaning of religious worship. If this were done properly, he felt it could be a pathway to the transformation of society.

Thurman's duties as dean of chapel also included a more general concern with the religious welfare of the Howard campus. His role was that of counselor, host, and spiritual adviser to the entire Howard community. He also organized student affinity and discussion groups that met at the chapel. These included a group on religion, one on interpersonal relationships, a *Nation* magazine study group, a poetry group, and community sings, among others. In the fall of 1939, for instance, Thurman's duties as dean of chapel included five appearances as preacher or reader in the chapel; at least seven "at homes" he hosted with Sue Bailey Thurman when he invited Howard students to visit them for informal discussions; three "twilight hour" worship services that involved special music and art; three special functions hosting visiting preachers; and three evenings hosting a supper club connected to the chapel.[60]

One of Thurman's main duties at Rankin Chapel was the preparation of the preaching schedule, which included both his own sermons and arranging for the appearance of appropriate guest preachers. Thurman seems to have preached about a quarter of the sermons at Rankin Chapel. In 1937–38, for example, he preached four of twenty-seven sermons and participated in several others. Johnson also preached four. In Thurman's last year as dean of chapel, 1943–44, he formally preached six times in twenty-three weeks and led three music services.[61] Because he so frequently preached elsewhere, Thurman did not preach extended sermon series, as he did later at the Fellowship Church and at Boston University.

Thurman's speaking style as a preacher was unique. He was at a great remove from the steady rhythmic cadence that characterized the preaching style often identified with the black church. To some extent he modeled his preaching style after that of Johnson, who was a noted orator but was more of a traditional speaker, modulating his voice, making dramatic emphases.[62] Thurman's oratory was of another kind—long pauses, lofty language (though he never used his erudition to impress or intimidate his audience), all delivered in precise, nonidiomatic English in his sonorous, deep speaking voice. His pace was slow and careful, his choice of topics often abstract (he rarely spoke on traditional Christian theological topics), and yet what came across was less his specific ideas than the profundity of his engagement with ultimate religious questions. Farmer has a succinct description of Thurman's preaching at Howard: "When Thurman occupied the university pulpit, Rankin Memorial Chapel was packed. Though few but theologians and philosophers comprehended what he was saying, everyone else thought if only they *had* understood it would have been wonderful, so mesmerizing was his resonant voice and so captivating was the artistry of his delivery. Those who did grasp the meaning of his sermons were even more ecstatic."[63]

Another description of Thurman's preaching style at Howard is provided by Evelio Grillo, a high school student of Cuban background that the Thurmans befriended in the late 1930s: "He spoke with a transfixing eloquence. He had an awe-inspiring command of the English language. He was understood by most people, for his sermons expressed feeling eloquently, were lucid, and above all, were poetic. He managed always to involve his audiences as he wove, with his expressive face, piercing eyes, and gracefully moving arms and body, a passage in a sermon that had vital meaning for him. He would struggle almost painfully as he introduced a theme, insisting that his auditors struggle with him for understanding. Once assured that the congregation was fully his, he poured forth with a waterfall of language, beautiful, ethereal, profoundly moving."[64]

Poetry was, as Grillo suggests, key to Thurman's homiletic style. Most sermons began or ended with his reading a relevant poem from his extensive poetry scrapbook. He wrote a correspondent in 1940, "I quote poetry in my addresses often because a good poem summarizes very often effectively in short compass what it would take many prosaic utterances to do."[65] Whether quoting poetry or not, Thurman eschewed the prosaic. A 1939 article about him in the *Crisis* had a similar perspective on the poetry in his presentations: "There are many people who will cancel everything to go hear Howard Thurman speak; his language is beautiful, his ideals and points of view intriguing. Most of all, people are overwhelmed by his silences, and marvel at how eloquent he can be without ever shouting or 'orating,' and his ability to get to rock-bottom issues."[66] To return to Grillo's description of Thurman preaching: "He was a large, very dark man, a powerful, inviting presence. He moved his whole body with a light arresting grace that complemented fully the beauty of his language and the music of his speech. His deep, melodic voice surrounded and enveloped the congregation, held by the sheer power of his presentation. While he projected himself as the deeply spiritual man that he was, his every sermon was also an exercise in virtuoso theater."[67]

What united Thurman's two roles at Howard, dean of chapel and professor of religion, was an effort to overcome the widespread perception held by many leading black intellectuals that religion was at best irrelevant to the struggle for black equality, if not a positive hindrance. To quote Farmer once again, when he arrived at Howard in the 1930s, "it was before religion occupied a central role in the black struggle, and before religious thinkers became intellectually respectable among the austere ranks of the black scholar."[68] The gulf between religious and secular black intellectuals at Howard was wide. If the university had a dominant intellectual approach, it was identified with the Division of

Social Science and especially its leading figures, E. Franklin Frazier, Ralph Bunche, and Abram Harris. It was Frazier who popularized the use of "black bourgeoisie" as an epithet—within a broadly nondogmatic Marxist analysis of the ills of American society that argued that the roots of racial oppression were basically economic. The black church was seen as a bulwark for the most conservative, reactionary, exclusive, antilabor, and stand-pat elements in African American society.[69] Frazier's hostility to religion was not a surprise to Thurman, who relates in his autobiography his astonishment on encountering Frazier's atheism during his undergraduate years at Morehouse.[70]

Thurman was broadly sympathetic to the political critique of Bunche and his peers, and in November 1934 he explicitly endorsed Bunche's critique of the first phase of the New Deal as a retrograde political development that, by providing government sanction to white supremacy, retarded the black struggle for equality.[71] Thurman had long been a critic of the black church, criticizing its "apocalyptic" vision and otherworldliness as early as 1927. He also endorsed Mays's two analyses of the institutional black church, *The Negro's Church* (1933) and *The Negro's God* (1938), which critiqued the traditional black church for its apolitical and anti-intellectual attitudes and became defining texts of black theological modernism.[72] While Thurman rarely wrote directly on political questions, his essay, published as "A 'Native Son' Speaks" in 1940—his own title was "The Negro in the City"—shows the impact of the critique of Frazier on Thurman's view of the Great Migration and the institutionalized black church, which he criticized for its distant, standoffish approach to the newcomers from the South. The essay ends with an endorsement of Bunche's call for interracial cooperation, especially through the labor movement, as the most effective way of advancing the interests of blacks. Thurman, like many of his peers at Howard, was consistent in his emphasis on integration and interracialism as the best way to achieve black equality.

Thurman was also convinced that religion had a crucial role to play in achieving this, but this required rethinking the nature of the Christian experience and reconceiving the nature of the church. In his lecture series "The Significance of Jesus" and "Mysticism and Social Change" and other sermons of the period, he outlined a conception of Christianity that emphasized God as a source of strength and conviction to the isolated and disenfranchised, personal commitment to social change, and an uncompromising struggle against the evil of an unjust society.

But for all that Thurman enjoyed his career at Howard, the intellectual excitement at being at the cynosure of African American intellectual life, and the satisfaction of being a mentor and inspiration to so many young minds, he also found Howard to be increasingly confining. By the late 1930s, Thurman was becoming restless at Howard. The reasons for this are not openly alluded to in the extant correspondence, beyond an amassing of complaints, petty and not so petty. Thurman's responsibilities at Howard were large, the pay and support inadequate, and his visibility not as great as some other positions would entail. It is not clear whether Thurman sought new positions or those with positions to fill sought him out, but by 1938 he was a person very much in demand.

One factor that undoubtedly contributed to his growing restlessness at Howard was the souring of his relationship with his longtime mentor and confidant, Mordecai Wyatt Johnson. The change from a friendship between mentor-protégé to an employer-employee relationship is frequently a difficult one, and both Thurman and Johnson were proud men, jealous of their prerogatives. At the same time, it is difficult to estimate fairly the extent of their estrangement—at least until the final break in 1946 that led to Thurman's resigning his position at Howard—because, as was generally the case, Thurman is circumspect in both his extant correspondence and his autobiography. Still, if one can read between the lines, it is possible to perceive a growing gulf between two men whose personal connection was at one time extraordinarily close and to discern that Thurman was thinking, with increasing urgency, about a future elsewhere.

After the first few years at Howard University, the Thurman-Johnson correspondence had lost its early banter. Their letters were for the most part proper and impersonal, sticking to the matter at hand with few personal asides. By the late 1930s, the correspondence between them largely consists of demands and complaints, such as a letter from July 1938 in which Thurman declares his profound regret at Johnson's decision not to allow university funds to pay Thurman's way to a conference. Thurman considers paying his own way but ultimately tells Johnson, "I do not think that it is worthwhile to put any more of my personal money in trying to develop my work here."[73] He subsequently complained to Johnson about his inability to put up speakers at Rankin Chapel at Howard's expense and the use of the chapel for classes.[74] When added to the correspondence, not directly addressed to Johnson, in which Thurman complains of the indignities heaped upon him by the Howard administration, the portrait emerges of a man who saw himself as beleaguered, put upon, and underappreciated by his employer.

Thurman was hardly alone in finding Johnson a difficult boss. If Johnson was acknowledged as one of the greatest educators and university builders of the middle decades of the twentieth century, he was also perceived as an autocratic and demanding chief executive, operating in an era in which there were few limits on the powers and prerogatives of university presidents, who often saw their task as shaping their institution in their own image. As Kenneth Manning has written, "Johnson wanted complete control over every department, from routine administrative matters to curriculum modifications to the broader goals and direction of the various programs. He had set about gaining this control by placing clear limits on the activities of the officers of his administration and the heads of academic departments."[75] Johnson had a clear vision of Howard as the premier African American educational institution, the "capstone of Negro education," and was ruthless in pursuing this vision. Kenneth Janken calls Johnson, fairly, an "enlightened despot."[76]

It is, however, not surprising that many of those who had to deal with him on the Howard faculty were more concerned with his despotism than with his enlightenment. In his history of Howard University, Rayford Logan, a frequent critic of Johnson, suggests that "very few of those who have known President Johnson hold neutral views about him; the vast majority are fervent admirers or bitter critics."[77] Logan was clearly in the latter category, complaining of Johnson's "Messianic Complex" and the fact that he saw his duties as including telling "E. Franklin Frazier the kind of sociology to write" and "Abram Harris the kind of economics to study."[78] Logan's views were common but by no means unanimous among the Howard faculty in the 1930s and 1940s. Benjamin Mays, for instance, in his autobiography offers a stout defense of Johnson, saying that his "respect for Mordecai Johnson increased mightily" during his years there and that he "never really knew why" Johnson engendered "such negative reaction" among some of his colleagues.[79]

Thurman's own feelings toward Johnson are somewhat difficult to gauge because of his natural circumspection; neither in his correspondence nor his autobiography does he offer a general evaluation of Johnson and their interactions. Thurman and Johnson occasionally exchanged letters after the former left Howard, and Thurman offered a eulogy at Johnson's funeral in 1975 (by a recorded message rather than in person). And while Thurman certainly grumbled at Johnson and his parsimonious and dictatorial ways, he does not appear to have been active among the opponents of Johnson on the Howard faculty in the mid-1930s. Still there can be little doubt that a declining relationship with Johnson, culminating in Thurman's being forced to leave Howard,[80] contributed to Thurman's growing sense by the early 1940s that his greatest challenges lay elsewhere.

Thurman was particularly sensitive in the late 1930s and early 1940s to the subtle but formative influence that outside institutions play in shaping the inner spiritual lives of those who come under their sway. This was again one of the themes of "The Significance of Jesus," and it was touched on in many of his sermons and addresses in this period. Thurman had spent almost his entire career in all-black institutions (with the exception of his three years of study at Rochester Theological Seminary), and if he recognized their necessity, he always felt uncomfortable about their role in American and African American society and believed that separate black institutions, despite the best efforts of those within them, would always carry the badge of inferiority. In 1938, speaking to graduating seniors at Tennessee A & I, a black college that later became Tennessee State University, Thurman asserted that "whatever the theory is, the fact is that the functional significance of education in our democracy is to guarantee and perpetuate things as they are now. . . . The need of education is to guarantee, perpetuate and establish order." He urged that graduates of black colleges needed to remember that black institutions affirmed an established order that was, at its core, radically unjust for those who were its members. Pride at graduation ought not to lead to complacency or a distancing from the masses of black folks who were unable to obtain a college education, and whatever satisfaction there is in being a big fish in a little pond needs to be tempered with the sense that "when we function as a minority," we are "not . . . people who are in control of society."[81]

The only way forward was to create new institutions. In the first section of "The Significance of Jesus," Thurman's dissatisfaction with existing religious (and political) institutions is the main theme. Jesus, after a consideration of the religious options available in first century C.E. Palestine—Pharisees, Sadducees, Zealots, Essenes—concluded they were all unacceptable in one way or another, and his alternative was to create his own religious course and direction.[82] This can be read as a veiled allegory of sorts for the dilemmas that faced Thurman and other like-minded persons in the late 1930s; none of the political or religious options really seemed appropriate. For Thurman, like Jesus, the way to deal with the problem was to start small and gather a tight-knit group of like-minded people to create alternative institutions. Thurman wrote of Jesus and his disciples that "standing within this group he projects himself into a world in which the common assumptions are radically opposed to his teachings."[83] With the backing and example of Jesus's disciples, his ultimate significance for Thurman is that he placed before the world "an impelling dream" and a way in which that dream could be translated into a "living community," and each partial realization of the dream would be a token of a possible broader transformation, of lives lived "without inner defilement and without self destruction."[84]

If Thurman was searching for a new type of religious community in the late 1930s, an alternative way and venue for religious expression, one that would, by the very fact of its existence, challenge America's racial status quo, he did not know precisely what he was searching for. In his personal life, he was a cautious and practical man, with two young daughters to support, and not the sort of person to turn his life upside down in pursuit of a whim. For a black academic such as Thurman, still completely shut off from mainstream colleges, the highest and most prestigious position that one could obtain would be the presidency of a black college. He was a most attractive candidate; young, dynamic, an ordained clergyman (most black colleges still had strong denominational ties), and a person whose reputation as a preacher and person of deep spiritual insight was already celebrated. In 1938 Samuel Archer, the acting president of Morehouse, tried to recruit Thurman to serve as his successor and return to his alma mater, but despite a strenuous courtship, Thurman declined the offer.[85] He was also sounded out for the presidency of Shaw University and for Florida Memorial College, the successor to his high school, which was in effect another of Thurman's alma maters.[86] He turned these down, along with other proffered offers of college presidencies, because they involved too much administration and fund-raising and were too far from what he really wanted to do with his life. In 1941 Thurman preached a trial sermon at Olivet Baptist Church in Chicago, one of the largest and most prestigious black Baptist churches in the United States, whose pastors often served as presidents of the National Baptist Convention, Inc. The sermon went well, and there are some indications that he was offered the position, though this remains ambiguous.[87] In any event Thurman did not get the job, and the candidate Olivet did hire in 1941, Joseph H. Jackson, was at the opposite pole to Thurman both politically and theologically.

But none of these positions would have directly challenged the racial status quo or the assumption, prevalent among most racial liberals, that at best blacks might be occasional visitors to mainstream institutions—there was no place for them among the permanent faculty or as permanent pastors—and that they were destined to spend their professional lives within black institutions. Thurman was determined to overcome these prejudices, which he tended to do through quiet negotiations and example setting rather than by making public demands. He sent his daughters to previously all-white boarding schools. He had worked for years to get his friend Henry MacCracken, president of Vassar, to set up student exchanges with Howard and admit black women to the prestigious all-women college.[88] In the 1940s his eldest daughter, Olive, became one of a handful of black students to attend the institution.

Thurman's motivations in wanting to desegregate white institutions were no doubt complex. He was proud of his talents and abilities, and he refused to be limited or pigeonholed as a result of his racial background. This was reflected in his reluctance to speak on "the race question" before white audiences, as if this was the only topic blacks were competent to speak on.[89] However, if he was interested in advancing his career, he also felt that he was no doubt in an excellent position to challenge the dominant racial orthodoxy. If someone like himself, who had spoken extensively before white audiences since his days at the Rochester Theological Seminary and had a wide following among white Christians, was not well positioned to help desegregate mainstream institutions, no one was. (An article about Thurman in the *Crisis* in 1939, describing his extensive speaking engagements at white colleges and universities, called him an "interracial minister plenipotentiary," whose message was making "friends

Howard Thurman. Courtesy of the Thurman Family and Arleigh Prelow/Howard Thurman Film Project.

Howard and Sue Thurman in Washington, D.C., Courtesy of the Thurman Family and Arleigh Prelow/Howard Thurman Film Project.

among young white men and women" who are "never the same after they have heard Howard Thurman.")[90] And as long as African Americans, no matter how talented, were obliged to remain within the world of black colleges and churches, black institutions would continue to be a sign of the legacy of slavery and a badge of inferiority. Only when blacks had an option and could freely choose to participate (or not) in black institutional life would they truly become full citizens.

If Thurman was restless in the early 1940s, and his thinking and reflecting was propelling him onwards, it was to an unknown and uncertain destination. But starting in the fall of 1943, there would be a new and sudden clarity. This volume concludes on the verge of his receipt of what he would call the "fateful letter" from the prominent Christian pacifist A. J. Muste, that would take him from his comfortable position as dean of chapel of Howard University, to co-pastoring a small, fledgling church in San Francisco, but one of the few churches in the United States that was established as an explicitly and avowed experiment in religious interracialism. This will be taken up in volume 3.

Whatever Thurman had accomplished at Howard, and whatever his attitudes toward Mordecai Wyatt Johnson, it is difficult not to sense in Thurman in the early 1940s a feeling of restlessness, ambitions not satisfied, and goals that were thwarted. If, personally, he felt himself drifting, in his religious writings he was increasingly emphasizing the importance of commitment as perhaps the key religious virtue. As Thurman wrote about the crucifixion in "The Significance of Jesus" in 1937: "For here is revealed that a man's life becomes meaningful and whole to the degree that he is willing to stake everything on a conviction that what he does when he is most himself has the approval and the imprimatur of the Highest."[92] For Thurman, central to his thinking since his return from South Asia in 1936 was the conviction that for representatives of American Christianity to hold their heads high to the rest of the world, the racism and segregation that was at its core needed to be overcome. To be true to his own deepest convictions, Thurman would have to "stake everything" on this belief.

Notes

1. Now in Pakistan.

2. HT, *With Head and Heart: The Autobiography of Howard Thurman* (New York: Harcourt Brace Jovanovich, 1979), 136 (hereafter referred to as *WHAH*). Thurman first wrote about his Khyber Pass vision in HT, "The Historical Perspective," in *The Church for the Fellowship for All Peoples* (San Francisco, 1947), 3, and for a wider audience in *Footprints of a Dream: The Story of The Church for the Fellowship of All Peoples* (New York: Harper and Brothers, 1959), 24 (hereafter referred to as *Footprints*).

3. To Ruth Cunningham, 18 January 1937, HTC-MBU: Box 3.

4. Luther E. Smith Jr., *Howard Thurman: The Mystic as Prophet* (Lanham, Md.: University Press of America, 1981), 27–30.

5. See, for example, Alonzo Johnson, *Good News for the Disinherited: Howard Thurman on Jesus of Nazareth and Human Liberation* (Lanham, Md.: University Press of America, 1997); C. Anthony Hunt, *Blessed Are the Peacemakers: A Theological Analysis of the Thought of Howard Thurman and Martin Luther King, Jr.* (Lima, Ohio: Wyndam Hall, 2005); Joseph Tucker, *Jesus' Strategy for Healed and Healthy Relationships: Major Emphases in the Christian Ethical Thought of Howard Thurman and Benjamin E. Mays* (New York: Vantage, 2001); Victor Anderson, *Creative Exchange: A Constructive Theology of African American Religious Experience* (Minneapolis: Fortress, 2008); and Victor Anderson, *Beyond Ontological Blackness: An Essay on African-American Religious and Cultural Criticism* (New York: Continuum, 1995). Walter Earl Fluker, *Ethical Leadership: The Quest for Character, Civility, and Community* (Minneapolis: Fortress, 2009); and Walter Earl Fluker, *They Looked for a City: A Comparative Analysis of the Ideal of Community in the Thought of Howard Thurman and Martin Luther King, Jr.* (Lanham, Md.: University Press of America, 1989).

6. Alton B. Pollard III, *Mysticism and Social Change: The Social Witness of Howard Thurman* (New York: Lang, 1992), 32.

7. Gary Dorrien, *The Making of American Liberal Theology: Idealism, Realism and Modernity: 1900–1950* (Louisville: Westminster/John Knox, 2003), 558.

8. Victor Anderson's critique is helpful in rethinking the relevancy and limitations of Thurman's contribution to a religiously inspired public ethic. In his illuminating essay *Beyond Ontological Blackness*, Anderson acknowledges the significance of Thurman's contribution to religious and cultural criticism in a racialized culture. He warns, however, that Thurman's notions of transcendence and community are problematic because the suppositions of order, continuity, and cooperative qualities of life that informed his universe of discourse can not be taken for granted in a postmodernist culture where grand metanarratives are suspect. He argues that "it is also conceivable that one may equally discover and produce counter-narratives from the same grounds. And these counter narratives can be as cynical and tragic as Thurman's is an ideally utopian narrative of world reconciliation and reformation of a lost primal community" (Anderson, 43). Victor Anderson, *Beyond Ontological Blackness: An Essay on African-American Religious and Cultural Criticism* (New York: Continuum, 1995), 38–50, 80–81, 159; see also chapter 4, "The Smell of Life: A Pragmatic Theology of Religious Experience," in Anderson's *Creative Exchange: A Constructive Theology of African American Religious Experience* (Minneapolis: Fortress, 2008), esp. pp. 115–135, where he provides similar critiques. From Thurman's perspective, however, the emphasis is on "the moral struggle," that is, the order, continuities, and cooperative processes of life as potential are wrecked by the ravages of human consciousness coming to itself and struggling to wrest goodness from the clutches of fate. For Thurman these are not binary, oppositional forces but one fluid center out of which opposition appears; the center of consciousness, being the Will of the One who is manifesting itself in varied and myriad forms of creative vitality and intelligence. Thurman's project does not avoid the tragic character of history, as such critiques suggest, but rather begins with the exigencies of history. Historical debt is the price exacted for knowledge, freedom, and possibility; it is the consequence of the birthing of conscious existence: the movement from primal innocence to the fore of new awareness of human possibility and freedom. "The transition from innocence to knowledge is always perilous and fraught with hazard," writes Thurman. HT, "When Knowledge Comes," in *The Inward Journey* (New York: Harper, 1961), 16–17, 18.

9. "There is a universal urgency for both personal and social stability. This urgency can find fulfillment along several lines. A fresh sense of history must be developed. All the events of our world must be placed in the context of incident that reveals their profound interrelatedness. History on this planet must be regarded not as individual happenings unrelated to social processes, but, instead, as overlapping patterns of group behavior brought into play by a wide variety of creative personal and impersonal forces at work in the world. History is not irrational; it has a deep logic and consistency. God is the God of history. He does not stand apart as some mighty spectator but is in the process and the facts, ever shaping them (in ways that we can understand and in ways beyond our powers to grasp) to ends that fulfill a great and good destiny for men. This is no idle or pious wish. Examine the past and behold the unfolding of the living process." *Deep Is the Hunger: Meditations for Apostles of Sensitiveness* (New York: Harper, 1951), 2.

10. Theophus H. Smith, *Conjuring Culture: Biblical Formations of Black America* (New York: Oxford University Press, 1994), 5–6, 58, 146–49, 162–74. According to Jeffrey Stout, the process of bricolage is the most viable candidate for retrieving, reappropriating, and reconstructing the varied moral strands that make up the national life. He points to leaders such as Thomas Jefferson and Martin Luther King Jr. as *bricoleurs* par excellence. Moral bricolage, according to Stout, is "the process in which one begins with bits and pieces of traditional linguistic material, arranges some of them into a structured whole, leaves others to the side, and ends up with a moral language one proposes to use" (Stout, 74). See Jeffrey Stout, *Ethics after Babel: The Language of Morals and Their Discontents* (Boston: Beacon, 1988), 191–242, 292; for a detailed account of Stout's argument, see 74-77.

11. See Bernice Johnson Reagon's assessment of Martin Luther King Jr. and other marginalized intellectuals who straddle and renegotiate worlds of common practice and tradition with foreign worlds of meaning. The outcome, for Reagon, is a new situation, a synthesis of sorts that allows for creativity, balance, and sanity. Reagon, "'Nobody Knows the Trouble I See'; or, 'By and By I'm Gonna Lay Down My Heavy Load,'" *Journal of American History* 78 (1991): 111–19. See also David Thelen's discussion of Reagon in "Becoming Martin Luther King, Jr.: An Introduction," *Journal of American History* 78 (1991): 15; for a fuller explication of this perspective, see Walter Earl Fluker, *Ethical Leadership: The Quest for Character, Civility, and Community* (Minneapolis: Fortress, 2009), 21.

12. HT, *The Creative Encounter: An Interpretation of Religion and the Social Witness* (New York: Harper, 1954), 20.

13. Ibid., 39.

14. Ibid., 33.

15. Ibid., 124. Thurman believed that the individual faced two demands of the religious experience. The experience must first give the individual a sense of *ultimate security*. This sense of being ultimately cared for and affirmed identifies the individual with all of existence as one created being among many others and establishes an ultimate or transcendent point of reference. The second demand is that the encounter with God must give the individual *personal assurance*, that is, he or she is dealt with at his or her most private and intimate center. This gives the individual a basis for understanding his or her own value and inherent worth as a child of God. Ibid., 30–31.

16. HT, *Footprints*, and Dennis Wiley, "The Concept of the Church in the Works of Howard Thurman," Ph.D. dissertation, Union Theological Seminary, 1988.

17. To Mordecai Wyatt Johnson, 20 September 1927, printed in volume 1.

18. St. Francis of Assisi (1182?–1226) was founder of the Franciscan Catholic religious order; Eckhart von Hochheim, commonly known as Meister Eckhart (1260–1328), was an influential mystic and religious writer; Jeanne-Marie Bouvier de la Motte-Guyon (1648–1717) was a mystic associated with the French Quietist movement.

19. Rufus M. Jones, *The Double Search: Studies in Atonement and Prayer* (Philadelphia: Winston, 1906). Thurman's language is remarkably similar to that of Jones. In *The Inner Life* (New York: Macmillan, 1916), Jones writes: "So, too, there is an outer way and an inner way and both are one" (viii–ix). He adds, "There is no inner life that is not also an outer life" (v). Compare those words with Thurman's later work, as in the line of dedication to Eleanor Lloyd Smith ("in whom the inner and outer are one") in *Meditations of the Heart* (New York: Harper, 1953), 5, or with his chapter headings in *The Creative Encounter:* "The Inwardness of Religion," "The Outwardness of Religion," "The Inner Need for Love," and "The Outer Necessity for Love." See also James E. Massey, "Bibliographical Essay: Howard Thurman and Rufus M. Jones, Two Mystics," *Journal of Negro History* 57 (1972): 190–95. Additionally see Rufus M. Jones, *Social Law in the Spiritual World: Studies in Human and Divine Inter-Relationship* (Philadelphia: Winston, 1904), in which this argument is more fully developed.

20. To Ruth Cunningham, 18 January 1937, HTC-MBU: Box 3.

21. "With Our Negro Guests," printed in volume 1.

22. "Good News for the Underprivileged," printed in volume 1.

23. Jones, *Social Law,* 154.

24. HT, "Mysticism and Social Change," printed in the present volume.

25. To P. O. Philip, 22 January 1937, HTC-MBU: Box 17. For other discussion of a student or teacher exchange with Alwaye and other Indian colleges, see From P. Oomann Philip, 17 July 1936, HTC-MBU: Box 17; From A. A. Paul, 22 July 1936, HTC-MBU: Box 17; and To A. A. Paul, 15 September 1936, HTC-MBU: Box 17.

26. Almost from the time of her tragic death, Juliette Derricotte's friends and colleagues thought of making as one of her legacies an enhanced connection between American blacks and Asia. Sue Bailey cosigned a tribute to Derricotte that stated that "her reception in the eastern countries was so significant that student leaders there expressed the wish that they might have a greater contribution of the Negroes of America to the life of the Orient" ("Tribute Is Paid to Juliette Derricotte, Noble Woman," *Chicago Defender*, 14 November 1931). Later, in 1947, Sue Bailey Thurman recalled "Juliette Derricotte, magnificent brown American, who in her thirty-four brief years demonstrated one vital truth to men. She might be called the perfect revelation of the lofty, tragic sense of values in life—shared by considerable numbers in all countries today—that the true lover of God must be challenged by the impossible." Jean Beaven Abernethy, ed., *Meditations for Women* (Nashville: Abingdon-Cokesbury, 1947), 97.

27. Sue Bailey Thurman, "The Indian Press and the Negro," *Norfolk Journal and Guide*, 27 June 1936.

28. An article she wrote shortly after her return from Asia, "India—The Perfect Museum," which opens, "It must have been in the mind of the great Creator of men and Places to make India the perfect reservoir of past and present things," probably gives a good sense of what her lectures were like. *Atlanta Daily World,* 17 May 1936. Sometimes she

gave a second, more overtly political lecture titled "The American Negro in the Press of Mexico and India." See "Mrs. Sue B. Thurman Interracial Worker to Talk at Olivet," *Chicago Defender*, 15 May 1937, and "Noted Lecturer Slated to Speak at Virginia U," *Chicago Defender*, 5 November 1938; for a printed version of the talk, see "The Negro and the Indian Press," *Atlanta Daily World*, 21 June, 1936.

29. For a sample of accounts of Sue Bailey Thurman's lectures, see "Eastern Atmosphere Prevails at Soiree [in Tulsa]," *Chicago Defender*, 14 May 1938; "Sue Bailey Thurman's Lecture in Florida Stimulates Group," *Atlanta Daily World*, 19 June 1938; "Derricotte Group Presents Exhibit," *Chicago Defender*, 20 April 1939; "Fund Reaches $1,800," *Pittsburgh Courier*, 23 July 1938; "Sue Bailey Thurman Will Be Heard at A.U. Monday," *Atlanta Daily World*, 17 July 1938.

30. Sue Bailey Thurman, "To the Patrons of the Juliette Derricotte Memorial Foundation and to Our Friends in India," 1 August 1938, Spelman College Archives, Atlanta.

31. "Derricotte Scholarshipees Back Home!," *Pittsburgh Courier*, 27 January 1940.

32. From Mordecai Wyatt Johnson, 22 September 1926, printed in volume 1.

33. For Johnson's role in reviving Howard, see Jonathan Scott Holloway, *Confronting the Veil: Abram Harris Jr., E. Franklin Frazier, and Ralph Bunche, 1919–1941* (Chapel Hill: University of North Carolina Press, 2002), 45–50, and Rayford W. Logan, *Howard University: The First Hundred Years, 1867–1967* (New York: New York University Press, 1969), 589–91.

34. From Emmett J. Scott, 9 March 1932, HTC-MBU: Box 20.

35. For an overview of Howard in the 1930s, see Holloway, *Confronting the Veil*; Logan, *Howard University*; and Walter Dyson, *Howard University, the Capstone of Negro Education: A History: 1867–1940* (Washington, D.C.: Howard University, 1941).

36. Logan, *Howard University*.

37. James Farmer, *Lay Bare the Heart: An Autobiography of the Civil Rights Movement* (New York: New American Library), 135.

38. Logan, *Howard University*, 83–86.

39. Ibid., 257.

40. Benjamin E. Mays, *Born to Rebel: An Autobiography* (New York: Scribner, 1971), 144.

41. Logan, *Howard University*, 314; Dyson, *Howard University*, 214.

42. Mays, *Born to Rebel*, 139.

43. For the history of the School of Religion through 1940, see Dyson, *Howard University*, 201–18.

44. Farmer, *Lay Bare the Heart*, 136.

45. George M. Marsden, *The Soul of the American University: From Protestant Establishment to Established Nonbelief* (New York: Oxford University Press, 1994), 335–38.

46. To Mordecai Wyatt Johnson, 20 January 1939, HTC-MBU: Box 9.

47. The information is based on available course catalogues, with the years 1932–33 through 1936–37, and 1942–43, lacking DHU-MS.

48. Farmer, *Lay Bare the Heart*, 135–36.

49. From Mordecai Wyatt Johnson, 8 October 1936, HTC-MBU: Box 9.

50. Dyson, *Howard University*, 68, 408; To Mordecai Wyatt Johnson, 20 May 1937, HTC-MBU: Box 9. Robert Russell Wicks (1882-1963) was dean of chapel at Princeton from 1928 to 1947. Charles W. Gilkey (1882–1968) was dean of chapel at the University of Chicago from 1928 to 1947.

51. To Mordecai Wyatt Johnson, 20 May 1937, HTC-MBU: Box 9.

52. To Mordecai Wyatt Johnson, 20 January 1939, HTC-MBU: Box 9. In the same letter, Thurman proposed that he become a full-time dean of chapel with the university paying his salary directly rather than his being paid from the separate funds, outside of the federal appropriation, used to pay salaries in the School of Religion. Thurman pointed to the position of military chaplains as a precedent. There is no evidence that Johnson ever acted on this proposal, which would have likely resulted in a salary increase for Thurman. Elsewhere Thurman argued that the chapel should be separate from the School of Religion. To Mordecai Wyatt Johnson, 20 May 1937, HTC-MBU: Box 9.

53. Marsden, *Soul of the American University*, 344–45. In 1948, 48 percent of colleges surveyed had mandatory chapel services.

54. Ibid., 359–62.

55. Raymond Wolters, *The New Negro on Campus: Black College Rebellions of the 1920s* (Princeton, N.J.: Princeton University Press, 1975), 73–75.

56. Benjamin E. Mays, "The Religious Life and Needs of Negro Students," *Journal of Negro Education* 9 (1940): 334.

57. Howard University, Annual Report, Dean of Chapel, 1940–41. DHU-MS.

58. *Footprints*, 25–27.

59. Ibid., 28.

60. Howard University, All-University Chapel Calendar, October-November-December 1939, DHU-MS.

61. Howard University, Annual Report, Dean of Chapel 1943–44, Andrew Rankin Memorial Chapel, printed in volume III; All-University Religious Services, Andrew Rankin Memorial Services, 1937–38, DHU-MS.

62. Richard I. McKinney, *Mordecai: The Man and His Message: The Story of Mordecai Wyatt Johnson* (Washington, D.C.: Howard University Press, 1997), 108–9; Logan, *Howard University*, 250.

63. Farmer, *Lay Bare the Heart*, 135.

64. Evelio Grillo, *Black Cuban, Black American: A Memoir* (Houston: Arte Público, 2000), 75.

65. To Lewis Douglass, 10 April 1940, HTC-MBU: Box 5.

66. G. James Fleming, "Preacher at Large to Universities," *Crisis*, August 1939, 233, 251, 289.

67. Grillo, *Black Cuban*, 75.

68. Farmer, *Lay Bare the Heart*, 135. For similar observations, see Marsden, *Soul of the American University*, 361–62.

69. See Holloway, *Confronting the Veil*.

70. *WHAH*, 40–42.

71. To Ralph Bunche, 9 November 1934, published in volume 1.

72. HT, "Higher Education and Religion," November 1927, printed in volume 1.

73. To Mordecai Wyatt Johnson, 13 August 1938, printed in the present volume.

74. To Mordecai Wyatt Johnson, 3 September 1938, HTC-MBU: Box 9; To Mordecai Wyatt Johnson, 1 August 1940, HTC-MBU: Box 9.

75. Kenneth R. Manning, *Black Apollo of Science: The Life of Ernest Everett Just* (New York: Oxford University Press, 1983), 211. Ernest Everett Just (1883-1941) was a biologist and the most noted scientist on the Howard faculty. Just's tortured career at Howard in the 1930s,

which included conflicts with Johnson over financial and educational matters as well as his leaves of absence, bears some similarity to Thurman's experiences.

76. Kenneth Janken, *Rayford W. Logan and the Dilemma of the African American Intellectual* (Amherst: University of Massachusetts Press, 1993), 204.

77. Logan, *Howard University*, 249.

78. Ibid. For a good overview of Johnson's conflicts with his faculty, see McKinney, *Mordecai*, 77–97.

79. Mays, *Born to Rebel*, 142.

80. In 1946, when Johnson demanded that Thurman either return to Howard full time or lose his position (Thurman had suggested splitting his time between the Fellowship Church and Howard), Thurman decided to become a full-time pastor in Francisco, see volume 3.

81. "Commencement Address Delivered at the A & I State College," 3 June 1938, printed in the current volume.

82. As noted in the headnote for "The Significance of Jesus I: Jesus the Man of Insight," much of the scholarship Thurman relies on in the series is unavoidably dated in its general thrust and its particulars.

83. "The Significance of Jesus V: The Cross of Jesus," printed in the present volume.

84. "The Significance of Jesus VI: [untitled]," printed in the present volume.

85. From Samuel H. Archer, 19 July 1938, printed in the present volume; To Samuel Archer, 26 July 1938, HTC-MBU: Box 1, printed in the present volume.

86. To Samuel Archer, 14 April 1936; From Nathan W. Collier, 9 December 1940, HTC-MBU: Box 3; To Nathan W. Collier, 6 January 1941, HTC-MBU: Box 3, printed in the present volume.

87. To S. W. Smith, 25 February 1941, and To S. W. Smith, 26 March 1941, both printed in the present volume.

88. To Henry MacCracken, 22 January 1940, printed in the present volume.

89. For Thurman 's reluctance to speak on race before white audiences, see To J. Barnard Walton, 12 December 1934, HTC-MBU: Box 22; To Ruth Cunningham, 18 January 1937, HTC-MBU: Box 3; and To B. F. Lamb, 16 May 1940, HTC-MBU: Box 12.

90. Fleming, "Preacher at Large to Universities," *Crisis*, August 1939, 233.

91. "The Significance of Jesus V: The Cross of Jesus," printed in the present volume.

Howard Thurman Chronology

The following chronology extends through July 1943 and is compiled from Thurman's correspondence, scrapbooks, and writings as well as secondary accounts of his engagements in newspapers. Undated items appear before dated items within their designated month and/or year.

1936

April

Returns with his wife to the United States; becomes only the third campus minister in the United States to be awarded the title dean of chapel.

26–29 April

Delivers three talks at Olivet Baptist Church in Chicago, "The Experiences of a Christian Ambassador to India," "Viewing the Occident and the Orient," and "The Contributions of Religion to Better Race Relations."

31 May

Gives commencement address at Shaw University, Raleigh, North Carolina.

4–5 November

Speaks on Gandhi and on "Class Distinctions Among Negroes" in a pair of chapel talks at Sale Hall Chapel at Morehouse College in Atlanta.

1937

17 January

Delivers "Ultimate Basis of Self-Respect" address for Interracial Vesper Service of the YWCA in Wilmington, Delaware.

18 January

Speaker for Interdenominational Ministerial Alliance Installation Service at Plymouth Congregational Church in Washington, D.C.

21 January–6 February

Under the auspices of the Student Christian Movement of Canada, tours colleges in Nova Scotia and New Brunswick.

11 February
Delivers address "Christianity and the Underprivileged" at Union Church in Berea, Kentucky, and at the University of Kentucky in Lexington.

March
Delivers series of sermons, "Jesus, the Man of Insight," at Pennsylvania State University in University Park. Suffers from nervous exhaustion; contemplates a complete rest from all activity over the summer. Poem "O God I Need Thee" published in a pamphlet released by the Board of Foreign Missions of the Presbyterian Church in the USA. Delivers four sermons at St. Antoine Branch of the Detroit YMCA for Holy Week sermons on the general topic of "The Kingdom of God in an Evil World." His individual sermons were "What Is the Kingdom Like?," "How May I Recognize the Kingdom?," "How Much Does the Kingdom Cost?," and "India's Challenge to the Negro."

16 April
Sue Bailey Thurman delivers a lecture and program, "The Beauties of Indian Civilization," at the Fifteenth Street Presbyterian Church, Washington, D.C.

18 April
Speaks about India during vesper service at Smith College in Northampton, Massachusetts.

1 May
Delivers address "What Am I . . . A Child of God" for the Third District Teachers' Association at Virginia Union University in Richmond, Virginia.

8 August
Speaks at Alabama State Teacher's College in Montgomery.

12-17 September
Under the auspices of the Student Christian Movement of Canada, delivers six lectures titled "The Significance of Jesus" at Lake Couchiching, Ontario.

26 November
Delivers "How Religion Tends to Solve the Meaning of Life" address to the J. F. G. Scholarship Club in Bethlehem, Pennsylvania.

4 December
Speaks to Laymen's League of the Unitarian Society in Gardner, Massachusetts.

10 December
Delivers "The Significance of Jesus to the Disinherited" address as the leader of Religious Emphasis Week at A & T College of North Carolina in Greensboro.

13 December
Speaks at the eighty-seventh anniversary exercises of John Wesley A.M.E. Church in Washington, D.C.

29 December
Delivers "Sources of Power for Christian Action" address for the National Methodist Student Conference at Centenary M. E. Church, South, in St. Louis.

30 December–2 January 1938
Delivers talks titled "Man and the World of Nature" and "Christian, Who Calls Me Christian?" at the National Assembly of Student Christian Associations, Oxford, Ohio.

1938

28 January
Speaks at discussion group addressing minority concerns at the South Parkway Branch of the YWCA in Chicago.

30 January
Delivers "What Shall I Do with My Life?" at the University of Chicago.

28–30 April
Delivers address "The Integration of the Ethical, Social, and Educational Program" at the fourth annual meeting of the National Association of Personnel Deans and Advisers of Men in Negro Educational Institutions at Shaw University, Raleigh, North Carolina.

Late May
Gives lecture titled "The Contribution of Baptist Church Schools to Negro Youth," subsequently published in *National Baptist Voice.*

3 June
Delivers commencement address at Tennessee A & I State College in Nashville, Tennessee.

26 June
Delivers sermon "Kingdom of God" at annual Northfield Young Women's Conference in Northfield, Massachusetts.

Late June–Early July
Speaks at the twentieth International Convention on Christian Education of the Toledo Sunday School Association in Columbus, Ohio.

15 August
Lectures at Religious Institute at Georgia State College in Savannah.

16–21 October
Speaks at the annual conference of the Federal Council of the Churches of Christ in America at University of Colorado in Denver.

December
Delivers a series of Christmas sermons at the Colgate Rochester Divinity School: "The Singing of Angels," "The Historical Quest," and "The Hope of the Disinherited."

1939

8 January
Preaches at the university chapel service held in the Strong Auditorium at the University of Rochester.

9 January
Along with others in Washington, D.C., signs petition asking for refuge for German children.

15 January
Preaches anniversary sermon at Mt. Olivet Baptist Church in Rochester.

22–24 January
Delivers address "The Implications of the Christian Religion for Canadian Students" at Queen's University in Kingston, Ontario.

13–16 February
Delivers four lectures titled "Mysticism and Social Change" during the annual convocation at Eden Theological Seminary in St. Louis.

February–March
Delivers four public lectures at Colgate Rochester Divinity School. The first, on 6 February, was "The Religion of Jesus and the Disinherited"; the other three, on 17 March, 24 March, and 31 March, on aspects of the "Christian message."

26 February
Delivers "The Modern Implications of Religion" address for the Campus Forum Series at Cornell University in Ithaca, New York.

29 March
Speaks at Clarissa Street YWCA in Rochester at Business Girl's League, in meeting sponsored by the Negro History, Art and Literature Group

10–13 April
Delivers a series of devotional lectures for annual spring convention at Colgate Rochester Divinity School in Rochester, New York.

23–30 June
Speaks at ninth annual Young Women's Conference at Russell Sage Chapel in East Northfield, Massachusetts.

26 November
Delivers "The Two Things That Unite Us" address for the young people's meeting at Grace Methodist Church in Wilmington, Delaware.

17 December
Delivers "The Quest for Peace" address at the Eastman School of Music in Rochester, New York.

1940

18 January
Speaks at meeting of North Carolina Council of Churches at the First Presbyterian Church in Greensboro, North Carolina.

4 February
Speaks for chapel service at Fisk University in Nashville, Tennessee.

11 February
Speaks at Interracial Sunday service at the First Baptist Temple in Youngstown, Ohio.

5 March
Delivers "The Quest for Peace" at Lenten service at First Presbyterian Church in Binghamton, New York.

12 March
Speaks at Homewood Friends Meeting at the John Hopkins YMCA in Baltimore.

11 April
Delivers "The Negro in the City" to the Chicago Roundtable of the National Conference of Christians and Jews, published in May under the title "A 'Native Son' Speaks."

11 May
Delivers "Whither, Negro Youth?" at twenty-fifth Annual Conference of the Organization of Teachers of Colored Children of New Jersey.

17 May
Speaker for first youth mass meeting sponsored by the Phalanx Fraternity of the William A. Hunton branch YMCA at the First Baptist Church in Roanoke, Virginia.

23 May
Delivers commencement address at Florida Normal and Industrial Institute in St. Augustine, Florida.

10 June
Delivers baccalaureate address for commencement exercises at Colby Junior College in New London, New Hampshire.

11 June
Delivers commencement exercise address at Knoxville College in Knoxville, Tennessee.

July
With Melvin Watson, Evelio Grillo, and Thomas Hawkins, attends Hubert Herring's summer seminar in Mexico.

12–25 August
Speaks at Central-Atlantic Conference of the United Christian Adult Movement in Massanetta Springs, Virginia.

28 August
Delivers "The Faith by Which We Live" address at Winona Lake Christian Assembly in Winona Lake, Indiana.

14 December
Preaches at Vassar College, his tenth appearance since 1928.

1941

9–12 January
Delivers "Patterns of Living" address during the religion symposium at Colby Junior College in New London, New Hampshire.

16 January
Delivers "Christian Fellowship and Inspiration" address for the Camden County Ministerial Association at the Broadway Methodist Church in Camden, New Jersey.

19 January
Speaks to Interdenominational Usher's Union of the District of Columbia.

9 February
Delivers "The Religion of Jesus and Our Modern Times" address at Miami University in Oxford, Ohio.

12 February
Speaks on "Our Underlying Spiritual Unities" at the Stevens Hotel in Chicago at the International Council of Religious Education in Chicago.

14–16 February
Speaks at conference on Student Leadership in Colleges for Negroes at Shaw University, Raleigh, North Carolina.

23 February
Preaches at Bryn Mawr College, Bryn Mawr, Pennsylvania.

28 February
Leads worship service at Rankin Chapel at the Conference on Theological Education and Labor, sponsored by the National Religion and Labor Foundation.

5 March
Speaks at the civic Lenten program at the First Baptist Church in Fulton, New York.

5-6 March
Speaks at noontime civic Lenten service in the Mizpah Auditorium in Syracuse, New York.

9 March
Preaches at Wheaton College, Norton, Massachusetts.

23 March
Preaches at Olivet Baptist Church, Chicago.

10–13 April
Speaker for Holy Week services hosted by the St. Antoine Branch YMCA in Detroit, on the general theme "The Hours of Crisis," with sermons titled "Father Forgive Them," "Father into Thy Hands," "My God, My God, Why Hast Thou Forsaken Me?," and "The Soundless Passion of a Single Mind."

27 April
Preaches at vesper service at Syracuse University in Syracuse, New York.

27 June–6 July
Serves as discussion leader at the twelfth annual Institute of International Relations on "Democracy, Religion and World Change" at Bryn Mawr College in Bryn Mawr, Pennsylvania.

17–19 August
Speaks on "The Three Illusions of Professionalism" at annual meeting of the National Hospital Association in Chicago.

31 October–November 1
Secretary-convener for annual meeting of the Fellowship of Religious Workers in Colleges and Universities for Negroes at Virginia Manual Labor School for Boys in Hanover, Virginia.

1942

14 February
Speaks at seventy-fifth anniversary celebration for Morehouse College.

27–28 February
Address conference on Teachers and Workers in Religion at Negro Colleges at Bennett College, Greensboro, North Carolina.

9–10 June
Delivers a series of talks, "The Religion of the Disinherited," at the Friends University in Wichita, Kansas.

5–15 July
Featured speaker at Institute of International Relations, Whittier College, Whittier, California.

10 October
Delivers "The Temptations of Jesus" sermon for the afternoon vesper service at Bennett College in Greensboro, North Carolina.

9–11 November
Delivers informal address, "Wartime and Post-war Race Relations," at Morningside College in Sioux City, Iowa.

17 November
Speaks to the annual meeting of Washington Association of Congregational-Christian Churches at the First Congregational Church in Washington, D.C.

1943
1 January
Speaks at community New Year's service at a Presbyterian church in Chapel Hill, North Carolina.

3 January
Delivers "He Is the Sign of Man's Attack" address for weekly vesper hour in the Duke Auditorium at the North Carolina College for Negroes in Durham, North Carolina.

7 February
Leads an interracial service at a white Presbyterian church in Chapel Hill, North Carolina.

13 February
Delivers "The Sign for Man's Attack" address for Race Relations Day in Hendricks Chapel at Syracuse University in Syracuse, New York.

14 February
Preaches at Hendricks Chapel at Syracuse University; reads poetry to student group at university; in the evening addresses an interracial group in Auburn, New York.

March
Delivers "Personal Religious Living" address at Mt. Vernon Methodist Church in Washington, D.C.

22–26 March
Preaches at the Lafayette Theatre in Detroit.

28 March
Preaches at Penn State University in College Park, Pennsylvania.

14 April
Speaks at Lenten sacred concert for the American University College of Arts and Sciences in Washington, D.C.

June
Visits Amache Relocation Camp in Amache, Colorado.

27 June–17 July
Featured speaker at Institute of Interracial Relations at Mills College, Oakland, California, and at Institute of International Relations at Whittier College, Whittier, California.

The Papers of Howard Washington Thurman

Volume 2

To Samuel Archer
14 April 1936
Washington, D.C.

On his return journey from India to the Unites States, Thurman hears about the recent death of John Hope on 20 February. In this letter Thurman informs Samuel Archer,[1] who succeeded Hope as president of Morehouse College, that Shaw University in Raleigh, North Carolina, is interested in Thurman as a candidate for their presidency.

My dear Friend:

You can imagine my state of mind when E. A. Jones[2] told me in Paris that Mr. Hope had rounded out his journey. My thoughts have been with you since that time and I am exceedingly anxious to have a good talk with you. It may be possible for me to come to Atlanta sometime within the next two weeks. If so, I shall come to Morehouse immediately.

I am sure you will be interested to know that I have been approached by one of the Trustees of Shaw University about the possibility of taking the presidency there. The conversations have been preliminary ones to be continued in a day or two. I don't know what you think of this proposition. I am not sure what I think of it in all its ramifications. However, I do not feel moved in that direction. My mind may change later but I have no great urge to go there. Of course, you will consider this in strictest confidence.

India was great, inspiring and depressing. More of that when we meet. Warmest personal greetings to Mrs. Archer and your sister.

Sincerely,
[*signed*] Howard Thurman
Dr. S. H. Archer
Morehouse College
Atlanta, Georgia

TLc. HTC-MBU: Box 1.

1. Samuel Howard Archer (1870–1941) was born in Virginia and attended Wayland Academy in Washington, D.C., and Colgate College in Hamilton, New York, graduating in 1902. He spent thirty-three years on the faculty of Morehouse College, serving as, at various times, professor of mathematics, football coach, secretary of the faculty, dean of the summer school, and purchasing agent as well as serving two stints as acting president before being named president in 1931. He held that position until 1938.

2. Edward Allen Jones (1903–81) received his BA from Morehouse College (1926); his MA from Middlebury College in French; his PhD from Cornell University in Romance languages and literature; and his diplôme de professeur de Français from La Sorbonne, Paris. He taught French at Morehouse from 1927 to 1979 and authored *A Candle in the Dark: A History of Morehouse College* (Valley Forge, Pa.: Judson, 1967).

To Mary Jenness

15 April 1936
Washington, D.C.

Thurman writes to Mary Jenness about the biographical sketch she was planning to include of him and Sue Bailey Thurman in Twelve Negro Americans,[1] *a volume of brief sketches intended for high school students; Jenness evidently had provided sketches of Howard and Sue Bailey Thurman that were too evangelical for their tastes. But while the chapter on Sue Bailey Thurman was dropped, Jenness responded to Thurman's complaints about the material on him, and the two soon met.*[2] *The final version of the sketch won Thurman's approval, and large portions, such as the young Thurman's encounter with Halley's comet, are told in his own words. Jenness's chapter stands as the first extended biographical portrait of Thurman in print.*

My dear Miss Jenness:[3]

I have read and reread the manuscript that you sent and it is my considered judgment that it does not give an accurate and true picture of the facts of my life and Mrs. Thurman's. Mrs. Thurman is completely unwilling to have her study used in this way and I am willing provided you can afford to have a personal conference with me at which time there may be recorded the salient facts of my own limited life. I note that in writing up the material which was at your disposal it has been necessary to give to it a propagandic flare using the material in a manner that will make a case for some particular theory of missions. I may be in error here. If you do not have the time to have the interview, I am suggesting that you abandon the idea of using our lives because a picture that is not true to the facts as we know them is worse than no picture at all.

I hope you understand the spirit in which I write this. By temperament I shrink from the whole idea of biographical story, and certainly do I find it impossible to entertain the idea of having my life considered as the product of any particular enterprise however good and noble it may be. For such a picture makes the complex life of the Negro too simple.

Sincerely yours,

[*signed*] Howard Thurman

Miss Mary Jenness

433 West 21st Street

New York, New York

TLc. HTC-MBU: Box 9.

1. Mary Jenness, *Twelve Negro Americans* (New York: Friendship, 1936). The volume included chapters on Thurman's friends William Lloyd Imes and Juliette Derricotte and concludes the latter chapter with an excerpt from Thurman's eulogy at her funeral.

2. Jenness later wrote that she was "very glad to have met you at last," From Mary Jenness, 10 May 1936, HTC-MBU: Box 9.

3. Mary Jenness (d. 1947), a graduate of Mount Holyoke and Columbia University, authored a number of books on Christian and missionary themes, often for children. These included (with Isabel Brown Rose) *Out of Yesterday into Tomorrow: A Course on India* (New York: Missionary Education Movement of the United States and Canada, 1930); *The Orient Steps Out* (New York: Abingdon, 1931); and *The Man Who Asked God Questions: George Washington Carver* (New York: Friendship, 1947).

From Seldon Matthews

25 April 1936

Rochester, N.Y.

Seldon "Red" Matthews,[1] *along with Dave Voss,*[2] *was Thurman's roommate in seminary. A longtime pastor in the Rochester area, Matthews remained in contact with Thurman through the years.*

Dear Howard,

You may be as great a man as Percy Barbour[3] when you get as far away from home as India—but to me will I remind you that we roomed together two years.

We have two of the finest negro fellows in Colgate Rochester this year! Tobin, I believe you have met.[4] "Chuck" Boddie, graduating next month is both brilliant, true and gracious.[5]

Now—I have your promise (in writing) to come to Rochester this spring. I expected you before this. I must know—and soon when to look for you. Some of our own plans await your decree so please put aside your unpleasant practice of procrastinating and post a prompt reply to this query.

Plenty to tell but it can wait till I see you so I'll just say, everything is going fine here.
Loyally
[*signed*] Red

ALcS. HTC-MBU: Box 12.

1. Seldon "Red" Matthews (1900–1946) received his BD from RTS in 1925, and he worked for many years as a Baptist minister in the Rochester area. Declining health led him to resign his ministry in 1941 and move to Los Angeles, where he worked as the president of a vitamin manufacturing company. In his autobiography Thurman described him as "an extrovert, with a cheerful countenance and easy grace, the kind of man who would become a good pastor greatly beloved by his parishioners." *WHAH*, 52.

2. David Voss (1898–1978) received his BD from RTS in 1925. He never worked as a minister but taught Latin in Toledo, Ohio, high schools for many decades. He remained friends with Thurman and was an active member of the Howard Thurman Educational Trust until his death. *WHAH*, 53.

3. Clarence Augustus Barbour (1867–1937), a graduate from Brown (1881) and RTS (1891), was pastor of the Lake Avenue Baptist Church in Rochester from 1891 to 1908 and then served as associate secretary of the religious work department of the International Committee of the YMCA. He was president of RTS from 1915 to 1928, where he was instrumental in the merger of RTS and the Colgate Theological Seminary to form the Colgate Rochester Divinity School. In 1928 he was named president of Brown University, where he stayed for the remainder of his life. Barbour was not a favorite of Thurman's: he had reprimanded Voss and Matthews for asking Thurman to be their roommate, and Thurman, after being elected class president, was told in a meeting with Barbour that "inasmuch as my people could not stand being completely accepted by white people, he wanted me to exercise great care that this honor which my classmates had bestowed upon me would not go to my head." HT, *Footprints,* 20.

4. Lucius M. Tobin (1898–1984) was a native of Greenville, South Carolina, and graduated valedictorian from Virginia Union University in 1923. He graduated from the University of Michigan with an MA in sociology in 1928 and earned a BD from Colgate Rochester Divinity School in 1938. In 1944 he became a professor of religion and philosophy at Morehouse College and pastor at Atlanta's Providence Baptist Church, remaining in the former position until 1954 and the latter position until 1969.

5. Charles Emerson Boddie (1911–97) had a distinguished career as a preacher and president of American Baptist Theological Seminary in Nashville. See Charles E. Boddie, *God's Bad Boys: Eight Outstanding Black Preachers* (Valley Forge, Pa.: Judson, 1972).

From Edgar S. Brightman
22 May 1936
Boston, Mass.

Edgar S. Brightman,[1] *a professor at Boston University and noted proponent of personalism, accepts Thurman's invitation to preach at Howard.*

Dr. Howard Thurman
Howard University
WASHINGTON, D.C.
Dear Dr. Thurman,

Your good letter of May 18[2] fortunately finds my schedule with an open date on January 31st, 1937, and I am very glad to accept your invitation to be your guest preacher at the All University Religious Service on that date.

Although it is still some time in advance, I should appreciate any suggestions either about the theme or the length of the sermon. Are there any subjects which your students have heard too much about, or not enough? Do the preachers ordinarily read or speak extemporaneously? Other things being equal, I prefer the latter. Are you going to wish (as I really hope you are not) for a summary of the sermon for publicity purposes? If you are, the sooner I know the awful truth, the better; please include a statement of the desired length. Shall I bring with me my academic costume for the occasion or not?

You must think me an animated question box, but I do like to get these items of red tape out of the way in order to concentrate on more important matters.

Looking forward with great pleasure to seeing you and Howard University, and wishing you continued courage and inspiration for your great work, I remain
Most cordially yours,
[*signed*] Edgar S. Brightman
ESB:JEN

TLS. HTC-MBU: Box 1.

1. Edgar Sheffield Brightman (1884–1953) received his BA and MA from Brown before obtaining an STB (1910) and PhD (1912) from Boston University. After teaching at Nebraska Wesleyan University and Wesleyan University, he returned to Boston University in 1919 as a professor of philosophy and spent the remainder of his career there. Brightman was noted for his theology of personalism, which promoted the social relevance of Christianity by bringing to life the personality of Jesus and showing how his love ethic could be applied to personal and social relationships. His books include *The Problem of God* (New York: Abingdon, 1930), *The Finding of God* (New York: Abingdon, 1931), *Moral Laws* (New York: Abingdon, 1933), and *A Philosophy of Religion* (New York: Prentice-Hall, 1940). In his final years, he was the chief academic adviser for Martin Luther King Jr. In 1946 Brightman became an "associate" of the Fellowship Church in San Francisco, writing Thurman that "the work of your church is one of the most important projects in American religion." From Edgar S. Brightman, 9 October 1946, HTC-MBU: Box 22.

2. To Edgar S. Brightman, 18 May 1936, HTC-MBU: Box 1.

From Carter G. Woodson
22 May 1936
Washington, D.C.

Historian Carter G. Woodson,[1] *still rankled by his dismissal from Howard University fifteen years earlier, refuses an invitation to speak at Howard.*

My dear Mr. Thurman:

I have your invitation to deliver at Howard University a religious address February 7, 1937. For two reasons I have to reply in the negative. Because of my irreligion I was dismissed from Howard University in 1920 by that elocutionary monstrosity, J. Stanley Durkee,[2] supported in this action by certain trustees who are still running that institution; and I have not been on the campus since that time. Negro History Week, moreover, is my most valuable time of the year which I reserve for service outside of Washington where the people are more interested in my work than the "segregated white persons of color" residing in the District of Columbia.

I am very much interested in you, however, and I am acquainted with your talented wife. Your trip to India must have been profitable. Inasmuch as I traveled in those parts thirty years ago your more recent account will be helpful to me in tracing developments in the East. Some day when you are in the city I shall be delighted to chat with you at your home. I am usually idle evenings until ten when I retire.

Sincerely yours,
[*signed*] C.G. Woodson
C. G. Woodson,
Director
Prof. Howard Thurman,
Howard University,
Washington, D.C.

TLS. HTC-MBU: Box 21.

1. Carter Godwin Woodson (1875–1950) received an AB from Berea College in Kentucky (1903) and a BA and MA from the University of Chicago (1908). In 1912 he became the second African American to receive the PhD from Harvard University. Woodson established the Association for the Study of Afro-American Life and History in 1915, and in 1916 founded the *Journal of Negro History*. In 1926 he founded Negro History Week, a commemoration of black achievement that evolved into Black History Month during the 1960s. He was the author or coauthor of nineteen books, including *The History of the Negro Church* (Washington, D.C.: Associated Publishers, 1921) and *The Mis-Education of the Negro* (Washington, D.C: Associated Publishers, 1933). Woodson later commended the efforts of Howard

and Sue Bailey Thurman to promote black American history at the Church for the Fellowship of All Peoples in San Francisco (*WHAH*, 158).

2. James Stanley Durkee (1866–1951) was the president of Howard University from 1918 to 1926. He received a PhD from Boston University (1906) and served as the pastor of Baptist and Congregational churches. Mordecai Wyatt Johnson succeeded Durkee as the first black president of Howard University in 1926.

From A. Ann Silver

23 May 1936
Boston, Mass.

A. Ann Silver,[1] *executive secretary for the Metropolitan Student YWCA, thinks of Thurman in the context of Boston physician and ethicist Richard C. Cabot,*[2] *who, in* The Art of Ministering to the Sick, *employed the phrase "the growing edge" as a metaphor for spiritual growth.*[3] *Cabot subsequently came to Howard to speak at Rankin Chapel, and Thurman eventually adopted and adapted the phrase "the growing edge" for his purposes; it would become the title of one of his books and the name of the newsletter produced by the Fellowship Church.*

Mr. Howard Thurman
Howard University
Washington, D.C.

My dear Howard Thurman:

We are still rejoicing in your having been with us and having shared with us the close of a rich year.

I thought of you the other day when I read a review of the book the art of administering to the sick by R. C. Cabot and R. L. Dicks. This comment concerns Dr. Cabot's philosophy of growth:

> "He stresses the fact that the soul has a 'growing edge,' and that all attempts to foster growth will fail insofar as they do not take that fact into account. This growing edge he finds at the point where the individual seeks an answer to some question of his own, and where what is offered corresponds to something he now wants to be."
>
> {Lend me your copy of this book}[4]

You never leave us but that we begin looking forward to the time when you will return to Boston. We hope so much that it will be possible for you to be with us sometime during the next academic year.

With best wishes to you and Sue, I am

As ever,
[*signed*] Ann Silver
Executive Secretary
AAS:EB

TLS. HTC-MBU: Box 19.

1. A. Ann Silver, a longtime friend of Thurman's, had a career within many progressive Christian organizations and, after her years in Boston, was involved in international relief work for the American Friends Service Committee in Philadelphia and the YWCA in Montreal.

2. Richard Clarke Cabot (1868–1939) was a physician and ethicist who for many years practiced at Massachusetts General Hospital and taught at Harvard University. He was one of the pioneers in the field of pastoral counseling.

3. Richard C. Cabot and Russell L. Dirks, *The Art of Ministering to the Sick* (New York: Macmillan, 1936). Cabot and Dirks introduce the notion as follows: "A person can assimilate spiritual food only when it feeds his 'growing edge.' A soul like a muscle grows from a frontier which registers the point reached thus far on its march into the unknown. Not many years ago it was discovered that we can cultivate a bit of human muscle or kidney outside the body and watch the details of its growth. The tissue puts out new columns of cells like the rows of bricks added as we build a brick wall. . . . The growing edge, jagged and irregular, is the surface out of which new cells sprout. . . . The soul has a growing edge. It can advance only from the point where just now it is," 13–14.

4. Thurman's handwritten insertion.

To the Hecht Company

23 May 1936
Washington, D.C.

Thurman had a personal policy of refusing to voluntarily patronize segregated institutions. This letter to Hecht's department store is one of his many polite, direct letters to institutions that refused equal treatment to blacks.

The Hecht Company[1]
F Street at Seventh
Washington, D.C.

Gentlemen:

Owing to your policy of discrimination against Negroes in your rest rooms, I hereby pay my bill and close my account.

Respectfully yours,
[*signed*] Howard Thurman
Encl.

TLc. HTC-MBU: Box 9.

1. Hecht's was for many decades Washington's best-known department store. Originally founded in Baltimore by German immigrants in 1857, it opened a branch in Washington in 1896, and the store at F Street and Seventh became a Washington landmark. Although it had the reputation for being generally hospitable to black customers, like almost all public establishments in the Jim Crow South, it had segregated dining facilities and bathroom accommodations. In 1951 the octogenarian Mary Church Terrell led a civil rights demonstration against Hecht's; the store fully desegregated the following year. In her honor the former store (now an office complex) at F and Seventh has been since 2003 known as Terrell Place. In 2006 the last Hecht's department store in Washington, D.C., was closed and renamed.

To John Nevin Sayre
26 May 1936
Washington, D.C.

In this letter to John Nevin Sayre,[1] chairman of the International Fellowship of Reconciliation (FOR), Thurman outlines his views on what the organization must do to combat racial injustice in the South and institute new possibilities for reconciliation. Thurman recommended bypassing the moderate and elite Commission on Interracial Cooperation in favor of grass roots interclass and interracial action.

Dear Nevin:

I regret very much that I have not been able to answer your letter until today, but when I tell you that a terribly crowded and hectic speaking schedule has been mine practically all the time since returning to the country you will understand my delay.

I am tremendously interested in the questions that your letter raise and I have two or three suggestions to make. In the first place, I think your concern relative to the effectiveness of the program of the Fellowship in the South is justified. In the second place, it has not been possible for the Fellowship to get close to the mind of the South during the past few years without running into areas of risk and danger which in themselves may not find justification. Shorty Collins[2] did an exceptional good job for the Fellowship among student and faculty people in the South. He was able to discover white people and Negroes who were interested in the ideals of the Fellowship but who were not known to each other. His activity served as a kind of catalytic agent bringing these people together. I think his strategy was sound in that he selected a particular area, mainly a student-faculty group, and worked within that area with a great deal of intensity. When the time was ripening for some form of action for reasons not related to this fact Shorty resigned.

Buck Kester[3] worked with a student group also but found a larger opportunity in the industrial and labor aspects of racial conflict. More and more his work was confined to these groups making contact with students and faculty people only by way of gathering inspiration and courage for the other job. The logic of the work that Buck Kester did leads, it seems to me, to a position somewhat similar to the one at which he arrived. The time has passed for the theoretical and the merely discussional approach to the question on group conflict in the South. There are several agencies at work on the theory of race relations. They are trying by slow processes of education and cultivation to bring about reconciliation and harmony. I refer to the Interracial Commission[4] and the various church groups. I do not think that the task of the Fellowship is in this area primarily, but it is in the area of action including propaganda. All of this by way of background for the suggestions that I have to make.

First, the Fellowship ought to concentrate its energies by confining its work of reconciliation to one segment of conflict in the South. It should give its good wishes to all work in the other areas but it should confine its own primarily to one particular kind of job.

Second, when that area is selected someone especially fitted by background, training, insights and "guts" should be commissioned to carry it through.

Third, the active interest and support of Negroes and white people in that section should be solicited and utilized.

Fourth, Negro and white students and faculties and a few courageous and intelligent ministers of both races could also be enlisted.

Fifth, representatives from the masses, particularly among Negroes, should be contacted. I have been deeply concerned for sometime because the message of peace to which we are committed and of which we are a part cannot be reduced to terms that are realistic to the ordinary man in the street. Despite all that we can do the peace movement in this country is essentially a "high brow" movement and that means that its effectiveness among the masses of the people is not as great as the energies put forth would justify.

You will notice that I do not mention a particular area. I hesitate to do so because I would not wish to put forward any pet idea of my own. There are several other things that I want to say but I shall have to put them off until a later time. I hope that this letter will give you some indication at least as to how I feel.

Sincerely,
[*signed*] Howard Thurman
Mr. Nevin Sayre
2929 Broadway
New York, New York

TLc. HTC-MBU: Box 19.

1. For additional information about Sayre, see the biographical footnote in volume 1.

2. George "Shorty" Collins (who stood six feet five), a Baptist minister, was the southern racial and industrial secretary for FOR in the early 1920s, where he first met Thurman.

He was Baptist campus minister at the University of Wisconsin at Madison from 1928 to 1957, and then held a similar position at San Jose State in California. Collins had a major impact on Thurman's intellectual and religious development. Thurman joined FOR when he was an undergraduate at Morehouse, and he later wrote: "In my encounter with the FOR, as exemplified in the life of one of its secretaries, Shorty Collins, I found a place to stand in my own spirit—a place so profoundly affirming that *I* was strengthened by a sense of immunity to the assaults of the white world of Atlanta, Georgia." Several years later, in September 1925, when Thurman was a student at RTS, at a retreat in Pawling, New York, Collins introduced Thurman to the works of Olive Schreiner. *WHAH*, 59, 265.

3. During the 1930s Howard Anderson "Buck" Kester, a prominent Christian socialist, was a leader in the Southern Tenant Farmers' Union (STFU) and the Fellowship of Southern Churchmen. He recorded his involvement with the STFU in *Revolt among the Sharecroppers* (New York: Covici-Friede 1936). For additional information about Kester, see the biographical footnote in volume 1.

4. The Commission on Interracial Cooperation (CIC) was founded in 1919 in Atlanta as a response to the increased racial tensions following World War I. Six white southern men met and chose Will Alexander as the organization's president. Soon a few prominent blacks and women, including John and Lugenia Burns Hope, were invited to join the group. Much of the early work in places such as Atlanta was dedicated to combating the Ku Klux Klan and the practice of lynching. While the CIC did not challenge segregation in the South, it did bring together blacks and whites to discuss racial problems and to plot strategies for improving relations between the groups. The Great Depression curtailed severely the work of the CIC. A shortage in funding forced the organization to rethink its strategy, and it concluded it could no longer afford to pay its field representatives. In 1944 the CIC abandoned completely its local committee structure and fieldwork and merged with the newly established Southern Regional Council.

To W. W. Mendenhall
23 June 1936
Pittsburgh, Pa.

On 25 May 1936 Thurman received a telegram from Rachel Timberlake, on the Philadelphia staff of the Student Christian Movement of the Middle Atlantic States: "Can you arrange come Blueridge for all or part of the national student secretarial seminar June twenty ninth to July thirteenth?"[1] The YMCA summer facility at Blue Ridge in North Carolina was segregated and a considerable affront to Thurman and other blacks associated with the Student Christian Movement.[2] He replied to Timberlake by telegram the same day: "Have had no previous knowledge and am quite embarrassed to find my name listed in publicity as one of the resources stop—dates listed are already taken regrets."[3]

Timberlake responded to Thurman by letter on 26 May, expressing her embarrassment at the mix-up and extending her "regret that it is impossible for you to come."[4] Thurman was therefore quite surprised when he subsequently received a letter from W. W. Mendenhall[5] *stating that the Student Christian Movement would be "honored to have you as one of our leaders."*[6] *Thurman declined attending, once again, in this pointed reply.*

My dear Mr. Mendenhall:

I am in receipt of your letter with inclosure under date of June 5. I am frank to say that it has caused me a great deal of concern because without any authorization from me some one (I do not know whose responsibility it is) has scheduled me for the seminar at Blue Ridge June 29 through July 13. This is a very serious blunder. Doubtless you know the attitude that Negro students and student leaders have taken towards the whole question of segregation at Blue Ridge and I need not rehearse it here. Suffice it to say that under no conditions would I be willing to attend any kind of meeting at Blue Ridge so long as it has its present policy of segregation. This is not to suggest that I would dictate to the administration at Blue Ridge, but it is to say that as far as I am concerned I could not keep my self-respect if I attended any kind of meeting there. You can see why to have my name publicized as one of the leaders at Blue Ridge under these circumstances is a gross injustice to say the least.

I hope you will not take this letter as a personal affront but it is a simple statement of fact. I would appreciate it very much if you can advise me as to who was responsible for this unauthorized use of my name. I know that it must have been due to an oversight.[7]

Sincerely yours,
[*signed*] Howard Thurman

TLc. HTC-MBU: Box 12.

1. From Rachel Timberlake, 25 May 1936, HTC-MBU: Box 21.

2. The YMCA summer facility in Blue Ridge, the creation of Willis D. Weatherford, first opened its doors in 1912. (The YMCA facility for Negroes, in Kings Mountain, North Carolina, also opened in the same year.) Although Weatherford was a leading southern moderate on racial issues, Blue Ridge was segregated from its start, with blacks limited to a separate dining and sleeping area and black delegates not given full status as conference members but listed as "program participants." There had been annual exchanges between the two conferences until 1928, when two Negro secretaries of the YMCA, Thurman's good friends Frank T. Wilson and Benjamin Mays, ended the practice of sending Kings Mountain delegates to the Blue Ridge. It was not until 1951 that the Blue Ridge facility was fully desegregated; see Benjamin E. Mays, *Born to Rebel: An Autobiography* (New York: Scribners, 1971), 125–30, and John Egerton, *Speak Now against the Day: The Generation before the Civil Rights Movement in the South* (Chapel Hill: University of North Carolina Press, 1994), 44–48.

3. To Rachel Timberlake, 25 May 1936, HTC-MBU: Box 21. Thurman was even blunter in writing two days later to a black national secretary of the YMCA, Celestine Smith: "Have discovered that I am advertised as leader at Blue Ridge Seminar. Stop—I do not know who

is responsible but the whole thing has been done without consulting me in any way whatsoever. It is a colossal fraud." To Celestine Smith, 27 May 1936, HTC-MBU: Box 19.

4. From Rachel Timberlake, 26 May 1936, HTC-MBU: Box 21.

5. William W. Mendenhall was from the early 1940s through 1954 director of religious work at Cornell University and thereafter spent three years in Greece on behalf of the Congregational Christian Service Committee.

6. From W. W. Mendenhall, 5 June 1936, HTC-MBU: Box 12.

7. Mendenhall quickly responded to Thurman and apologized for the confusion. From W. W. Mendenhall, 25 June 1936, HTC-MBU: Box 13.

From Alice Sams

June 1936
Daytona Beach, Fla.

The relationship between Thurman and his mother was deep and abiding. In this letter she speaks about news from home and of her plans to visit soon. As Thurman notes elsewhere, the India experience and much of what followed was outside her life's experience, but she accepted it all with a quiet grace.[1]

My dear Son I thank you so much for the dollar as you sent with out me telling you ofcourse I need many things but I relise how high everry thing is now that we haftir have so I don't want you to spend any thing on me the man that have growing children to feed now hafter spend some you money I know you got broke on your India trip so I am trying to let {you} be free to get as far a head as posible and I want you to rest you braines and mind as much as you can everry 3 person here are playing some kind of nombers

It is gambling so far as I can see. And even some of the preachers are doeing It James have been put in Jaile three times about It the lass time he was put in he had played the luckey no. and they paid him one thousand and four hundred dollars while he was in DE Land Jaile and he paid him selfe out and he have not been in Jaile since. I wanted to tell Madeline to don't buy A mattress some one have been sleeping on please she might get some germs from It I will come up there for a few weeks I hate for you to hafter send the money but that will be my only chance because Bro. Jimes[2] is not willing for me to come and he would say he had no money to waist on the train So I ~~wou wou~~ would not ask him I want him to pay up all of my insurrence a head he tried to split when I told {him} but I don't care any thing about that of course If he would It agree to It nicely I would like Much better but that not him only as he is forced I will try to ready by the 15 of August. the school opens around the 14 or 15 of Sept he is cleaning the ground now I think he will out to the School this winter again I am geting where I feel my age more and so I am verry happy to have you and Madeline ~~and and~~ think of helping me to rest If you just be half as nice to me as I was to Mama

I will be satisfide I can wait on my own yet but I may live long enough to be like Mama was before she died but I am trying to treat everry body right I wish you could see the [*illegible*] letter Moes wrote to Leve here is his Address You can get your friend to visit him please and tell us how he is please but the best of All he is a converted man love to the family Anice is up but not so well Olive did not write me pray for me be good and Careful rest all you can
[*signed*] Your Mama

ALS. HTC-MBU: Box 198.

1. *WHAH*, 155–56.
2. James Sams, Alice's husband.

From Susan Ford Bailey

5 July 1936
Dermott, Ark.

Susan Ford Bailey's[1] *letter to her son-in-law makes brief mention of Thurman's financial difficulties, after taking a year's leave of absence with no pay from the university for their Asian trip, and the need to spend the summer of 1936 in a strenuous series of speaking engagements.*

Rev. Howard Thurman

Dear Son

Your wife and children are here, and I enjoy their company very much. But there is a vacant space. We miss your presence. Of course money must be scarce with you and I can not ask you to come—any way because I know what financial Strains mean. But you must try to come to see me when you can make it convenient, for I love you as well as these. Be sure that you do not over work yourself. Your health is worth more than any thing else. Your tribe is well and full of noise and never fail to let it out. Ann is the Idol of the community and she is vain enough to enjoy it. She is an unusual Baby, Olive is the drawing card for the children of the neighborhood They all want to be with Olive
With much love I am your devoted
[*signed*] Mama Bailey

ALS. DHU-MS: Box 4046.

1. See biographical note in volume 1.

From A. A. Paul

22 July 1936
Maitri, Kilpauk, Madras
India

A. A. Paul, general secretary of the Federation of International Fellowships in India, reflects on the racial divide in Christianity, potential world conflict, and emerging efforts to bring about greater understanding between religions.

Dr. Howard Thurman,
Associate Professor of Christian Theology,
Howard University,
Washington, D.C. U.S.A.

My dear Dr. Thurman,

I hope you got all the letters and the bundle{s} of literature that I sent to you since you left India. I suppose that after getting to America you have been busy visiting the student centres and sharing with your constituency the experiences you had while here in India. I suppose it will take three or four months before you are through with that and that then you would be free to write and tell me about things.

I was very much grieved to read about the recent union of the three great Methodist Bodies of the U.S. A. when your community was put off in a separate fold of their own![1] Fancy a thing like this happening in the year 1936! However, there it is.

How far away we are from the Message of Christ. I am exceedingly sorry about this and I wish the white Christian leaders would recognise the absurdity and the silliness of an action like this. Is this a forecast of the coming conflict between the whites and the coloured in the world? It is very difficult to escape the thought that the world is slowly but surely marching towards a conflict between the colourless and the coloured.

In this atmosphere one feels so happy that efforts are being made in several parts of the world, not necessarily through the Christian Churches, to bring about closer understanding and cooperation between the various religions.

I suppose you have heard about the World Congress of Faiths[2] which was held in London recently at which some outstanding leaders of thought of the various religions spoke. In the "Hindu" of Madras, in its issue of the 20th. July was published a talk that Dr. S. Radhakrishnan,[3] the famous Indian Philosopher gave to the Congress. It really is a super address. I am sending you a copy of it. I feel that ~~we~~{you} must read it particularly because you are interested in our own Fellowship Movement here in India.

I wonder if, after getting to America either you or Mrs. Thurman did anything in connection with the starting of an International Fellowship Movement in America. You remember that both of you were deeply interested to do that when you were here. I shall be glad to know what you are doing and what success you are meeting with.

We are still thinking of you. You will be glad to know that Kumari, my daughter, has passed the S.S.L.C. Examination which was held in April last and has been admitted into the Women's Christian College with Physics, Chemistry and Natural Science as her optional subjects, preparing herself for medicine. The other children also are doing well.

Hoping to hear from you when you have the time,
Yours Very Sincerely,
[*signed*] A. A. Paul
AAP/SVV.

TLS. HTC-MBU: Box 16.

1. The Methodist Church, uniting the Methodist Episcopal Church, the Methodist Episcopal Church, South, and the Methodist Protestant Church, was created in 1939, though this merger relegated blacks to the Central Jurisdiction, a segregated jurisdictional conference based strictly on race. The Central Jurisdiction was abolished in 1968.

2. The aim of the World Congress of Faiths, held in London in July 1936, was "not to create one new synthetic religion, but to generate understanding and a sense of unity between the religions of the world." "World Congress of Faiths: Promotion of Peace," *Times* (London), 27 May 1936.

3. Sarvepalli Radhakrishnan (1888–1975) was a leading Indian philosopher, educator, and interpreter of the Vedanta. He later enjoyed a prominent political career, serving as India's ambassador to the Soviet Union (1949–52), vice president (1952–62), and president (1962–67). The talk sent to Thurman was probably "The Supreme Spiritual Idea," presented at the World Congress of Faiths on 5 June 1936.

From A. Philip Randolph

2 November 1936
New York, N.Y.

At the meeting on 6 December, A. Philip Randolph's[1] *union, the International Brotherhood of Sleeping Car Porters, received its charter from the American Federation of Labor as the AFL's first all-black union. Thurman chaired the meeting, at which Howard University Secretary Emmett J. Scott*[2] *was the principal speaker. In Thurman's remarks he was quoted as stating "the Brotherhood of Sleeping Car Porters is one of the most significant steps that have been taken in the direction of attempting to raise our standard of living," and he praised the union for overcoming the many difficulties that had stood in its way.*[3]

My dear Friend:

Just a word of remembrance and to hope that you and the family, the wife and youngster, are enjoying the best of health.

Now the Brotherhood of Sleeping Car Porters plans to hold a big labor Mass Meeting in Washington on Sunday afternoon, December 6 at the Florida Avenue Church. We hope to make this mass meeting big and significant and to bring to the Negro worker the importance of their developing an interest and participating in the labor movement, since the large majority are workers.

Mr. M. P. Webster,[4] Chairman of the General Executive Board of the Brotherhood, and myself and possibly Edward F. McGrady[5] of the Department of Labor will be the speakers.

May I request you to serve as the chairman of this meeting? I assure you I shall appreciate it immensely. It will be a pleasure to see you and the wife again. I am sending you under separate cover a copy of The Black Worker,[6] which is published by the Brotherhood.

May I hear from you at your earliest convenience?

Fraternally yours,
[*signed*] A. Philip Randolph
A. Philip Randolph
International President
BS&AU
12646

TLS. HTC-MBU: Box 17.

1. Asa Philip Randolph (1889–1979) was born in Crescent City, Florida, and grew up in Jacksonville, where he graduated from the Cookman Institute in 1907. After moving to New York City in 1911, he became active in black socialist politics and formed the International Brotherhood of Sleeping Car Porters in 1925. His call for a rally by blacks in Washington, D.C., in 1941 led to the formation of the March on Washington Movement; although the rally was called off at the last minute, it led to Executive Order 8802, which established the Fair Employment Practices Commission (FEPC).

2. Emmett Jay Scott (1873–1957) was born in Houston and attended Wiley College without graduating. After working as a journalist, in 1897 he became Booker T. Washington's personal secretary and right-hand man. In 1912 he became secretary of Tuskegee Institute, remaining in that position until 1919, serving as special adviser to Secretary of War Newton D. Baker on colored troops during World War I. In 1919 he became secretary of Howard University, remaining in the position until his resignation in 1938.

3. "Porters Granted A. F of L. Charter," *Baltimore Afro-American*, 12 December 1936.

4. Milton P. Webster (1887–1965) was the longtime first international vice president of the Brotherhood of Sleeping Car Porters. See William H. Harris, *Keeping the Faith: A. Philip Randolph, Milton P. Webster, and the Brotherhood of Sleeping Car Porters, 1925–1937* (Urbana: University of Illinois Press, 1991).

5. Edward F. McGrady (1872–1960) worked as a pressman in Boston before becoming active in union activities, eventually becoming president of the Massachusetts State Federation of Labor. In 1933 he was appointed assistant secretary of labor, leaving in 1937 to become vice president in charge of labor relations for the Radio Corporation of America (RCA), retiring in 1951.

6. *The Black Worker*, the official organ of the Brotherhood of Sleeping Car Porters, was published quarterly from 1929 to 1968.

To Sherwood Eddy
9 November 1936
Washington, D.C.

The Delta Cooperative Farm in Hillhouse, Bolivar County, Mississippi, established in the spring of 1936, was a remarkable attempt to point toward new ways of economic organization and racial interaction in the Deep South. It was a project of the interracial Southern Tenant Farmers' Union (STFU), founded by tenant farmers and sharecroppers in eastern Arkansas in 1934. In March 1936 some of the leaders of the STFU, including union president H. L. Mitchell and Howard Kester, decided to establish a cooperative farm.[1] *(There was much interest in cooperatives among progressives and black intellectuals at the time as nonrevolutionary alternatives to capitalism.)*[2] *Unable to find suitable land in Arkansas, with the financial assistance of Christian socialist Sherwood Eddy,*[3] *they purchased a two-thousand-acre farm in Mississippi. The cooperative farm received much attention from the socialist and left Christian circles in which Thurman traveled; Norman Thomas and Reinhold Niebuhr were among its most prominent advocates. Thurman worked with Eddy to find students at Howard who were capable of and willing to assist at the Delta Cooperative Farm,*[4] *and Thurman's involvement with the project reflected his lifelong interest in practical interracial activities and his interest in the late 1930s in alternatives to capitalism.*

The Delta Cooperative Farm faced a number of problems, though. It quickly ran into economic difficulties and was near bankruptcy after the 1937 season. These financial troubles were compounded by disputes among the trustees over the farm's direction and broader problems in the STFU between communist and socialist factions. The Delta Cooperative Farm continued until 1942; a sister farm eighty miles to the south, Providence Cooperative Farm, lasted until 1956.

My dear Sherwood:

I am writing for two things: first, I am very desirous of getting some up-to-date information about Hill House, Mississippi. I have not heard anything in a long time. I am wondering if it would not be a good idea to try to interest our students and some of our faculty in maintaining a teacher down there for a year or two. I want, if possible, that a vital connection between our campus and Hill House be maintained. Let me hear from you on this point, please.

The second thing that I want to say has to do with the possibility of your coming down here for some kind of spiritual meeting. We could arrange a dinner or something at which you would have an opportunity to meet the students and some of the faculty. You have not visited Howard University in a long time and we are exceedingly anxious to have you. Please advise me as to the possible dates that you will be available and the cost.

With kindest personal greetings, I am

Sincerely yours,
[*signed*] Howard Thurman
Dean of the Chapel
Mr. Sherwood Eddy
347 Madison Avenue
New York, New York

TLc. HTC-MBU: Box 6.

1. For accounts of the STFU and the Delta Cooperative Farm, see Donald H. Grubbs, *Cry from the Cotton: The Southern Tenant Farmers' Union and the New Deal* (Chapel Hill: University of North Carolina Press, 1971); Howard Kester, *Revolt among the Sharecroppers* (New York: Covici, Friede, 1936); Robert F. Martin, *Howard Kester and the Struggle for Social Justice in the South, 1904–77* (Charlottesville: University Press of Virginia, 1991), 86–108.

2. For African American cooperatives in the interwar years, see John Hope II, "Rochdale Cooperatives among Negroes," *Phylon* 1 (1940): 39–52 and W. E. B. Du Bois, "Dusk of Dawn" (1940), *Writings* (New York: Library of America, 1986), 706–15.

3. Sherwood Eddy (1871–1963) was born in Leavenworth, Kansas, and was an 1896 graduate of Yale University He went to India as a YMCA secretary, and in 1910 became the Asia secretary of the YMCA, retiring in 1930, though he continued to have an active career as an exponent of a progressive Christian internationalism. He founded the annual Sherwood Eddy Seminars in 1921, an experiment in international education.

4. See from Sherwood Eddy, 14 April 1937, printed in the current volume, and from Prentice Thomas, 15 October 1937, HTC-MBU: Box 21.

REVIEW OF ALBERT SCHWEITZER, *INDIAN THOUGHT AND ITS DEVELOPMENT*

DECEMBER 1936
WASHINGTON, D.C.

Thurman's review of Indian Thought and Its Development[1] *indicates his admiration for Schweitzer*[2] *and his long interest in Indian culture. According to Schweitzer, Indian thought is more otherworldly, more spiritual, and less doctrinaire and dualistic than Western thought. Although Thurman praises Schweitzer's writing style and his inclusion of a wide range of Eastern religions, he dissents from Schweitzer's criticism of contemporary Indian religious thinkers.*

Any book published by Albert Schweitzer is an event of significance, for his is one of the world's great minds. In *Indian Thought and Its Development* he examines the ground of Indian religious thought and traces its development from the ancient Vedas to its flowering in the minds and lives of contemporaries like Gandhi, Tagore[3] and Bose.[4]

The distinguishing marks between western and Indian religious thought are two. The West tends toward a world-view that is life and world affirming; while Indian thought moves in the direction of world and life negation. In the second place, Indian thought is monistic and mystical; while western thought is dualistic and doctrinaire. He shows with brilliant skill how the claims of two world-views have made their demands upon individual and group interpretations of religion in India and with what results. His appreciation of the major contributions of Hinduism, Buddhism, Jainism and Islam is heartening in its fairness and comprehensiveness.

One of the most interesting things about the volume is the restraint and simplicity with which it is written. A technical knowledge of the history of religion is hardly necessary in order to assure a rather comprehensive understanding of the points at issue and the points discussed. This is rewarding and stimulating reading.

In his discussion relative to the way in which modern Indian thinkers force the old texts of their sacred writings into the service of their own doctrines or spiritual discoveries, Dr. Schweitzer is quite severe. He seems to overlook the fact that this tendency is inherent in the very effort by which a religious thinker seeks to affirm spiritual solidarity with the race. He makes a plea for humility on the part of the Indian thinker as he faces the West with his contribution. Even as he does this one is conscious of the same attitude in western thought in the light of which Dr. Schweitzer makes his judgment.

Woman's Press 30, no. 11 (1936): 573.

1. Albert Schweitzer, *Indian Thought and Its Development* (New York: Holt, 1936).

2. Albert Schweitzer (1875–1965), born in Alsace, achieved renown as a musician, musicologist, and theologian before studying medicine and establishing a hospital in Lambaréné in French Equatorial Africa (now in Gabon) in 1912. A renowned humanitarian, he received the Nobel Prize for Peace in 1953.

3. For additional information on Rabindranath Tagore, see the biographical essay about Thurman in volume I.

4. Subhas Chandra Bose (1897–1945) was a Bengali nationalist, rival of Gandhi, and a leading official of the Congress Party in the 1930s. He served as president of the party in

1938, though Gandhi forced him from his position. Never an advocate of nonviolence, his opposition to British imperialism during World War II led him to flee India and form alliances with Germany and Japan. In 1943, in Japanese-occupied Singapore, he organized the Indian National Army to fight against the British in South Asia. He died in an airplane crash in 1945.

From Herbert King

31 December 1936
New York, N.Y.

Thurman's close friend Herbert King[1] *writes about the financial problems with his position as associate secretary of the YMCA at the National Council of Student Christian Associations.*

Dear Howard,

Thanks for the telegram which was phoned to me from Philly. Sorry I can't come to Washington. This finance business of the Student Division is running me crazy.

Don't jump sky high when I tell you that I'm using your name in a letter to Florence Reed[2] and David Jones.[3] I've thought it through carefully and it won't hurt you or indicate any change of mind or appraisal on your part, as regards Miss Reed especially. I couldn't think of any other Council person's name to use. Please be sweet and don't be angry.

Thanks for your gift and for the letter to Murray which he shared with me. Fill in this blank for the $25<u>00</u> if you actually think you can raise the $15<u>00</u> extra from your budget. It will help—but <u>don't</u> if you aren't able. <u>I</u> <u>mean</u> <u>that!</u>

Am going through with this thing this year. What a tragedy that having found the thing which for the next few years {can} give me my best opportunity and which I fundamentally enjoy doing and to have such violent hate of this financial aspect of it (with all its collateral branches) that takes from me something I've cherished so long. I think, Howard, it may be only fear of insecurity that keeps me at it, frantic as I am, here in the midst of the year. Today I am sorry for so many things.

Stay with me—stick by me—God knows I say this with every bit of me—I need you, Howard, as never before. I'm still näive—I didn't know life could be quite like this. Don't worry though . . . please . . . things will come out finally some way, I believe—which keeps me going—along with the knowledge of your love.

Ever
[*signed*] Herb.

ALS. HTC-MBU: Box 10.

1. William Herbert King (1906–66), generally known as Herbert King, was born in Atlanta and was a 1927 Morehouse graduate. He received his B.Div. from Union Theological Seminary in 1930 and then served as minister at Plymouth Congregational Church in Washington, D.C, from 1930 to 1933. An active pacifist and socialist, he was associate chairman of the United Youth Conference Against the War in 1932 ("Delegates to Conference against War," *Chicago Defender*, 10 December 1932). After obtaining a master's in sacred theology from Oberlin in 1934, he taught at Hampton Institute from 1934 to 1936, and was associate secretary of the National Student Council of the YMCA from 1936 to 1944. In 1946 King became pastor of the Grace Congregational Church in New York City, and he earned an EdD from Columbia Teacher's College in 1951. In 1958 he became a professor at McCormick Theological Seminary in Chicago, where he remained until his death. King was probably Thurman's closest friend in the 1930s and 1940s. After the death of Thurman's first wife, Katie Kelley, King accompanied him to Europe in the summer of 1931, and the two men were in frequent contact over some of their most private concerns. In 1944 King was the first person recommended by Thurman to be the pastor of what became the Fellowship Church. Their friendship, for reasons unknown, seems to have cooled in the later 1940s and 1950s. King was not mentioned in Thurman's autobiography, a striking absence.

2. Thurman's enmity to Florence Matilda Read (1886–1973), his former supervisor as president of Spelman College, was well known to his friends. For additional information about Read, see the biographical footnote in volume 1.

3. Probably David Dallas Jones, who was from 1926 until his death, president of Bennett College in Greensboro, North Carolina.

To Herbert King
5 January 1937
Washington, D.C.

Thurman replies to King, lamenting the decision that combined the Negro and white divisions of the Student Christian Movement.

My dear Herbert:

I regret very much that it is not possible for me to write the kind of personal letter that I want, but this will have to do. I am deeply concerned about the fact that you have been made to feel that you must raise the budget for Negro work. This is a fundamental violation of the understanding that was prevalent when Negro Student work became a part of the Student Division. My frank feeling is that it would be much better if the National Student Division dropped Negro work completely disavowed any responsibility providing in some joint mannor the kind of aggregate leadership that they feel their students need. It is a rotten piece of hypocrisy for you to be made to feel that it is your responsibility as a Negro Secretary to raise your budget. The old arrangement was at least honest in its segregated policy.

I have sent you my pledge and hope to pay it before the first of May. I ought to be coming through New York sometime Friday night enroute to Northfield.[1] I shall get in touch with you. Best of real wishes.

Sincerely yours,
[*signed*] Howard Thurman
Dean of the Chapel
Mr. Herbert King
347 Madison Avenue
New York, New York

TLc. HTC-MBU: Box 10.

1. Northfield Seminary for Young Ladies in Northfield, Massachusetts.

From Alice Sams
9 January 1937
Daytona Beach, Fla.

Alice Sams writes her son a post-Christmas letter, telling him of the events in her life. Like all of her letters, this letter displays her selflessness, deep Christian faith, and abiding love for her children.

My dear son I was verry glad to hear from you I had just said I would wait and if no word came from you in the maile I would write and find out if the oranges and sweet bread[1] got there how did Sue leave her Mama I am not going to hint things to worry about but the way things are going in this city a person hafter worry or think of things a little serious I went to town the other day and a big police was station an City hall down one week yesterday they have been fussing down Town those are things that we hafter think of some times and the church is runed by politick just like the city and county and there is verry little Justice but I thank God It is among the whites and not Colored and whites they had all sorts of guns and pistol Knives[2] verry glad you adopeted daughters[3] was there though the holidays glad my poor daughter had a good Christmas dinner I wish so that I could have been there with my two children and thir family I am ~~sendi~~ sending a crate of oranges son are for Madeline and her fam you will hafter wash them before you use them I was two tired to wash them I walked to the city and back and brought the box back So I was all used up and I thought I would have got them off yesterday but Mr Brant had to work yesterday afternoon verry glad of all you all sent me for Christmast Levebaby is liveing with his wife mother a while James is still in jaile[4] I have not been down there to see him Thornlon say he is the cook down there and perhaps If we let him stay there a ~~h~~ long time he will stay out I hope you or Madeline will allways regard God law though shall not steal and not kick against the law of the city that what James trouble pray for

Kiss the darling daughter {for me} mind don't over doe you selfe My ~~son~~ Son and tax you mind two much there was a lady to ~~church~~ church lass Sunday night who use to go to hear you when you went Detroit Michigan seemingly verry glad to see you Mother tell Madeline to write me a note to My Daughter Susie Bailey Thurman I hope you had a large table because It takes all most a whole big table to hold the deckerration on days like Christ did you have a turkey and plumbuding and all sorts of food glad you did get back to Washington for Christmast I thought you let Ann stay with her grand Mam Bailey well I hope to get my furnture paid for this winter I hope you will and tell all all about Christmast present by next Christmast I got curtain up in the frount room and dinging room shade in the bath room I am doeing fine don't you think bought a hat and some gloves a white cotten dress to wear on the deaconess board they require us to wear cotton dresses so I cant wear the one you all sent me to wear to Atlanta

Kiss the family for me be sure to wash the oranges because they are verry dirty let me know when they are out because they are droping on the ground and wisting Most of my young chickens died God bless you I Heln Harris have some kind of school Job in the county

[*signed*] Your mother Alice

ALS. HTC-MBU: Box 162.

1. Sweet bread was a type of Christmas cake containing raisins and molasses, popular in Scotland, Newfoundland, the Caribbean, and the American South. Alice Sams, according to her son, "was a creative and imaginative cook" who spent much of her working life cooking for white families. Thurman's highest praise of a culinary accomplishment was that "it is worthy of Mamma Alice." *WHAH,* 14–15.

2. Alice Sams was referring to the confrontation at Daytona Beach City Hall in the opening days of 1937 between the Florida National Guard and the Daytona Beach police force, part of a feud between the outgoing governor of Florida, Dave Sholtz, and the former mayor of Daytona Beach, who was forced to resign on 10 December 1936 and was replaced by his wife, Irene Armstrong. When Governor Sholtz sought to remove Armstrong from office in the final days of his term, the confrontation ensued, with four companies of national guardsmen facing ninety police officers armed with pistols, shotguns, and riot gear who were protecting her. The matter was resolved when the incoming governor, Fred P. Cone, revoked the ouster order against Edward Armstrong, and in March 1937 Irene Armstrong resigned in favor of her husband, who resumed office as mayor. "Guns Keep Woman in Post as Mayor," *New York Times*, 3 January 1937; "Woman Mayor Resigns," *New York Times*, 5 March 1937.

3. The reference to 'adopted daughters' is unclear. Neither of Thurman's daughters was adopted, though Sue Bailey Thurman was not Olive's biological mother.

4. James Sams, Alice's husband.

To Samuel Williams
14 January 1937
Washington, D.C.

Thurman gives Samuel Williams[1] advice on whether to study for his graduate degree in theology at Howard or at a predominantly white seminary.

My dear Samuel Williams:

I am in receipt of your letter under date of January 6. I understand quite sympathetically the problem that you face and am writing you my opinion. In the first place, if you have money, then your situation is at once altered by the fact. You could go to any one of several Eastern institutions and have a grand experience. In some ways there are advantages in larger and older Eastern theological seminaries that are not to be found in Howard University. Too, there is the added advantage of spending a part of your academic career associating intimately with white students in an atmosphere that is not constantly loaded with dynamite. However, Howard University offers a very excellent opportunity for you to get a foundation in the sense of thorough and expansive theological education. In addition to these facts, it will not be as costly as in some other places. We have a good staff and Washington abounds in more opportunities than even you will take advantage of if you came. In addition to all the above, there is a decided advantage in studying religion with minds that happen to be encased in Negro bodies.

If you can afford it economically, go East and get a good comprehensive theological training. But, have no illusions; you must have some money. If your circumstances are limited, come to Howard University and get a thorough training in religion in an atmosphere in which survival value of all your idealism will be comprehensively checked. Whatever you decide to do, please get after it at once.

My sincerest greetings.

Sincerely yours,
[*signed*] Howard Thurman
Dean of the Chapel
Mr. Samuel W. Williams
253 Mildred Street
Atlanta, Georgia

TLc. HTC-MBU: Box 21.

1. Samuel Woodrow Williams (1912–70) was born in Sparkman, Arkansas. He earned a BA from Morehouse in 1937, BD and MA degrees from Howard University, a PhD from the University of Chicago, and a DD from Arkansas Baptist College. In 1947 he returned to Morehouse to teach philosophy and was chairman of the Department of Philosophy and

Religion from 1947 to 1970. He was also assistant pastor of Friendship Baptist Church from 1947 to 1954 and then pastor from 1954 until his death. At various times during his years in Atlanta, he served as chair of the Atlanta Community Relations Commission, as well as president of the Atlanta NAACP.

To Max Yergan

15 January 1937
Washington, D.C.

In this letter inviting Max Yergan[1] to speak at Howard University, Thurman states that he "did not know what it was to wrestle with hate" until his travel to India, an indication of how his experience in the Negro Delegation was leading him to rethink the meaning of the political and religious response to oppression and imperialism.

My dear Max:

I have wanted to see you ever since you returned to the country. Sue and I would like to have a good long talk with you about many things. Since we saw you last, we have been to India and we have seen for ourselves. The only thing that I can say in passing is that I did not know what it was to wrestle with hate until my experience in that country. I may add that I am not thinking of anything that was directed at me as a person but the complete futility that is present in the mind when one sees what it is that Imperialism truly involves.

Would you be willing to come down to Howard University to speak at a Vesper that is yet to be arranged sometime in February, say February 14? We can only give you $35, as this is the amount that our budget can stand. We would like for you to speak from a topic from your own choice and wording and to plan some time, say the next day, Monday, when you can talk ~~kindly~~ {quietly} and informally with some friends. The service will be held in Chapel. The setting will be good, and we want the service vigorous and challenging. Sue joins me in urging you to come and so does President Johnson.

Sincerely yours,
[*signed*] Howard Thurman
Dean of the Chapel
Mr. Max Yergan
347 Madison Avenue
New York, New York

TLc. HTC-MBU: Box 22.

1. For additional information about Yergan, see the biographical footnote in volume 1.

To Max Yergan
19 March 1937
Washington, D.C.

Thurman expresses his interest in traveling to Africa, which would be a theme in his correspondence for the next several years before the worsening world situation would make this impossible. His interest in Africa dates back to talks from Christian missionaries who gave talks in Daytona's black churches.

My dear Max:

Just a note to thank you for your good letter and to say how very happy both Sue and I were to have you here and to talk at length about things of mutual concern.[1] You may be interested to know that I had occasion to see Canon Stokes[2] the other day and casually mentioned my desire to visit Africa sometime within the next two years.[3] His interest in it was immediate, and he said that he would be very glad to use his office and influence to help me get into the country and give me personal letters to interested people. When we meet, I want to talk with you about what this involves.

Sue joins me in genuine greetings to you.

Sincerely yours,
[*signed*] Howard Thurman
Dean of the Chapel
Mr. Max Yergan
8 West 40th Street
New York, New York

TLc. HTC-MBU: Box 22.

1. For a summary of the discussion between Yergan and Thurman, see To Beverly Oaten, 23 March 1937, HTC-MBU: Box 15.

2. Anson Phelps Stokes Jr. (1874–1958), an Episcopal priest, was canon of the National Cathedral in Washington from 1924 to 1939. For many years he was board president of the Phelps-Stokes Fund, a philanthropic organization that concentrated on African and African American projects. His published works include *Report of Rev. Anson Phelps Stokes on Education, Native Welfare, and Race Relations in East and South Africa* (New York: Carnegie Corporation of New York, 1934) and *Negro Status and Race Relations in the United States, 1911–1946: The Thirty-Five Year Report of the Phelps-Stokes Fund* (New York: Phelps-Stokes Fund, 1948).

3. On the voyage from Marseilles to Colombo, Ceylon, in 1935, Thurman stopped in Port Said on the Mediterranean side of the Suez Canal and made a port of call at Djibouti in French Somaliland, in sub-Saharan Africa. However, he would not make an extended trip to Africa until 1963. For the history of Thurman's attitudes toward Africa, see *WHAH*, 193–211.

From Sherwood Eddy
14 April 1937
New York, N.Y.

After expressing uneasiness with taking money for speaking at Rankin Chapel, Sherwood Eddy seeks Thurman's advice on the recruitment of a Negro student to work at the Delta Farm in Hillsdale, Mississippi. Eddy prefers someone with experience in the Deep South.

My dear Howard Thurman:

I felt troubled about receiving the honorarium of $50 from Howard for my very small service there. To me it would be like drinking water from the well of Bethlehem by David. My race has so long defrauded your race that I feel I can never repay my debt by a long life of service. I doubt not that this is Government money. Nevertheless, I do not feel I can use it personally. I have written to Sam Franklin[1] and he cordially agrees with me in the plan of using it to defray the expenses for one Negro student who will serve on our Farm this summer with Harold Colvin's[2] group. I will write and tell Harold Colvin that the money is available for one such person and to consult you and others in the selection of the best single individual we can find. Very much will depend upon the first student who works in this capacity. If there is no trouble this summer, no visit from the Vigilantes, and no violence, then we shall have established a precedent and will not be so likely to have trouble in the future. They will work out their own relationships on the Farm without difficulty, I believe, but the first man who goes down should, in my judgment, be not a sensitive person from the north, primarily concerned with the issue of social equality, but should recognize the backwardness and prejudice of that region of the deep south as well as the legal status that forbids the teaching of social equality in the state of Mississippi. He or she should be prepared to spend their leisure time with their own people. We shall have to take extra precaution for this one first year. After that I do not anticipate any trouble. It is a time when precedents will count.

I understand Harold Colvin is sick at present, from overwork, but when he is well I will ask him to take up with you and others the question of the right person to work in this group on the Farm this summer.

With sincere regards,

Ever yours,

[*signed*] Sherwood p

P.S. After dictating above I received yours of April 12th in which you speak of two candidates for the Farm. I think I saw this young man who is in the theological school and with his wife wishes to spend part of the summer on the Farm.[3] I believe he is from that part of the country. In general, a man from the deep south would be better than someone from the north who does not know conditions there so well. But it is a question rather of the person than of place. Which of the two do you think would be the safer man, the stronger and better man, who could make the largest contribution to the Farm? Would you feel absolutely safe with the better of these two, or should we look further for an ideal man?

E:P

Copies to: Sam Franklin

Harold Colvin

TLS. HTC-MBU: Box 6.

1. Samuel Franklin Jr. (1902–94) was born in Dandridge, Tennessee. A staunch Presbyterian, Franklin was a graduate of Maryville College, McCormick Theological Seminary, and the University of Edinburgh in Scotland. Franklin was Eddy's secretary before becoming a missionary to Japan in 1929. He left Japan in 1934, and in 1936 he became director of the Delta Farm, an interracial cooperative project founded by Eddy in Bolivar County, Mississippi. He served there until entering the military as a chaplain during World War II. Rick L. Nutt, *The Whole Gospel for the Whole World: Sherwood Eddy and the American Protestant Mission* (Macon, Ga.: Mercer University Press, 1997), 107, 118–19, 278.

2. Harold W. Colvin (1896–1995) was born in Omaha, Nebraska, and raised in Topeka, Kansas. He graduated from Washburn College in 1917 and, after a year at Yale Divinity School, joined the Army in 1918. Colvin became a YMCA secretary in 1919 at the University of Illinois, where he served for one year, until he took a position as the boys' work secretary of Salina, Kansas. In 1923 he returned to the University of Illinois, this time as campus program director. Colvin remained active in YMCA work throughout his professional life. He also continued in college whenever possible. He spent the summers of 1933 and 1934 at the University of Chicago and the summers of 1935 and 1936 at Teachers College, Columbia University. After being invited to join the PhD program at Columbia, Colvin conducted his fieldwork in the summer of 1937 at the Delta Farm. He recruited and led a group of college students from across the country to work at the farm, and each evening he conducted debriefing sessions, the content of which became the core of his dissertation.

3. The young man is probably Coleman Leroy Hacker (1910–1994).

From Melvin Watson

14 April 1937

Raleigh, N.C.

A protégé, Melvin Watson,[1] relays a secondhand account of a preaching engagement where Thurman left the audience spellbound. There is also discussion of Watson possibly going to teach at Alwaye College in India.

Dear Doctor,

I was in Atlanta over the week-end for the "Y" Council meetings. We regretted very much your absence. Richard McKinney[2] was there also and he told me that you preached at Union[3] last week until all the place got cloudy. It seems that the occasion was characterized by bench-walking,[4] literal and intellectual. I was greatly impressed when "Mac" told me that you left your little papers and cards at home!

This news about you made me anxious to know definitely whether it will be possible for you to make Shaw or not. You have already written that you plan to come, but I want to check on you. I want you to come both for our students' sake and for mine. I need to talk with you about the summer. You haven't sent me any more India news and I don't know just how matters now stand.[5] If I'm not to go to India then I need to go over with you possible uses of the summer. This means that if you are not coming to Raleigh, then I must make arrangements to visit Washington at some convenient time. Let me hear from you!

Much love to Sue, Olive, and Anne.

As ever,

[*signed*] Monk.

ALS. HTC-MBU: Box 21.

1. Melvin Watson had studied under Thurman at Morehouse, and he was at this time a professor of religion and dean at Shaw University in Raleigh, North Carolina. For additional information about Watson, see the biographical footnote in volume 1.

2. Morehouse alumnus Richard McKinney was completing his S.T.M. at Andover Newton Theological School. For additional information about McKinney, see the biographical footnote in volume 1.

3. Virginia Union University.

4. An idiom referring to ecstatic worship, and more generally to all forms of emotional worship practices, in the black church. Watson was referring to the latter sense, and was using it with considerable metaphorical license.

5. Thurman wrote P. O. Phillip of Alwaye College on 22 January 1937, suggesting Watson's candidacy for the Alwaye Fellowship. HTC-MBU: Box 16. For reasons that are not clear, Watson never went to Alwaye.

To Ralph Harlow

19 April 1937

Washington, D.C.

One gets a glimpse of Thurman's psychology as a preacher in this letter to Ralph Harlow,[1] as Thurman laments how poor a sermon he recently delivered at Smith College.

My dear Ralph:

I am enclosing my check for $10 to cover the advance which you and Marian let me have yesterday. Please accept my appreciation for this consideration.

I am very anxious to have you know that I appreciate tremendously the opportunity to visit with you. My one regret was that it was so short.

President Seely[2] and I had quite a talk on the train last night, and he, out of a clear sky, asked my reaction to an idea that he had in mind relative to an undergraduate student exchange between the University and some Negro institution. It was quite a coincident and to me tremendously exciting.

I do hope that I shall have a chance to come to Smith College again because in my ten years as a preacher the sermon that I gave in the Chapel yesterday was the worst exhibition of which I have been conscious. For some strange reason my mind did not click.[3] I was deeply moved by the opportunity the responsiveness of the group and I felt at the end a deeply humiliated man. I am therefore really anxious to have a opportunity to do a better job. I write this quite frankly even though it may seem on the surface a bid for an invitation.

The session on India in the evening was a little better.

Within the next two or three days I am going in to have a talk with President Johnson about his proposal. Remember me very kindly to Marian.

Sincerely yours,
[*signed*] Howard Thurman
Dean of the Chapel
Prof. Ralph Harlowe
Smith College
Northampton, Massachusetts

TLc. HTC-MBU: Box 162.

1. Samuel Ralph Harlow (1885–1972) was born in Boston. He graduated from Harvard in 1908 and from Union Theological Seminary in 1912. Harlow earned MA and PhD degrees from Columbia University and Hartford Theological Seminary, respectively. He was a missionary in Turkey and taught college in Beirut until the U.S. entrance into World War I led him to France as a YMCA secretary for American servicemen. After spending a year in Africa as a delegate for the World Student Christian Federation, Harlow joined the faculty of Smith College in 1923. Active in leftist political movements, in 1932 he ran unsuccessfully for the House of Representatives on the Socialist Party ticket headed by his good friend Norman Thomas. Harlow also served on the board of the NAACP and was an active member in the American Christian Palestine Committee, a group that supported the establishment of the state of Israel.

2. Possibly Laurens Hickok Seelye, who was president of St. Lawrence University in Canton, New York, from 1935 to 1940.

3. Ralph Harlow disagreed, writing, "personally, I thought your chapel talk the best we have had this year. From experience I have come to feel we cannot be sure of our own judgments." From Ralph Harlow, 9 May 1937, HTC-MBU: Box 22.

To Mordecai Wyatt Johnson

20 May 1937
Washington, D.C.

Thurman presents his concept of the role of the dean of chapel at Howard to university president Mordecai Wyatt Johnson.[1]

My dear Mr. President:

I am herewith submitting a memorandum in re my interpretation of the function of the office of the Dean of the Chapel of Howard University. First, the main function is the conduct of the preaching services in the Chapel and personal consultation with students. In connection with these two there follow very closely the responsibilities for the development of the religious life of the University generally.

Second, all undergraduate religious organizations should head up in the office of the Dean of the Chapel. The general and specific sponsorship of such organizations should be through his office.

Third, the relationship of the office of the Dean of the Chapel with the personnel and health offices of the University should be that of one dean to another. The office of the Dean of the Chapel should cooperate with all of the personnel offices in matters in which his knowledge and advice may be especially helpful.

I may add generally that I do not think of the office of the Dean of the Chapel in an administrative sense. I think that he should have the privilege of attending the meetings of the Administrative Council and that he should be a member of the Faculty Committee on Student Activities. These are the general functions of the office as I see them. I am convinced that the office will define itself specifically as the work develops. We must realize that we are pioneering in this field and there are no precedents established. There are only two Deans of Chapels in the United States aside from the office here. At both of these universities, Princeton and Chicago, the functional significance of the job is very loosely defined. Please let me come in to see you about this very soon.

Sincerely yours,
[*signed*] Howard Thurman
Dean of the Chapel
President Mordecai W. Johnson
Howard University

TLc. HTC-MBU: Box 9.

1. For additional information about Johnson, see the biographical footnote in volume 1.

To Harold B. Ingalls
24 May 1937
Washington, D.C.

Thurman discusses how his distress at the common Indian conceptions of American blacks led him and Sue Bailey Thurman to start, and to a large extent fund by themselves, the Juliette Derricotte Scholarship Fund.

My dear "Pete":[1]

I regret very much that November 28 is the best that I can do with complete confidence. I think there is a bare possibility of my coming sometime in the late spring but it is so remote that I dare not depend on it. If you want to take a chance, I am game but it is not a very promising possibility. I shall hold November 28 until I hear from you.

With reference to the students going to India this is the situation. We found that the Indian people for the most part as well as the other people with whom we came in contact had been so completely victimized by anti-Negro propaganda that their minds were made up about us long before we appeared on the scene. Much of the propaganda was deliberate and thought out and has been going on over a long period of years. Sue and I decided that inasmuch as our presence in India had helped to dispel much of the error that had settled in people's minds relative to Negroes, it would be a very fine thing if it were possible for one or two Negroes to spend from three to six months in one or two institutions of learning. It would be a flesh and blood answer to propaganda. This is the first point. The second point, the students kept asking us while we were in the country last year, "Why didn't you bring an undergraduate, someone who is chronologically closer to us and who would participate more fully in our undergraduate life than your responsibilities will permit?" Therefore, we felt that in all fairness to the total picture an undergraduate from one of our colleges should go to India as early after our return as possible. In the third place, we have found since our return that a great deal of genuine stimulation can be given to Negroes as a whole through their knowledge of the struggles of other people in other parts of the world. The undergraduate going to India, living there in one or two places for six months would get even more first-hand insights than we were able to get and would be in a position to provide a great deal of inspiration to college students upon her return.

To this end Sue has given lecture-recitals over the country in an effort to raise the required amount. She is still short of all that she needs to complete the project. Whatever consideration your committee is able to give will be a very definite contribution to a significant enterprise. Sue has not gone out to solicit funds, choosing rather to earn the money. A few interested persons, however, have contributed merely on the basis of their interest, for instance Douglas Steere[2] sent her $35.

Anna Vivian Brown and Marian Martin of this University are the two girls. Marian Martin is being supported outright by Sue while Anna Vivian Brown's father is paying the cost of her travel, and Sue is responsible for her scholarship in Woman's Christian College in Madras. I hope this covers everything.

Please let me hear from you on the preaching date. Be assured that if I can get a hot minute, I shall take a death defying life leap for a respite at Northfield. Our love to you and Betty.

Sincerely yours,
[*signed*] Howard Thurman
Dean of the Chapel
Rev. Harold B. Ingalls
Northfield Seminary Church
East Northfield, Massachusetts

TLc. HTC-MBU: Box 9.

1. Harold B. Ingalls (1902–77) received his BD from Yale University in 1936, the same year he was appointed chaplain at Northfield Seminary. He also served as associate secretary of the National Council of the YMCA (1948); secretary of the Urbana, Illinois, YMCA (1950–58); and envoy to UN talks (1951), author of "Howard Thurman: Being a Few Highlights On an Interesting Life," *Intercollegian* 58, no. 6 (1941): 137–138.

2. Douglas Van Steere, a renowned Quaker and religious philosopher, taught at Haverford College. For additional information about him, see the biographical footnote in volume 1.

"KEEP AWAKE!"

JUNE 1937

In this sermon Thurman writes of the place of spirituality or disciplined spiritual practices as resources for ethical life. Thurman addresses the role of character as a form of personal conduct aligned with one's highest values. He also challenges intellectual smugness that prevents one from seeing the beauty and magic of the commonplace and asserts the need for some overarching purpose that gives to life a transcendent vision and noble character.

From hour to hour keep awake. Luke 21:36.

It is a common truth expressed many times that the key to the meaning of life, as the individual finds that meaning, is within. All of life's meaning is not found within the individual but an indispensable part of it is found there. Part of a sentence on the outside of the railway station in Washington reads: "He who seeks the wealth of the Indies must carry the wealth of the Indies with him."[1] There is current in India the story of the musk deer. It is said that in the springtime the musk deer is haunted by the odor of musk. He seeks it everywhere. There are times when the questing becomes terrible in its agony. He runs over hills, jumping streams and rivulets with his nostrils dilating and his body aching with desire, confident that around the next turning he will discover musk, the object of his quest. This goes on until at last he falls exhausted, with his tiny head resting on his still more tiny paw, to discover that the odor of musk is in his own hide. "Go where you will from Benares to Mathura; if you have not found your own soul, the world is unreal to you."[2]

It is altogether necessary that we should guard well our inner life lest by our attitudes and our deeds the meaning and the significance of life recede into the background as we proceed into the future.

I call your attention to three simple but important attitudes that students sometimes take toward life which tend to destroy for them its moral significance.

I

First, the failure to recognize the fact that there must be a basic harmony between one's personal conduct and the ideals which one recognizes as most worthful for him. When my personal conduct fails to exemplify increasingly my own sense of the highest, the meaning of life tends to disappear. It is this which Jesus calls the unpardonable sin; you remember the incident. His family sought to excuse him from the judgment of his enemies by saying that he was a little out of his mind. But the Pharisees said, in substance: "His mind is all right, but he is full of the devil; and it is by the power of the devil that he casts out devils." Jesus, overhearing the conversation, replied: "You do not talk as sensible men. A house divided against itself cannot stand. If you keep saying that I am casting out devils by the power of the devil, you will commit the unpardonable sin."[3] This is to say, if you continue calling a good thing bad, you will eventually arrive at a place which makes it impossible for you to distinguish between that which is good and that which is bad. You will precipitate yourself into a twilight world of values in which meanings are obscure.

When I was a boy, my mother forbade me to shoot marbles "for keeps." It happens that I had sisters who found some mysterious use for all the marbles that I could accumulate. One day when I went to my cigar box I found that it was empty. I slipped out of the back yard and went down to the corner in quest of a certain boy. He was notorious in our community for his poor skill with marbles. But he always had many marbles because his parents were well-to-do. When I found him, I borrowed a few marbles from him and engaged in a game "for keeps." As soon as I returned home, my mother, hearing my footsteps on the porch, called to me. My heart leapt to my throat. Great was my relief when she said, "I want you to run an errand." But all through the day and the next day there was a gulf between her and me. She was the same lovely person as always; but now she was seen by me to be not my mother, but my judge. This relationship between us obtained because in my private life I had accepted a course of conduct that was unworthy of my own sense of that which was right and ethical.

The same fundamental idea is illustrated in Shakespeare's "Macbeth." Macbeth had the idea that he was a man of destiny. He communicated this idea to his wife. Together they swam across Scotland in seas of blood, tying laurels to their brows with other people's lives and other people's heartstrings, until at last Macbeth *was* the first man of the land and Lady Macbeth *was* the first lady. Their friends began disappearing; their enemies multiplied. Macbeth became prematurely old and Lady Macbeth became diseased in mind. She was always trying to wash Duncan's blood from her hands—blood that was not on her hands, but in her mind! At last, exhausted, she gave up the ghost. An attendant came to Macbeth announcing that Lady Macbeth was dead. His reply was profoundly significant:

> She should have died hereafter;
> There would have been time for such a word,—
> Tomorrow, and tomorrow, and tomorrow,
> Creeps in this petty pace from day to day,
> To the last syllable of recorded time;
> And all our yesterdays have lighted fools
> The way to dusty death. Out, out, brief candle!
> Life's but a walking shadow; a poor player,
> That struts and frets his hour upon the stage,
> And then is heard no more: It is a tale
> Told by an idiot, full of sound and fury,
> Signifying nothing.[4]

Why was life to Macbeth a tale told by a fool, a sounding brass and tinkling cymbal with no meaning? Because in his private life he had violated his best ethical judgment.

Is life to you a grinning skull and crossbones? Out of the depth of its meaninglessness to you, do you cry: "There is no God; no sin, no future life, nothing but the survival of the fittest and every man for himself"? Perhaps life is a grinning skull and crossbones to you because you insist upon trying to separate your personal conduct from your world of values.

II

A second attitude which may tend to destroy the meaning of life for students is the one that says: "I am smart, smart, smart. You can't fool me. I know a great deal. I have been almost everywhere, and the places where I have not been, I have read about. I am a really intelligent person, with no illusions." This attitude makes it very difficult if not impossible for a man to learn very much from ordinary, commonplace experiences of living. It was not an accident that Oscar Wilde said, "There is always room in an unlettered man's mind for a great idea."[5]

I remember once doing a group of discussions on religion at a certain institution in the east. I was very much impressed by the rather "smart" contributions of a particular freshman. At the end of my last discussion he accompanied me to my room. As we walked across the campus, I asked him, "Do you come from a religious or churchgoing family?"

He said: "Yes, my mother and father are Methodists."

"And you?" said I.

He stretched his little freshman shoulders back and said, "I am inclined to be rather atheistic."

Bless his little heart! There was only one thing wrong with him, and that was that he was standing at dawn attempting to describe the colors of the sunset; not a typical case, rather extreme. But it is illustrative of a mood that is deadly. If a man has lived to the fulness of his years and comes at last to the end with a sober conclusion that after going up and down many highways he has found nothing of meaning and significance in life, I can only say to him that such has not been my experience. But for one to anticipate all the totality of his experiences in the future by accepting prematurely a judgment with reference to the future, viewed as an end-result, is stupid, to say the least.

> They thought him a magician, Tycho Brahe
> Perhaps he was. There's magic all around us
> In rock and trees, and in the minds of men,
> Deep hidden springs of magic.
> He that strikes
> The rock aright, may find them where he will.[6]

Some years ago during a week of prayer service at a certain state college I noticed an elderly, baldheaded, crippled man who occupied a front seat in the chapel. He was horribly misshapen, stumbling through the years supported between two huge crutches. At the end of the last address he offered to bring me a gift in appreciation for the inspiration that had come to him in the services. He said, "I shall call at your room tonight at 11." During the afternoon I made inquiry as to his name and other particulars. I was told that he earned his living by mending shoes for the men in the college. My informant knew only his nickname. A few minutes before 11 he knocked at my door. Entering, he placed his crutches on the floor and held himself up by holding to the back of the chair. It was then that he said, calling me by name, "Do you like Shakespeare?"

"Yes."

"What is your favorite play?"

"Hamlet."

To my utter amazement he read to me from memory the entire first act of "Hamlet." And then at my dictation he went through many scenes of various

Shakespearian tragedies. Just an old cripple, earning his living by mending shoes for men, most of whom, had never taken the time to tap his amazing resources. There *is* magic all around us, but to the "smart" man there is little of meaning in the commonplace.

Is life growing dingy on your sleeve? Perhaps it is because you have never taken the time to learn from the simple things by which your life is surrounded and which are trumpet-tongued with meaning and values.

III

The third attitude that may destroy the meaning of life for a student is one in which he refuses to identify himself in complete surrender with some cause, purpose or movement—which cause, purpose or movement is more important than the particular fortunes of his little life. All of us are frequently oppressed by our apparent insignificance in the midst of the vastness of the universe. The old theology that made man the center of the universe was built upon the kind of astronomy which made the earth the center of the solar system. Man therefore became the center of the universe. Modern astronomy says that this vaunted earth is but a tiny speck of stardust whirling mathematically through space. We live in the western half of that tiny speck of stardust. We live in the northern part of the western half of that tiny speck of stardust. We live in one country in the northern part of the western half of that tiny speck of stardust. We live in one city in one country in the northern part of the western half of that tiny speck of stardust. And, for the most part, we live in one room in one city in one country in the northern part of the western half of that tiny speck of stardust; so that by the time we get to the spot which we actually occupy, it tends to be a vanishing quantity. The net result is that we are oppressed by the littleness of our lives, and the meaning that we find in life is often comparable to our interpretation of our individual significance in the vastness of the universe. It seems to me, then, that we are under great obligation to find something in our world, some cause or purpose to which we may give ourselves in utter devotion.

Some ants through many generations constructed an ant mound. At last, only one tiny grain of sand was needed for one unfinished spot. It happened that in line of duty an ant delivered this one grain of sand to the unfinished spot. As he put it in its place, he arose on his haunches and cried: "My antheap I have built. My view, my world, my me!" The wind stirred in the valley below the antheap and mounted up over its crest, sweeping the vaunting ant to destruction on the other side; *but the antheap remained.*

The full impact of the demands of Jesus upon the life of the individual registers at this point. His references to the pearl of great price, to the treasure in a field which a man sells in order to buy, the necessity for letting the dead bury their own dead, the absolute insistence upon the fact that family and friends must be considered in the light of the demand of God:[7] it is a stern insistence, but it is the great door to the meaning of life. Happy is the man who has become the captive of a great commitment. If you would know the meaning of life and keep that meaning fresh and vital in your own experience, look about you; select some cause, some great purpose; identify yourself with some overwhelming need, give yourself to it in abiding enthusiasm and in complete devotion—something that is capable of stirring you to the depths; something that looms before you as of more importance than the fact of life or death, something which becomes for you the call of God. Our times are pregnant with vast, aching needs. It may be the plight of the sharecroppers in the weary bottoms of the black belt; it may be the threat of war that is increasingly imminent with the passing days. It may be the loneliness and desolation of men and women held within dingy prison walls. It may be the withering tide of secularization that quietly strangles the soul of Christian institutions. It may be the despair of the jobless and the hunger of the unemployed. Find what it is to which you can give yourself in complete devotion and do this knowing that it is *not* nothing.[8]

If life has no meaning for you, it may be that it is because your character is always at war with your ideals, or it may be that your conceit keeps you from exposing yourself to the ministry of the commonplace, or it may be that your pride and insensitiveness keep you from identifying yourself with some cause or some deeply moving purpose which may be the call of God.

> I saw a man pursuing the horizon;
> Round and round they sped.
> I was disturbed at this;
> I accosted the man.
> "It is futile," I said,
> "You can never"—
> "You lie," he cried,
> And ran on.[9]

"From hour to hour keep awake."

Christian Century Pulpit, June 1937, 125–27.

1. See "Barren or Fruitful?" printed in volume 1.

2. See "The Perils of Immature Piety," printed in volume 1.

3. A paraphrase of Matt. 12.

4. William Shakespeare, *Macbeth,* act 5, scene 5.

5. This is a paraphrase from Oscar Wilde's *De Profundis*. The exact quote reads: "In the soul of one who is ignorant there is always room for a great idea." Oscar Wilde, *De Profundis and Other Writings* (New York: Penguin Books, 1986), 169.

6. The opening of section 5 from Alfred Noyes, *Watchers of the Sky* (New York: Stokes, 1922), 64. The Dane Tycho Brahe (1546–1601) was the leading astronomer in the generation before the invention of the telescope.

7. Citing Matt. 13:45–46 and Matt. 8:21–22.

8. This is a paraphrase of Olive Schreiner. The exact quote reads: "This is all you can do; but do it; it is not nothing." Olive Schreiner, *Stories, Dreams, and Allegories* (New York: Stokes, 1923), 170.

9. Stephen Crane, *Prose and Poetry* (New York: Library of America, 1984), 1306; originally poem 27 in *The Black Riders and Other Lines* (1895).

From Juanita L. Harris
25 July 1937
Washington, D.C.

Juanita Harris's letter deals with the role of Japan in international affairs, a matter of considerable debate among African Americans in the 1930s. Many African Americans were pleased to see Japan challenge the Western monopoly on imperialism, especially given the virulent racism then prevailing toward Asians and the more general presumption among whites in the United States that non-Western peoples had neither the ability or will to engage with the Western imperial powers on an equal basis.[1] *At the same time, though, there were many African Americans who were disturbed by Japanese aggression against its Asian neighbors. The engagement in Northern China in the vicinity of the Marco Polo Bridge between Japanese and Chinese forces on 7 July 1937, a skirmish that is generally seen as the opening battle of World War II, made the question of the evaluation of Japanese intentions more urgent. Harris's comments reflect the common assumption at the time among many blacks that the rise of Japan was an opening chapter in an international racial war between whites and blacks.*

Dear Sir:

Recently, I was in a discussion of Current Events, and I made this statement: I should be glad for Japan to conquer China, because if she does not the white man will. Further, since Japan has foresight enough to discern that the white man is trying to do so himself, I feel that Japan is acting wisely; however some persons disagree, but I am a Negro, and I want to see the darker Races become as strong as possible.

Although, many people think that it is impractical to think of the white Races uniting against the dark Races, I feel that the white Races have been congenitally united against the dark Races. I note too that the "Baltimore Sun" and the "Times" have certainly publicized the fiftieth Anniversary of Mound Bayou.[2]

Therefore, since I have just completed my first year college at Howard University, I am taking the liberty to write to you, because I have complete confidence in your judgment of the matter. Moreover, I will deem it an irreparable favor, if you will answer my letter stating your views in this matter. I thank you sincerely.

Yours very truly,

[*signed*] (Miss) Juanita L. Harris

HTC-MBU: Box 24.

1. For African American attitudes toward the Japanese in the 1930s, see Marc S. Gallicchio, *The African American Encounter with Japan and China: Black Internationalism in Asia, 1895–1945* (Chapel Hill: University of North Carolina Press, 2000); Gerald Horne, *Race War: White Supremacy and the Japanese Attack on the British Empire* (New York: New York University Press, 2004); and David Levering Lewis, *W. E. B. Du Bois: The Fight for Equality and the American Century, 1919–1963* (New York: Holt, 2000), 388–421.

2. The all-black community of Mound Bayou was founded in the Mississippi Delta in 1887. Its anniversary celebrations were noted in the *New York Times* ("Negro City to Celebrate: Mound Bayou, Founded by Ex-Slaves, to Mark 50th Year," 8 July 1937). For a history of Mound Bayou, see Janet Sharp Hermann, *The Pursuit of a Dream* (New York: Oxford University Press, 1981).

To Juanita L. Harris

10 August 1937

Washington, D.C.

In his response to Harris's letter, Thurman provides one of the most interesting summaries of his political views during the late 1930s. Thurman never expressed sympathies with Japanese imperialism and later condemned the Japanese invasion of Korea the following month in his "Significance of Jesus" series.

My dear Miss Harris:

I have delayed replying to your good letter of July 25 because I am on vacation. I am very much interested in the discussion which you had and would like to have the opportunity to talk with you on the whole thing. Perhaps we can do so in the fall. I am inclined to agree with your position relative to Japan. It is true that there is a great struggle going on in the Far East, including Africa, between the subject darker races and the dominant white races. I am opposed fundamentally to imperialism, whether the imperialist be black, yellow, white, or any other color. Naturally, I would stand in opposition to what seems to me to be the facts relative to Japan's invasion of China. My sympathy is with China, while my pride is with Japan, as she commands increasingly a position of power in the Oriental world. As a member of the darker races, viewing the problem from the relationship between Japan and European powers, I am pro-Japanese. As a pacifist, I am opposed to the whole sordid struggle that is going on between China and Japan.

You will note how hard it is for me to give a clear-cut position because of the dilemma that I face as an under-privileged man.

I agree completely with your remarks on the point of the predominant attitude of the white race towards the darker races. I am convinced from my experience, my reading, and my reflection, that there is a deeply-~~lined~~ {lying} effort on the part of the white race as a whole to hold the darker races in subjection, if not in complete servitude.

I shall be glad to talk this through with you in the fall. Thank you for writing.
Sincerely yours,
[*signed*] Howard Thurman
Dean of the Chapel
Miss Juanita L. Harris
137 T Street, N.W.
Washington, D.C.

TLc. HTC-MBU: Box 24.

To James Sams
1 September 1937
Washington, D.C.

Thurman's mother Alice married James Sams in 1917 after the death of her second husband, Alex Evans. While Thurman speaks fondly about Saul Solomon Thurman and Evans in his autobiography, he writes sparingly about his less amiable stepfather, Sams: "Mr. Sams was a devout churchman. He had a clever and original mind and was engaged in several business ventures when he married Mamma. We children did not feel as close to him as to Mr. Evans."[1] *Thurman speaks bluntly to Sams in this letter, written during a visit by Mamma Alice to Washington, D.C.*

My dear Brother James:

I have planned writing you for a long time, but kept putting it off because I thought that I would be coming home this summer and I could talk to you face to face. But I decided against coming home because I knew that the only way that Mamma would get any vacation from the wear and tear of the preparation of three meals a day for you would be for me to have her come up here. For some reason that I do not understand, the idea seems never to have occurred to you to give her any rest.

I am writing you very frankly as man to man, and I want you to think about what I am going to say. I have known you intimately for more than twenty years, and you will recall the circumstances under which the present arrangement with you and Mamma was made. You made all kinds of promises about what would happen if you were permitted to move back to 614 Whitehall Street. I was looking after the supporting of Mamma and taking care of the running of the house myself. Ten years ago I told her that as long as I lived and had my health and any kind of job she would never have to work again. I wanted her to live at home with her chickens and her garden, with her prayer meeting and her friends. I was not interested in uprooting her and having her live with me because if she did she would naturally want to help take care of the children and do other things in the house. This arrangement was working nicely when she and I agreed that we would take you at your word one more time. Now what has happened? For the first few months you were a changed man. You tried to be what any husband and man ought to be in his home. But for a long time now you have been getting worse steadily. In the first place, Mamma cooks three meals a day for you. This means spending a good part of every day in a hot kitchen in hot Florida weather. But this is not enough. You have let your attitude become nastier and nastier. In other words, I am convinced now, Mr. Sams, that you are a mean man, and I am writing you to say that I, as my mother's son, am not going to stand by and let you worry her to death. I have nothing against you as a person, but I love my mother and I am going to take care of her. She will not suffer, and I am not going to let you or anybody else make a door mat out of her. She has not asked me to write you, nor has she talked to me freely about the situation, but I have seen enough and I have gathered enough from an occasional remark to know what the situation is, because I lived in that situation when I was a boy.

I have found out one thing, however, that in my opinion may be responsible for the highhanded way that you are doing. You have had your name placed back on the deed for the property, and now you feel, I suppose, that nothing can be done with you regardless to what you do. I will not discuss this point with you now, but I want you to realize that you are making a very great mistake if you are thinking this way.

You are getting older every day and it will not be many years before you will be an old man. You have lived your life in a community with people who have long since lost their love and neighborly feeling for you. Your own children will not take care of you when you are so you cannot work and it seems to me, Mr. Sams, that common sense would make you try to win the love of your wife's children, so that they would want to see you cared for until the end of your days. Now, this is just ordinary horse sense. But, instead of doing this, you seem to take delight in doing things that will turn them against you. You ought to realize with your wisdom of the world and your experience that you will not be loved for unkindnesses to our mother.

Now, how does this look? You are my mother's husband. You have been her husband for more than twenty years. In addition, you are a professed Christian. You read the Bible, you pray, you talk about religious convictions, and your faith. And yet, Mamma has been here two weeks and you have not written her a single letter. You have not done this because you are mad that she came up to visit her children and grandchildren. In my opinion that is a very ungracious and un-Christian way to act. Now, I have never interfered with Mamma's personal relationships with you. I want her to be happy and I am going to see to it as much as in my power to guarantee that that thing happens. She will be going home this week, and I want you to change your way of doing while it is possible to do so. I would like to feel in going home that I had a mother and a father there who were glad to see me and who were happy. But, frankly, I do not feel that way now, and I want you to try to straighten up.

I am not mad with you, nor do I have anything in me against you, but I am insisting that you treat my mother as a husband should. That is my only concern. And if you cannot do this, or are not willing to do it, then I want to know so that I shall know what next to do. I am always running into nice things that I think you would enjoy reading, things on the Bible and on religion, things that will help you in your thought and in the position to which we are all permitted—the bringing of the Kingdom of God in the world. But I do not feel like sending anything down there to you because you just have not played square. You have not kept your promise to me. There is nothing in this that is meant to try to frighten you, but it is rather an appeal to your heart that any son would make to a man who stands in his life where a father ought to stand.

Sincerely yours,
[*signed*] Howard Thurman

TLS. HTC-MBU: Box 19.

1. *WHAH*, 16.

"The Significance of Jesus I: Jesus the Man of Insight"
12 September 1937

In late January and early February 1937, Thurman made a tour of colleges in Nova Scotia and New Brunswick at the behest of the Student Christian Movement of Canada. Thurman's time there was a great success. Although he admitted being "quite exhausted" afterward, the reports of his speaking tour were uniformly laudatory.[1] *The Canadians wanted a return engagement. Margaret Kinney of the Canadian Student Christian Movement wrote to Thurman on 20 February 1937 to invite him to speak at their annual conference of students from Ontario and Quebec at YMCA Park at Lake Couchiching, about ninety miles north of Toronto that September, with his emphasis to be "the significance of Jesus, his teachings, his life, death and resurrection." They requested that Thurman provide five or six presentations of one hour each.*[2]

After some deliberation Thurman accepted the offer, and did so knowing his personal resources were at a low ebb. In the first half of 1937 Thurman was physically and spiritually exhausted because of the arduous speaking schedule he had undertaken since his return from India. His physician recommended a summer of almost complete inactivity. This enabled him to prepare the "Significance of Jesus" series with great care, and very unusually for him, he wrote out the lectures so that they would consist of "precisely what I want to say and the way I want to say it."[3] In the carefulness of its preparation, its length, and the centrality of the topic to Thurman's concerns, "The Significance of Jesus" was his most important religious statement to date.

The original plan of seven lectures proved a little too ambitious. Thurman wrote out the text of the first five lectures, while the sixth was delivered extemporaneously from notes and survives only as an edited transcript. Thurman was very proud of the work, and he later boasted to his friend Herbert King of compliments he had received for his talks. Thurman planned to expand the lectures and have them formally published, but he reluctantly agreed to let his manuscript be mimeographed and distributed to conference participants.[4] For many of those lucky enough to receive a mimeographed copy, it became a cherished possession.[5]

Word of Thurman's lectures reached Scribner's, one of the leading publishers of religious books, and an editor asked Thurman for a copy to evaluate but ultimately turned down the manuscript.[6] Despite Thurman's continued efforts during the late 1930s and early 1940s, the lectures were never reprinted beyond the small mimeograph edition from the conference. While some of the words and ideas contained in "The Significance of Jesus" saw the light of day in other contexts, in many ways these lectures form a unique work in Thurman's output, a summation of his writings to date with a constellation of religious and political concerns specific to its time, the late 1930s.

Although the topic of "The Significance of Jesus" was chosen by the conference organizers, it was one that was congenial to Thurman, and one that was at the heart of the liberal theology, what Albert Schweitzer famously dubbed the "quest of the historical Jesus."[7] "The Significance of Jesus" was not an attempt to write a biography of Jesus, but it was as close to a "life of Jesus" as Thurman ever wrote, systematically discussing the major events in his life, describing Jesus not as a supernatural being but as a man, a Jew in first century C.E. Palestine. And part of this involved, crucially, Jesus coming to terms with the complex political situation in which Palestinian Jews were obliged to live.

In some ways the opening lecture in the series, "Jesus the Man of Insight," was an extension of Thurman's first effort to describe the social context of early Christianity in his 1935 lecture "Good News for the Underprivileged." And while there is overlap and explicit borrowing from that essay, and both essays look forward to the 1949 Jesus and the Disinherited, *there are also significant differences.*[8] *Unlike those works, Thurman in "Jesus the Man of Insight" does not concentrate on the dichotomy between Jesus and Paul and the importance of Roman citizenship but instead places Jesus within the framework of religious sectarianism in Palestine in the late Second Temple period. Thurman sketches the options that Jesus did not follow, explaining why he was neither a Zealot, a Sadducee, a Pharisee, or an Essene. Thurman argues that Jesus rejected all of these options in favor of a search for the divine, which Thurman here defines as the "creative purpose out of which life arose" and toward which "all aspects of society are constantly under [its] judgment," the implications of which are elaborated in the subsequent lectures.*

Thurman's emphasis on the social context of the life of Jesus reflects the historicism of much contemporary scholarship on the Hebrew Bible and the New Testament. "The Significance of Jesus" was influenced by many works that sought to re-create the political and social situation in Palestine in the first century C.E. *Palestine, such as* Jesus: A New Biography *by University of Chicago professor Shirley Jackson Case.*[9] *Much of the scholarship Thurman relies on in the first lecture in "The Significance of Jesus" is unavoidably dated in its general thrust and its particulars. Contemporary scholars, are, as a rule, far less confident than Thurman in thinking Palestine's religious factions can be best understood by an analysis based on class and political allegiance. But in all of Thurman's writings on the historical Jesus, sociological interpretation forms at best an outer scaffolding on which he presents his true concerns; how can a person living under the scrutiny of God live a moral life in a society that is profoundly irreligious and un-Christian?*

One of the striking aspects of "The Significance of Jesus" is the radicalism of Thurman's social commitments. As always was the case with Thurman, he shied away from explicit political arguments, but in the critique of existing social institutions and private property and contemplation of insurrection it marks itself as very much a work of the 1930s. It is also Thurman's first extended effort to come to terms with the implications of Gandhi and Gandhianism. Although the Indian pacifist's name is never mentioned, Thurman attempts to place the struggle for socially transformational nonviolent action in a personal spiritual context and Christian framework. "The Significance of Jesus" combines an effort to reconsider the life of Jesus from the vantage of a radical, modernist view of his life and ministry with the cause of nonviolent protest, in a way that few theologians, white or black, had done before him. Thurman's interest in the social origins of Christianity did not reduce religion to political involvement. His argument here, and in many other places, was the reverse, that genuine religious commitment leads inevitably to social involvement and activism. This theme was first stated with clarity and at extended length in "The Significance of Jesus."

To some, God and Jesus may appeal in a way other than to us. Some may come to faith in God and love, without a conscious attachment to Jesus. Both nature and good men besides Jesus may lead us to God. They who seek God with all their hearts, however, some day in their way meet Jesus.[10]

Jesus, the 19th Century and After

Christianity is an historical faith, the result of a movement that was started in time, by an individual located in history. For the purposes of our discussion during these hours, I am asking you to approach the life of Jesus stripped bare of much that is metaphysical and theological and mystical. Let us begin with the simple fact that Jesus of Nazareth was a Palestinian Jew. Did it simply happen that as a result of some accidental collocation of atoms this human being came into existence, so conditioned and organized within himself that he became increasingly a perfect instrument for the embodiment of a set of ideals of such alarming potency that they were capable of changing the calendar, redirecting the thought of the world, and placing a new sense of the rhythm of life in a weary nerve-broken civilization? Or was there something unique in the great womb of the people out of which he sprang that made of him the logical funding of a long development of racial experience, ethical in quality and spiritual in tone? But the fact is that whatever may be the far-flung reasons therefore, Jesus was a Jew.

He was a poor Jew—so poor that his family could not afford a lamb for the birth presentation to the Lord, but had to secure doves instead. Is it too daring to suggest that in his poverty he was the symbol of the masses of men so that he could truly be Son of Man more naturally and accurately than if he had been a rich Jew? He was a poor Jew.

As a Jew, Jesus was a member of a minority group, underprivileged and to a great degree disinherited.[11] As Shirley Jackson Case[12] says, "Palestine had fallen into the hands of the Romans in 63 B.C. Henceforth the yoke of the foreigner had grown constantly heavier, while his desecrations of the Holy Land multiplied. Although Rome had permitted Herod the Great to rule as King of the Jews (37–4 B.C.), his professed loyalty to the Jewish religion had not checked the rising tide of heathen defilements in God's sacred territory. Taxes collected from the people were freely expended for building temples in honor of Emperor Augustus, even within Palestine itself, and characteristic Roman entertainments were staged almost under the shadow of the Jewish temple at Jerusalem. In the two chief cities of Palestine, Jerusalem in Judea and Sepphoris in Galilee, foreigners, with their wares and customs were almost as much at home as were Jews. People in authority, who enjoyed the king's favor, might approve of his cosmopolitanism, but the devout Jew, yielding allegiance only to God as his king and ruler, viewed the situation with disgust and righteous indignation.

Herod's death in 4 B.C., was the signal for outraged Jews to act. A certain Judas, heading a band of Galilean revolutionaries, seized weapons from the royal armory in the capital, Sepphoris, and attempted to establish once more Jewish autonomy under the protection of God. But presently, the people of Sepphoris were to pay dearly for their ambition. Roman soldiers, aided by the army of King Aretas of Arabia, destroyed the city, slaughtering or carrying into captivity its inhabitants. During the next quarter-century, under the patronage of Herod Antipas, to whom the Romans assigned control of Galilee (4 B.C.–39 A.D.), Sepphoris was magnificently rebuilt. It continued to be the royal residence until Tiberias was founded (about 25 A.D.), and it still blended in its life as a Jewish city those foreign elements that defiled the purity of God's chosen land and people."

While this tempestuous chapter in Jewish history was taking form, Jesus was growing to manhood in the neighboring village of Nazareth, scarcely an hour's walk from Sepphoris.[13]

Inasmuch as Jesus did not live his life in a vacuum, but was in certain important particulars a child of his time, it is quite necessary for us to assume that he was a part of the psychological climate of his age. This is not an attempt to explain Jesus, for "explanations" of a spiritual genius, or any kind of genius for that matter, whether they be in terms of his psychological pattern or in terms of his historical setting, fail to be very significant for the simple reason that they do not explain the one thing most worth knowing—why the particular genius in question differs from others whom the same explanation would fit. Any explanation of Jesus in terms of the social or economic forces of his time must inevitably explain his contemporaries as well. It may explain why he was a particular kind of Jew, but it does not explain why the other Jews were not Jesus. And that is, after all, the most important question, since the thing which makes him most interesting is not the way in which he resembled his fellows, but the way in which he differed from all the rest of them. Jesus inherited the same traits as countless other Jews of his time. He grew up in the same society, and yet he was Jesus—and the other Jews were not. Often we escape into history or psychology or economics and we hesitate to face the problem which remains when history or psychology or economics has done its uttermost. All three are useful in their way; the danger is in forgetting what that way is.

Such considerations, however, should not blind us to the importance of a careful analysis of some of the major problems of his period, so as to see the relevancy of certain of his emphases.

There is one overmastering problem that the underprivileged always face—what must be their attitude towards their master, their oppressor? Whatever the practical question is, whether one of vocation or one of marriage, or whatnot, it is all finally related to the attitude that must be taken towards the controllers of the society. I remember once hearing a young Korean girl, an undergraduate at a certain American university, give a most significant address. She was scheduled, along with a Japanese gentleman, to discuss her interpretation of American education as an undergraduate with a foreign background and culture. He was scheduled to discuss American education viewed in retrospect after ten years out of Harvard. When she got up to speak, she said, "I am scheduled to talk to you about my impression of American education as an undergraduate from a foreign land. But there is only one thing that a Korean has any right to talk about in public, and that is freedom from Japan."[14] For several minutes she made a most impassioned plea for freedom. She ended her address with these searching words, "If you see a little American boy and you ask him what he wants, he says, 'I want a penny to put in my bank' or 'to get some candy' or 'to buy me a whistle.' But if you see a little Korean boy and you ask him what he wants, he says, 'I want freedom from Japan.'" This seems to be illustrativ~~r~~e of the kind of atmosphere in which Jesus must have moved.

It should be observed further, that inasmuch as Judaism was a civilization, a culture, and a religion, touching every problem with which the individual Jew had to do, it should be instructive for us to inquire in this preliminary statement as to what solutions were offered to the common people within the Judaistic tradition. There were at least five remedies offered. There was the method of violent revolt as advocated by the Zealots. They believed that the only thing that the Roman could understand and appreciate was seeing his own blood flow in the streets of Palestinian cities. He had built his empire on violence, bloodshed, refined brutality; and it was the only thing that he respected. They were adherents of assassination and armed rebellion and were violently opposed to new cultures alien and foreign. They loved liberty better than life. The expression attributed to Patrick Henry of American Revolutionary days, "Give me liberty, or give me death!" could very easily have been the battle cry of the Zealots. As Simkhovitch points out, "The rebellion of the Jew against Rome rather begins with the power of Rome over the Jews; and in the same degree as the Roman power over the Jews increased, did the political reaction against that power, the revolution against Rome, increased and spread. The Jewish revolutionists against Rome were called by the Romans bandits or robbers. Later they were called 'scitarri' (men with knives).[15] As a matter of fact, they were religious patriots who were fighting and dying for their country. Their reason was simple and direct. Would God permit his people to perish as they gave themselves over to the defense of the Holy City, the Temple? Ultimately, Jehovah would triumph."

Such was their faith. It was in the midst of wars, rebellions, outbreaks, and riots that Jesus lived his days. He saw Jews swimming or floating through Palestine in seas of blood, trying to tie the laurels of Roman subjection on their brows with their own heart strings fashioned out of their own precious blood. Jesus evidently did not agree with them, even though he accepted a Zealot as one of his disciples.[16] I have often wondered why. Speculation at this point is fascinating, but profitless.

Second, there was a solution offered by the Sadducees. This group of people stood in a strategic position in the organized life of the Jews. They represented the ruling class. From their numbers came the High Priests; and most of the economic security derived from contemporary worship was their monopoly. They belonged to the privileged class, and their contacts with Roman officialdom gave to them a sense of security that the other Jews did not have. Their position was maintained, to some extent at any rate, by the strong arm of the Roman government, so that their fate was tied up more intimately with the fate of the Roman Empire, and naturally they wanted its star to remain in the ascendancy. Theologically, they differed from the Pharisees, because they did not believe in the bodily resurrection of the dead. They hated spiritual idealism, and the messianic concept, so that it had no earthly significance, and they were of the acute opinion that there was a desert and a sea between authority of the old traditions and the law.[17] Any disturbance of the established order meant upsetting their position. They loved Israel, but loved their comforts and luxuries more. They had made their peace with Rome, and the enemies of Rome were their enemies. Personally, I am inclined to the speculative position that they did not love the Romans, but they were clever enough to see that the only way they could guarantee and perpetuate their own position was to stand in firm opposition to revolutionaries and to radicals. Anyone who came with a message that would send a thrill through the broken-hearted, the destitute and cast down, would have them to reckon with. Jesus could find no common cause with the Sadducees.

The Pharisees were baptized–legalism.[18] They believed profoundly in the eternal significance of an historically revealed law. To phrase it in the language of some of our contemporaries, they were the defenders of the faith, once for all time, delivered to the Saints. They were as anxious to observe the interpretations that had grown up around the law as the law itself. In fact, their position at this point was consistent, for the law was what it was interpreted to be, and the interpretation, if it were to be valued, must be on the same footing as the law itself.

It was the Pharisees' insistence upon ceremonial law that made it possible for Judaism to persist as a culture, a religion, and a civilization. Standing at the center of literal Jewishness, they fought off every attempt at innovation and the like. They saw clearly that if the Jews were to remain a race, they would have to protect themselves from the Hellenistic influences by which they were surrounded.

In order to do this it was necessary for them to carry their environment with them, and it is to the credit of the vitality and power of the Pharisees that Judaism has persisted as a culture in an endless series of foreign environments and foreign soils. To them the Messiah was to be a human son of David. He would reign on the earth. One must understand the formalism of the Pharisees to appreciate the significance of many of the teachings of Jesus. I need not burden you with this point with comments in defense of their position. They felt that if the Jews kept God's law, God would take care of them. The only way to handle their enemies was to have no intimate dealings with them. One of the most striking scenes in the cinema "Ben Hur" is that one in which a Roman legion marches by, and as the last soldier passes a proud Pharisee with folded arms and eyes smoldering with the utmost contempt, without a shift of his facial muscles, spits at the heel of the receding legionary, a consummate touch portraying in one sweeping muscleless gesture all the spiritual pride and self-sufficiency of a people in whose foreheads were the marks of destiny.[19] Their solution was to have no contact, except in the most formal matters, no respect for the Roman dog. Obey Jehovah's law and Jehovah would fulfill the deepest desires of one's heart. There was much in the Pharisees' position to which Jesus could not subscribe, and their solutions of the problem could not be accepted by him because of its narrow exclusiveness.[20]

There were the Essenes. They were a group numbering something over four thousand, and according to Philo, residing chiefly in monastic colonies around the Dead Sea. They lived a communal life, sharing all things in common and eating their meals at a common table. They were not unlike contemporaneous religious communities. They sought to be self-contained through crafts and farming.[21] Pliny says that "their membership is steadily recruited from the large number of people who resort to their mode of existence because they are wearied with life's struggle with the waves of adversity."[22]

Fundamentally, they were ascetic, having all of their relationships guided by three great loves–love of God, love of virtue, and love of man. They felt no profound concern for the problems incident to the national life of the Jew. In a sense, they were mystics, and the net result of their mysticism ended in pessimism. As mystics, they were life-negating, rather than life-affirming.[23] If you were to classify them in contemporaneous terms, they would be regarded as escapists, feeling, perhaps, that if one withdrew from the filth and struggle and anxiety incident to commerce and fame and honour, there would, in that act of withdrawal and consecration, be released in society a spirit which would cause a ground swell that would shake the very foundations of that which was evil and iniquitous. Jesus could be no Essene.[24]

With this as a background, and with all of these solutions teeming in his mind, Jesus leaves the inspired moment of the baptism and goes alone into the wilderness. I think it was clear to him at his baptism that he was forced to make a religious and spiritual approach to the problem. It is reasonable to suppose that he saw that as a religious man bent upon summarizing all aspects of life: personal, national, and social, in terms of the inexorable demands of his faith, he could renounce the world—withdraw from it—with the firm conviction that contact with the world at any point would make for contamination. Under such a circumstance, he would seek to save a remnant and leave the rest to a fated end. This note seems to creep through his life at various periods in his career. He saw also that he might live his life in the glow of the past glory of his religious background, to make it his mission in life to urge his fellowmen to recapture a lost radiance. He saw also that he could become a reconciler of man to man, being careful to take no position that would antagonize his fellowmen. He would then be all things to all men; he would not stand in judgment against society, but would be the creative harmonizer. However, it seems clear that he decided to interpret the world and life in terms of some creative purpose out of which life arose and that all aspects of society are constantly under the judgment of such a purpose. As such, his life and his teaching would be simple, direct, always under this inexorable scrutiny of God. All men are children of God, and as such must live their lives under his Divine scrutiny. This is true of the Roman, the slave, the Pharisee, Sadducee, Zealot, Essene—all men. There is not escape. With this fundamental commitment, I believe, sending him originally into the wilderness, he faces the temptations of his career.

"The new mother, when she looks down at the little head upon her breast, whispers in her heart: Oh, may you seek after truth. If anything I teach you be false, may you throw it from you, and pass on to higher and deeper knowledge than I have ever had. If you are an artist, may no love of wealth of fame or admiration and no fear of blame or misunderstanding make you ever paint, with pen or brush, an ideal or picture of external life otherwise than as you see it; if you become a politician, may no success for your party or yourself or the seeming food of even you nation ever lead you to tamper with reality and play a diplomatic part. In all the difficulties which will arise in life, fling yourself down on the truth and cling to that as a drowning man in a stormy sea flings himself on to a plank and clings to it, knowing that, whether he sink or swim with it, it is the best he has. If you become a man of thought and learning, oh never, with your left hand be afraid to pull down what your right has painfully built up through the years of thought and study, if you see it at last to not be founded on that which is; die poor, unloved, unknown, a failure—but shut your eyes to nothing that seems to them the reality."[25]

Olive Schreiner

TD. HTC-MBU: Box 112.

1. For background to the tour, see From Beverly Oaten, 24 November 1936, HTC-MBU: Box 15; To James C. Taylor, 21 January 1937, HTC-MBU: Box 21; From Beverly Oaten, 5 February 1937, HTC-MBU: Box 15; and To Beverley Oaten, 8 February 1937, HTC-MBU: Box 15. Thurman was in the Maritimes from 21 January to 6 February.

2. From Margaret Kinney, 20 February 1937, HTC-MBU: Box 10.

3. To Robert Holmes, 26 May 1937, HTC-MBU: Box 9. See also, Quinton Dixie and Peter Eisenstadt, *Visions of a Better World: Howard Thurman's Pilgrimage to India and the Origins of African American Nonviolence* (Boston: Beacon Press, 2011), 129–30.

4. To Herbert King, 25 September 1937, printed in the current volume.

5. In 1949 Thurman received a letter from a Canadian missionary in Angola who had been present at Lake Couchiching, writing that she still had his "messages on the Significance of Jesus among my books and pamphlets and every now and again I read them again. As a matter of fact, I was asked to take five of the morning worship periods at our annual Mission council meeting in April, and I quoted freely from some of your talks." From Amy E. Shauffler, 31 July 1949, HTC-MBU: Box 19.

6. From W. L. Savage, 21 February 1938, printed in the current volume.

7. Albert Schweitzer, *The Quest of the Historical Jesus: A Critical Study of Its Progress from Reimarus to Wrede* (London: Black, 1910).

8. HT, "Good News for the Underprivileged," printed in volume 1; HT, *Jesus and the Disinherited* (New York: Abingdon-Cokesbury, 1949).

9. Shirley Jackson Case, *Jesus: A New Biography* (Chicago: University of Chicago Press, 1927). Shirley Jackson Case (1872–1947), a longtime professor at the University of Chicago, was one of the leading figures in historical New Testament scholarship in the first half of the twentieth century. For Case and his impact, see Gary J. Dorrien, *The Making of American Liberal Theology: Idealism, Realism, and Modernity, 1900–1950* (Louisville, Ky.: Westminster/John Knox, 2003), 190–99.

10. Heinrich Weinel and Alban G. Widgery, *Jesus in the Nineteenth Century and After* (Edinburgh: Clark, 1914), 405.

11. Most of the lecture until this point was taken verbatim from "Good News for the Underprivileged."

12. Shirley Jackson Case, *Makers of Christianity: From Jesus to Charlemagne* (New York: Holt, 1934), 3–4.

13. Ibid. The passage from Case ends here, after the close of the quotation marks.

14. This occurred at the quadrennial convention of the Student Volunteer Movement in Indianapolis, 28 December 1923–1 January 1924; see HT, *Jesus and the Disinherited,* 21–22.

15. Vladimir G. Simkhovitch, *Toward the Understanding of Jesus and Other Historical Studies* (New York: Macmillan, 1921), 7–8. Although Thurman does not close the quotation for another four sentences, the passage from Simkhovitch ends here.

16. Simon, according to Luke 6:15. Questions about whether the Zealots described in Josephus in the period of the Jewish Wars (66–73 C.E.) were the same faction as the sicarii (to use the more common spelling), about whether they existed as an organized faction at the time of Jesus, and about the meaning of Simon's description as a "zealot" has long been debated by scholars of first-century Palestine and the New Testament.

17. Although the Sadducees are mentioned in the New Testament, the Mishnah, and Josephus, they remain a somewhat shadowy group, largely defined in the historical sources by their enemies, with few if any extant writings or figures clearly identified with the faction.

18. Thurman's meaning is unclear. Although the practices of the Pharisees, as viewed through the classic texts of rabbinic Judaism, did employ the mikveh or ritual bath for reasons of purification (such as after contact with a source of contamination, menstruation, or seminal emissions), ritual immersion was not used as a general sign or rite of faith.

19. *Ben-Hur* (1925), directed by Fred Niblo, starring Ramon Novarro and Francis X. Bushman, based on Lew Wallace's novel, *Ben-Hur: A Tale of the Christ* (New York: Harper, 1880). The silent film was Metro-Goldwyn-Mayer's first real success and inspired their popular 1959 remake.

20. Thurman here follows the traditional Christian views of the Pharisees, drawn from New Testament texts, that criticize, as here, their "legalism," "formalism," and "narrow exclusiveness." This view of the Pharisees has largely been rejected by recent scholarship, which has emphasized their flexibility and creativity at a time of wrenching change and has seen them as the source of most of the innovations associated with late Second Temple Judaism, including the belief in the bodily resurrection of the dead and the codification of the oral law. See Jacob Neusner and Bruce Chilton, eds., *In Quest of the Historical Pharisees* (Waco, Tex.: Baylor University Press, 2007).

21. Philo, "Every Good Man Is Free," in *The Works of Philo*, trans. C. D. Yonge (Peabody, Mass.: Hendrickson, 1993), 689.

22. Pliny the Elder, *Natural History*, trans. H. Rackham (Cambridge, Mass.: Harvard University Press, 1951), 5.73.

23. The reference here is to Rufus M. Jones, *Social Law in the Spiritual World: Studies in Human and Divine Inter-Relationship* (Philadelphia: Winston, 1904), 149. For the impact of Rufus Jones on Thurman, see Walter E. Fluker, *They Looked for a City: A Comparative Analysis of the Ideal of Community in the Thought of Howard Thurman and Martin Luther King, Jr.* (Lanham, Md.: University Press of America, 1989), 25–28.

24. Thurman of course was writing before the discovery, in 1947, of the Dead Sea Scrolls, near Qumran, in what is the now the West Bank, which has revolutionized knowledge of the Essenes. The general scholarly consensus (from which there are dissenters) holds that the most likely source of the scrolls was an Essene community at Qumran. Far from being quietist or apolitical, many of the texts reveal a fervid apocalypticism and an eagerness at the approach of the end-time. For a review of the argument for Essene authorship and an analysis of the theology of the scrolls, see James VanderKam and Peter Flint, *The Meaning of the Dead Sea Scrolls: Their Significance for Understanding the Bible, Judaism, Jesus, and Christianity* (San Francisco: Harper San Francisco, 2002).

25. Olive Schreiner, *From Man to Man; or Perhaps Only . . .* (New York: Harper, 1927), 158; reprinted in HT, ed., *A Track to the Water's Edge: The Olive Schreiner Reader* (New York: Harper & Row, 1973), 153.

"The Significance of Jesus II: The Temptations of Jesus"

13 September 1937

Thurman interprets the three temptations of Jesus in Matthew as reflecting the contrasting obligations of body and spirit and the ever-present temptation to overvalue one at the expense of the other.[1] *His analysis of the first temptation warns of the danger of purely material satisfaction and argues that even the realization of a just economic order, but one without "beauty and comradeship and righteousness," would be an example of living "by bread alone." The second temptation was to provide the illusion that exceptional people or exceptional circumstances could somehow transcend the usual workings of nature. In his analysis of the third temptation, following many authors in the progressive tradition, notably Lincoln Steffens and Reinhold Niebuhr, Thurman argues that without a transformation of society's institutions—what he calls here "the framework of relationships"—personal goodness or spiritual power will be unavailing. He also criticizes the opposite tendency, that a social transformation will be sufficient to make individuals "instruments of positive weal." For Thurman the temptations of Jesus are the same temptations that tend to lead people astray in the formation of an authentic Christian radicalism.*[1]

Monday

I shall deal with the temptations in the order that they were given in Matthew, and I shall waive the critical question as to whether they belong at the beginning of his career or whether they represent a summary of his entire career and were placed at the beginning in the record because of a systematic reflection upon the subsequent meaning of his life.

> Matthew 4:1–4
>
> Then was Jesus led up of the spirit into the wilderness to be tempted of the devil. 2. And when he had fasted forty days and forty nights, he was afterward an hungered. 3 And when the tempter came to him, he said, If thou be the Son of God, command that these stones be made bread. 4. But he answered and said, It was written, Man shall not live by bread alone, but by every word that proceedeth out of the mouth of God.

After this vigil Jesus was hungry. The fact could have doubtless been duplicated all over Palestine with this important exception—many of his fellows were hungry through no choice of their own. They were hungry because necessity had confronted their universe with an invincible gesture. By their fellows they had been shut off from free and necessitous participation in the basic creature demands for survival. On the other hand, Jesus was hungry because he had foregone these demands under the impelling power of a great concentration. He was caught in the agonizing grip of a great challenge—what shall I do with my life? What must be for me an adequate disposition of my life?

Wrestling in the wilderness seemed strangely trivial and irrelevant. The quest in its practical bearing was this—how fundamentally important is bread, is feeding the hungry? It is true that man cannot live on bread alone—of course this means that he must have bread, but should this be his major concern? Only a hungry man could face this question realistically. It is very simple often—to quote the Zulu proverb—for "full belly child to say to empty belly child, 'Be of good cheer.'" The danger for a hungry man in such a reflection is that the importance of food may be greatly over-emphasized, for it is very natural to idealize possessions which we are denied.

With reference to the problem before him Jesus reached an amazingly significant conclusion—man must live on bread but not bread alone. There is more besides, and it is this more besides, that reveals the true stature of the man. Men must have food, yes, admitting this, and seeing the practical significance of this in terms of actual survival, what then? He must let the bias of his life be on the side of those needs that cannot be adequately included in creature demands. The problem for us is at once clear. As a religious man, what must I do in the face of the pressing demands of men for creature needs? I must not make the error of giving myself over to the meeting of these needs alone, but even as I recognize realistically the physical needs of men, I must let my bias be on the side of his deeper concerns; I must give priority to their desires and yearning that can never be met by a full stomach or by all the economic security available in the world. The major emphasis must not be an either-or one but rather a both-and emphasis with a positive bias in favor of that which is deeper than food. My interests in creature needs must be genuine and practical, but I must see these needs as things which may stand clearly in the way of the realization of the higher ends of life. Feed the hungry, yes, and always; but I must know that man is more than his physical body. There is something in him that calls for beauty and comradeship and righteousness.

Matthew 4:5–7

5. Then the devil taketh him up into the holy city, and setteth him on a
pinnacle of the temple, 6. And saith unto him, If thou be the Son of God,
cast thyself down: for it is written He shall give his angels charge concerning
thee; and in their hands they shall bear thee up, lest at any time thou dash
thy foot against a stone. 7. Jesus said unto him. It is written again, Thou shalt
not tempt the Lord thy God.

In this experience Jesus is facing the problem of one of life's great illusions—the illusion that exceptions are made in the operation of natural consequences on the basis of character concentration. The tempter suggests to him that if he were to go to the pinnacle of the temple and cast himself down, the operation of what we characterize as natural law would be ineffective in dealing with him—the normal working of the law would be interrupted in his behalf and God would perform on the spot a miracle. For, he quietly whispers, the world of nature is not really orderly.

Jesus' reply was very striking. He said in substance that if I go to the pinnacle of the temple and cast myself down, I will break my neck, son of God to the contrary, notwithstanding. And he who presumes to disregard the ordinary processes of nature, tempts God. His choice here was on the side of the normal, natural working of the simple laws of life demanding nothing of them that dared to stretch them out of shape. To do so would have been to deceive himself and to have created a spiritual problem for which no solution could have been found.

The bearing of this choice upon the lives of students is at once clear. I have had students who during an entire semester did not pay much attention to the simple direct, natural operations in the classroom: who fulfilled none of the day-by-day requirements relative to their work. Then, when the day of judgment arrived—examinations—they came into the classroom, read the questions and expected, by some beyond-the-natural operation, to participate in complete knowledge and understanding of the questions raised. In other words, they expected a miracle. What they received was what they had rated—failure. It is a terrible truth that life does not have a habit of making exceptions in our case even though we may be good in general, even though our fathers may be great men and our reputations of outstanding merit. Let us not be deceived by the great illusions, but let us see the finger of God moving in the natural unfolding of antecedants and consequences.

Matthew 4:8–11

> 8. Again, the devil taketh him up into an exceeding high mountain and sheweth him all the kingdoms of the world, and the glory of them; 9. And saith unto him, All these things will I give thee, if thou wilt fall down and worship me. 10. Then saith Jesus unto him, Get thee hence, Satan; for it is written, Thou shalt worship the Lord thy God, and him only shalt thou serve. 11. Then the devil leaveth him, and, behold, angels came and ministered unto him.

In this experience the tempter strikes at the centre of the dominant passion of Jesus to bring society under the acknowledged judgment of God and thereby insure its purification. More and more as he lived, he became the embodiment of this great desire. He thought of himself as the example of the judgment and of the salvation of God. The tempter said to him, "Behold the kingdoms of the world. You want them to become the kingdom of God. They belong to me." It seems to me that the full realization of the thought came to Jesus with tremendous shock. His reasoning may have been, "God created me. God created the world of nature. God created all mankind; therefore, God is the creator of the relationships that exist between men." At this point the devil suggested, "You may be logical, but you are not true. I made the relationships between men." In the subsequent awareness of the far-reaching significance of this fact, Jesus cautioned his disciples, "Behold, I send you out as lambs among wolves. You must be wise as serpents and as harmless as doves." And again he said, "Rejoice when men persecute you for my sake for it means that you are making inroads on territory that is foreign to the will of God."

It seems to me that that experience reveals one of the potent fallacies of Orthodox religion, namely, that the world can be made good if all the men in the world as individuals become good men—after the souls of men are saved, the society in which they function will be a good society. This is only a half-truth. Many men have found that they were caught in a framework of relationships evil in design, and their very good deeds themselves have developed into instrumentalities for evil. I suggest that you read the autobiography of Lincoln Stephens to find wide-spread verification of this position.[2] It is not enough to save the souls of men; the relationships that exist between men must be saved also. To approach the problem from the other angle is to reveal what seems to me to be the basic fallacy in certain types of social radicalism. The assumption is that after relationships between men are saved, then the individual men will thereby become instruments of positive weal. This is a half-truth. The two processes must go on apace or else men and their relationships will not be brought under conscious judgment of God. We must, therefore, even as we purify our hearts and live our individual lives under the divine scrutiny, so order the framework of our relationships that good men can function in a good framework to the glory of God.

the job

"But, God, it won't come right! It won't come right!
I've worked it over till my brain is numb.
The first flash came so bright,
Then more ideas after it—flash! flash!
I thought it some
New constellation men would wonder at.
Perhaps it's just a firework—flash! fizz! spat!
Then darker darkness and scorched pasteboard and sour smoke.

"But, God, the thought was great,
The scheme, the dream—why, till the last charm broke
The thing just built itself while I, elate,
Laughed and admired it. Then it stuck,
Half done—the lesser half, worse luck!
You see, it's dead as yet—a frame, a body—and the heart,
The soul, the fiery vital part
To give it life is what I cannot get.

I've tried—
You know it!—tried to snatch live fire
And pawed cold ashes! Every spark has died.
It won't come right. I'd drop the thing entire–
Only—I can't! I love my job.
You who ride the thunder—
Do you know what it is to dream and drudge and throb?
I wonder.

"Did it come at you with a rush, your dream, your plan?
If so, I know how you began.
Yes, with rapt face and sparkling eyes.
Swinging the hot globe out between the skies,
Marking the new seas with their white beach lines,
Sketching in sun and moon, the lightning and the rains,
Sowing the hills with pines,
Wreathing a rim of purple round the plains!
I know you laughed then, as you caught and wrought
The first swift, rapturous outlines of your thought.
And then—
Men!

"I see it now,
O God, forgive my pettish row!
I see your job. While ages crawl
Your lips take laboring lines, your eyes a sadder light.
For man the fire and flower and centre of it all—
Man won't come right!
After your patient centuries,
Fresh starts, or castings, tired Gethsemanes
And thense Golgothas, he, your central theme,
Is just a jangling echo of your dream.
Grand as the rest may be, he ruins it.

"Why don't you quit?
Crumble it all and dream again! But no;
Flaw after flaw you work out revise, refine—
Bondage, brutality, and war and woe,
The sot, the fool, the tyrant and the mob—
Dear God, how you must love your job!
Help me, as I love mine."
—Badger Clark[3]

TD. HTC-MBU: Box 112.

1. The temptations of Jesus were a favorite theme of Thurman, one he would revisit many times, definitively in *Temptations of Jesus* (San Francisco: Lawton Kennedy, 1962).

2. Much of this lecture was reused by Thurman in his sermon "What Shall I Do with My Life?" *Christian Century Pulpit*, September 1939, 210–11.

3. Lincoln Steffens (1866–1936), one of the most prominent muckraking journalists of the early twentieth century, conducted celebrated investigations of municipal corruption and other social ills. In *The Autobiography of Lincoln Steffens* (New York: Harcourt, Brace, 1931), he frequently criticizes reform politics as being too focused on morality and argues that the problem of politics was economic, not moral. Thurman knew Steffens and, in *Jesus and the Disinherited*, 52–53, discusses a conversation they had.

4. In Badger Clark, *Sky Lines and Wood Smoke* (Custer, S.D.: Chronicle Shop, 1935). Charles Badger Clark Jr. (1883–1957) was a prominent western and cowboy poet who was named the first poet laureate of South Dakota in 1937.

"The Significance of Jesus III: Love"
14 September 1937

Thurman's third lecture distinguishes two types of love, the "personal and intimate" and the "social and more impersonal." The former type of love is characterized by a deep sympathy between two persons, while social love for Thurman grows out of a "deep, persistent energetic self-regard" or an expansion of self-love. Thurman's lecture is primarily concerned with the consequences of the second kind of love, which he sees as a form of social glue, a "self-identification" by which a person extends a concern with self-preservation to include one's partner, offspring, extended family, or even one's community, nation, or race. In some ways Thurman's two types of love stand in stark opposition; social love forms tight self-regarding communities, disdaining the outsider; to be contrasted by a love of genuine sympathy, going beyond the self-protective categories we all form, with the Good Samaritan as a model for intimate or sympathetic love.

What is most striking about this lecture, unique in Thurman's works, is the extended condemnation of private property. For Thurman private property is an extension of self-love to include one's possessions. An identity with one's possessions leads to defending one's property as one's life; Thurman uses as an illustration the factory owner who does not hesitate to hire gunmen to kill striking workers. When property becomes a value and end in itself, Thurman argues, genuine Christian love and deep regard for another becomes impossible, because "when property becomes sacred, personality becomes secular."

Thurman is not content to make an abstract case against private property. He argues that the usual ways sensitive Christians deal with this problem, by such strategies and compromises as trying to live simply or giving away excess possessions, are mere self-delusions, because the underlying problem remains unchanged. The only Christian response is directly political, "to put himself squarely against the possession of all personal property and to recognize it as a thing making for evil in the world," and to work for changing public opinion and legislation that would seek its abolition. Only in this way could a society be created in which all love is "without self-interest, sufficiently expansive and comprehensive to include everybody in the world." In Thurman's ideal world, that is, the selfishness of "social love" would disappear.

Thurman's familiarity with a wide range of progressive opinion helped inform the third lecture of "The Significance of Jesus." At the time of "The Significance of Jesus" he was close to the Socialist Party, which had a strong Christian pacifist orientation.[1] *There is some evidence of Thurman's interest in Communism: a book on Communism and religion (by a Communist) that he found "scintillating";*[2] *an odd article about a Thurman speech in the* Richmond News-Leader *in 1937 headlined "Claims Communism Is Help to Church";*[3] *and some friends, such as Max Yergan, who were in the Communist orbit. But Thurman kept his distance from any ties or affiliations with Communists or Communist organizations, and if Thurman was a socialist, it was of a nondoctrinaire, non-Marxist persuasion. In the end the lecture is less about the nationalization of the means of production than the creation of a society where personal possessions and private property did not crowd out essential human values. Thurman's vision of a society without private property owed as much to Gandhi as to conventional socialist thinking, and if the lecture has a motto it is the Gandhian catchphrase here favorably quoted by Thurman: "He who has more than he needs is a thief."*[4]

The central emphasis of the teaching of Jesus centers upon the relationship of individual to individual and of all individuals to God. There are numerous passages which are illustrative of this teaching at different points. So profound has been the conviction of Christians as to the ultimate significance of his teaching about love that they have rested their case, both for the validity and the supremacy of the Christian religion on this point. When some one asked Jesus what is the meaning of all the law and the prophets, he gave those tremendous words of Judaism, "Hear, O Israel, the Lord thy God is one, and thou shalt love the Lord thy God with all thy mind, heart, soul, and strength. Thou shalt love thy neighbor as thyself."[5] So that it seems that Jesus also rested his case finally on this point. It is my purpose in this lecture to discuss the meaning of this radical doctrine of love both from the point of view of the structure of social relationships and that of personal piety.

Love is the intelligent, kindly, but stern expression of kinship of one individual for another, having as its purpose the maintenance and furtherance of life at its highest level. Self-love is a kind of activity having as its purpose the maintenance and furtherance of one's own life at its highest level. All love grows basically out of a self regard and is in essence the exercise of that which is spiritual. If we accept the general proposition that all life is one arising out of a common center: God, all expressions of love are acts of God. Hate, then, becomes a form of annihilation of self and others–in short, suicide. Violence is animal and atheistic because it denies the unity of life and defeats its maintenance and furthermore on the highest levels. It is for this reason that hatred and bitterness, self-violating as they seem to be, in the last analysis are apt to destroy both the hated and the hater. In Jesus' insistence that the normal ethical relationship between men is love, he reflects most accurately the very heart of God. To be true to this insight means ultimately the extension of one's self until all life is included and the individual loses himself in that which is vast and inclusive of all.

There are two levels on which love as Jesus saw it operates, the personal and intimate; the social and more impersonal. On the personal level, love grows out of a knowledge that is intimate, increasingly complete, but inexhaustible. It is small wonder that for a long time men have been of the conviction that perfect knowledge and perfect love are two aspects of one whole. Wherever contacts are primary and are enveloped by the warmth of fellowship, there is engendered in the mind a quality of understanding that is sympathetic, wholesome, and often redemptive. Hate is not possible when one man enters into intelligent sympathy with another. If I were to summarize this teaching in one categorical passage, I would say contacts with fellowship lead to an understanding that is sympathetic. Sympathetic understanding expresses itself in the exercise of a good will. Good will dramatized in a man or a woman is love walking on the earth.

Now, on the impersonal level, love for other-than-self grows out of a deep, persistent energetic self-regard. At the center of my life there is a hard purpose to live. I am caught in the upward surging of a great passion to guarantee the perpetuation of my days and to transmit my life through my kind. It is for this reason that the doctrine of self-defense is one of such meritorious significance among all peoples. Men are held guiltless when they destroy life that threatens their own life. I think this is the reason that a doctrine of reverence for life cannot long persist if it does not substitute compassion for indifference as an ethical attitude. Because of this desire to live, the mind is alert to take advantage of almost every situation on behalf of self-interest. Some years ago, I read a very thrilling description of a certain kind of buck rabbit that lives in the Arizona desert, that sleeps all day with one eye wide open. Because of this persistent demand that self be guaranteed and that self-interest be placed first, there is provided one explanation at least as to why it is so difficult to destroy the tendency toward deception in human life.

Devotion to those ends that tend to guarantee the fulfillment of my own life become ethical and religious. The most striking illustration that I know is that of the fable of the frog and the yeast cake. The frog and the yeast cake were seated on a park bench. Some one dropped water on the yeast cake and it began fermenting. The more it fermented, the more it crowded the frog, and presently, in desperation, the frog said, "Yeast cake, why don't you stop pushing me off the bench?" The yeast cake said, "I am not pushing you, I am growing." Back of all imperialism, back of all exploitation, is often this fundamental passion that urges the individual to guarantee and to perpetuate himself, his family, his group or class.

It seems reasonable, therefore, to say that whenever we observe love in action among men, we see self-identification at work. I do not love until I succeed in extending myself so as to include the object of my devotion, so that the same things that work in me on behalf of my own preservation become operative now in me with regard to the other-than-myself that has been included in this extension of myself. For instance, when a man marries, he identifies himself with another, and then when there are children, there is a further extension of oneself so as to include them. And it is very instructive at this point that love is not possible between parent and child until there has been sufficient time to develop this network of relationships by which the parent works out his self-extension with the child. Careful analysis of the emotional reaction of almost any parent to the first appearance of the child will bear this point out. And then, little by little, there is the extension of oneself to include those fictitious family relationships such as cousins and aunts and uncles. And then it may be widened further to include, less intensively, those who are part of one's race, or one's nation or one's club. To illustrate, in times of economic crisis, it becomes necessary to contract one's self-extensions. If the crisis is of an economic nature, one's self-extension will include only those to whom one is tied by immediate blood relationships. If a choice has to be made between one's mother and one's grandmother, the possibilities are that one chooses one's mother. And if times get still harder and one has to choose between one's mother and one's wife, the possibilities are that one would choose one's wife; and on it goes.

The bearing that this whole framework of relationships has upon our economic life is profoundly interesting and significant. As we know, in society there is not an atmosphere of mutual trust except in certain aspects of credit. Society must have signatures and guarantees for security, and ways of penalizing those who violate them. Hence, there are oaths and all kinds of laws to make men do what trust alone ought to make them do. This is directly traceable to the concept of private property. This conception recognizes personal prerogatives and gives them precedent over social weal. It is built upon an assumption that all social security for individuals is ultimately guaranteed by individual initiative and certain political prerogatives. The moment that property becomes private, it becomes an extension of the self, the ethical basis for the . . . Whatever there is upon which the subsistence of those with whom I have identified myself depends becomes at once a part of the self-extension. For instance, let us begin with the individual. The money that I have by which I support my family is referred to by me as my money. The job that I have that makes possible a measure of economic security is my job. It becomes a part of the extension of myself. The years that a man spends in school to prepare himself to be a physician becomes a part of himself, and when he exchanges it in the open market, he expects to get for it economic units, which economic units guarantee and perpetuate himself. So that if he exchanges his services with any individual, that person becomes his patient. All of these exchanges are viewed as his practice. And anyone who threatens to take away from him his patients threatens his life. And he may be able to go into a court of law to defend the private property rights that he has in his patients.

Now, the same thing is true with the business man. That upon which he depends as a guarantee of his economic survival becomes an extension of himself. It becomes his private property, and any individual who threatens to disturb his security threatens his life. Hence, men feel quite justified in importing gunmen or thugs to kill defenseless strikers in a factory, or in using the police of the state to keep their property intact against individuals who would, in their self interest, make inroads on this property. Property becomes sacred only when it has already become private; and when property becomes sacred, personality becomes secular. If a choice must be made, then, between property and personality, at all costs, property rights must be protected. Sacredness of property, then, renders individuals in society who are without property, without security. It makes individuals possessing property identify their status and their significance with the amount and value of the property they possess. They seek to organize themselves for defense against all efforts towards distribution and confuse all sharing with those outside their property class as either charity or philanthropy. Any conception of love, therefore, must fit into their property demands. It must not disturb individual or group security. Trust outside of the group and often within it becomes a highly precarious problem; for any man may easily become a threat to any other person's security or to any other person's property, just as an ideal of social action must always be balanced by the bearing that a specific act of justice may have upon property rights, upon security.

The demand, therefore, of Jesus that men love each other is in fundamental opposition to the grounds of security for men in the modern world. It attacks private property, for it demands the willingness to renounce all personal claims to possession if the need arises. It puts one's property at the mercy of the welfare of those who have no property rights in one's possessions. To recognize this demand is to render one economically insecure in a world in which economic security is interpreted as the right of individuals.

The Christian finds that it is necessary for him to compromise with this demand. He shares his surplus. He draws a very fine line between all he needs to guarantee his security on a level, sometimes arbitrarily chosen, and what he may put at the disposal of the needs of his fellowmen. He may accept the dictum "he who has more than he needs is a thief,"[6] but will give to the interpretation a meaning that completely nullifies the far-reaching significance of the demand. Almost all efforts to live the simple life break down at this point. Rough, rigorous effort is not exercised in reducing one's needs to the simplest possible terms. Self-deception is one of the hounds of hell that dog the footsteps of all who would be true to the highest. If I accept the Christian compromise, I must steadily reduce my personal demands. But Jesus quietly insists "He who does not hate mother, father, sister, brother, cannot be my disciple."[7]

Ultimately, experimenting with this principle will lead an individual to put himself squarely against the possession of all personal property and to recognize it as a thing making for evil in the world and to work in all ways for legislation and for public opinion that would make private property impossible. "No slave can belong to two masters, for he will either hate one and love the other, or stand by one and make light of the other. You cannot serve God and mammon. Therefore, I tell you, do not worry about life, wondering what you will have to eat or drink or about your body, wondering what you will have to wear. Is not life more important than food, and the body than clothes? But you must make his kingdom and uprightness before him, your greatest care, and you will have all these other things besides."[8] That time will come in society only when the security of each individual is guaranteed by all individuals. So long as any man threatens my security I cannot trust him, for he is outside of my self-extension. If I cannot trust him, then love is impossible between us. It seems to me, therefore, that the Christian in the modern world is called upon to work out a scheme of political organization and machinery designed for the managing of social life on this basis. Then, and not until then will love as an ideal become the will of society and the personal practice of it a practical procedure in widespread social relations. Certain attitudes that are now considered exceptional and belonging only in a minister's sermon would be day by day life in the world.

Let us apply this quite practically now. In the first place, the response of men to any form of human need would be instantaneous and effective. The story of the good Samaritan would be normal, rather than unique as life is now lived. As a matter of fact, it would not be necessary for a man to accumulate possessions. In the second place, a man's life with regard to everybody would be covered with a wide series of simple gratuitous deeds of unasked-for kindness. When I was a boy, Christmas was the most important single day in the year. From Thanksgiving Day to December 24, I was a model son. I anticipated all of my mother's needs, so that i[t] became singularly unnecessary for her to make any suggestions either as to decorum or as to things she wanted done around the house. My insight was uncanny. But after Christmas Eve had passed and the Christmas toys had been distributed, I became a boy again. The attitude that I maintained for a period of four or five weeks is one that should be characteristic of the Christian with reference to everybody if he loves without self-interest, sufficiently expansive and comprehensive to include everybody in the world. And finally, it would mean an expression on the part of everybody which makes for respect for personality. The best illustration of what Jesus means here is found in that interesting story of a woman taken in adultery.[9] We waive the critical question as to the authenticity of this story, but here was a woman taken in adultery. The men who had brought her to Jesus said, "We caught her in the act. The law says she should be stoned. What do you say?" Jesus was such a gentleman that he could not look at the woman, covered as she was in her shame. He said, "Let the man among you who is without sin cast the first stone." He marked on the ground. After hearing no screams, seeing no expressions of violence, he looked at the woman, saying, "Where are those thine accusers?" for all the men had gone away, and his look now upon her would not cover her with shame. "Does not any man condemn thee?" "No man, Lord." "Neither do I. Go into peace and sin no more." Jesus met the woman where she was and treated her there as if she were where she should have been. When we love, that is what we do. We meet people where they are, and we treat them there as if they were where they ought to be, and by so doing, we believe them into the fulfillment of their possibilities and love becomes an act of redemption. We place a crown over their heads that they are always trying to grow tall enough to wear.[10]

"From the mysterious drawing together of amoeba to amoeba, their union and increase, on through all the forms of sentient life, and in the life of the very vegetable world, the moving original power is always this stretching out, uniting, creative force . . . shaping itself in the union of male and female, of begetting with their begotten; drawing together creatures of like and unlike kinds, bringing into all the forms of friendship and union and love, it lies at the root of existence; it shapes the petals of flowers, not for death but to call the insects to such their sweetness and carry fertilizings to one another; it sings in the songs of all songbirds calling to their mates; it blossoms into human speech; to kill man might have been silent; but to communicate with and bind himself to his fellow, child to mother, mother to child, the sexes to reach each other, man to reach man belonging to his social organism, man was obliged to blossom into speech. Everywhere this binding, moving, creative force moves at the very heart of things, growing more and more important and complex and the creatures mount into the scale of life, till it reaches its apotheosis in the artist . . . Men have so recognized that this creative (and not the destructive) power was the fount and core of life that in all ages they have tended to call the highest intelligence they could conceive of, and therefore their supreme God, 'the great Creator': and their devils have been destroyers. It is false to say that the mighty jaw and the mighty claw and the stomach that is never filled and is always seeking to fill itself are the fundamental moving power in life—'Tis love that makes the world go round, the world go round, the world go round.'"[11]

Olive Schreiner

TD. HTC-MBU: Box 112.

1. In November 1936, when his friend Ralph Harlow, chaplain at Smith College, told him that he was running for Congress as a candidate of the Socialist Party, Thurman replied, "I am very glad that you are carrying out your convictions relative to the way that religion works in the political affairs of men. I only wish that I myself were located in a community where that sort of activity would be possible for me." To Ralph Harlow, 6 November 1936, HTC-MBU: Box 9.

2. See To T. J. King, 12 March 1935, HTC-MBU: Box 10, discussing Julius Friedrich Hecker, *Religion and Communism: A Study of Religion and Atheism in Soviet Russia* (London: Chapman & Hall, 1933), as one who comes "to Communism steeped in the piety of Methodism, and the combination is rare and scintillating."

3. "Claims Communism Is Help to Church," *Richmond News-Leader*, 10 April 1937, in which Thurman is quoted as stating "the present program of the Communists in America should be of great value to the organized church." Thurman may have been misquoted (or not.) Certainly there is no evidence of Thurman ever having expressed similar sentiments.

4. Thurman restated the argument in this lecture in a sermon at Boston University on 19 October 1938, "The Perils of Preaching the Love Ethic of Jesus" (HTC-MBU: Box 17), and in "Vital Christianity in a Disordered World," *Intercollegian and Far Horizons* 56 (February 1939): 88, 104.

5. Mark 12:29–31, quoting Deuteronomy 6:4–5; Leviticus 19:18.

6. In the spring of 1935, before Thurman left for India, Madeleine Slade (1892–1982), the upper-class English woman who as Mirabehn became a member of Gandhi's personal ashram and entourage, gave a lecture at Howard on this subject. Thurman recalls in his autobiography, "For days afterward, half in jest but with an undertone of seriousness, one student would say to another, 'You are a thief, look at your clothes!' Or 'Are you a thief? You must be, with all that food on your plate!'" *WHAH*, 106–7.

7. Luke 14:26.

8. Matt. 6:24–26.

9. John 7:53–8:11.

10. A recurring statement for Thurman. The statement is also inscribed on the monument in his honor at Morehouse College. This may be its first appearance in his work.

11. Olive Schreiner, *From Man to Man; or Perhaps Only . . .* (New York: Harper, 1927), 189–90, reprinted in HT, ed., *A Track to the Water's Edge*, 174–75.

"THE SIGNIFICANCE OF JESUS IV: PRAYER LIFE OF JESUS"
15 SEPTEMBER 1937

In this lecture Thurman discusses the prayers of Jesus and portrays him as "one who enjoyed God and prayed out of sheer love of him." Thurman argues that the act of Jesus praying to someone and something other than himself is an "overwhelming argument against the tendency to make Jesus and God identical. If Jesus were God, when he prays he is playacting, or shadowboxing." Thurman would have agreed with his main source for this lecture, Walter Bundy, who suggested that Jesus was "the perfect prayer" and that, in praying to God, "Jesus learned the divine will and found the personal power to perform it."[1]

I have often wondered at the effort of people to understand Jesus appreciatively by merely analyzing the records and subjecting them to the rigorous standards of historical criticism. There is much to be said for what may be gained from such methodology, but in my opinion, the key to the understanding of Jesus is in his experience with God focused in a deep prayer life. Perhaps this is the reason that is responsible for the fact that the humble and the devout seem to be able to penetrate his character with much more deftness and skill than the sophisticated and the learned. Jesus was a man of prayer. In times of great turmoil, stress, strain in times of deep joy, he sought new depths for his spirit. In Newman's "Dream of Gerontius"[2] as you remember, the soul is taken on a sight seeing tour through heaven. It at last comes to a place that gives rise to a great deal of bewilderment. Upon inquiry, the soul is told that "over there" is where God is. The soul says, "I have always wanted to see God." And the angel is greatly perturbed because the soul does not know that for which it asks. Finally, it is turned over to another angel called the Angel of Agony. This angel prepares the soul for the presence of God. The soul is ushered finally into the presence of God, and—there is a great stillness, like the stillness of absolute motion. And then, the soul cries aloud to be taken away to some remote place where it might recover from the sight of God. But this is not what Jesus experienced. To me, the great contribution that Jesus makes in his life of prayer to all who observe that life is this: Here is one who enjoyed God and prayed out of sheer love of him. It was a demonstration of prayer on the upper reaches of experience.

But let us examine some of the prayers of Jesus. First there is the prayer at baptism. Luke's text reads: "Now it came to pass, when all the people were baptized that Jesus, also having been baptized and praying, the heaven was opened, and the holy spirit descended in bodily form, as a dove, upon him, and a voice came out of heaven, 'Thou art my beloved Son; in thee I am well pleased.'"[3] Here is the first great step in the public career of Jesus. John has been preaching a message of repentance, and Jesus joins the throng of those who come to participate in the preparation of the new age. Definitely, John is calling men to repentance. Does Jesus come to him because he feels a sense of sin? It is my opinion that Jesus does not interpret himself as being one whose life is without dependence for guidance and strength upon God. I do not know why he came to John; I only know that he came. My own religious conviction is that he came to John for two reasons: first, John's was the clearest note on the horizon, a note in which he saw unmistakably clear the finger of God. Looking at the inexorable demand of God for absolute perfection in human life, Jesus becomes acutely aware of his own sense of spiritual and moral inadequacy. Driven by these two things: a challenge to get ready for a great moment in history and to seek a more complete surrender to God, he comes. While there, he gets a confirmation that the course that he is undertaking has the approval of God. And, ladies and gentlemen, to have the approval of God placed upon your life and your vocation is the be-all and end-all of existence. Jesus may fail, but at this moment he is conscious that he is working in the right direction, and the stars in their courses pull for him.

The second prayer is found in Mark: "And in the morning, a great while before day, he rose up and went out and departed into a desert place, and there prayed. And Simon and they that were with him followed after him; and they found him and said unto him, 'All are seeking thee.' And he saith unto them, 'Let us go elsewhere into the next towns that I may preach there also, for to this end came I forth.'"[4] Jesus has had a very full day. It has been a day crowded with numerous activities which have made upon him vast demands. He is confronted with a great crisis. He has healed the sick, cured men of disease; he has been given the emotional and irrational gratitude and enthusiasm of the crowds. There stretches out before him in fascinating glimpses an intriguing career, which career is strikingly like the temptation he refused when he was challenged to turn stones into bread. In his previous life he had been a carpenter, apparently living an obscure, simple existence. He feels now the thrill of riding on the crest of the wave so that his name is on the lips of the man in the street. He would be a success. And then, he remembers the baptism. He remembers the wilderness. The fight is on. It is intimated in Mark's account that he had been wrestling with this thing all night. He gets up a good while before day and goes out in a lonely place to pray. His mind is in a fog. He wants to see once again the illumined finger of God against the blackness. It is his mission in life to which he must be true, and whatever comes between that and him must be destroyed. It is the echo of struggles like this that makes him say, "If your eye offend thee, pluck it out, if thy right hand offend thee cut it off."[5] He wants a clearness of insight, the power to see the basic and ultimate purpose of God, for himself. He turns then, in trembling devotion to God in prayer. We are not given the words, but when morning comes, peace has settled in his spirit, the tempest is clear, his spirit is at rest. He sees what it is that he must do, and he tells Simon Peter, "Let us go elsewhere into the next towns that I may preach there also, for to this end was I born."[6]

The third prayer is reported by Luke only: "But he withdrew himself in the desert and prayed."[7] Here there is the story of the healing of the man with leprosy. The multitudes press upon Jesus after this, and he withdraws to pray. There is no content indicated relative to the prayer, and we assume here that it was a prayer not unlike the second one noted. He must keep his course clear. He must not be taken away from his goal, even though it means a greater tension within his spirit. And I may throw in here in passing, that the question of directing one's life is scarcely ever permanently settled. In all the great decisions of life men act on the basis of evidence that is not quite conclusive, and subsequent experience is apt to precipitate the crisis all over again. Sometimes it happens to the nth. degree of intensity; other times not so much. But it is never completely and finally settled.

The fourth instance is found in Luke. It is recorded that Jesus spends the whole night in prayer, and in the morning, he gathers his followers and from them he chooses twelve. "And it came to pass in these days that he went out into the mountain to pray; and he continued all night in prayer to God. And when it was day, he called his disciples; and he chose from them twelve."[8] He is obviously aware that he cannot trust completely his own mind in this matter. He is frail; he is fallible; and he wants to be assured that God gives his approval to this choice. It is not magic that is at work here. He has associated with these men; he has reasons to believe that he understands them pretty well. But he wants to put at the disposal of his mind and his experience the best resources of religion. He wants to feel that what he is doing in this regard is the expression of the will of God. He wants the catalytic agents to crystallize the precipitate. It is a clear expression of his rational dependence upon God.

The fifth is found in Matthew and Mark. It is the experience that follows after the feeding of the five thousand. "And straightway he constrained his disciples to enter into the boat, and to go before him unto the other side to Bethsaida, while he himself sendeth the multitude away. And after he had taken leave of them, he departed into the mountain to pray."[9] Let us assume the literalism of this for a moment. Jesus is exhausted. He is tired of eyes, and he turns to God for rest. "I come to thee at last, O Lord, for rest, with heart and mind and soul oppressed."[10] It seems in this prayer, as in so many of the others, Jesus needed to have his spirit restored and reenforced by basking himself in the complete presence of God.

The sixth is found in Luke. This is the great Caesarea Philippi experience. "And it came to pass, as he was praying apart, the disciples were with him: and he asked them, saying . . ."[11] After his prayer, the motive for which is not given, Jesus questions his disciples about the impression he was creating among men.

Doubtless the questions were but an echo of his struggle in the prayer experience. Was he succeeding or failing in being true to his basic commitment? Or it may have been the expression of fear on his part, lest he was beginning to feel too confident that he was in the right path. Or he may have been driven from his prayer experience to seek a social "other-than-self" reference by which he could more objectively gauge his progress and development.

The seventh is peculiar to Luke also. It is the transfiguration experience. He is taking fateful steps which hasten a climactic end. He withdraws into the mountain with Peter and James and John to pray. "And it came about eight days after these sayings, that he took with him Peter and John and James, and went up into the mountain to pray. And as he was praying, the fashion of his countenance was altered, and his raiment became white and dazzling."[12] It was perhaps a prayer that he would be able to keep his feet on the ground, a prayer that would enable him to keep his head and not go to pieces under the withering concentrated attitude of his enemies. We do not know what happened at the transfiguration, but if you grant the authenticity of the incident, we do know that it was obviously a mystic experience of tremendous moment. To have the countenance changed under the impelling power of great emotion is nothing new, nor is it unusual. Jane Steger tells how a friend of hers experienced such tremendous light in her countenance on one occasion that it frightened her dog.[13] It was Cowper[14] who says somewhere that at times in prayer he is so full of the spirit of God that it seems as if he would die because of excess of joy.

The eighth is also peculiar to Luke. "And it came to pass, as he was praying in a certain place, that when he had ceased, one of his disciples said unto him, 'Lord, teach us to pray, even as John also taught his disciples.'"[15] It is a record of the impression that Jesus, in an act of prayer, made upon his disciples. It is the only thing that they ask him to teach them how to do. It is the crowning tribute to thc qualitative but overt significance of the prayer life of Jesus as his disciples observed it in practice.

The ninth is the Gethsemane experience. We have here the reported content of his prayer. "And they come unto a place which was named Gethsemane: and he saith unto his disciples, Sit ye here, while I pray. And he taketh with him Peter and James and John, and began to be greatly amazed, and sore troubled. And he saith unto them, My soul is exceeding sorrowful even unto death: abide ye here, and watch. And he went forward little, and fell on the ground and prayed that, if it were possible, the hour might pass away from him."[16] Comment on this is unnecessary. All men of the spirit know what this means. "We kneel, how weak; we rise, how full of power!"[17]

I want us to examine now the concrete content of the recorded personal prayers of Jesus. I shall not deal with the Lord's prayer, around which much of discussion and controversy has arisen, but I shall deal with those in which the didactic element is almost entirely missing. In Matthew and Luke we find these words:

"I thank thee, O Father, Lord of heaven and earth, that thou didst hide these things from the wise and understanding, and didst reveal them unto babes: yea, Father; for so it was well-pleasing in thy sight."[18]

It is a prayer of praise in which Jesus expresses great exaltation. It belongs essentially to the literature of piety, and to the personal religious experience of Jesus. It is almost a shout of exaltation. One cannot understand it, viewing it outside the experience itself. It has the same quality of that greatest of utterances of exaltation: "I know that my redeemer lives!"[19]

The third prayer, counting the Lord's prayer as the first, is a prayer of intercession. It is found in Luke:

"Simon, Simon, behold, Satan asked to have you, that he might sift you as wheat; but I made supplication for thee, that thy faith fail not."[20]

It is an utterance to his friend, springing out of a heart of great affection and what he has asked for himself so many, many times he now asks for his friend. Wobbling, impetuous, irrational, constant, on-the-heights, in-the-depths Peter, his friend. Jesus prays for him that in all the crises of life he might be true to the centre of the soul. There is another prayer of intercession found in Luke.

"Father, forgive them; for they know not what they do."[21] It is a prayer in which Jesus puts himself into the blindness and prejudices and fears of his destroyers and makes them articulate with helplessness in the presence of which, the deepest stirrings of the mercy of God are poured forth in a never-ending stream. What men did not know to ask for themselves Jesus asked God for. You will recall that Stephen died with the same words on his lips.[22]

Then, there is the prayer in Gethsemane, to which we have already referred.

"Abba, Father, all things are possible unto thee; remove this cup from me: howbeit not what I will, but what thou wilt."[23]

Stripped bare of everything, to quote Bundy: "In it there is no doctrine, no dogma, no theology, no soteriology. To seek to fit such a prayer into a system or scheme of salvation is to tear out its heart. In this prayer there is no fanaticism seeking a tragic fate; there is also no fatalism that goes to its end in a feelingless fashion. Jesus' Gethsemane prayer is the spontaneous outburst of a torn human heart that can reconcile itself to its fate only because such appears as the divine will. This conviction becomes a religious certainty which issues in an heroic submission. Jesus' submission in Gethsemane is his supreme religious act . . . "the most exalted attitude ever attained by a human religious subject." It is small wonder that Professor Heiler calls this prayer "the highest and purest prayer in the history of religion, the sublime summit in the history of prayer," or, as Hooffding says, it is "the most profound religious word that was ever uttered."[24]

With all of this I agree with all of my passionate endeavor. I have already referred to the prayer, "My God, my God, why hast thou forsaken me."[25] And, so, ladies and gentlemen, we see by an examination of the internal evidence that prayer was a central emphasis in the religion of Jesus. The prayer life of Jesus in my opinion is the overwhelming argument against the tendency to make Jesus and God identical. If Jesus were God, when he prays he is playacting, or shadow-boxing. If he were not God, then the prayers become the normal language of his heart and mind as they sought constantly to walk on the earth by the light in the sky. In all the withering vicissitudes of life Jesus affirms the fact that "the best way to handle scars, after you have seen them straight, is to remember things big enough to wipe them out."[26] To him God is the answer to the deepest needs of human life; and if I were as sure of God as Jesus was, God would become for me the answer to my deepest needs.

TD. HTC-MBU: Box 112.

1. Walter E. Bundy, in *The Religion of Jesus* (Indianapolis: Bobbs-Merrill, 1928), 208. In this lecture, Thurman closely follows the scheme laid out by Bundy in *The Religion of Jesus*, first discussing the nine instances which are "Jesus' Retreats for Prayer," and then the seven instances in which the Gospels record the words of Jesus's prayers, with the Lord's Prayer being the only overlap on the list. The second list concentrates on the passion narrative, including Jesus's "last seven words" from the cross (The Religion of Jesus, 189–209). If Bundy was agnostic on the divinity of Jesus (*The Religion of Jesus*, 331), Thurman goes further arguing that the prayer life of Jesus is the key to understanding not only who Jesus was, but who Jesus was not.

2. A poem written in 1865 by John Henry Newman (1801–90), the well-known Roman Catholic cardinal and theologian. The poem is probably best known as the text of the oratorio of the same name by the English composer Edward Elgar.

3. Luke 3:21–22. See also Matt. 3:13–17 and Mark 1:9–11.

4. Mark 1:35–38. See also Luke 4:42–43.

5. Matt. 5:29.

6. Mark 1:38.

7. Luke 5:16.

8. Luke 6:12–13. See also Matt. 10:1 and Mark 3:13.

9. Mark 6:46; Matt. 14:23.

10. This does not appear to be a biblical quotation but is adapted from a work of suffragist and progressive reformer Edith Houghton Hooker (1879–1948): "I come to Thee at last, O Lord, for rest / With wasted years, with mind oppressed." Edith Houghton Hooker, *Life's Clinic: A Series of Sketches Written from Between the Lines of Some Medical Case Histories* (New York: Association Press, 1918), 56.

11. Luke 9:18–21. See also Matt. 16:13–20 and Mark 8:27–30.

12. Luke 9:28–29.

13. Jane Steger, *Leaves from a Secret Journal: A Record of Intimate Experiences* (Boston: Little, Brown, 1926). Steger was the pseudonym of Margaret Prescott Montague (1879–1955),

a West Virginia native, who wrote many novels and books of personal reflection, most of which were published under her own name. Thurman later preached on *Leaves from a Secret Journal* in his 1949 sermon series, "Men Who Walked with God."

14. William Cowper (1731–1800), an English poet and evangelical Christian who underwent severe episodes of depression.

15. Luke 11:1.

16. Matt. 26:36–44; Mark 14:32–42; Luke 22:40–46.

17. From an untitled sonnet by Anglican archbishop and poet Richard Chenevix Trench (1807–86). Trench, *The Story of Justin Martyr and Other Poems*, 5th ed. (London: Parker, Son & Bourn, 1862), 252.

18. Matt. 11:25–26; Luke 10:21.

19. Job 19:25.

20. Luke 22:31–32.

21. Luke 23:34.

22. Thurman seems to be confusing Luke 23:34 with Luke 23:46, "Father, into thy hands I commit my spirit," which is paraphrased by Stephen in Acts 7:59: "and they stoned Stephen, calling upon God, and saying, Lord Jesus, receive my spirit." Both are derived from Psalm 31:5, "Into your hands I commit my spirit."

23. Mark 14:36.

24. Friedrich Heiler, *Prayer: A Study in the History and Psychology of Religion* (New York: Oxford University Press, 1932), 123. Both quotes in Heiler's text are attributed to "Höffding," presumably the Danish philosopher and theologian Harald Høffding (1843–1931).

25. Matt. 27:46; Mark 15:34.

26. From Mary Ellen Chase's novel *Mary Peters* (New York: Macmillan, 1934), 200.

"THE SIGNIFICANCE OF JESUS V: THE CROSS OF JESUS"
16 SEPTEMBER 1937

In this meditation on the cross of Jesus, Thurman sees the crucifixion as "the inevitable result of the life that he lived." We all live in societies that contain evil, with which we must compromise to survive. For Thurman "the good man is a man who definitely and concretely reduces the area of his compromise, while the bad man is one who increases the area of his compromise." But when society closes in on the core of a person's life, the moral individual has no choice but to let their life go, like Socrates and Jesus. As Thurman says, "the cross teaches us that there are some things in life that are worse than death." Although, as Thurman points out, disciples and followers play a critical role in the lives of all creative religious leaders, in the end all truly religious persons are profoundly alone, and on the cross Jesus was stripped to the "literal substance of himself." In his final cry, "My God, My God, why hast Thou forsaken me?" Jesus was "surer of God than God was of him." The ultimate message of Jesus's cross for Thurman is that it "revealed that a man's life becomes meaningful and whole to the degree that he is willing to stake everything on a conviction that what he does when he is most himself has the approval and the imprimatur of the Highest."

Thurman's lecture on Jesus's cross was typical in his religious writing in its avoidance of the standard Christological categories. This is a crucifixion of a man who dies without certain knowledge of his fate, without redemptive or expiatory suffering for the sins of mankind, and without a resurrection. Instead Thurman's Jesus is a person whose life is shaped by deep convictions, by refusal to countenance the concessions to dominant society and their abettors. It is a person whose most profound beliefs are shared and bolstered by the support of close friends and who had learned to follow those beliefs, without compromise, to wherever they led. It is the model of an emerging social type, the pacifist or the civil rights activist. Although Thurman makes no reference to his experiences in India, in many ways it is a portrait of Jesus as an advocate of Satyagraha, using deep religious convictions and willingness to undergo personal sacrifice as the basis for creating a movement and effecting social change. This was a consistent theme in Thurman's reflections of the late 1930s on the religious roots of social change.[1]

> "Life is hard, it is brutal, it is unjust, it is immoral / You do not think so now, / This is your springtime, your halcyon days / But times will come when you must sit in the sepulchers of gloom / And watch your dreams go silently to dust, / Times when you must look upon the decayed corpse of all your illusions; / Times when you will realize that pain and grief and broken faith / and unrequited love are not merely the imaginings / of pessimistic philosophers and sentimental lady moodists, / But hideous realities that come unexpectedly and unbidden into / the happiest lives. / You will stand in the twilight of all your idols, / You will know that divine omnipotence and divine mercy cannot be reconciled. / You will lift up your eyes and your voices unto the hills and / the only answer will be the echo of your wailing plea for pity. / It is then you must have recourse to that universal and unalterable / faith that 'Somehow far off discordant sounds are wed, / somewhere far off the broken rays converge.' / Under the inspiration of that faith which requires / An almost divine fortitude you will carry on / You will believe, as others have before you, / That the promethean fire that burns in the heart of every real man / Cannot be extinguished by the waters of adversity. / You will thrill to the realization that pain and privation / and penury are negligible, that even death is a little thing

In the blackness of the gaunt eventual and . . . you will voice / the dauntless challenge . . . T'isn't life that / matters, it's the courage you bring to it. / And when you have found the strength to say that, you / will stand once more in the Sunshine" (*Fugitive Papers,* Russell Gordon Smith, 1930),

This morning I propose to talk about the problems which centre around the Cross of Jesus. You will recall that in our discussion of the temptations, I pointed out that Jesus discovered rather early that he was a centre of great disturbance and confusion to the faith into which he was born. He cautioned his disciples, "Behold, I send you out as lambs among wolves.[3] Rejoice when you are persecuted for righteousness' sake.[4] Fear not those who can kill the body, but rather fear God, who can send both soul and body to Gehenna.[5] I come not to bring peace but a sword."[6] I shall not attempt to deal with any of the more technical and critical problems which centre around the Cross, but rather, I shall deal with the bearing of the following fundamental proposition on the significance of the event: When a man refuses to conform to prevailing customs and conventions, he at once puts himself on record as opposed to the established order. The best setting I know for the picture of what Jesus was up against is found in this remarkable passage from Olive Schreiner:

"For on that broad road of opposition to law and authority, along which stream the millions of humanity too low to grasp even the value of laws and institutions about them, resisting them from an ignorant and blind selfishness which makes them believe they are improving their own conditions by violating them, there are found walking men of a totally different order—white-robed sons of the gods with the light on their foreheads, who have left the narrow paths walled in by laws and conventions, not because they were too weak to walk in them, or because the goals towards which they led were too high, but because infinitely higher goals and straighter paths were calling to them—the new pathfinders of the race! These men, who rise as high above the laws and conventions of their social world as the mass who violate them fall below, are yet inextricably blended with them in the stream of souls who walk in the path of resistance to law. From the monk Telemachus, who, springing into the Roman arena to stop the gladiatorial conflict, fell, violating the laws and conventions of his society—a criminal, but almost a god—up and down all the ages man has been on earth there have been found these social resisters and violators of the accepted order, the saviours and leaders of man on the earth to higher forms of life."[7]

Let us review some of the central events in the career of Jesus to see if we can find the raison d'etre of this phenomenon. Here was a young man, a Jew, of humble parentage, a craftsman and a peasant who, for some reason that remains forever a mystery, begins moving among his fellowmen, the living embodiment of disturbing ideas. In the first place he refused to be bound by many of the legalistic demands of his own religion, moving among people who were committed to a whole series of legal minutiae such as:

> "Women are forbidden to look in the glass on the Sabbath because they might discover a white hair and attempt to pull it out, which would be a grievous sin. . . . A woman may walk about her own court but not in the street, with false hair. Similarly, a man was forbidden to wear on the Sabbath wooden shoes studded with nails, or only one shoe, as this would involve labour. . . . A person might go about with wadding in his ear, but not with false teeth, nor with a gold plug in the tooth. If the wadding fell out of the ear it could not be replaced. As regards false teeth, they might fall out and the wearer might then lift and carry them, which would be sinful on the Sabbath. . . . But anything which formed a part of the ordinary dress of a person might be worn also on the Sabbath, and children whose ears were being bored might have a plug put into the hole. It was also allowed to go about on crutches or with a wooden leg, and children might have bells on their dresses, but it was prohibited to walk on stilts."[8]

But I need not burden you further with details of this sort. Think of what anger and fear he must have aroused when this young man said, "Man is greater than ceremony, man is greater than the Sabbath." I have referred to the strong position that he took with reference to the woman taken in adultery. It is quite conceivable that good sincere men would look upon him as a dangerous character, whose teachings were filled with evil omen for that which represented to them much of the heart of religion.

Again it seems that he was intent upon associating with the wrong kind of people. He found more of the evidences of religion among the insecure, the outcasts, the conscious sinners, than among those who felt themselves called upon to protect position and status. Children loved him, and I can imagine that there was always a group of village boys hanging around this teacher and his knot of disciples. And this leads to another very important observation. The disciples of Jesus served him as protection from the deadly power of his environment. Time and time again in retreat, in quiet fellowship, he found assurance in their midst that gave to him an objective validation for the rightness of his position. Perhaps this is the reason why all religious founders gather about themselves disciples. It is not so much that there is fear that their teachings will die, for the God-conscious man is sure at this point, but he must have an other-than-self reference which will be a social echo of the voice of God. Standing within this group he projects himself into a world in which the common assumptions are radically opposed to his teachings. If he did not have such a group footing for him, the possibilities are he would be pushed away from his moorings and destroyed. A man finds such a thing some times within the intimate circle of his family life, some times within the intimate circle of a close fellowship.

The Cross of Jesus, then, seems to me to be the inevitable result of the life that he lived. It presents to us the fundamental question as to how far one may go in the matter of compromising in defense of an end that he sees. As a general thing men are apt to be moral and religious as they move away from the areas of their security. As they go toward the centre of their security they are apt to be evasive, irreligious, immoral. It is a real question as to how far an individual can go without compromising his ideals. I do not think that a man can live in a society of which he does not approve without some measure of compromise. The good man is a man who definitely and concretely reduces the area of his compromise, while the bad man is one who increases the area of his compromise. The principle in the matter is this: Keep the compromise away from the centre of one's conviction. When society closes in on an individual and he is forced to compromise his life it is much better to die. You will recall that this is a central point made in the trial and death of Socrates. It is an issue at stake in that stimulating passage in Ibsen's "Wild Duck," in which he has one of his characters to point out that the wild duck when wounded, sinks himself to the bottom of the pond, fastens his feet to the growing vegetation there, and chooses rather to give himself up to the spirit of the water than to accept life on any terms that life may offer.[9]

This leads me to the first thing that we learn from the Cross of Jesus, namely, there are some things in life that are worse than death. Stephen Benet in his "John Brown's Body," makes Abraham Lincoln liken himself unto an old weary hunting dog who must hang on to what he gets until the end. In a memorable passage he says:

> "Therefore I utterly lift up my hands
> To You, and here and now beseech Your aid.
> I have held back when others tugged me on,
> I have gone on when others pulled me back,
> Striving to read Your will, striving to find
> The justice and expedience of this case,
> Hunting an arrow down the chilly airs
> Until my eyes are blind with the great wind
> And my heart sick with running after peace.
> And now, I stand and tremble on the last
> Edge of the last blue cliff, a hound beat out,
> Tail down and belly flattened to the ground,
> My lungs are breathless and my legs are whipped
> Everything in me's whipped except my will.
> I can't go on. And yet, I must go on."[10]

It would be completely irrational to say that Jesus was not confronted with the precarious nature of the choice which he had made. This is the full-orbed meaning of the prayer in the garden of Gethsemane, and before that, the utterly striking picture of Jesus coming out of Jericho, approaching the forks of the road, one leading to Jerusalem, the other leading back to Nazareth. Perhaps with fists clenched, with face set, he pushed ahead of his disciples, turning resolutely down the way that lead to Jerusalem and to death. The gospel writer says when his disciples looked at his face they were frightened. Without morbidity, without a martyr-complex he chose rather to be destroyed than to relinquish his right to be true to his deepest self. Yes, the cross teaches us that there are some things in life that are worse than death.

It teaches us, further, that there is a fundamental difference between failure on the one hand, and being mistaken on the other. "I have some times thought it would be a terrible thing if, when death came to a man or woman, there stood about his bed, reproaching him, not for his sins, not for his crimes of commission and omission toward his fellowmen, but for the thoughts and the visions that had come to him, and which he, not for the sake of sensuous pleasure or gain, had thrust always into the background . . . And then, when he is dying, they gather round him, the things he might have incarnated and given life to—and would not. All that might have lived, and now must never live for ever, look at him with their large reproachful eyes, saying, 'We came to you; you, only you, could have given us life. Was it worth it?' It has come upon me so vividly sometimes that I have almost leaped out of bed to gain air—that suffocating sense that all his life long a man or a woman might live striving to do his duty and then at the end find it all wrong."[11] Not to be mistaken in the central commitment of his life was his master concern. Not whether he should succeed, or fail, but whether he is right in what he undertakes to do is the point. Of course, Jesus was concerned about the impression that he was making on his fellowmen, as evidenced in his enquiry of his disciples, "Who do men say that I am?" He wanted men to believe in him, and the measure of his faith in himself was the measure of what he desired of others with reference to his commitment. And perhaps his greatest contribution was the fact that he created in other men a faith in himself, but his problem lay deeper than that. "Am I right in what I am undertaking?" The baptismal experience, the many recorded recurrences to prayer to know the will of God, the transfiguration and at Gethsemane—all find their meaning in this act of his to know the will of God. For he knew that if he were mistaken, then all other achievements of his life were trivial and meaningless. There came a time when he had to put this conviction over against all the testimony of his environment. His friends began moving in ever-widening circles away from him as the crisis approached in Jerusalem. The masses of the people under the skillful guidance of his enemies, blinded by profound political and social and economic frustrations, turned against him. One by one his disciples deserted. Stripped to the literal substance of himself, he stood alone on the naked vitality of his rightness in the course that he had taken. In that amazing, daring audacious cry of his on the Cross, "My God, My God, why hast Thou forsaken me?," we see him saying in that agony that he was surer of God than God was of him. This is the ultimate triumph of his spirit and he rested the subsequent significance of his end to the unfolding centuries of tomorrow and tomorrow and tomorrow.

It is small wonder that the Christian religion has sought to view the whole life of Jesus in the light of Calvary and the Cross, a shameful symbol of his death. It is my considered judgment that Jesus of Nazareth becomes a saviour in his death. For here is revealed that a man's life becomes meaningful and whole to the degree that he is willing to stake everything on a conviction that what he does when he is most himself has the approval and the imprimatur of the Highest. This is the meaning of that well-known spiritual "Were you there when they crucified my Lord? Sometimes it causes me to tremble, tremble, tremble. Were you there when they crucified my Lord?"

> "Yes: I am alone on earth: I have always been alone. My father told my brothers to drown me if I would not stay to mind his sheep while France was bleeding to death: France might perish if only our lambs were safe. I thought France would have friends at the court of the kings of France; and I find only wolves fighting for pieces of her poor torn body. I thought God would have friends everywhere . . . Do not think you can frighten me by telling me that I am alone. France is alone; and God is alone; and what is my loneliness before the loneliness of my country and my God? I see now that the loneliness of God is His strength: what would He be if He listened to your jealous little counsels? Well, my loneliness shall be my strength too: it is better to be alone with God: His friendship will not fail me, nor His counsel, nor His love. In His strength I will dare, and dare, and dare, until I die. I will go out now to the common people, and let the love in their eyes comfort me for the hate in yours. You will all be glad to see me burnt; but if I go through the fire I shall go through it to their hearts for ever and ever . . . O God that madest this beautiful earth, when will it be ready to receive Thy sainst? How long, O Lord, how long?"
>
> From "Saint Joan"
> By Bernard Shaw[12]

TD. HTC-MBU: Box 112.

1. See, for instance, "Christian, Who Calls Me Christian?" printed in the current volume.

2. *Fugitive Papers of Russell Gordon Smith* (New York: Columbia University Press, 1931), 118–19. Russell Gordon Smith (1892–1929) was an instructor of sociology at Columbia University; his fugitive papers were published posthumously, after he committed suicide. Thurman arranged the conclusion of Smith's essay "Fraternity" to form a poem.

3. Luke 10:3.

4. Matt. 5:10.

5. Matt. 10:28.

6. Matt. 10:34.

7. Olive Schreiner, *From Man to Man; or Perhaps Only . . .* (New York: Harper, 1927), 174; reprinted HT, ed., *A Track to the Water's Edge*, 162.

8. Alfred Edersheim, *The Life and Times of Jesus the Messiah*, vol II (London: Longman, Green, 1883), 778–779. Edersheim (1825–1889), a converted Jew who became a minister in several British denominations, wrote this passage to demonstrate, "the terribly exaggerated rules of the Rabbis, and their endless, burdensome rules about the Sabbath," 773. Given his apologetic purposes, it is not surprising that Edersheim's accounts of rabbinic Sabbath restrictions are without nuance; some of the rules he cites are mere suggestions, and challenged by other rabbis in the same sources, and some of his descriptions unduly emphasize their farcicality. For the Talmudic tractates Edersheim draws on, see Jacob Neusner, *The Talmud of the Land of Israel, A Preliminary Translation and Explanation: Volume 11, Shabbat* (Chicago: University of Chicago Press, 1991); Jacob Neusner, *The Mishnah: A New Translation* (New Haven, Conn: Yale University Press, 1988), 179—207 (Tractate Shabbat).

9. Henrik Ibsen's (1828–1906) *The Wild Duck* premiered in 1884.

10. Stephen Vincent Benét, *John Brown's Body* (Garden City, N.Y.: Doubleday, Doran, 1928), 219–20. The last line quoted by Thurman anticipates the well-known quotation from Samuel Beckett's *The Unnamable* (New York: Grove, 1958): "I can't go on. I'll go on."

11. Schreiner, *From Man to Man*, 458–59, reprinted in HT, *A Track to the Water's Edge*, 197–98.

12. George Bernard Shaw, *Saint Joan: A Chronicle Play in Six Scenes and an Epilogue* (New York, Dodd, Mead, 1924), 94.

"THE SIGNIFICANCE OF JESUS VI: [UNTITLED]"
17 SEPTEMBER 1937

This sixth and final talk in the series was actually numbered as the seventh; seven lectures had been planned, but only six were delivered. Thurman's lack of time to complete the work is apparent here. He did not prepare his comments in advance, and the talk teems with textual difficulties. Additionally while the five earlier talks are in pretty good shape, the last talk, taken down by stenographers as it was delivered,[1] *has Thurman's handwritten corrections on the mimeograph versions, including his recommendations for the excision of several long passages. The editors have prepared a version that emphasizes readability, following Thurman's final thoughts on its wording.*

As the closing address in the series, Thurman focused on the final chapter of the story of Jesus, his resurrection. Thurman is skeptical of the resurrection as a physical or metaphysical phenomenon and argues that the significance of the death of Jesus is that his followers did not take death as an excuse to abandon their discipleship; the significance of the resurrection and the other miracles of Jesus was in "the impression that Jesus made upon many people who knew him well."

For Thurman the ultimate message of Jesus has two main components: first, that everything that is alive is connected in its (and their) "aliveness" and that every living thing requires respect; second, that artificial divisions between people were abhorrent in the eyes of God and that artificial and arbitrary distinctions, made to oppress one class of humans, must be fought against. The final message of Jesus is the need for struggle, not against "the power of evil but evil power in the world." This is a struggle not against individuals but against the social forces that keep evil in place. Thurman argued it was the underlying forces, the "invisibles—invisible powers, invisible networks, intimacies, of which the individual is but an agent"—that had to be defeated.

In his conclusion, for the first time in the series, Thurman turned his attention to racial oppression at home and abroad and the need for dedicated opponents of evil in society to be unstinting in their fight against it (though only in ways that respect the sanctity of all life). The significance of Jesus for Thurman is that his example points to a better world, a "new community," and a way to achieve it, "without inner defilement and without self destruction."

(Closing address by Dr. Thurman at Couchiching), Friday

We now come to the end of our series of reflections together about the significance of Jesus Christ and before I attempt to summarize and point up what we have been saying together during these days I think it would be altogether fitting that some statement should be made relative to the Resurrection. There are several things which impress me about the accounts of the Resurrection. The first is that the accounts themselves are amazing in their lack of that which is grotesque and fantastic. How truly unlike those attempts to tell the world something about the childhood of Jesus of which you have either read or heard—the stories, for instance, that are found in some of the records of how Jesus as a little boy was playing with some other boys and making clay pigeons. Because one of the other boys made a pigeon which was more perfect in outline than the one made by Jesus, he commanded his pigeon to fly away. Or how when he was playing hide-and-seek he simply did a fade-away act.[2] Fantastic stories! And certainly in connection with the Resurrection the stage was all set for a wide series of fantastic manoevres on the part of one who had returned from the dead. But the accounts of the Resurrection are amazingly sober. The second thing that impresses me is that the accounts seem to belong to the before-Calvary life of Jesus. In other words the accounts do not seem to be inconsistent with what his disciples knew him to be. Of course you can see at once what the psychologist would do with that. Thirdly, I have been able to find no completely satisfying and rational explanation of precisely what happened. The question is simple, you see, if miracles are accepted on their face value. If it is true that they are accepted on their face value then of course the sky is the limit—anything can happen. But is seems to me that in the second temptation Jesus is quite wary of confusing himself and his career with that of a conjurer or some kind of juggler.[3] He takes his position on the side of the normal processes as they work out in the world. "I ask no dream, no prophet ecstacy, no sudden rending of the veil of clay, . . . But take the dimness of my soul away."[4] The important thing, (and this is almost an aside, not quite)—the important thing, it seems to me, about the miracles is the fact that they reveal the qualitative significance of the impression that Jesus made upon many people who knew him well. It is not important to me whether Jesus walked on the water—personally I don't think he did; it makes no difference. But the important thing to me is that they said that he did it; which is, in my opinion, the measure of the significance of the impression that his personality made upon their minds. And that to me is the important point. Incidentally, your mother, for instance, thinks that you are a much better person than you know yourself to be. We always claim more for our friends than they dare claim for themselves but what we claim for our friends is in some very definite measure a revelation of the quality of the impression that they have made on us and that impression is as much a part of the total picture as the person himself is. No one knows exactly what happened but it is historically authentic that something <u>did</u> happen—something of momentous significance!

Now why do we know that something happened? In the first place the disciples were a broken, discouraged, disheartened group. They had returned to their before-Jesus activities. Fear had done its perfect work and I can hear Peter say in terms of the American College student "Well, that's that! I go back to fishing." The same group of men now became transformed into a powerful, courageous, dynamic company. Their explanation was "Jesus is alive." We may not agree with that explanation. Or we may be forced to agree with it! What proof did they give? Not these stories in the Bible—they are important perhaps but that was not the proof they gave. The proof was the <u>change</u> that had taken place in their outlook—in their lives. That was the proof. They rested their case not on the miracle; that is where I think the Church has made one of its great errors. They rested their case not on the miracle but they rested their case on the new <u>motivation</u> that they had received. It was an appeal to a personal experience—the ultimate seat of authority in the human heart. It was this new motivation that was their final argument. The thing that has defied all the contrary arguments from the time of Celsus[5] up to the present moment is the pragmatic results in the lives of men arising out of this new motivation. A living character cannot be disputed. Now what is the meaning of all this?—one sentence. There is but one argument then for the Christian religion—one—and that is the Christian life—what some in this conference have been calling the witness—the Christian witness—what the Quaker calls the Quaker testimony and if there is no life, if there is no witness, if there is no testimony, all the theology, all the ethics, all the preachments, all the prayers, all the hymns are filthy rags.

Now to move into the second part; the final pooling of what we have been trying to say in our moments together. What then is the significance of Jesus for our day? I should like to read something from "The Terrible Meek."

> "And so we go on building our Kingdoms—the kingdoms of the world. We stretch out our hands, greedy, grasping, tyrannical to possess the earth. Domination, power, glory, money, merchandise, luxury, these are the things we aim at; but what we really gain is pest and famine, grudge labour, the enslaved hate of men and women, ghosts, dead and death-breathing ghosts that haunt our lives forever. It can't last, it never has lasted, this building in blood and fear. Already our kingdoms begin to totter. Possess the earth! We have lost it. We never did possess it. We have lost both earth and ourselves in trying to possess it; for the soul of the earth is man and the love of him, and we have made of both a desolation.
>
> "I tell you, woman, this dead son of yours, disfigured, shamed, spat upon, has built a kingdom this day that can never die. The living glory of him rules it. The earth is his and he made it. He and his brothers have been making and moulding it through the ages: They are the only ones who ever did really possess it: not the proud, not the idle, not the wealthy, not the vaunting empires of the world. Something has happened up here on this hill today to shake all our kingdoms of blood and fear to the dust. The earth is his, the earth is theirs and they made it. The meek, the terrible meek, the fierce agonizing meek, are about to enter into their inheritance."[6]

Our first important consideration is this: Jesus placed before man a great creative ideal—an ideal which was the logic of the assumption that the source of all life is one—God. Now that automatically affirms the kinship between man and man and I think the kinship between all living things. It is no accident that the prophets envisioned a time when the lion and the lamb should lie down together—when a little child should put his hand over the hole of an asp and not be stung.[7] It is the logical deduction from this fundamental assumption that Jesus makes about the common origin of life. I think that the Christian then is obligated to have a reverential <u>and</u> compassionate attitude towards all forms of life. Of course it makes for a certain amount of morbidity, I guess. Sometimes I walk along the road crushing ants, crushing insects—all unconsciously—not because I need them in order to live but because they get in my way and I don't think about it. Perhaps that is why we should say grace at meals. Not so much because we are thankful to God, because so very often gratitude is furthest removed from our minds; but when we eat we are accepting the life sacrifice of cows, of pigs, of cabbages and potatoes. Who are we that a cabbage that enjoys the sunlight and the rain and the fresh air should give up its life in order that our stomachs should be full? Who are we that we should make that kind of inexorable and absolute demand upon something that is alive in its own right,—that it should yield its aliveness in the interest of my aliveness. Therefore when I eat I should bow my head in reverence for I am standing in the presence of that which is of unspeakable sanctity—life that is yielding itself in my behalf. Thus the free act of living and the perpetuation of life places upon the individual a great moral obligation so that even if he cares nothing about religion, if he cares nothing about God, if he is not conscious of all the moral and ethical significance of Jesus Christ, even if he ignores all that, to be alive in the world and subsist on other life places upon him a definite moral responsibility, that if he is a man he dare not ignore. Now what is this ideal? It is a dream,—yes, it is a dream of a kingdom, of a realm of friendly men in the midst of a friendly world of nature.

In the second place Jesus, you see, not only gives us this ideal—this dream that springs out of this assumption that he makes about the nature of life, but he also demonstrates and points out a technique by which this dream may be realized in the world. He calls it love. We talked about love one morning so I need not go over that. But it is a technique by which the dream might be translated into practical terms of human experience.

There is a further word I want to add to what has been said. In the achievement of this dream, in the achievement of this ideal, struggle is inevitable. It is important to point out this because when we think about love in the Christian religion we are apt to become merely sentimentalists. In the achievement, then, of this end—this ideal, struggle is inevitable. Now why, why is struggle inevitable? Because the organization of society is such that this primary fact of kinship and unity, that is the underlying assumption of Jesus' dream which to him was God's dream, is ignored. Struggle, then, is inevitable because the individual who is trying to translate this ideal in terms of practical reality in the world comes into conflict with a society that is organized on another principle, a principle that repudiates the fact of kinship and the fact of brotherhood that grew out of this basic trunk-line assumption that Jesus makes about the nature of life. Now the individual, then, in the second place, acting on the basis of this assumption, finds that there are powers and principalities and systems that are entrenched and that individuals functioning in these systems and in these organizations are but puppets in the hands of an invisible power. We do not like to think that there is a kingdom of evil but there is. So that even if I destroy the individual representative of a society or way of life that repudiates this ideal of Jesus—if I destroy all the individuals as they come up, knocking their heads off, there will always be men coming up to take their places because the individual Christian is not fighting against individuals, he is struggling with invisibles—invisible powers, invisible networks, intimacies, of which the individual is but an agent. To illustrate: two days ago I read in a Toronto paper that Bishop Heard of the African Methodist Episcopal Church in the United States died. He was eighty-eight years old.[8] I was impressed by the fact that he died last Sunday because last summer he experienced precisely the thing that I am talking about here. He was an official delegate from his church to the World Conference at Edinburgh. He had arranged for his living before he left New York City through some travel agency. But when he arrived in Edinburgh he was not permitted to claim his reservation. Eighty-eight years old, he had to sit all night in a lobby of a hotel because he could not find a bed. I was interested in his statement to the press when he came back. He pointed out very clearly the thing that I am saying here. He said that the task of the church is one which must enlist it in a struggle against not the power of evil but evil power in the world. Of course, the next day there were many individuals who extended to him the courtesies and hospitality of their homes. But the individual hotel keeper who would not let him claim his reservation was not a bad man—no, but he was the epitomization of one of the forms of the Kingdom of Evil. I am not excusing him but pointing out clearly that he was an agent, a representative of evil and if he had been destroyed there would have been others and others and others and others to take his place. The Christian attempts to project his ideal into the midst of a world that is organized on other than principles of kinship and brotherhood. He demonstrates that he cannot escape conflict. It is for this reason that I am always amazed when I see people admitted into the church and no clearly defined statement is made to them relative to the fact that they are enlisting in an enterprise that involves struggle in the world.

Well, what must be done? What must the Christian do with this fact? Obviously he must see to it that what he condemns in society he does not permit to grow and flower in himself. That is the thing. As Olive Shreiner states it:

> "You cannot, by willing it, alter the vast world outside of you; you cannot perhaps cut the lash from one whip; you cannot stop the march of even one armed man going out to kill; you cannot perhaps strike the handcuff from one chained hand; you cannot perhaps even remake your own soul so that there shall be no tendency to evil in it; but one thing you can do—in that

> one, small minute, almost infinitesimal spot in the universe where your will rules, there, where alone you are as God, strive to make that you hunger for real. No man can prevent you there. In your own heart strive to kill out all hate, all desire to see evil come even to those who have injured you or another; what is weaker than yourself try to help; whatever is in pain and unjustly treated and cries out, say, 'I am here.' I, little, feeble, weak, but I will do what I can for you."[9]

That is the first step but that is not enough. As an individual I share the guilt of my society—of my class in society. Therefore, I must exhaust all possible means, and this is important, that do not conflict with my ends, for defeating the kingdom of evil. And this means that I must put my creative mind to work at the devising of strategies, personal strategies and group strategies for the achievement of these ends. And doubtless I shall find them falling into two or three classes. There are those that belong in the general classification of moral suasion, moral appeal, an attempt to awaken individuals to some kind of consciousness of what they are doing, an attempt to make articulate individual and social conscience with reference to sin, with reference to invalidation of this ideal of Jesus. As Anatole France says of Emil Zola, "He was a moment of the conscience of man."[10] Moral suasion, yes, but it is important to point out that moral suasion is limited by the amount of moral atrophy that has taken place in a man. I may be patient; I may keep working and trying and keep appealing and appealing and appealing on the assumption, of course, that all men are children of God—those instruments of evil, as well as those who are suffering because of evil. I shall endure, hoping that moral suasion will finally cause dead things to come to life.

That is a possible position for the Christian. He will not stop at number one but he may stop at number two. Number one attempts to see that he will not encourage in himself what he condemns in society. And number two attempts to see that he will exercise moral suasion in an effort to awaken a conscience in oppressors. He will brood over the hearts of men until there is a stirring, the stirring of consciousness both of sin and of sonship in their hearts—like the Spirit of the Hive hovering over the bees.[11] But if I am going to be realistic I must see very clearly that if I keep on or if an individual keeps on calling a good thing a bad thing, if an individual keeps on acting as if a bad thing, that he knows he is doing, is really a good thing, he will eventually so confuse his sense of ethical values that he will not be able to distinguish between the bad and the good. So that when you are exercising moral appeal on such individuals you do not have many hooks to hang it on; they have taken out all the screws.

In the next place I may recognize a conflict of loyalties at this point. Here I confess the ice is apt to be very thin. There may be a conflict between my loyalty to the ideal of brotherhood, viewed with reference to the oppressors and the ideal of brotherhood, viewed with reference to the oppressed. I must take sides. The oppressors are my brothers which fact is as true and realistic as the other one namely, the sufferers are my brothers. I am apt to be caught between the recognition of fundamental kinship with the powerful and the pull of the needy—the silent, dumb articulation of the oppressed. An aspect of the issue is set forth quite graphically in "The Green Pastures."[12] I may say in passing that the author is giving no true or factual description or interpretation of the religious life of Negroes in his portrayal. This must be said in all fairness. At any rate the incident I have in mind is the one in which God is being forced to reconsider his decision to leave man to his fate in the world. God has decided to give up the world. Man is so sinful that He cannot do anything with him. He decided to stay in heaven. He won't come down to earth any more. So He is seated at His desk attending to His problems of another nature but every now and then a shadow falls across the room. The door is open, you see, and there is a shadow—a man walks in front of the door but he won't come in; the shadow finally begins to penetrate God's mind, to penetrate his emotions so that He is worried and turns to Gabriel and says "Why doesn't he come in? Who is it? What does he want?" Gabriel says that it is Hosea—one who loves men and he won't come in but he keeps walking up and down in front of the door so that his shadow will disturb you and make you change your mind about man. Then God gets up and walks over to the window and looks out across the vastness. Presently there comes up from the earth the cry of a man, Hozdrool—a man who cries out to God and nothing can stop him. He simply has become a maniac begging God to come down to do something about man. God, then, caught between the terrific agitation of the man on the earth and the silent, relentless, penetrating pressure—quiet, persistent pressure of Hosea, finds that He must do something. Conflict is present, you see, between loyalty to His determination to give man up and loyalty to the pull of the needs of men and He reverses His decision and affirms His loyalty to the needs of man and comes back to earth. Now this is the second possibility—that in the conflict between two loyalties I may decide that I cannot wait. There is too much agony, too much hunger, too much poverty and misery everywhere, too many flagrant denials of kinship and brotherhood all along the line. I cannot wait for this thing to work out. Something concrete must be done <u>now</u>. I must give my testimony more positively. If I decide that the suffering of the oppressed demands sacrificing the time element then I am forced to resort to pressure more drastic. To wait for moral pressure to work its perfect work may be too late. The oppressed may be annihilated meanwhile.

I may resort to the exercise of some form of shock, the function of which is to tear men free from their alignments in the kingdom of evil, to free them so that they may be given a sense of acute insecurity and out of the depths of their insecurity they may be forced to see their brotherhood with the oppressed. Men do not voluntarily, my friends, relinquish their hold on their place without being uprooted, uprooted by something from without or by volcanic eruption from within the man, from within the group. It is not until something becomes movable in their situations that men are spiritually prepared to embrace the ideal of Jesus. That is why when the young man came to Jesus seeking life, he said "Keep the law," and the young man said "But I have kept the law all my life." "The thing you lack is you have a false sense of security. Get rid of that. Cut yourself free and then you will see what the meaning of the Kingdom is."[13]

The final thing in an attempt to answer the question what must I do in the light of all this: when I have exhausted all the strategies that are permitted to me by the rigorous demands of my own ethical ideal with reference to brotherhood, with reference to what Jesus really means to me, when I have exhausted all the strategies that are permitted to me by the rigorous demands of my own rigorous sense of the ideal, then I try to select the moment when the supreme sacrifice of my life will be my ultimate contribution to the Kingdom of brotherly man. As for me, I believe it is better to be killed than to kill and I think the spirit of God will help an individual decide when is the best moment for martyrdom, so that martyrdom will be an act of the profoundest redemptive significance rather than death, merely.

Not only does Jesus give to us a great creative ideal and a method for its realization but he also calls attention to a dynamic by which we may seek to overcome. He calls it God, Father. That is why I cannot understand individuals who say I can accept, I see the ethical teachings of Jesus but I cannot be bothered very much with his religion. They are inseparable as I think of it; for Jesus knew, even as Aristotle knew, that for man to see the right thing is not for him to do the right thing. Now the human spirit, as Jesus demonstrated it, makes a two-fold demand on life with reference to God. First that God be creator—vast, majestic, powerful, almost impersonal; also that God be intimate, primary, personal. For Jesus, faith taught him what he knew about God and experience corroborated it. His faith was an act of knowledge. His faith taught him three very central things about God. It taught him first that God is. He could not prove it but it may be that we only try to prove things of which we are not sure. If you had a friend who was always trying to prove that she was your friend you would get uneasy. His faith taught him also that God was near. God was not in the sky or high above men—"In the year that King Uzziah died I saw the Lord, high and lifted up."[14] Jesus funded all the religious insights of Israel and the prophets; with them he erected one vast pyramid, scaled the heights of it to bring God down out of the clouds. He found Him to be an intimate part of the struggles of life—"Speak to Him, thou, for He heareth; and spirit with Spirit can meet. Closer is He than breathing, nearer than hands or feet."[15] Finally his faith taught him that God is love. This is the most stupendous affirmation of which the human spirit is capable. For in a world in which there is this organization of evil—where there is so much that depresses and casts down and so little that builds up and inspires; where A must kill B before B is strong enough to kill A—a world of blood and violence, bitterness and hate, the dumb inarticulate misery of the masses whose silence is only heard by God, in such a world how can a sane mind say—God is love? What does Jesus mean? This is what he means, that when I love I seem to have in my hands a key that unlocks the meaning of life. Thus I will do gladly for love's sake what no power in heaven or hell could make me do if I did not love and when I love the sun seems to shine more brightly, the colour of the leaves is a richer green, for somehow I have tapped a source that whispers to me the secret of the mystery of existence. Whatever else God is He must be like this. When I think about Him, I do not start with power for that would lead me to an endless series of limitless difficulties but I start with love. For here I seem to be precipitated into the centre of all the meaning that there is in life. When I find myself gripped by the terrible hold of an almighty affection, I know I have come under God's spell. What then is the significance of Jesus? He places before the world an impelling dream, growing out of a fundamental interpretation of the meaning of life—human life—all life; a methodology by which that dream might be translated into living power—in a living community; he points out a dynamic available to men by which they may stand in the universe, and also a power by which they may be able to work out a wide series of anticipations of the new community without inner defilement and without self destruction.

> "I will fly in the greatness of God as the marsh-hen flies
> In the freedom that fills all the space 'twixt the marsh and the skies:
> By so many roots as the marsh-grass sends in the sod
> I will heartily lay me a-hold on the greatness of God:
> Oh, like the greatness of God is the greatness within
> The range of the marshes, the liberal marshes of Glynn."[16]

TD. HTC-MBU: Box 112.

1. To Herbert King, 25 September 1937, printed in the current volume.

2. Both tales are found in the pseudepigraphical Infancy Gospel of Thomas, not to be confused with the Gnostic Gospel of Thomas, and probably dates to the early second century CE.

3. Matt. 4:5–7.

4. From the second stanza of the hymn "The Holy Spirit" (1905) by John W. Baume.

5. Celsus, a Greek anti-Christian writer of the second century C.E., who is primarily known through Origen's riposte, *Contra Celsum.*

6. *The Terrible Meek* (New York: Harper, 1912) is the best-known play of Anglo-American playwright Charles Rann Kennedy (1871–1950). The play, with Christian and

pacifist themes, attracted a good deal of attention, and Kennedy personally sent one thousand copies of the work to political and religious leaders worldwide.

7. Isaiah 11:6, 8.

8. William Henry Heard (1850–1937) was born a slave in Elberton, Georgia. He served a term in the South Carolina legislature in 1876 and was minister-resident and consul-general in Liberia from 1885 to 1889. He was ordained in 1870 and became an A.M.E bishop in 1908, assigned to West Africa, where he served until 1912. He thereafter served as A.M.E. bishop for the first district, which included New England and the mid-Atlantic states. When Bishop Heard arrived at the World Faith and Order Conference in Edinburgh in early August 1937, he was denied admittance to one of the best hotels in Edinburgh because "American tourists refused to register at hotels" that catered to blacks. Heard found other accommodations, and on his way back to the United States, in Glasgow, he met with Sir John Simon, the chancellor of the exchequer, who offered him an apology. Heard died in Philadelphia a month after his return to the United States. "British Regret Jim Crow Insult: Bishop Was Barred from Hotel in Scotland," *Chicago Defender,* 14 August 1937; "Simon Decries Hotel Snub to U.S. Negro in Scotland," *New York Times,* 9 August 1937.

9. Olive Schreiner, "The Dawn of Civilization," *London Nation and Athenaeum*, 26 March 1921; quoted in HT, ed., *A Track to the Water's Edge,* xxxii.

10. The French belletrist Anatole France (1844–1924), recipient of the Nobel Prize for Literature in 1921, made this remark at the funeral of Emile Zola (1840–1902), one of the leading French novelists of his time. He was referencing Zola's stalwart role in the Dreyfus Affair, in late-nineteenth-century France, when Captain Alfred Dreyfus (1859–1935) was accused of espionage. The case, rife with anti-Semitism, became a cause célèbre. On 13 January 1898 Zola published his famous "J'accuse" in the newspaper *L'Aurore*, which asserted that high-ranking government and military officials were covering up the truth about the case.

11. The phrase "spirit of the hive" was coined by the Belgian author Maurice Maeterlinck (1862–1949), the 1911 recipient of the Nobel Prize for Literature, in *The Life of the Bee* (New York: Dodd, Mead, 1901), 39.

12. Marc Connelly's (1890–1980) play *The Green Pastures* (New York: Farrar & Rinehart, 1929), which depicts stories of the Hebrew Bible from the perspective of a naive African American folk religion. Thurman is recounting a version of God's monologue that occurs at the end of act 2, scene 6. *The Green Pastures* won the Pulitzer Prize in 1931 and was made into a film in 1936. The play was controversial among African American intellectuals, who found the image of black life somewhat condescending, and it is rather surprising that Thurman cites the play here, since he offers a very mixed judgment on the play; in 1951 he complained of the play's "relentless hammering of stereotypes" and offered his "considered judgment that a revival of The Green Pastures cannot be justified." To Willard Johnson, 18 May 1951, HTC-MBU: Box 9.

13. The parable of the rich young man, at Matt. 19:16–22, Mark 10:17–22, and Luke 18:18–23.

14. Isaiah 6:1.

15. From "The Higher Pantheism" (1869), by the English poet Alfred Tennyson (1809–92).

16. From "The Marshes of Glynn" (1878), by the American poet Sidney Lanier (1842–81).

To Herbert King
25 September 1937
Washington, D.C.

Thurman writes to his good friend Herbert King, expressing his satisfaction with his recent delivery of the "Significance of Jesus" series.

My dear Herb:

You are some bozo! You knew I was coming back from Canada on Monday, and yet you deliberately absented yourself from New York City so that it would not be possible for us to get together. I call that a flagrant insult for which no pardon is possible.

I have heard from eight of the sixteen people about the retreat of religious workers and the tentative date is the weekend of November 12–14. I hope you will pin this date down if possible. Again, the Lincoln-Howard conference is set for the weekend of October 23rd, at Lincoln.

The lectures went off in grand style and they are insisting that I let them keep the manuscript so that it may be neatly mimeo-graphed and bound and distributed to all those people at the conference who signed up for them. The cost will be seventy-five cents. I hesitated about this a long time, because I think that the whole thing should be reworked and published. This will certainly be done, I hope, within the next twelve months. I gave only six lectures. The last one was taken down by three stenographers and I revised it before I left. With reference to the temptations, the professor of New Testament at Emanuel College at the University of Toronto[1] told me that in his twenty-five years as a New Testament scholar he had not encountered an interpretation that was as effective and original as the one which I gave to the third temptation. Coming from him this was something of first rate significance.

Let me hear from you please. The year opens up in grand style and we are all very happy.

With devotions,
[*signed*] Howard Thurman
Mr. William Herbert King
347 Madison Avenue
New York, New York

TLS. HTC-MBU: Box 10.

1. John Hugh Michael (1878–1959) was an ordained Wesleyan minister from England who began his teaching career as professor of New Testament at Victoria University in 1913. He later moved to Emmanuel College until his retirement in 1943. He is the author of *The Epistle of Paul to the Philippians* (New York: Doubleday, 1927).

"The Sources of Power for Christian Action"

29 December 1937
St. Louis, Mo.

Thurman delivered "The Sources of Power for Christian Action" at the National Methodist Student Conference, held 28–31 December 1937, in St. Louis. The conference was part of the unification movement within American Methodism, which sought to repair the divisions caused a century before by the fight over slavery and the Civil War. In 1938 the three main Methodist denominations, the Methodist Episcopal Church, the Methodist Protestant Church, and the Methodist Episcopal Church, South agreed to merge and form the Methodist Church. This occurred the following year, though blacks were relegated to the Central Jurisdiction, a new segregated division within the church. All of these developments were under consideration at the time of the December conference. On 26 May 1937 Thurman accepted an invitation to attend the conference, serve on the leadership commission, and act as a "resource person" for a session titled "The Sources of Power and the Means of Finding Them."[1] Although Thurman was not a Methodist, he was well-known to Methodist youth organizations. While there were African American delegates to the conference, he was the only African American to address the assembly.

Thurman's preparation for the St. Louis conference ran into a complication in July when he received an invitation to deliver two addresses and lead a workshop that same week at the National Assembly of Student Christian Associations to be held in Oxford, Ohio. Thurman was very interested in speaking at the latter conference and wrote on 10 August to H. D. Bollinger, one of the organizers of the Methodist meeting, asking to be released from his obligations. (For details see the introductory note to "Man and the World of Nature.")

Bollinger replied that he would accede to Thurman's wishes, but he urged Thurman to attend at least part of the Methodist conference because he thought that Thurman's presence could be a positive influence on the question of the status of blacks in the unified church. Bollinger explained that it was important that the "Negro leadership of this particular student conference shall be of the very best caliber that our country affords" and that "the Negro speakers not be limited, as so often was the case, to speak on race relations."[2] Bollinger's letter could not have been more perfectly designed to appeal to Thurman's views on his lecturing before mixed race audiences, and he agreed to speak at the Methodist conference, taking an evening train to Oxford after his address.[3]

Thurman spoke on techniques for applying "Christian idealism to unideal and unchristian situations." (A few days later in Oxford, in "Christian, Who Calls Me Christian?" he gave another version of the same talk.) However, the appearance in St. Louis became more of a lesson in race relations than either Thurman or his hosts intended. The organizers had made an agreement with the Marquette Hotel that while blacks might attend the conference, they would be unable to eat or lodge there. Thurman, unaware of this, was met at the train station on his arrival from Washington and escorted to the hotel, where he had breakfast and then gave his first talk. When he returned to the dining room, he was informed that while an exception had been made for breakfast, he would not be served lunch. They offered to feed him in the room of one of the white guests. Thurman said this was unacceptable. He left and had lunch with one of his students living in St. Louis. He returned to the Marquette Hotel for his evening lecture, and before his prepared remarks, he told the audience what had happened earlier in the day and that their denominations had made all of those present complicit in the action of the hotel. "The time will come when you are in the same position as the men who made this commitment on your behalf. When that time comes I want you to remember this experience."[4] *(This was not included in the summary of the talk published by the National Methodist Student Conference.) Still very angry, after the lecture he made his way to the railroad station and left for Oxford.*

It is necessary at the outset to raise a fundamental question about the why of Christian action and the meaning of Christian action.

Wherever there is action there is struggle. Struggle has a most important place in the experience of the Christian because he is ever desirous of injecting into his own person and into his own sphere of influence a principle of life and an ordering of life which stand in contradistinction to the society in which he lives and moves and functions. For the Christian sees that society is organized on other than principles of kinship and brotherhood.

He sees that the strong do live by bleeding the weak. He sees that fear and dishonesty run the entire frantic gamut of our culture and our daily living. He sees institutions dedicated to high and holy ends, finding themselves as literal instruments of violence and exploitation in the world. He see before his very eyes the degradation of ideals, of reverence and respect for life and personality. He sees himself functioning in a state that has given itself over to cheap political conniving and skullduggery. He sees his own government arming for protection against enemies, visible and invisible, and a large share of his own funds going to support engines of war against which, as a Christian, he is dedicated to struggle.

What, then, is Christian action in the presence of such conditions? The first answer is this: As a Christian I must see to it that what I condemn in society, I do not permit to grow and flower in me.

This observation has to do with personal piety, without which there can be no sound basis for Christian action. There can be no substitute, for I must not be a liar to myself.

But mere personal piety is not enough. Even if my heart is pure, my motives are above reproach and, as far as my personal action is concerned, it is unequivocal and positive—this is not enough. I share the guilt of my age, of my society, of my race. Therefore I must exhaust all possible means that do not conflict with my ends for bringing about the kind of society in which it is possible for men in large groups, without external limitations, to experience the good life.

This means that I must put my creative mind to work to devise techniques, personal and group, for the achievement of these ends. Doubtless I shall find these falling into two general categories.

The Technique of Moral Appeal

There are those that belong under the general classification of moral suasion, moral appeal; an attempt to awaken individuals to some kind of definite consciousness as to what is the meaning of their action. In other words, an attempt to make articulate individual and social conscience with reference to sin.

It is of desperate importance to point out that moral suasion has a serious limitation in the amount of moral atrophy that has taken place in the mind and character of the person who is to be aroused. I may be patient. I may keep working and persuading and appealing on the assumption that all men are the children of God. I may endure, hoping that moral suasion will finally cause dead things to come to life. And yet I may be disappointed.

Always, as a Christian, I must be essentially and intensely realistic in my understanding of the nature of my task. The Gospels contain an interesting account about the unpardonable sin. Jesus' family sought to excuse Him before His enemies by saying that He was a little crazy—not terribly insane, but just a little off. The Pharisees said, "No, He has sense, perhaps, but He is full of the devil, and it is by the power of the devil that He casts out devils."

Jesus, hearing the discussion, said: "You do not talk like sensible men. A house divided against itself cannot stand. If you continue saying that I am casting out devils out by the devil, you will commit the unpardonable sin;"[5] that is, if a man continues to call a good thing bad, he will eventually arrive at a place at which it will be impossible for him to determine that which is good from that which is bad. In other words, such a person will experience quite definitely moral and spiritual atrophy.

So many of us in the modern world must spend our time doing with our hands and with our lives what we cannot affirm with our hearts and minds as that which is right, that we find ourselves precipitated into state of mental and moral confusion as to the ethical significance of life. And from moral and mental confusion we drift into varied states of lethargy and indifference, yielding ourselves more and more to the instruments of evil in our world. I must bear these facts in mind when I consider the first type of action that is available to me as a Christian, namely, moral suasion.

A Conflict of Loyalties

The second type of action is even more difficult. I may recognize a conflict of loyalties in me that will make a decision relative to what is positive Christian action in a given situation very difficult to determine. For instance, there may be a conflict between my loyalty to the ideal of brotherhood viewed with reference to the weak, and my kinship with them, and the ideal of brotherhood viewed with reference to the strong and my kinship with them.

I may be forced to take sides. The strong are my brothers, which fact is as true and realistic as the other one, namely, the weak are my brothers. I am likely to be caught between the recognition of fundamental kinship with the strong and the desperation of the weak, the silent dumb articulation of the oppressed. Or it may take the form of a conflict between a completely ethical demand of my religion that I wash my hands of the doers of iniquity and leave them to go their recklessly destructive way, feeling that there are some types of struggle even God does not demand of me as a believer. By temperament, by training, by background, I may say this type of action is not for me, and to all the pull of the needy who are on the receiving end of the violence of the wicked, I may turn a deaf ear—if I can. Or, like the Jehovah of "The Green Pastures,"[6] I may reverse myself and affirm my loyalty to the needs of men.

But here is the second possibility in the conflict between two loyalties: I may decide that I cannot wait for the thing to work itself out. There is too much agony, too much hunger, too much poverty and misery everywhere, too many flagrant denials of kinship and brotherhood all along the line. Something concrete must be done now. I must give my testimony as a Christian more positively. If I decide that the suffering of the oppressed demands sacrificing the time element, then I am forced to resort to some form of pressure more drastic and more immediately devastating and arousing than mere moral pressure.

What do I do then? I may resort to the exercise of some form of shock, let us say by organizing a boycott, by organizing widespread non-cooperation, by engineering nonviolent strikes. The function of these techniques is to tear men free from their alignments to the evil way, to free them so that they may be given an immediate sense of acute insecurity, and out of the depths of their own insecurity they may be forced to see their kinship with the weak and the insecure.

Men do not voluntarily relinquish their hold on their place without being uprooted; uprooted by something from without or by volcanic eruption from within the man, from within the group. It is not until something becomes movable in the situation that men are spiritually prepared to apply Christian idealism to unideal and unchristian situations.

But to take one more step, when I have exhausted all the techniques that are permitted to me by the rigorous demands of my own Christian ideal with reference to kinship, when I have exhausted all the techniques that are permitted by the rigorous demands of my own rigorous sense of the ideal, what then? I shall try to select the moment when the supreme sacrifice of my own life will be my ultimate contribution to the kingdom of brotherly men.

As for me, I believe it is better to be killed than to kill, and that the spirit of God will help an individual decide which is the best moment for martyrdom, so that martyrdom will be an act of the profoundest redemptive significance rather than death, merely.

The Spiritual Resources I Need

What, then are the spiritual resources necessary for the kind of Christian action I have described? I am conscious that in this area even my *thinking* is hedged about by limitations, vast and profound. But it seems to me that there are four fundamental resources available to the individual in this connection.

First, there is the strength that comes from a great cause and a man's loyalty to it. If there is indirection, indecision, and a lack of concentration of life on some all-inclusive commitment, spiritual resources available in a high cause and man's relationship to it are cut off. A great commitment gives to the details of an individual's life great and significant relevancy.

There is available to me all of the resourcefulness and the power that is inherent in the cause to which I am committed. Furthermore, the cause draws out of me all of the inherent resourcefulness of my own spirit. I will do for its sake what I will not do for my own.

(I may pause here to point out that one of the pitfalls of a great commitment is that it is apt to make a man insensitive to some of the nobler, gentler virtues such as thoughtfulness, kindness, and consideration, when these virtues seem to weaken him with reference to the fulfillment of his purpose. It is for this reason that a man dedicated to God sometimes is as hard to live with as a man dedicated to the making of money.)

Loyalty to a great cause to which one is committed releases in the individual many of the psychological and spiritual resources needful for sustained achievement. It makes for freedom of mind, for a kind of orderly recklessness of action; it makes courage possible, and it robs man of his fear of death. But this is not enough.

The second great resource for the Christian is in the career and the example of Jesus Christ. He has identified Himself, it seems permanently, with the best that the mind can conceive of as it contemplates the good life for itself and for society. And when I, as an individual, independent of Jesus, achieve a sense of purposefulness and high ethical motivation in my own character, it seems as if I become a fellow-worker with Him. Even though I may not come out of a tradition of which He is a part, or I may not bow my knees at the altar what is dedicated to His service; when I am most myself with reference to my highest ethical conception of the way of life, He becomes by brother.

In the contemplation of this vision of which He is the embodiment Jesus ceases to be the peculiar product of any particular age, or any particular race, or any particular school of thought. He at once rises to such staggering heights that He becomes the product of all the ages and a benediction to all the races of men. The great doctrine of the church, the communion of saints, becomes significant and realistic in His fellowship. I need not add more about His resourcefulness in a specific sense.

The third resource is fellowship with men and women of my own kind who are a part of the same quest. It is significant to me that founders of great religions, as well as leaders in any significant cause, find it essential to have disciples. This is true, not because they are fearful lest their insights will not be transmitted to subsequent generations, but because they must have as a present intense reality a little world in which the validity of all they live for can be felt and realized. It is in the form of fellowship that men come to understand the nature of the ideals of their lives.

Christians projecting themselves into an unchristian society, working to transform it, are likely to be overwhelmed by a majority opinion which negates the things for which they stand. For Christian are merely men and women after all, and it is a particularly precarious move to feel that the majority of one's fellows are wrong and only you are right. The Christian, therefore, must have the springs of his life fed by a fellowship of kindred spirits in which he can bathe himself and get refreshment and reorganization for the tasks to which he is committed in the world.

The Highest Resource

The ultimate spiritual resource for Christian action, of course, is God. And I say this with cold objective deliberation. For many of the tasks to which we are committed it will be enough to get the inspiration and the strength that come from the consciousness of high endeavor. For many of the things that we have to do, it will be enough to know that we have entered actively into fellowship with Jesus Christ. For still other tasks we may find all the resources needful in a sense of communion with a select group of like-minded seekers and achievers of the good life for themselves and their age. But, fundamentally, in the task that calls for the complete transformation of the world and the redemption of man and society from evil only an infinite source of strength and power can meet the demand.

To state it categorically, only an infinite resource can meet an infinite need. And particularly is this true when one comes face to face with the deep abysmal churnings of evil resident in one's own life and character. For the same thing that the Christian is seeking for himself, namely salvation from evil in particular and the root of evil in his own spirit; there must be something that can absorb all the limitations of one's life, limitations of personality, limitations of thought, limitations of action, limitations of desire, and it seems to me that God is the only answer.

And how is this true? It is true because in the first place I must have a guarantor of my deeds, a guarantor of my values in the clear lucid light of which I can see myself as I am, stripped bare of all pretense, of all subterfuge, of all artificiality. And once I have seen it, I know what it is that I seek and I know what it is that society needs. I know then what is the be-all and the end-all of living.

Prayer, which offers the method does several things for me. It grows out of an imperative urgency of trust. It enables me to keep fresh in my spirit the dedication to which my life is given. It provides a sense of power that makes courage and purposefulness possible for one as limited as I am. It gives abundance of freedom and joy because it destroys fears. It clarifies the conflicting issues that naturally arise out of any form of action, so that against the darkness of the age I can see the illumined finger of God guiding me in the way that I should go, so that high above the clash of arms in the conflict for position, for rights, for status, for place, for priority, I can hear speaking distinctly and clearly to my own spirit the still small voice of God, without which nothing has meaning quite, with which all the rest of the journey, however difficult, however painful, however devastating, will be filled with a music all its own and even the stars in their courses and all the wooded world of nature participate in the triumphant music of my heart.

Students Ask and Dean Thurman Answers

R.C. Morgan (Rust College): If codes like the Mosaic law, or others, have become obsolete, is it possible to reinterpret them so that they will be helpful to present society?

Dean Thurman: I do not think we have any choice about it; we must interpret them in the light of our own experiences and our own needs. After we understand a little about the words that they had to say to the particular generation in which they started, we must accept the responsibility of reinterpreting in our own language, in terms of our own social experiences, the meanings of religion from the past. If we do not do that it has no meaning for us.

A Student*: If Jesus is a revelation of God, why must we go one step further to discover God as a source of power?

Dean Thurman: Very often the needs of my life are far more terrific than any less-than-ultimate source can help. That is, there are times in my own experience when I must have what is to me a sense, not of the presence of Jesus Christ, important as that is, but a sense of the presence of God Himself. And in my mind and my own experience, those two things are not necessarily identical. I simply speak for myself.

Marvin Wilkening[7] (Southeast Missouri State Teachers' College): How can we put moral approval on that which we know to be immoral?

Dean Thurman: I do not know how we do it; I only know that we do. We tend to be moral and religious, as we move away from the areas of our security. And we tend to be immoral and irreligious, as we move toward the center of the areas of our security. And you don't have to do that long before you discover that, well, really the thing is not so bad; I mean, it is not as bad as it seems. We find ourselves putting the *imprimatur* of our character on the bad things that do not seem so bad. Or, we hold our moral judgment in suspense, and say now, "Well, I will do this. I will go through the motions; but I am not going to put my *imprimatur* on it." The trouble is, I am what I do, including my reservations.

T. Otto Nall, ed., *Christian Students in a Changing World: Report of the National Methodist Student Conference* (N.p.: National Methodist Student Conference, 1938), 37–44.

1. From H. D. Bollinger, 18 August 1937, HTC-MBU: Box 3.
2. To A. R. Elliott, 25 August 1937, HTC-MBU: Box 6; Anne Schockley, "Interview with Howard Thurman," Fisk University Oral History Project (17 August 1973), tape no.3.
3. Ibid.
4. See *WHAH*, 166–67; From W. McPherson, 6 January 1938, HTC-MBU: Box 13; and for additional information, To H. D. Bollinger, 19 January 1938, printed in the current volume.
5. This story is found in Matt. 12:24–25, Mark 3:23–25, and Luke 11:14–19.
6. See "The Significance of Jesus VI," printed in the current volume.

*The reporter was unable to hear the name of the student and his university in several instances.

7. Marvin H. Wilkening (1918–2006) was a 1939 graduate of Southeast Missouri State Teachers' College and received his MS and PhD degrees in 1943 and 1949, respectively, from Illinois Institute of Technology. He was a member of a research group at the University of Chicago that achieved the first sustained nuclear chain reaction. Wilkening operated the neutron detector on 2 December 1942, which showed proof of that achievement. Wilkening was a veteran of the U.S. Army's Manhattan Project, and from 1948 until his retirement he taught in the Physics Department at New Mexico Institute of Mining and Technology.

"Man and the World of Nature"
30 December 1937–2 January 1938
Oxford, Ohio

The National Assembly of Student Christian Associations met at Miami University in Oxford, Ohio, from 27 December 1937 to 2 January 1938. It was a very large meeting, with 1,350 delegates and other personnel in attendance representing some 320 institutions of higher learning from forty-three states and foreign countries.[1] *Thurman was one of six members of a distinguished "evening team" who presented talks to the assembled body of delegates.*[2]

Thurman's two lectures before this assembly, "Man and the World of Nature" and "Christian, Who Calls Me Christian?" are reprinted here.

Thurman's participation in the event had initially been in doubt: he was already committed to appear at the National Methodist Student Conference convening in St. Louis from 28 to 31 December[3] *when he was invited to speak by Roland Elliott, the executive secretary of the National Assembly of Student Christian Associations (whom Thurman knew well from their extensive dealings during the planning of the Pilgrimage of Friendship to South Asia). Elliott asked Thurman to be one of the facilitators for the conference-wide discussions on "the structure or content of the Christian faith and its critique of the contemporary situation,"*[4] *and Thurman very much wanted to accept. On 10 August he wrote H. D. Bollinger, one of the leaders of the Methodist group, explaining that the invitation to help lead the assembly of Christian associations was "very difficult to refuse," in part because of the visibility and also because his first obligation was to "our own students who will be present." He asked to be released from his obligation in St. Louis, though, adding somewhat abashedly that "it is the first time in my life that I have been in a position that makes me play off one invitation against another." A compromise was eventually effected, and Thurman was able to appear at both conferences.*[5] *(His address at the Methodist meeting, "The Sources of Power for Christian Action," is also printed in the current volume.)*

While the lectures and deliberations at Oxford covered a wide range of topics, the main focus of the conference was the social involvement of Christians in the dangerous and difficult world of the late 1930s, and the conference found the American Christian Student Movement at the apogee of its most politically radical phase. Resolutions held for, among other things, the institution of "Marxian socialism" in America (through "gradual changes to our economic system") because "capitalism today is unchristian" and because "private ownership of the means of production gives men power over the lives of others. Considerations of profit force men to ignore human values." Another report called for the "rejection of war as a method. Opposition to any program of collective action entailing military sanction," and 47 percent of delegates declared their "refusal to support the government of the U.S.A. in any war that it may undertake."[6] Many of the talks directly addressed the political and social situation, such as Rose Terlin's "Students and World Crisis" and John Bennett's "How Can a Christian Determine Goals and Methods of Action?" So do Thurman's lectures, but typically he did so obliquely, without offering direct political commentary.

"Man and the World of Nature" was one of Thurman's most original pieces of the 1930s, opening a vein of argument that was largely absent from progressive Christianity: religion as ecological critique. Thurman's interest in evolutionary biology, drawn from his own nature mysticism and the work of Olive Schreiner, was of long standing, and this strain in his work is deepened in this lecture. Drawing from recent discoveries in psychology and biology, Thurman pioneers a "new ethic" that "will be a kind of reverence for all expressions of life," a recognition of compassion for all living things, and the ethic that follows from this recognition. Thurman posits a fundamental alienation from nature in traditional religion and in modern American society and argues that the effort to subdue nature is based on a "false kind of dichotomy" that separates man from nature and artificially enhances human aggressiveness. Thurman takes pains in this essay to avoid the sentimentalizing of nature, arguing that nature is "an unceasing struggle with cruelty, pain and death" but that by recognizing our "at-homeness in the world" we will acknowledge and release our inhibitions and harness our deepest and least understood impulses. This synthesis of our higher and lower selves, Thurman argues, is fundamentally a religious quest. Thurman's essay should be considered in any effort to construct an "African American environmental tradition,"[7] though it probably can be more securely located as a pioneer statement of the argument that traditional Christianity imbued its adherents with a will to dominate nature, an argument closely associated Thurman's good friend

Lynn White Jr., author of "The Historical Roots of Our Environmental Crisis" and other works.[8]

"Man and the World of Nature"

I am the legatee of fierce desires;
A strange bequest of sundry hopes and fears,
Loves, hates and hidden smoldering fires,
Have come to me unsought far down the years
From those whose name I bear; themselves the heirs
Of time, and race, through every bygone age
Of man. And I am not myself, but theirs
Who so devised this jumbled heritage.

Yet I thank God and thank him with a song,
That he gave me a will that is my own
And made me free to choose the right or wrong
And fight; and fashion life as I shall choose.
And with this gift I sigh for no man's shoes,
Nor envy any king upon his throne;
So fare I forth intent at last to be
Master, not slave, of my strange legacy.[9]

I want you to think with me tonight about man and his relation to the world of nature. I have written on this piece of paper the gist of what I have to say. I would like to read that first:

When religion for perfectly good reasons of its own succeeded in convincing man that he was of a completely different order of being, it gave to him a kind of conceit that has remained with him down to latest time. Once there was made a vast gulf between man and nature, with nature being symbolic of all that is evil in life, man was cut off from his major source of vitality. Man was viewed as a pilgrim, temporarily domiciled on the earth, but the earth was merely a point of preparation in time and space for a life that was envisioned beyond time and space.

The contribution of psychology and biology to Christianity at this point is very significant. These two sciences in particular have made modern man see that he is part of nature; in a very definite sense he is nature. They have located his impulses which he calls evil in his own past and made them a part of the very life of man, natural and normal. They have not minimized the conflicts within him, but man is more conscious of his responsibility, even as he becomes more aware of his essential helplessness at certain points. His mistakes are made not because he is human, but because he has not yet become human. He now sees the relevancy of the demand of the Christian religion that he must become perfect.

Even casual reflection upon the evolution of conscious life on the planet reveals an unceasing struggle with cruelty, pain and death. There is struggle in nature. Somehow nature seems to be blind to man's private world of hopes and fears and dreams and ambitions. Much of human life is spent in trying to put the face of a man on the world of nature so that there will be something in nature to which man may speak and something which may answer him in his moments of deepest distress and deepest pain.

But the sense of isolation that man feels in the presence of the cruelty in nature is one that doesn't quite escape even the most callous-minded individual. The complete terror that comes to the human spirit as it sees itself a part of the world of nature and yet separate and distinct from it, particularly in moments of strain and agony, is something that staggers the imagination. Nature cannot hear men cry; therefore men have decided that nature must be an enemy. So they fight against nature. They become defiant. They affirm their significance in the presence of this impersonal world of nature through a delusion. Their minds have separated themselves from it, you see, so they do not see themselves as a part of the world of nature.

> There was a man who went to the wilderness for a home,
> Building a cabin, grubbing out brush, breaking sod.
> The first year drought withered his grain and parched his meadows.
> Plague came the twelvemonth after, and his cattle were bone-picked
> carcasses and a stench on the wind.
> And in the third year there was hail.
> Out of the green windows of that cruel mowing
> He lifted grimed fists to heaven
> And laughed . . .
> Laughed . . .
> As he shouted:
> "God! Listen to me, God. I'm telling you!
> I'll beat you yet!"[10]

This is man girding his loins for a life and death struggle with his enemy nature. Then one day man discovers that nature is not his enemy; that as a matter of fact nature, in the light of the false kind of dichotomy that is in his own mind, simply does not take him into account at all—which is even worse, for men cannot stand being ignored.

Then if he keeps on thinking about it, keeps on judging the facts of his experience, hoping that somewhere in their midst there will come a fleeting glow of illumination that will point to a solution to his problem as far as nature is concerned, he discovers that he is a part of nature and that every judgment that he passes upon nature is a judgment that nature passes upon itself.

What he does nature is doing. The gulf between him and nature becomes in many of its important aspects a trick of his mind. But he doesn't stop there. There is going on within him a struggle that is similar to the one that he sees in nature. There is cruelty resident in him. There is—with apologies—brutality in him. There are impulses that come from he knows not where, impulses that work against what he most desires when he is most himself.

He finds that more and more there is laid upon him the necessity for working out some kind of synthesis between these warring elements within him, turning to psychology, to psychiatry, and to something else, trying to get light that will help him understand, help him locate and define what it is that is taking place within him, even as he continues experimenting with new and different types of syntheses, harnessing this impulse, giving it wide range within zones of agreement, utilizing this particular instinct, let us say—if there be such things left—in a manner that will be of service to something else that has taken ahold of him now, an idea, a creative synthesis that takes the form in his mind of an ideal, a destiny, a purpose, a significance.

It is at this point that modern man stands most in need of the strength and the guidance and the insights of religion. For we have not yet evolved ethical insights that belong to the human animal, who is trying to work out a synthesis of all the varied impulses within him. The ethical insights that we have are built for the most part upon the false line that was drawn in the past between man and nature.

Now that a bridge has been built between man and nature by the aid of the two sciences that I mentioned (and several others for that matter), it remains a task of the modern Christian man and woman to work out ethical insights that are in keeping with this new synthesis.

There are two statements in this connection then, with which I shall close. One of the important results of this new ethic will be a kind of reverence for all expressions of life, with a corresponding demand for compassion with reference to them; and secondly, it will make for an at-homeness in the world and release the inhibitions that are due to the thinking that we have done relative to the essential temporary nature of what Keats calls "this veil of soul-making."[11]

I am a part of nature, plus a deeply lying tendency or manifestation of synthesis. And the key to my ultimate significance is found in the synthesis as well as in the ground of nature in which this synthesis has a firm root.

Heir of the kingdom 'neath the skies
Often he falls, yet falls to rise
Stumbling, bleeding, beaten back
Holding still to the upward track
Playing his part in creation's plan
Godlike in image, this is man.[12]

"Man and the World of Nature," in *New Directions for Campus Christian Action* (New York: National Intercollegiate Christian Council, 1938), 22–25.

1. *New Directions for Campus Christian Action* (New York: National Intercollegiate Christian Council, 1938), 181. Thurman's two lectures are reprinted from this volume: "Man and the World of Nature," 22–25, and "Christian, Who Calls Me Christian?" 71–77.

2. The other members of the "evening team" were Edwin Ewart Aubrey, Professor of Christian Theology and Ethics, University of Chicago Divinity School; John C. Bennett, Associate Professor of Christian Theology, Auburn Theological Seminary; T. Z. Koo, Secretary of the World Student Christian Federation; Rose Terlin, Secretary of the World Student Christian Federation; and Henry P. Van Dusen, Dean of Students, Union Theological Seminary.

3. To Roland Elliott, 4 August 1937, HTC-MBU: Box 6.

4. From Roland Elliott, 7 July 1937, HTC-MBU: Box 6.

5. To H. D. Bollinger, 10 August 1937, HTC-MBU: Box 2; From H. D. Bollinger, 18 August 1937, HTC-MBU: Box 2; To Roland Elliott, 25 August 1937, HTC-MBU: Box 6.

6. *New Directions for Campus Christian Action*, 126–141.

7. See Kimberly A. Smith, *African American Environmental Thought: Foundations* (Lawrence: University Press of Kansas, 2007). Smith does not mention Thurman.

8. Lynn White Jr., "The Historical Roots of Our Environmental Crisis," *Science*, 10 March 1967, 1203–7. White was president of Mills College in Oakland from 1943 to 1958 and helped Thurman arrange for the publication of several books in the mid-1940s.

9. William Woodford Rock, "Heredity," *Christian Century*, 7 May 1925, 597.

10. Ted Olson, "Laughter," in *A Stranger and Afraid* (New Haven, Conn.: Yale University Press, 1928), 43.

11. In John Keats's letter to George Keats, 21 April 1819, though in the original "the vale of Soul-making."

12. The poem can be found in sources such as Robert Scott and William C. Stiles, *Cyclopedia of Illustrations for Public Speakers* (New York: Funk and Wagnalls, 1911), 446, where the poem is credited to an unknown author.

"Christian, Who Calls Me Christian?"

30 December 1937—2 January 1938
Oxford, Ohio

"Christian, Who Calls Me Christian?" was Thurman's second lecture delivered at the National Assembly of Student Christian Associations, most probably on 1 January 1938. It stands as one of his most powerful and pointed statements of the period.[1] *With resonances of "The Cross of Jesus," the fifth lecture of the 1937 "Significance of Jesus" series, as well as "Sources of Power for Christian Action,"*[2] *Thurman argues that to bring about needed social change, at times one must select "a method of shock" so that "the oppressor or the instrument of evil in society . . . may temporarily be dislodged from his security." This, Thurman argues, always carries with it the implicit possibility of offering one's life as "the sacrifice*

supreme," and he concludes that "it is a great creative spiritual act to know when the moment for martyrdom has arrived." These tasks are best accomplished "as a result of a sustained relationship with an inner group of like-minded, like-dedicated people." All of this is predicated on hearing, in moments of quiet reflection and prayer, the soft but unmistakable voice of God. "In moments of profound meditation I become sometimes for one transcendent moment only," writes Thurman, "a central part of the purpose of life." Thurman's argument here, as in several other of his writings of the 1930s, links elements of Gandhian pacifism, his mystical appreciation of nature, and the progressive Social Gospel into a unique amalgam that pointed the way toward a generation of social protest.

Thurman's two addresses before the National Assembly of Student Christian Associations were very well received. His old friend, George "Shorty" Collins, who had not seen Thurman in a number of years, wrote him after hearing him at Oxford, "I had wondered, as we all do, what might have happened to your ideas and to your spirit, in view of all the situations through which we have gone. It meant much to me that you have gone on growing in the direction which I had thought and hoped you would. You are one of the prophets of the day."[3] Similarly a 1941 article about Thurman contained the following reminiscence of his appearance: "Oxford—the 1937 National Assembly of Student Christian Associations. Thirteen hundred of us from all over the map in hushed silence as we reached out for his words and sought contact with his soul. 'Christian, Who Calls Me Christian?' was the topic, and many of us went away wondering just why anyone should call us Christian."[4]

"Life does not grow more simple with the passing years, but its deeper needs are unchanging. The secret of peace is not to be sought at the end of the road, but in the spirit in which we journey. It is to be sought in the consciousness of the sustaining love of a God who is committed to a real participation in all our strife; who does not release us from the battle, but who shares the fight; who does not set us free from the possibility of pain and tears, but who feels the hurt of our wounds, the salt bitterness of our sorrow; who spends himself not only with us but for us, and in the travail of redemptive passion anticipates the victories of the spirit. And, finally, whatever pilgrimage we undertake must be undertaken, in spite of the interior loneliness of all great spiritual processes, in the comradeship of our kind and all well-being must always be our goal. We are never to forget that we are all so tied up in one bundle that peace and reconciliations in which others are not involved are quite impossible. The note of service must be deepened and in our care for those who lie wounded or broken along the road we shall forget

> our own wounds and our own weariness. So conceived, so reinforced, life is never impossible, but does indeed become, so these books and leaders teach us, an adventure whose greatness is its own best justification and whose difficulties may become for the faithful and discerning but stairs of ascent to radiant and triumphant regions."[5]

Christian, who calls me Christian? May each of us raise that question with himself tonight. Christian, who calls me Christian?

What I have to say is divided into two sections; it is my faith that the two sections are related to each other.

In the first place I want you to think with me for a little while about the steps involved in action for Christians, or for those who live in anticipation of becoming Christians tomorrow and tomorrow and tomorrow. In the first place, as a Christian I must not permit to grow and flower in my own heart and life what I condemn in society or in my fellow man. I must be rigorously honest with myself there. I must not permit my mind to do clever tricks with me so that I shall give to my own sin and my own weaknesses high and holy names as I pour out invectives and condemnations upon those same things in society and in other people around me. It may be that I cannot take the handcuffs from one single prisoner; it may be that I cannot stop a single man who is going out to kill his brother; it may be that I cannot dry up the springs of the tendency toward evil in my own heart. But in that intimate, primary, solitary world in which my will is as the will of God, I must see to it that all the things for which I hunger most are real. And as I look out upon the world, it there is something, some one, weaker that I, must say, "Here I am, limited, weak, perhaps confused, but I give my hand to you. It is the best that at I can do and I must do it."

If I let flower in my own heart what I condemn in society and in my fellow man, Christian, who calls me Christian? But that isn't enough. With reference to society, I stand under certain obligations. I must devise methods and techniques and ways, personal and group, by which it will be possible for an increasingly large number of people to live the good life in time and space without external limitations; and the techniques and the methodologies available to me as a Christian fall into two or three general categories. I shall mention them.

The first one, of course, is moral appeal. I shall try to make articulate in my fellow man a sense of the significance of his own actions. I shall brood over him as the spirit of the hive broods over the apiary. I shall try by moral suasion to woo him into a sense of sinfulness and into a sense of sonship. But I must be very conscious that moral suasion has one rather important limitation, and that is the amount of moral atrophy that there is in the life of the individual who is to be persuaded to the good life.

For moral suasion to be effective there must be hooks on which to hang it; and if the individuals have constantly violated their sense of values, their sense of the right, their sense of the worthfulness in their daily actions, then this sense of right, this sense of worthfulness, this sense of the ethical meaning of life becomes weak, and even weaker. If I am making a moral appeal to men who have destroyed, in part at least, the ground of their moral values, I am driven perhaps either to desperation or to profound frustration; but if I am not willing to exercise to the limit of my power moral suasion upon men in the interest of the redemption of themselves and of society—Christian, who calls me Christian?

The second category has to do with the conflict of loyalties. The oppressor, the strong, the powerful, are my brothers, even as the weak and the cast down are my brothers. Perhaps under the circumstances I must choose between brothers; but I must be clear as to the significance of what I am doing. Or I may decide that I cannot wait for a sense of kinship and a sense of brotherliness to arise in the hearts of men as a result of the overmastering expression of kinship and brotherliness and love that arise in my own heart. I may decide that I must resort to something drastic in order that things may become movable in the situation, that good might work its work, and that suffering may be relieved and oppression may be done away.

It is then that I select—if this is possible—a method of shock that falls within the limitation of my Christian ideal; some form of pressure more drastic and more immediately devastating than moral pressure. And what is the purpose of this? That the oppressor or the instrument of evil in society toward whom I direct my pressure may temporarily be dislodged from his security so that for one breathless moment or for one breathless week he becomes the brother in experience with the insecure and the weak; and while he is in that condition it may be that the spirit of God can take advantage of the looseness of his situation and effect another combination before he settles down again.

But when I have exhausted all means available to me, when I have exhausted everything, and it becomes necessary for me to register, with all of my passionate endeavor, my complete disapproval of an evil world, by offering my life as the sacrifice supreme because it is the logic of all that I have been doing; when that moment comes it is very necessary, I think, for me to be sensitive to the difference between merely dying and martyrdom. It is a great creative spiritual act to know when the moment for martyrdom has arrived.

You know that passage in John Brown's Body—the striking lines about a man at Pigeon Creek who earned his living by selling hounds. There was an old dog who enjoyed "lying in a piece of sunlight at the kitchen door." People would come around and say, "Why don't you sell this old dog? Why do you keep the old dog and sell all the puppies?" And the man's reply was this:

No—he ain't much on looks or much on speed,
A young dog can outrun him anytime—
Outlook him and outeat him and outleap him.
But, Mister, that dog's hell on a cold scent
And once he gets his teeth in what he's after,
He don't let go until he knows he's dead.
Then Abraham Lincoln says:
"Therefore I utterly lift up my hands
To You, and here and now beseech Your aid.
I have held back when others tugged me on,
I have gone on when others pulled me back,
Striving to read Your will, striving to find
The justice and expedience of this case,
Hunting an arrow down the chilly airs
Until my eyes are blind with the great wind
And my heart sick with running after peace.
And now, I stand and tremble on the last
Edge of the last blue cliff, a hound beat out,
Tail down and belly flattened to the ground,
My lungs are breathless and my legs are whipped
Everything in me's whipped except my will.
I can't go on. And yet, I must go on."[6]

If I am not willing to do that—Christian, who calls me Christian?

Now what are the sources available for that kind of qualitative living? First, there is the strength that comes from a great cause, and a man's loyalty to it; even our most ordinary task becomes profoundly significant under the clear light of a great and creative commitment. There is the freedom of mind that comes with a great commitment. It causes an orderly recklessness of action and it robs a man of the fear of death. I think sometimes it is difficult for an intellectual to experience this thing. I feel rather often—perhaps I feel rather than think it—that the kingdom of evil must be held by fanatics; the gains that the fanatics make can be held by the intellectuals.

There is the power that comes from fellowship with Jesus Christ. He becomes for us not the product of any age or any race or any school of thought, but a great benediction to all the races of men. There is also, of course, the power that comes from fellowship, and a primary contact with God. There are some tasks to which our hands are set that can be done under the aegis of a great commitment. There are some tasks to which our hands are set that can be accomplished as a result of a consciousness of fellowship with Jesus. There are some tasks that can be accomplished as a result of a sustained relationship with an inner group of like-minded, like-dedicated people.

But in the great task which involves the transformation of the world, and the redemption of the individual human spirit from evil, only primary releases from God may apply. For the task is infinite, and only an infinite power can address itself to an infinite need. We get this in the life of meditation and prayer and discipline; in moments of quiet I hold, at the center of my spiritual focus, the cause to which I am dedicated. This gives an abundance of freedom and joy because it destroys fear—fear of failure, fear of death, fear of being misunderstood, fear that I am mistaken in the thing that I am undertaking, fear that all my life long I might live for a cause only to find at the end that the cause is wrong. *In moments of profound meditation I become sometimes for one transcendent moment only a central part of the purpose of life.*

Finally, this kind of discipline clarifies the conflicting issues that naturally arise out of any form of action, so that against the darkness of the age I can see the illumined finger of God guiding me in the way that I should go, so that high above the clash of arms and the conflict for position, for rights, for status, for privilege, for place, for priority, I can hear speaking distinctly and clearly to my own spirit the still, small voice of God without which nothing has meaning, quite: with which all the rest of the journey, with its joy, with its pain, with its devastating brutality, all the journey will be filled with a music of its own, and even the stars in their courses and all the wooded world of nature will participate in the triumphant music of my heart.

If I do not know what that means, in terms of power necessary for the transformation of life and of systems—Christian, who calls me Christian?

I would like to close, then, by reading this to you:

"But, God, it won't come right! It won't come right!
I've worked it over till my brain is numb.
The first flash came so bright,
Then more ideas after it—flash! flash!
I thought it some
New constellation men would wonder at.
Perhaps it's just a firework—flash! fizz! spat!
Then darker darkness and sour smoke

"But, God, the thought was great,
The scheme, the dream—why, till the last charm broke
The thing just built itself while I, elate,
Laughed and admired it. Then it stuck,

Half done—the lesser half, worse luck!
You see, it's dead as yet—a frame, a body—and the heart,
The soul, the fiery vital part
To give it life is what I cannot get.
I've tried—
You know it!—tried to snatch live fire
And pawed cold ashes! Every spark has died.
It won't come right. I'd drop the thing entire–
Only—I can't! I love my job.
You who ride the thunder—
Do you know what it is to dream and drudge and throb?
I wonder.

"Did it come at you with a rush, your dream, your plan?
If so, I know how you began.
Yes, with rapt face and sparkling eyes.
Swinging the hot globe out between the skies,
Marking the new seas with their white beach lines,
Sketching in sun and moon, the lightning and the rains,
Sowing the hills with pines,
Wreathing a rim of purple round the plains!
I know you laughed then, as you caught and wrought
The first swift, rapturous outlines of your thought.
And then—
Men!

"I see it now,
O God, forgive my pettish row!
I see your job. While ages crawl
Your lips take laboring lines, your eyes a sadder light.
For man the fire and flower and centre of it all—
Man won't come right!
After your patient centuries,
Fresh starts, or castings, tired Gethsemanes
And tense Golgothas, he, your central theme,
Is just a jangling echo of your dream.
Grand as the rest may be, he ruins it.
"Why don't you quit?
Crumble it all and dream again! But no;
Flaw after flaw you work out revise, refine—

Bondage, brutality, and war and woe,
The sot, the fool, the tyrant and the mob—

Dear God, how you must love your job!
Help me, as I love mine."[7]

"Christian, Who Calls Me Christian?" in *New Directions for Campus Christian Action* (New York: National Intercollegiate Christian Council, 1938), 71–77.

1. For background, see "Man and the World of Nature," printed in the current volume.

2. Both talks are printed in the current volume.

3. From George "Shorty" Collins, 18 January 1938, HTC-MBU: Box 4.

4. Harold B. Ingalls, "Howard Thurman: Being a Few Highlights on an Interesting Life," *Intercollegian,* April 1941, 137–39.

5. Gaius Glenn Atkins, *Pilgrims of the Lonely Road* (New York: Revell, 1913), 338–39. This is the concluding paragraph of the book. Thurman used the same passage in his 1938 sermon "Kingdom of God," printed in the current volume.

6. Stephen Vincent Benét, *John Brown's Body* (Garden City, N.Y.: Doubleday, Doran, 1928), 219–20. The same passage was also cited in "The Significance of Jesus V: The Cross of Jesus," printed in the current volume.

7. In Badger Clark, *Sky Lines and Wood Smoke* (Custer, S.D.: Chronicle Shop, 1935). This same passage is also cited, with minor textual differences, in "The Significance of Jesus II: The Temptations of Jesus," printed in the current volume.

Poetry: "Adventure," "The Melody," "Vision," and [Untitled]

1938

The following poems are taken from Thurman's 1938 journal. In the poem "Adventure," the speaker ruminates on nature as a source of mystical reflection that leads to God. "The Melody" is an expression of personal agony and a cry to God, interrupted by a group of students singing a Negro spiritual. In "Vision" the speaker expresses a sense of personal weariness that is transformed through his experience of God, and "Untitled" offers a reflection on silence in the midst of personal exhaustion. Collectively these highly personal, private poems provide insight into Thurman's brooding spirit and convey the mystic's experience of encounter with God.

"Adventure"

A night so wild with the
glory of the moon
that the earth covered its face

with
Silence.
On the pathway of my mind
long long thoughts run riot.

They are quieted; not by the
beauty of the moon
On the covered face of the earth—
But by the passionate swelling
of awful harmony:
"De ole sheep, they know the way.
Young lambs must find the way.

My heart whispers to God;
"Let me always be the young lamb."

"The Melody"

All night I lay across my bed—
No rest—no sleep:
Naught but the utter agony
of despair.
I cried to God—
The answer: Bold awful silence.
Along the walk outside my
window,
a group of men—
Students in a Mission School—
return
From breakfast.

Suddenly, as if in answer to my
all night cry,
They wooed the silence into song:
"I'm so glad trouble don' las' always,—
O my Lord, O my Lord, what shall I do?"

"Vision"

Last night I climbed my attic stairs
Alone as the shadows deepened.—
The moments passed.
I was aware of His presence.

The way over which I had come in
the day's journey—
Tired, groaning beneath the weight of
ancient ills,
Choking with the dust of dullness
and despair—
The way over which I had come in
the day's journey
Was radiant with the light of the
meaning of Life.
I wept.—
Through my tears, I begged
God for the journey.

[Untitled]

I journeyed
to a hilltop at close of day
Darkness stole upon the valley beneath
as sleep on a tired brow.
Silence, pursuing me all the day
Wont at last as exhausted I lay at his feet . . .
No sense of senses, time-space—all
awareness of self spread out til
I and all around me run together
In one expansive streaming liquid
~~silence~~ quiet.

. . . .

Suddenly with a start—time began
The heavy cares of the years seemed
lighter now—
God so near
I was radiant
With his light!

AD. HTC-MBU: Box 170.

From Mordecai Wyatt Johnson
7 January 1938
Washington, D.C.

A light note from Mordecai Wyatt Johnson about a forthcoming gathering on his farm.

Dear Mr. Thurman:

Please put on your calendar Friday, January fourteenth for a trip to the Johnson farm in Virginia with President Nelson[1] and the undersigned. The understanding being that you will cook, Nelson will eat and I will wash the dishes. As soon as I hear from Mr. Nelson I shall let you know.

Sincerely yours,
[*signed*] Mordecai W. Johnson
Mordecai W. Johnson
President
Professor Howard Thurman
Dean of the Chapel
Howard University

TLS. HTC-MBU: Box 9.

1. William Stuart Nelson (1895–1977) received a BA from Howard University in 1920, a BD from Yale in 1924, and attended the Sorbonne and the University of Berlin before joining the faculty at Howard. He became president of Shaw University in 1931 and then president of Dillard University in New Orleans in 1936. Nelson served at Dillard until 1940, when he became dean of religion at Howard, where he remained for the rest of his academic career.

To H. D. Bollinger
19 January 1938
Washington, D.C.

Thurman responds to a letter of apology sent by H. D. Bollinger,[1] after the incident in St. Louis in late 1937 in which Thurman was denied service at a hotel at which he had just delivered an address. (For details see the introductory note to "The Sources of Power for Christian Action.")

My dear Dr. Bollinger:

I was very glad to get your letter under date of January 7th. I am sorry that I missed seeing you. I had a very very terrible headache that had been with me since Christmas Eve, and the fact that I did not have lunch aggravated my feeling. The result was I found a Negro restaurant, had a quiet dinner, and then came down to the railway station and waited until I could go to bed at nine o'clock. My train did not leave until nearly midnight, but I was in bed from nine-thirty on.

I am very sorry that the incident took place because recovery from such things is most difficult. I appreciate profoundly your very fine letter and the spirit in which it was written. It reveals on your part an extremely sensitive spirit, and to me this is heartening.

The incident makes one or two things very clear. In the first place, it dramatizes all over again that in matters affecting race relations absolutely nothing can be taken for granted. It is for this reason that confidence and trust are so difficult to obtain between Negroes and white people. The framework of the relationships is so completely without high ethical quality that even the most simple ethical advances challenge the entire society. The statement in your letter that is most heartening to Negroes is the one in which you say "the best that I can do is to pledge myself all the more to the practice of Christian brotherhood in such future assemblies as our church may hold." You are right. This is the best that you can do. And I am sure that there will be ways in which we can be of immeasurable help to you.

I have read the material on the Wesley Foundation very carefully and I appreciate its philosophy and what it is undertaking.[2] There is one practical problem, however. Inasmuch as the Asbury Church is a long distance from the campus, some place nearer the campus will have to be found if the work is to be effective. Our students cannot get downtown very often. It will not be possible for the activities to be located on the campus because the Trustees of the University have not opened the campus to any denominational religious emphasis. I am sure you appreciate what is involved there. I had a conference with Mrs. Anderson the other day about the whole matter and I think something can be done. You may be assured that I as dean of the Chapel I shall give to the Wesley Foundation at the University every possible help and cooperation, for after all, the tasks to which we are committed are one and the same.

Please give me a ring when you are here so that we may have a chance to get together.

Sincerely yours,
[*signed*] Howard Thurman
Dean of the Chapel
Dr. H. D. Bollinger
740 Rush Street
Chicago, Illinois

TLc. HTC-MBU: Box 2.

1. Hiel Devere Bollinger (1898–1981) was a leader in the Methodist Church for many decades and the author of *The Student at Prayer* (Nashville: Upper Room, 1960), among

other works. He also served as a leader of the National Methodist Student Conference held in St. Louis, Missouri, in December 1937.

2. The Wesley Foundation is a Methodist college campus ministry, with its first chapter established at the University of Michigan in 1886. Originally called the Wesleyan Guild, its name was changed to the Wesley Foundation in 1923.

FROM WILLIAM M. ASHBY

2 FEBRUARY 1938
SPRINGFIELD, ILL.

William Ashby,[1] executive secretary of the Springfield, Illinois, Urban League, applauds Thurman for preaching about religious convictions during a sermon at the chapel of the University of Chicago.

Dear Doctor Thurman:

I want to tell you how thoroughly I enjoyed your sermon, delivered Sunday last at the University of Chicago religious services. If I was incapable of thoroughly understanding it purely from the point of view of homiletics, there is, on the other hand, one thing which I very thoroughly grasped. It was your sense of fitness.

I have observed over and over again that when our ministers are fortunate enough to get the chance to appear before audiences such as was yours, they invariably seek to bring in some aspect of the race problem. Indeed, too often they go into ravings and rantings and excoriations which are very harmful. I hope you will understand that I do not fail to recognize that the problem is a serious one and, therefore, keeps us ever conscious of it, but, on the other hand, it is my thought that when one seeks to preach a sermon, his object should be just as you did—preach the sermon.

I feel reasonably certain that you will be remembered longer and more kindly for the intelligent and serious presentation of your subject than you would have been had you taken a part of the time pointing out to your audience the injustices which we suffer and for which we are so rarely willing to take the blame. Do let me know if you are going to speak in these parts again and if the sermon is to be broadcast.

Yours very truly,
[*signed*] William M. Ashby
Executive Secretary.
WMA:M

TLS. HTC-MBU: Box 1.

1. William M. Ashby (1889–1991) was executive secretary of the Springfield, Illinois, Urban League from 1932 to 1944. A native of Virginia and a graduate of Lincoln University

(Pa.) and Yale, he became in 1916 New Jersey's first African American social worker and established, several years later, Urban League branches in Newark and Elizabeth. He returned to Newark after his time in Springfield and remained active in civic affairs. He was the author of several books, including a novel, *Redder Blood* (New York: Cosmopolitan, 1915), a play, *The Road to Damascus* (Boston: Christopher, 1935), and his autobiography, *Tales without Hate* (Newark, N.J.: Newark Preservation and Landmarks Committee, 1980).

To Mordecai Wyatt Johnson
3 February 1938
Washington, D.C.

Thurman informs President Johnson of his plans to spend the 1938–39 academic year on sabbatical at Colgate Rochester Divinity School.

My dear President Johnson:

I am herewith complying with your request that I state my plans for a Sabbatical, including suggestions as to the disposal of my work in my absence.

The Rauschenbusch Foundation[1] of the Colgate-Rochester Theological Seminary has offered to furnish comfortable living quarters for me and my family in the Missionary apartments and to make a slight cash consideration of perhaps two hundred dollars, in exchange for which I shall give a series of short chapel addresses before the student body during each semester in residence, and I shall be presented in one formal lecture during the year in the auditorium. This will provide an opportunity to me and my family to be together for the winter comfortably housed in a place providing excellent educational facilities for the children. I shall have the opportunity to work independently in the library and under the guidance of Dr. Robbins in the field of mysticism.[2] I shall be able to do this if the customary provision of one half of my salary is provided while I am on leave. This arrangement will provide for ample relaxation and rest from the tension under which I have lived for the past few years.

With reference to my work here, Dean Mays[3] and I have talked a little about the possibility of inviting Mr. Kelsey,[4] a graduate of Morehouse College, an honor graduate of Newton Theological Institution, and at the present time a Ph. D. matriculate at Yale University. He is a young man whose father you know. I am reasonably certain that he would be able to take care of my classes, and with the proper kind of help he would be able to hold together the student work that I have undertaken. In my opinion he could meet both requirements as well as a younger man at the salary that would be available for him. I take it that the university would not be willing to pay him more than approximately half of my own salary.

There is a counter suggestion as to the disposal of my time next year that is being made about me from another source.[5] Inasmuch as no formal proposal has been given to me, I do not think it in order to include it in my own suggestions to you. If there is any question that you would like to have me clear up please advise me.

Sincerely yours,
[*unsigned*]
Howard Thurman
Dean of the Chapel
President Mordecai W. Johnson
Howard University

TLc. MWJ-DHU-MS: Box 9.

1. The Rauschenbusch Foundation was established in 1929 at the Colgate-Rochester Divinity School in memory of the late Walter Rauschenbusch (1861–1918), a leading figure in the Social Gospel movement. The Rauschenbusch Lectures were given annually during Alumni Week at the school. Writing to B. R. Brazeal on 28 July 1938, Thurman elaborated on his plans for Rochester: "My special responsibility will be to give the devotional addresses each semester, to give the devotional addresses in connection with the Spring Convocation" (HTC-MBU: Box 2). Thurman also had a number of speaking engagements planned for the year, including an appearance at the Los Angeles Sunday Evening Club and the lecture series that became "Mysticism and Social Change."

2. Henry Burke Robins.

3. Benjamin E. Mays was the dean of the School of Religion at Howard. For additional information about Mays, see the biographical footnote in volume 1.

4. George Dennis Sale Kelsey (1910–96) earned his AB degree from Morehouse College (1934), a BD degree from Andover-Newton Theological School (1937), and his PhD from Yale University (1946). Kelsey taught religion and philosophy at Morehouse from 1938 to 1948 and was also director of the Morehouse School of Religion beginning in 1945. He left Morehouse in 1948 to work for the National Council of Churches as associate director of the field department. Kelsey remained there until 1952, when he joined the faculty at Drew University.

5. Thurman is probably referring to efforts to recruit him for a one-year position with the YMCA World's Committee in Europe, which is the topic of subsequent correspondence.

To William M. Ashby

7 February 1938
Washington, D.C.

Responding to Ashby's letter of February 2,[1] *Thurman is pleased to get corroboration of his decision to focus on spiritual questions in his sermons.*

My dear Mr. Ashby:

It has been a long time since I have received a letter with which I was in more complete accord. The sentiments which you expressed are fundamentally my own. I refer particularly to the fact that I "preached the sermon," which I was scheduled to do. For several years now it has been my policy to stick to my "last."

My training and main interest are in the field of religion. I do not accept invitations to discuss the race question; not because I do not think that the race question needs to be discussed, but I am determined to make my contribution along the lines of my preparation and my chosen field of activity. I cannot do this if I become merely a propagandist or a sociologist. This is to reflect no discredit upon anyone who sees it differently. I simply give my judgment. So characteristic has this become of me that out of the invitations that I receive each year, almost never is there one asking me to do anything other than preach or speak on some religious question.

It was kind of you to write as you did.

Sincerely yours,
[*signed*] Howard Thurman
Dean of the Chapel
Mr. William M. Ashby
Springfield Urban League
234 South Fifteenth Street
Springfield, Illinois

TLc. HTC-MBU: Box 7.

1. From William M. Ashby, 2 February 1938, printed in the current volume.

"INDIA REPORT"
10 FEBRUARY 1938
WASHINGTON, D.C.

One of Thurman's obligations as chairman of the Negro Delegation to India, Ceylon, and Burma was to prepare a final report to the sponsoring committee. He had, by the summer of 1936, already prepared the lecture "What We May Learn from India," from which a good deal of the India Report is drawn.[1] *However, because of his own exhaustion, the demands of speaking engagements he undertook to compensate for his unsalaried sabbatical, and his obligations at Howard University, completion of the report was delayed until early 1938, when he sent a copy to Helen Morton of the National Student Council of the YMCA.*[2] *Because there is considerable overlap between the "India Report" and "What We May Learn from India," and the latter has been recently reprinted,*[3] *the editors are only including the report here, with notes that indicate the major divergences between the two documents. There are several drafts of the India Report. The editors are publishing what appear to be Thurman's final thoughts on the wording.*

The report opens with a discussion of Thurman's initial reservations about undertaking the tour of South Asia and then focuses on his observations on India and the status of Indian Christianity and the relation between social, ethnic, and political structures and the role of religion. Throughout the report there are comparisons, explicit and implicit, on the possible implications for Christianity in the Indian subcontinent for American and African American Christianity.

In many ways "What We May Learn from India" is more pointed in its political judgments, but the India Report is more personal and frank (though Thurman refrains from reopening the personnel controversies that led to considerable tension in the planning for the Negro Delegation). Thurman was reluctant to have the report circulated further. When Paul Braisted, the general secretary of the Student Volunteer Movement and an expert on Indian education, wished to use excerpts to prepare a delegation for a conference in Madras, Thurman informed him, "The report is very confidential and I trust you will make no use of it that would be a violation of the delicate relationship that obtains between the Movement and the Government or the Movement and Missionary Enterprise." Still Thurman took pride in the report's forthrightness, telling Braisted: "I tried to be honest and objective, bearing in mind my obligations to my own religious convictions. I think that fact is evident in the report itself. If it is not, I have failed completely."[4]

Introduction

When the invitation came to me to be the leader of a proposed pilgrimage of friendship to India, I felt that under no circumstances would it be possible for me to accept. Thereupon, the first invitation was graciously declined. But the committee was persistent, and through its special representative, Miss Winifred Wygall,[5] I had a rather exhaustive discussion, raising all of the questions that had troubled my own mind. After a long talk with her and hearing her replies relative to my questions, I felt that the undertaking fell within the range of my own life purposes.

It may be in order to review the major considerations which stood squarely in the way of my acceptance. In the first place, I am an American Negro, a member of a relatively underprivileged minority in American life. Organized religion, for the most part, feels it necessary, so to make its peace with the powerful of the earth, that in the last analysis it is often against the weak and with the strong. The question then was "How could I, a member of an exploited race in America, be a part of this delegation and at the same time be true to my interpretation of the genius of the Christian religion as over against the prevailing attitudes of organized expressions of that religion." When I was assured that I would be completely free to make any interpretation of the meaning of the religion of Jesus Christ as I, myself, had discovered that meaning, my course was clear.

Second, I had certain misgivings that led me to believe that we would be considered as the spearhead of some kind of evangelistic movement from the West. At this point, I do not wish to be misunderstood. I am quite definitely and concretely committed to the Christian way of life, but I was convinced that any effort which led us to be used in any mass evangelistic appeal would be decidedly unfortunate. I may say in passing that our position in this matter had to be explained over and over again in our journey through the country.

Our party consisted of four persons: the Reverend Edward G. Carroll and Mrs. Phenola Carroll,[6] his wife, Mrs. Sue Bailey Thurman, and the chairman, her husband. Mr. Carroll is a graduate of Morgan College and Yale Divinity School, and came to the Delegation from the active pastorate. Mrs. Carroll is a graduate also of Morgan College. Mrs. Thurman is a graduate of Oberlin College and brought to the delegation a background of several years as National Student Y.W.C.A. Secretary and rather wide travel both in the Americas and Europe. We were a congenial group whose personalities clashed but little, and we found much personal enrichment in our sustained contacts with each other. As chairman of the delegation, I am happy to say that at no time was there serious conflict either as to assignments or as to general or specific plans relative to the successful fulfillment of our commission. Without this high grade cooperation and understanding, the pilgrimage would not have been possible.

We left New York September 21,1935, on the Ile de France. The party consisted of the Carrolls, the Thurmans, and the Thurman children and their aunt. We accompanied our children to Geneva, where they were set up for the winter. The Visser't Hooft's[7] were very helpful to us and extended a wide variety of simple deeds of gratuitous kindnesses. One long conference with Dr. Visser't Hooft, who was at that time fresh from a visit to India, helped a great deal in preparing my mind for certain attitudes among Indian Christians. After some thirty days we arrived in Colombo, Ceylon, October 21.

Character of the Report

We spent a total of one hundred thirty days in the country.[8] Our schedule was very full. In addition to carrying the major load of addresses, interviews, and conferences, I had to do all of the correspondence on schedules with the cities to which we were going. It was necessary also for me to keep accurate accounts for the India Movement, of all monies advanced me by them and send these accounts periodically to Mr. Ralla Ram.[9] This meant that there was literally no time to do the systematized studying of Indian life and problems that I desired. I had one advantage, however. My experience in America as an American Negro had prepared my spirit for much that I was to see. Having spent several years as a student in a mission school, there were many things that I understood at once while visiting a mission college, which things would have to be explained to the average visitor. I was determined also not to discuss or deal with questions of a political nature; our understanding was clear at this point before leaving this country. In preparation for going to India I had read many books. Being a student of religion, I had for a long time been interested in the various dominant religions of Indian life; I had talked with as many Indians in this country as it had been my privilege to meet; I made a journey across the continent to spend one day with Muriel Lester in order to get a feel of the Indian spirit through her mind and words and heart.[10] With all of these things in my background, I felt that I could approach the life and the struggles of the Indian realistically and yet with understanding, sympathetic and profound. I am very conscious of the extremely complicated character of the problems of India and of the limitations of understanding that my Western culture affords as it stands in the presence of the East. Therefore, I approach with deep modesty and definite caution the setting down in order my reaction and summarizing report of the pilgrimage.

My report is divided into the following parts: Christianity in India; the Indian Christian; the Missionary; the Student Christian Movement of India, Burma, and Ceylon; Indian College Students; Racial Attitudes; the Caste System; and Indian Religions.

Christianity in India

I shall begin with Christianity in India. My purpose here is not to give a complete outline of the background of the Christian movement in India, but I shall deal rather summarily with the whole problem. According to the tradition, Christianity through the Syrian Church has been in India since the first century. Whether it is a fact that the Church was started by St. Thomas near the close of 100 A.D., it is well authenticated that the Syrian Church has had a continuous life since the sixth century.[11] The locale of the Syrian Church for the most part is in Travancore, an Indian state, and the Malabar area across the Ghats on the southwestern coasts. The history of the Church has not been too impressive for it has concerned itself with its own internal development and has given but scant attention to questions of development among the non-Christian religions. This assumes that the Christian religion normally is a missionary religion. I was informed that some of the churches in the Syrian tradition or fellowship had taken over certain customs from their Hindu neighbors, such as the recognition of caste and the like. I saw very little evidence of this sort of thing during our crowded and brief sojourn to Travancore.[12]

I was impressed with the Syrian Christians wherever I found them. They seemed to me to be without doubt among the most independent and forward-looking Christians to be found in all of India. I was struck by their high self-estimate and the way that they in recent times are emphasizing an indigenous Indian Christian experience. The only Christian college that I visited that is supported outright by Indian funds is the Syrian Christian College at Alwaye. The staff and its program are largely indigenous

Western Christianity came into India by way of the Portuguese who established the hierarchy of the church through their political possessions. The spearhead of this movement was St. Francis Xavier.[13] Under the mission of propaganda in the seventeenth century the papacy began its large and influential work in the country. Between 1911 and 1923 the Roman Catholic population of India increased by more than three hundred thirty-two thousand, while the Protestant increase over the same period was five hundred forty-seven thousand. Protestant Christianity came into India about 1813.

I was deeply impressed by the denominational cleavages of the Protestant Christian movement. Let us look into the picture. Among the Baptists there are English, Canadian, and American Baptists; the Methodists include the Wesleyan, the Free Methodist of America, and the Methodist Episcopal Church; the Lutheran include the United Lutherans of America, the Church of Sweden, the Basel Church, the Leipzig Mission, the Missouri Evangelical Mission, and the Danish Society; there are the Disciples of Christ, the Seventh Day Adventists, the Mennonites; among the Congregationalists are the American and the British, the Scandinavian, Swedish, Free Church of Finland, and the London Missionary Society; among the Presbyterians, the United Church of Canada, the Canadian Presbyterians, the Welsh Calvinistic Methodist, and, in addition to all of these, the Salvation Army, some holiness sects of the Church of Scotland, the Anglican Church, and the Y.M.C.A. and the Y.W.C.A.[14] For the most part these groups have their own tenets, doctrinal positions and differences, politics and policies. They are united in some important particulars: They have in them many manifestations of the Western culture, out of which they come, and are for the most part represented officially by white persons. Second, they all claim loyalty to Jesus Christ and certain aspects of his teachings. Third, the sacred book of all of them is the Bible, for they are interested in the spiritual salvation of the Indian.

Inasmuch as sixty-eight out of every one hundred Indians are Hindus, the dominant culture pattern of the land is Hindu.[15] This is particularly true in the South of India and as far as my observations went was definitely true in the cultural centers of the North. India as the home of Hinduism. Now, Hinduism is a religion, a culture, and a civilization. In that respect it is like Judaism. The genius of Hinduism seems to me to be synthesis-making. It possesses amazing powers of adjustment and is profoundly elastic. In the vast palaces of Hindu faith there seem to be many unoccupied rooms. To all and to any new face Hinduism says "Come in. Your room has been reserved for you for many ages. Make yourself at home." It determines many details of dress, it presses its imprimatur upon social customs and ceremonials; it provides names for its children, and sets up the conditions under which society itself is operated. Many of its laws determine the economic life of its devotees and the disposition of property. It decrees what shall happen to the body after death and the fate of the widow and the children. It is indeed a culture and a civilization.

The genius of Christianity tends to be exclusive. It is an either-or-genius. Its demand is absolute with reference to all other faiths. It, too, to a much less degree than Hinduism is a culture, a civilization, and a religion. I was not conscious of this until I went to India. It seems to me that Christianity has projected itself into the country as a civilization whose culture patterns it has developed from its environment as it has sought to become at home in the West. I do not see how this could have been otherwise. The representative of Christianity in a foreign country brings his customs, his mode of dress, his language, his diet, his entire psychological environment, in addition to his mission, which are all more or less defined as an integral part of his faith. Almost everything he does is a manifestation of all these things and as he is a missionary it means that his religion in its social expression cannot be separated from the society of which it is a part. He must demand then of his Indian convert that his break with his Indian religious culture patterns be drastic and complete. It means also that as far as Hinduism is concerned one who leaves the faith should be considered a dead man. It is the same principle operating in both. Thus, such an Indian changes his name and becomes the first generation of a new family tree. He is given a Christian name. Now precisely, what is a Christian name? He is married by the use of a Christian ceremonial. He gives his wife a Christian wedding ring and takes her on a Christian honeymoon. The break with his past culture is practically complete. The meaning of this will be suggested in another part of the report.

The Christian missionary faces a very peculiar dilemma. As I have pointed out, he comes into the country as a product of Western civilization and of such culture as he has been able to absorb. He propagates a faith which to him is personal and ultimate. It is apt to be, however, a faith built upon certain definite assumptions relative to the established order of which he is a part. If he is British it is a faith that is apt to be built upon the assumption of empire. If he is some other kind of European, including the American, it is a faith that is apt to be built upon the assumption of the supremacy of his religion, his civilization, his race. The missionary cannot ever escape the fact that the ruler of India is not only like him as to race, but is also a Christian. I am not proposing to discuss the merits or demerits of British rule. It would be a very discourteous thing to do, having been the recipient of so many fine kindnesses by officials of all kinds. The message of the missionary and for the most part his activities must be limited by the fact of his kinship, identity, race in faith with the ruler. To fail to acknowledge this is to be unrealistic and hypocritical.

I was impressed with the highly theological and orthodox quality of Christianity in the country. Naturally as one who has given his life to reflection in this field, I would notice it. There seems to me to be at least two reasons why this is true. In the first place, when a missionary religion operating in a new environment is seeking to make converts in the midst of a very old culture and religion, it is necessary for it to establish its position as rapidly as possible by defining its terms and especially its categories in contrast to the definitions and the categories of the faiths by which it is surrounded. The converts must be given formulae that are easily manipulated so as to defend their position on the shortest possible notice. The psychological climate of the converts is charged with antagonisms and attacks, very often, and the bullets of their faith must always be available; hence, the tremendous emphasis upon concrete definition. This tendency makes for over simplicity, conservatism, and almost a quaint kind of "cocksureness." For those familiar over a long period of time with the meaning and the developmental genius of religion it is easier for them to pass through rebirth after rebirth as they grow in the richness of the power of their faith. For them to have a growing idea of God is entirely possible without an apparent apostasy. But for the convert to shift his position before he has become completely conditioned is to seem to be backsliding. I had to understand this so as to appreciate and not be hurt by the apparent disappointment of some of the Indian Christians because of the, to them, irregular method of presenting the Christian message which we employed. I remember once in Kandy, after I had delivered a religious address based upon a certain Negro spiritual, an Indian friend said, "Oh, but you did not call my Master's name!" After we talked about the whole thing he was satisfied. I do not wish to generalize too completely at this point. There were many exceptions. I am trying to call attention to the problem as a whole.

The second reason for the strict and rigid definitive policies of Christianity in the country is due to the fact that it cannot afford to countenance the political effects resulting from a very liberal interpretation of the social implications of the Christian message. The major concern in the last analysis and often in the first must be to perfect and redeem the individual's relation to his God. I found many instances of highly devoted, conscientious missionaries who were sacrificing their health, their strength, themselves, for the masses of the people, many who were healing the sick, feeding the hungry, administering in a wide variety of ways to the social need of the people. They were doing all of these things, even as their doctrine became increasingly rigid, increasingly orthodox. Only it should be said in all fairness that unless a missionary had a firm absolute conviction as to the eternal rightness and supremacy of the Christian religion, defined in the most rigid and exclusive terms he could hardly hope to fulfill the demands of the missionary enterprise. The Western supporters of this enterprise must be assured that many souls are being saved. There must be no substitute for this.[16]

I found few illustrations of Western Christians who impressed me that the Indian was accepted without reservation as a brother. Naturally, coming out of the West where all my life I had been victimized by racial separateness and segregation within the Christian Church, I was acutely aware of every sign of it that I saw in India. Among many of the Western Christians, there is a keen sensitiveness to limitations at this point. Among many others I found few evidences of it. I visited only one Roman Catholic college. After the address the presiding Father emphasized the fact that there was no difference in his Church between Indian and European, or between black and white. In subsequent conversation it was his boast that the Roman Catholic Church of India recognized no class distinction in its clergy as between Indian and European. Movements in India pointed towards the union of Protestantism, movements that are gradually bringing about a larger share of equality and leadership, movements that are making for the development of an Indian Christianity—all of these are encouraging signs on the horizon.[17] As a Christian minister and one who loves Jesus, I do not see how it is possible for a Christian institution that has made its peace with the world, that represents so many vested interests, can hope, as things stand at the moment, to give a living interpretation of the Christian religion which springs out of the heart of Jesus of Nazareth, who was a member of an underprivileged disinherited group in a Greco-Roman world. Here and there are glorious illustrations of individuals who have transcended to amazing degrees the limitations of cultures and civilizations and have exemplified a quality of life, timeless and all-embracing. Those individuals as I found them in India do not belong to race, or class, or strata, but are a part of an invisible kingdom for which the bleeding heart of a stricken world languishes, not only in India, but everywhere.

The Indian Christian

Very little remains to be said specifically about the Indian Christian. In the section of this report on Christianity, I have pointed out the fact that Indian Christianity comes out of an immediate or remote culture which is foreign to the culture of this newly embraced faith. The dominant culture pattern of India is Hindu. When the Indian Christian begins to make his religion at home in the country he finds that he must make use of certain forms, social and cultural, which according to his profession of faith are anathema to him. So that one finds the Indian Christian today singing Western hymns for the most part, wearing Western clothes very often, and inclined to think of the God of the Christian religion in terms of the ideology of the dominant controlling European of his country. He is naturally sensitive to the fact that his Church is supported by funds that come from the West, that many of the leaders are Western men and women, that the interpretation that he has received of Christianity belongs essentially to a modern culture.

The economic dependence of the Indian Christian upon the West tends to rob him of independence of thought, and action based upon the dictations of his own heart and mind. He impressed me particularly as feeling this very keenly, and in some quarters there was very deep resentment. When we were in quarantine in Lahore I had an occasion to talk, through an interpreter, with a man who had been recently converted to Christianity from Mohammedanism. He asked me if I could help him in developing his Christian life. I made several suggestions, one of which was a careful study of the Sermon on the Mount and its application to his personal life. He told me that he could not read. I suggested learning to read, whereupon he said his hours were so long that the only time he had for such would be on Sunday. And then he added, "You see, I work very long hours in the shop, so that my condition will not be like the condition of some of my friends who have recently come into the faith. I do not ever want to go to the missionary begging for bread. It will not help my religious faith."

One of the most wholesome movements among Indian Christians is the increasing independence of the Church of Western Influence.[18] The Indian Christian strikes me as being singularly a man who is half way between two worlds. Over and over again as I observed him I was reminded of Carl Sandburg's description of flying fish: "Child of water, child of air, wing thing, fin thing; I have lived in many half worlds myself, so I know you."[19] It remains to be seen what will really happen when the Christ of the Indian road[20] treads the streets of Calcutta and Madras and sits by the roadside in the Indian village.

The Missionary

It is very difficult to measure the contribution that the missionary has made to the life of India, Burma, and Ceylon. First, I want to express wholeheartedly our thanks to all the missionaries who in any way contributed to our health and well-being while we were in the country. In almost every place they put at our disposal their homes, their beds, their food, their thoughtful attention. Particularly were they kind and gracious to the ladies in the delegation, supplying them with many of the personal touches that only ladies can completely appreciate. Relative to the country from which they came originally, they shared themselves with us freely. It was but natural that we would have some misgivings about the possible treatment we would receive from American missionaries, knowing how dominated our land is with racial prejudices against us. I am happy to say that with but one exception we experienced none of the thing we would have experienced in our own country. One very fine American missionary as he welcomed us into his home said, "I am so glad that I can express my real Christian feeling to you here in a way that would be well nigh impossible in our own country." Too much thoughtful praise cannot be given to the missionaries at Lahore, particularly the members of the faculty of Isabella Thoburn College, for their care for all of us, and particularly Mrs. Carroll, during her experience with yellow fever.[21]

My impression of the missionaries is divided into three parts. In the first place, for the most part, they are highly consecrated and devout as far as their devotion to the cause of Christianity as they saw it is concerned. Second, they were for the most part benevolent in their attitude towards the Indians, but very few times was I convinced of their love for the Indian stripped bare of condescension. My impression was borne out at this point by numerous intimate conversations with many Indians from almost every walk of life. Third, I found myself wishing over and over again that more of the finest flowers of our Western culture were engaged in the missionary enterprise. In my opinion, if such were true it would heighten the qualitative significance of everything that is being done.

It is not my purpose to deal in personalities, but I cannot forgo the opportunity to pay a special tribute to the life and services of the late Dr. Vale of Miraj.[22] It was a benediction breathing peace to observe the faces of Indian men and women and children of all religions and castes become illumined with beams of joy when they saluted Dr. Vale on the street. I think this moved me as deeply as anything I saw during the entire pilgrimage. Whatever one may think of his theology the people in this town impressed me as loving and honoring the spirit of a man who for twenty-five years had been in their midst, the incarnation of a healing ministry.

I sympathize with the missionary as he faces the spiritual problems of his personal life in the land. Think what it must do to a man who in his own country could not afford one servant at all to find himself transported to another land where life is so cheap that he may have many servants, so that it is not necessary even for him to bone his fish at the table unless he so desires. To the weak such a thing is suicidal, and may God have mercy on his soul! He comes from another country, by blood and birth he is a member of the ruling class, by commitment of life he is devoted to Jesus of Nazareth whose teachings cannot be compatible with much to which the missionary must give his approval in order to function. He has all of the prestige of power as he tries to live humbly; he represents economic security to people the masses of whom are insecure and many of whom are hungry; he must live without arrogance, even as he is called upon to uphold the dignity of the white man in that part of the world. To such a task only the most powerfully rugged individuals as to mind, spirit, intelligence, and culture should be sent. It is not enough merely to want to help the Indian, and to desire to preach the Gospel to him. Only man and woman who as Odysseus stand head and shoulders above their fellow men in their own land in the midst of their own culture should be sent as apostles and sharers in the life of a great people like the Indians.

The Student Christian Movement

I want to begin this section on the Student Christian Movement by paying a tribute to Reverend A. Ralla Ram, the general secretary of the Movement for India, Burma, and Ceylon. I found him to be a man of tremendous energy, thoughtful and sensitive to all of our needs, gracious in every conceivable manner. He extended himself without limit in an effort to make us at home in his country. Through an indefatigable series of concentrated efforts he made India conscious of our coming and of our presence. It was largely through his instrumentality, directly and indirectly, that some of the finest people in every community were brought to our attention and were apprised of our coming. I wish to take this opportunity on behalf of the entire Indian delegation to pay a special tribute to our generous friends. I wish also to express our wholehearted gratitude to the other members of his staff—Mr. Duraisamy, Mr. Matthews, Mr. Devanesan, Miss Matthews, Miss S. Isaiah, and Miss Gavin. All of these friends became the embodiment of the finest expression of Indian hospitality by doing all in their power to enrich our experience and to provide manifold opportunities for contacts and for services. A special word is due Mr. Matthews, Mr. Devanesan, and Mr. Duraisamy, who traveled with us when we were in their respective territories. They took from my shoulders responsibilities relative to the handling of tickets, the checking of luggage, and things of that sort. I cannot refrain from having a special word of thanks for Miss Gavin, who took charge of us in Calcutta and who saw to it that many of our physical needs were met. She secured a home in which Mr. Carroll could convalesce from his sinus infection. She thoughtfully provided means of recreation for us. She sensed our needs, often without our having to express them. She was always gracious, always kind, always thoughtful.

Our schedules were handled in each locale by a local committee made up usually of the local president of the S.C.M. and citizens either of the school or Church fellowships. I found these local chairmen anxious to help in every way possible so that we could get a fairly complete picture of Indian life and problems. Long before we arrived at the particular town or city a program of work and entertainment was outlined. It always included seeing the places of interest and meeting some of the important Christian and non-Christian leaders of the community.

Some words are in order relative to the Movement itself, I shall list briefly my outstanding impressions. In the first place, I was surprised to find the Movement so small. But this is not really surprising when one remembers that slightly less than one Indian out of every one hundred is Christian. The Student Christian Movement is quite definitely a minority movement among students. In many of the large universities and larger colleges it is but a fragment of the total student body. The most flourishing all-Indian student organization is the Student Union, a non-religious, non-sectarian student organization. For its size and its age (for the Student Christian Movement is very young in India) it possesses amazing vitality.

Second, I was impressed by the fact that there is a very close tie between the missionary and the Student Christian Movement, a much closer tie than is true between the Church and the Student Christian Movement in America. On some of the campuses the president of the local chapter of the Movement is a missionary. In my opinion one of the most needful developments in the Movement is that which would make for a closer tie between Indian Christian college graduates, both on college and university faculties, and in other walks of life, and the Student Christian Movement itself. It stuck me as being decidedly unhealthy for the Movement to be dependent upon the missionary enterprise for much of its adult local leadership. One can understand how inevitable this close tie up would be in the early days of the Movement, but for it to continue much longer would be to stifle its growth. This is true not through any fault of the missionaries operating in the schools, but because of an increasing and inevitable Christian national consciousness that is a part of the normal development of the people. To be a thoroughly Christian movement it need not be a missionary controlled movement. If it is to appeal in any widespread manner to the use of India it must be an <u>Indian</u> Christian Student Movement.

The third thing that impressed me was the definite awareness of the Movement that it was a part of the World Christian Student Federation. Everywhere we went we encountered an awareness of the worldwide nature of the Student Christian affiliation. This is so different from what we had all of us been accustomed to in our own country.

Fourth, the Movement was much more evangelistic in its emphasis than I had anticipated. In fact, that was the major emphasis in all of the program activity that we encountered. The reasons for this are not unlike the reasons for its presence in the Christian Church in the country. If the pilgrimage of friendship was a disappointment at any point it was in connection with the whole question of evangelism. May it be said to their great credit that at no time was there present any tension relative to the depth of their disappointment in us at this point. It was not that we believe less in evangelism, but rather that our interpretation of evangelism differed profoundly from the one to which the Indians themselves were accustomed.

The Indian College Student

In many respects we found the Indian college student not unlike students of our own country. They were young, for the most part idealistic, troubled. My specific impression of them is as follows: First, they were very sensitive to the needs of their own country. They evinced often a very keen intelligent appreciation of the processes, nationally, that were at work, politically, socially, economically. Second, they were inclined to be less mindful of distinctions as to caste, which distinctions were a part of their early life and their community background. Third, they were restless under the yoke of certain of the customs, particularly those customs having to do with relationships between men and women and the whole question of arranged marriages. Fourth, the Christian students particularly, and many of the Hindu students whom I met, were very zealous in their concern to do something about the village life. I met students, particularly in South India, who had spent a part of their holiday living and working in village reconstruction. Fifth, they were all vitally troubled about questions of employment. Having traditions which vetoed any form of manual labor for the educated and conscious of the fact that there were more than enough young people already filling the needs incident to clerkships and other "white-collared" jobs, the future presented very little hope. This is one the great problems of the educated Indian. Sixth, they were deeply interested in hearing about the American Negro and everywhere we went there were expressed desires to know more about us and to develop through the years closer cultural and spiritual contacts. It is for this reason, together with several other considerations, that Mrs. Thurman and I were responsible for sending two undergraduate young women to spend six months in several Indians colleges during the year 1937–38.[23]

Before I close this section I wish to express on behalf of the delegation and the entire American Movement our profound appreciation for all the little and the big things, the courtesies, the smiles, the good food, the huge audiences, for the gifts—for everything—of which we were the simple but appreciative recipients.

Racial Attitudes

As we contemplated undertaking the pilgrimage there was very much of concern as to how we would be received by the Indians. This concern was based upon two facts. First, it had been our experience that Indians who came to America to study soon found it to their advantage to have as little to do with Negroes as possible. They came to America to take advantage of whatever educational and cultural privileges they could obtain here, and to return to their own country. If they associated too intimately with Negroes, or if they were thought to be Negroes by the American white men, they would be subject to the same disabilities, civic and what not, to which the American Negro is subjected. Of course there were exceptions, men who had come and who had built very firm lasting friendships with Negroes. But as a general thing there was very little contact. Many Negroes, therefore, regarded the Indian as someone who would not wish to associate with him, but who rather wanted to be white. There was a general impression also that the Indian considered himself so very superior to the Negro that we would not be well received on a mission such as ours.[24]

The second cause for concern was much more grave. I can best illustrate it.[25] One day an Indian law student asked me, "What are you doing here?" I said, "What do you mean?" He said, "What are you doing here? I know what the publicity says about the pilgrimage of friendship from the students of America to the students of India. But that does not answer my question. What are you doing here?" "This is what I mean," he said. "More than three hundred years ago your African forebears were taken from the West Coast of Africa by slave traders who were Christians; in fact, not only was the name of one of the English slave vessels "Jesus" but one of your very celebrated Christian hymn writers who wrote 'How Sweet the Name of Jesus Sounds to a Believer's Ear,' was a dealer in the slave traffic.[26] You were sold in America to other Christians. You were held in slavery three hundred years by Christians.

You were freed a little more than seventy years ago by a man who, himself, was not a Christian, but who was the spearhead of certain political, economic, and social forces, the full significance of which he himself did not quite understand.[27] And for seventy years you have been lynched and burned and discriminated against by Christians; in fact I read one incident of a Christian Church service that was dismissed in order that the members may go to join a mob, and after lynching came back to finish their worship of their Christian God. Now, here you are over here as a Christian. You will pardon me, Sir, I do not wish to seem rude and disrespectful to you, a visitor in our midst, but in my opinion you are a traitor to all the darker peoples of the earth and I wonder what you, an intelligent man, would have to say for yourself." I knew that we would have to face such a searching examination if the Indians were frank and honest with us, and it became the second ground of concern. Believing as I do that the Christian religion has a fundamental significance for the underprivileged and the disinherited, that has been my approach to the whole study of the history of the faith. It was from this point of view that I replied to the lawyer.

I am happy to say that the Indians were enthusiastic in their response and in their welcome to us and at no time were we ever conscious of any form of condescension or inference on account of race or color. I feel confident that the pilgrimage heightened the respect and regard that the Indian of culture and refinement has for the Negro peoples, and certainly gave to us, and through us, thousands of American Negroes, a deeply personal appreciation for them.

We were naturally interested in the interracial attitudes and relationships as obtained particularly between Europeans and Indians. We noticed certain forms of discrimination as between Indian and European, discrimination based upon race and not religion. For instance, a Student Movement secretary who was traveling with us up to Masulipatam found it impossible to occupy a room in the section reserved for Europeans at the Bezwada Junction. The Indian guard gave our party rooms for the night in European section but when our friend wanted to move with us, he was told very sternly by the guard, "You know you are not allowed in here!" I was strangely reminded of my home land.[28] We were told in subsequent discussions about this that instances of that sort are not as numerous as in previous years. To illustrate how much progress has been made in this whole matter: In a long conversation with a certain Indian judge, he told me that he remembered a time when in the _____ Church there were two pulpits, one high and elevated, the other on the level with the floor. Only the European minister, or someone like him, could preach from the high pulpit. The Indian preacher had to preach from the floor pulpit. Such conditions are not to be found today.

Roughly speaking, there are three broad classifications of the population: European, Anglo-Indian or Eurasian, and the Indian. For obvious reasons those people at the top are European, which, if one may speak of a difference in privileges, stands at the most advantageous position in the country. They have most of power and most of privilege. In that classification are to be found the controllers of the society. Now, next to them are the Eurasians. They are of mixed parentage and as I understand it moved for a long time in separate social stratification. This stratification was guaranteed by certain economic privileges such as the monopoly in telegraph and railway services. Their dress is European, their manner and customs for the most part tend to be European, and their speech for the most part is English. Their attachment is more definitely with the European side of their background, rather than with the Indian. They are a buffer between the European and the Indian. I was not favorably impressed by the average attitude of the European towards the Anglo-Indian. The third group is the Indian. He is the native of this country and he is the masses. Whatever disadvantages there may be in the total picture, for various reasons he is apt to be more completely the victim. I was happy to discover in various parts of this county the beginning of what seems to be a close sympathy between the Indian and the Anglo-Indian in a disposition to recognize the fact the fate of one is the fate of all. I was fascinated by the distinction made between the Indian and the Anglo-Indian because it has certain significance for the problem that exists between the American white man and the Negro. Prior to and for perhaps a decade after the Civil War there was a keen distinction made between the mulatto Negro and the black Negro, a distinction made by the master because the mulatto was the offspring of slave and master. The terrific social pressure under which the South struggled incident to the ravages of the Civil War caused the ruling class to have little time to pay careful attention to the differences between the black and the mulatto. The fate of one became the fate of all. The crime was to have any Negro blood whatsoever. Now that our culture is quite mature and we are through pushing back frontiers as to land, it is not necessary to be definitive with reference to minorities in society. There is a well defined manifestation which makes for an increasingly keen distinction between mulatto and black people on the part of the ruling class. The tendency is to give preferential economic treatment to the mulattoes. With this summarizing statement one can see why I was particularly interested in the thing that I saw there.[29]

We were asked many times if the condition of the Indian and the condition of the American Negro had anything in common. Superficially, many Indians, as well as Europeans in India, said that the only thing comparable in India to the American Negro's situation was the untouchable. Once I was introduced in a public meeting by an Indian who had been to America. He told how a white man had refused to shake hands with the Negro American and as he observed the spectacle he thought of the great throngs of untouchables in Hinduism in his own country. This generalization overlooks certain important factors. In the first place, the American Negro, along with all other Americans, is the direct and indirect descendant of immigrants who took the land from the American Indian, the indigenous fold. We are all engaged in the process of becoming one nation on soil that a few centuries ago was foreign to our ancestors. This is not true of the Indian.

Second, the political ideal of America is in favor of practices that are democratic in the genius and before which undemocratic practices such as discrimination can be condemned as antithetical and immoral. The democratic dogma is central to the political ideal of the new country. This is not true in the same sense in India. Third, both the American Negro and the white man are definitely committed to the same Christian ideal of brotherliness, which ideal is a part of the culture, for America claims to be a Christian land. In such an affirmation it exposes itself to the searching judgment of the most radical social teachings in existence. This is not a Christian country as far as its practices are concerned, but the ideal which is accepted provides the more underprivileged members of the society with a powerful weapon of defense. This is not true in India.

The fact is that both of these large sections of the darker races are temporarily disadvantaged. How long this disadvantage shall continue cannot at the moment be accurately determined.

The Caste System

The caste system presents a very interesting spectacle to a person coming from a different country. I do not presume to pass a judgment upon its functional significance. I do not know enough about India to determine whether caste is good or bad for that land. On the surface of it, it seems to me very bad in many ways. But this is a superficial and uncritical judgment. I cannot say the same thing about untouchability. If untouchability is a fundamental part of the caste system, then my judgment must include it as well. I think that untouchability is a very very terrible thing because it destroys every vestige of self-respect on the part of the outcast. I was in the Malabar district and one evening after retiring I heard someone knocking gently at my door. I turned the light on and went to the door, and there I saw the head of a little boy peering up at me—he must have been twelve or fourteen. He said, with his head down, "I have listened to your words and I have come in the night to ask if there is hope for me. I am a nobody, a less than nothing, but your words give me hope. Tell me, can I be anything, ever?" Because they have been despised over so many many decades they have come to despise themselves. I salute Gandhiji[30] with all my heart for the supremely significant work that he is doing in that area. It is my opinion that the genius of the Christian religion has in it that which is capable of the vast redemption of the untouchables, but so long as Christianity is paralyzed and impotent in the presence of the color bar and in the presence of all kinds of racial and class distinctions in the West, it seems to me sacrilegious for it to boast about its power to redeem the untouchables from their desperate lot. This is not meant to be a personal affront to the individuals in India who are working within the Christian tradition for the salvation of the untouchables. I saw many expressions of purest devotion on their behalf. I shall never forget the thing that I saw in Hyderabad in the experimental community there. God bless all efforts of that nature. But unless a man stands on the receiving end all the iniquity that can be reeked upon him because of social status or color, he will glibly talk about the way institutional Christianity can work miracles for the untouchables.

Indian Religions

I had personal contact with only four of the religions of India, Burma and Ceylon, except Christianity: Hinduism, Mohammedanism, the religion of the Parsis, and Buddhism. I visited only Mohammedan, Hindu and Buddhist places of worship. With reference to Hinduism the following things are outstanding in my mind. It seems to me to be a very sad religion. The devotees seemed heavily burdened. This may be due to the Indian temperament. I am not sure. Even the music stirred emotions of sadness in me as no music that I have ever heard has done. There was something grim about the worship that frankly I do not understand. Always Hindu temples tugged at my heartstrings, not because they were not Christian churches, but because they seemed so devoid of joy and hope. Second, the hold that their religion has on the masses of the people utterly amazed me. There seemed to be no executive secretaries sending out numerous letters and mimeographed sheets reminding the people of their obligations; their feast days were celebrated without pressure being exercised in order to make the people turn out; their ceremonials seemed a part of their life. Third, I was impressed with the richness of its lore and the careful but startling purity of its mystic insights. In another part of the report I have discussed certain aspects of Hinduism more thoroughly.

MOHAMMEDANISM

It was my good fortune to be present in Calcutta when the Midan was filled with thousands of Mussilmen assembled for the preparation of breaking a fast.[31] There were the rich and the poor, the educated and the uneducated, those who stood high and those who stood low in the community—they were all there, side by side, without distinction. Only one who has lived my kind of life can know the thrill that a spectacle of this sort gives. The Mosques always inspired me. There was something about them that gave me a feeling of vastness and cleanliness, both things spiritual. I found the Mussilmen apt to be less friendly than the Hindu. I appreciate and understand the reason for this. Perhaps this was due to the fact that as Christians we seem to be greater traitors to Mohammendanism due to our African background than to Hinduism. I seemed to be more aware of the existence of Purdah[32] in Mohammedanism than in Hinduism. The fact that every Mussilman whom I met seemed to me to be a missionary out to make converts for his faith gave me great respect for him. I had encountered this in my own experience at home. Two incidents stand out. Years ago when I was doing religious education in a city church in the state of Virginia I came into the Young People's Society one evening and to my amazement heard an African gentleman make a most passionate plea to these young people for Mohammedanism. His one point of emphasis was the fact that Mohammedanism made no distinction as to race or color among its adherents. He ended with this significant remark, "Allah laughs aloud in his Mohammedan heaven when he looks out upon the First Baptist Church, colored, and the First Baptist Church, white."[33] Since returning to America I was giving a series of Lenten addresses in Detroit, Michigan, during Holy Week. At the close of the Good Friday service, among the people who tarried to speak was a man who gave me an envelope. When I opened it some time after I found it to be an application card for me to sign, signifying my willingness to become a Mohammedan.[34]

PARSIISM

I did not visit a Parsi[35] place of worship, but I met a large number of them in North India, particularly in Bombay and Hyderabad. In my contact with them, there was nothing from their conversation or manner that made me know their religious faith was different from mine. I found them intelligent, appreciative, thrifty.

Buddhism

My first contact with Buddhism, other than in New York City, was in Ceylon. I visited many Buddhist temples. Buddhism impressed me as being full of resiliency, unapologetic, powerful, but cold. It seems to me to be the most relaxed of all the religions I encountered. I was particularly impressed with what I saw at the Buddhist temple in Rangoon.

To summarize, India is the land that abounds in religions. In some ways it seemed to be God-intoxicated. Despite all of the superficialities and leaches that are present in all developed religions, more than any other place that I have known India seems capable of grasping completely a religion that inspires overwhelming personal sacrifices and complete moral and ethical devotion.

TD. Reel 134, "Negro Delegation to India, 1934—1936," YWCA of USA Records, Sophia Smith Collection, Smith College, Northampton, Mass.

1. Thurman delivered "What We May Learn from India" at a meeting of the National Council for Religion in Higher Education in November 1936. It was printed as *What We May Learn from India: Report of the Eleventh Week of Work, 1936* (New York: National Council on Religion and Education, 1936), 25–28. Thurman also delivered a talk with this title at the Race Street Forum in Philadelphia in early 1937.

2. From Helen Morton, 2 February 1938, HTC-MBU: Box 12.

3. Walter Earl Fluker and Catherine Tumber, eds., *A Strange Freedom: The Best of Howard Thurman on Religious Experience and Public Life* (Boston: Beacon Press, 1998), 200-210.

4. From Paul Braisted, 28 June 1938, HTC-MBU: Box 2; To Paul Braisted, 6 July 1938, HTC-MBU: Box 2. See Paul Judson Braisted, *Indian Nationalism and the Christian Colleges* (New York: Association Press, 1935).

5. Winnifred Wygal was a professional staff member with the YWCA for two decades. For additional information about her, see the biographical footnote in volume 1.

6. See the biographical footnotes in volume 1 for additional information about Edward G. Carroll and Phenola Valentine Carroll.

7. Willem (Adolf) Visser't Hooft (1900–85), the general secretary of the World Student Christian Federation in 1932, resided in Geneva, Switzerland. See volume 1 for additional biographical information about him.

8. The trip actually spanned a total of 140 days in three separate British colonies, Ceylon, India, and Burma.

9. Augustine Ralla Ram (1888–1948), born in the Punjab region, the son of Brahmin parents who had converted to Christianity. He graduated from the Saharanpur Theological Seminary (run by the United Church of Northern India, a combined Presbyterian and Congregationalist denomination) in 1915 and later served as a chaplain to Indian troops overseas (serving in 1919 in Iran and Iraq) and as a pastor in Allahabad, and in 1928 he was named general secretary of the Student Christian Association of India, Burma and Ceylon,

staying in the position until 1947, in which capacity he made numerous overseas trips to Europe, North America, and Asia.

10. For information about Muriel Lester, see the biographical footnote in volume 1.

11. Current scholarship holds that Christian missionaries visited India by the end of the second century C.E. and an indigenous Indian church was established during the fourth century. The native Indian church has always been relatively small (1,180,000 in the 1931 census) and generally known as the Syrian Church, from the language of their scriptures, Sryiac, a dialect of Aramaic. Syrian Christians in India are often known as Thomas Christians.

12. Travancore is now in the Indian state of Kerala.

13. St. Francis Xavier (1506–52), an original member of the Jesuits and a close associate of St. Ignatius Loyola, engaged in extensive missionary work in India in the 1540s, with his activities focused on Goa, a Portuguese possession on the west coast of India from the mid-1500s through the 1960s.

14. For a history of Protestant missions to India, see Kenneth Scott Latourette, *A History of the Expansion of Christianity, vol. VI: The Great Century in Northern Africa and Asia A.D. 1800–A.D. 1914* (New York: Harper, 1944), 65–214; Stephen Neill, *The Story of the Christian Church in India and Pakistan* (Grand Rapids, Mich.: Eerdmans, 1970); and *Directory of Christian Missions in India, Burma, and Ceylon, 1934–1935* (Nagpur, India: National Christian Council, 1934).

15. In the 1931 census of India, there were 239,195,140 Hindus and 77,677,545 Muslims among a total population of 352,195,140. (This census included the current nations of India, Pakistan, Bangladesh, Nepal, and Bhutan.)

16. In "What We May Learn from India," Thurman states that "almost everywhere I encountered what amounted to fear, practically, of the social emphasis of Christianity." *Strange Freedom*, 204.

17. During the first half of the twentieth century, various Protestant missionary movements in India sought to integrate their efforts to avoid duplication or rivalries between denominations. The South India United Church, an alliance between the Congregationalists and Presbyterians, was formed as early as 1909, and a similar alliance created the United Church of Northern India in 1929. These churches later combined with the Anglicans and other denominations to form the Church of South India in 1947 and the Church of North India in 1970.

18. For efforts to assert indigenous control of the Protestant churches in India (and related organizations such as the Student Christian Movement and the YMCA), see Neill, *The Story of the Christian Church in India and Pakistan*, 142–45, and Hans-Ruedi Weber, *Asia and the Ecumenical Movement, 1895–1961* (London: SCM, 1966), 143–63, and passim. For rising Indian Christian sentiment against foreign missionaries, see George Thomas, *Christian Indians and Indian Nationalism, 1885–1950: An Interpretation in Historical and Theological Perspectives* (Frankfurt: Bern/Cirencester, U.K.: Lang, 1979).

19. "Flying Fish," in Carl Sandburg's *Smoke and Steel* (New York: Harcourt, Brace & Howe, 1920), 189. Thurman's version slightly differs from the original.

20. A reference (and typically for Thurman, a rather caustic one) to E. Stanley Jones, *The Christ of the Indian Road* (New York: Abingdon, 1925).

21. In the "detailed schedule" for the India trip, printed in volume 1, Thurman states that Phenola Carroll developed a case of scarlet fever, which is far more likely than yellow fever, which was very rare in India.

22. Charles E. Vail (1881–1935) was director of the American Presbyterian Hospital and its associated medical school in Miraj.

23. The two women were Marian Martin and Anna Vivian Brown. The students went to India under the auspices of the Juliette Derricotte Memorial Fund for Undergraduate Study in India, which was initiated by Sue Bailey Thurman, who delivered a number of lectures to raise money for the fund. But much to the fury of Sue Bailey Thurman, Anna Brown would leave the program after only a few months, and publicly denounce its policy of only sponsoring Negro students as "racialist," Sue Bailey Thurman to Anna Brown, 1 August, 1938, HTC-MBU: Box 2. In 1939 Betty McCree, from Fisk University, and Margaret Bush, of Talladega College, spent a semester in India at Rabindranath Tagore's school, Santiniketan. The program was disrupted by World War II and did not resume. Sudarhsan Kapur, *Raising Up a Prophet: The African-American Encounter with Gandhi* (Boston: Beacon, 1992), 93, 188–89.

24. Since becoming a naturalized American citizen was far more difficult if you were classified as "non-white," many darker-skinned immigrants took great pains to emphasize that they were not African Americans. Joan M. Jensen, *Passage from India: Asian Indian Immigrants in North America* (New Haven, Conn.: Yale University Press, 1988), 246, 269. American blacks resented this practice.

25. This incident occurred in Colombo, Ceylon, presumably with a Ceylonese student or lawyer. For more details see the discussion in "Colombo Journal," printed in volume 1.

26. John Hawkins (1532–95), one of the pioneers of the English slave trade, used *Jesus of Lübeck* as his flagship in his slave expedition on the Guinea Coast in 1567–68. The English minister and hymnodist John Newton (1725–1807) was active in the slave trade for a number of years and was the author of "How Sweet the Name of Jesus Sounds" and other hymns, including "Amazing Grace." He eventually denounced the slave trade and became an active leader in the antislavery movement that resulted in the abolition of the British slave trade in 1807.

27. Abraham Lincoln was not a church member, though his rhetoric was steeped in the cadences of the King James translation of the Bible and he often made striking use of religious language and imagery in his speeches. The analysis of Lincoln as waging the Civil War for reasons largely unrelated to the freedom of the slaves was a standard view in progressive historiography, to be found in works such as Charles and Mary Beard, *The Rise of American Civilization* (New York: Macmillan, 1927), and other works.

28. In "What We May Learn from India," Thurman said the refusal to let the Indian stay with them "reminded me a great deal of the 'land of the free and the home of the brave.'" *Strange Freedom*, 206.

29. This essay and the related "What We May Learn from India" were some of the few times Thurman, who was dark-skinned, wrote on the question of skin-color prejudice within the African American community. In "What We May Learn from India," he expands the argument to claim that it was poor whites who took power after Reconstruction, leading to an evisceration of the distinction between former field slaves and house slaves and the related distinction between darker and lighter skinned blacks. Thurman's view of the post-Reconstruction segregation as a revenge of poor whites against blacks owes much to W. E. B. Du Bois's writings on history. See *The Souls of Black Folk* (Chicago: McClurg, 1903), 357–47, especially "Of the Black Belt," 439–55; and *Black Reconstruction in America* (New York: Atheneum, 1962), praised by Thurman during his India pilgrimage. In a talk during

the fall of 1936 at Morehouse College, "Class Distinctions among American Negroes," Thurman argued that the overt and vicious racism of the immediate post–Civil War era had been replaced by a subtler but just as vicious racism that often favored lighter-skinned blacks. This custom could be codified into law: "When our civilization has completely shaken down, and all the minority groups have been located and defined and labeled, what is there to guarantee to us that what has happened in South Africa and India shall not happen in the America? . . . Racial distinctions in India are sharply defined and rigidly observed. Provision is made for the protection of all who have European blood in their veins, no matter how irregular this blood relationship may be." "Dr. Thurman Sees Danger of Class Distinction Among American Negroes," *National Baptist Voice*, vol. 20, no. 43 (14 November 1936). Thurman went on to note that he found Indian newspapers full of disparaging stereotypes about African Americans and suggested that one benefit of African Americans traveling overseas to places such as India was to provide "a living refutation of the lies that have been spread."

30. Honorific reference to Mohandas K. ("Mahatma") Gandhi.

31. The gathering in the Maidan, the largest public park in Calcutta, was for Eid-al-Fitr, the celebration at the end of the month of Ramadan.

32. The practice of veiling women's faces and covering their bodies whenever they are in public.

33. In 1924 and 1925 Thurman worked as an assistant pastor at the First Baptist Church of Roanoke, Virginia, and was ordained at the church in 1925.

34. The encounter in Detroit was most likely with an early member of the Nation of Islam, which was founded in Detroit by Wallace Fard in the early 1930s.

35. Parsiism is an alternative name for Zoroastrianism.

From William L. Savage

21 February 1938
New York, N.Y.

Thurman's growing reputation as a religious thinker led William L. Savage[1] *of Charles Scribner's Sons to request to see one of his manuscripts. Thurman sent his 1937 lecture series, "The Significance of Jesus." Savage's reply was not particularly encouraging, but Thurman remained undaunted and requested a follow-up visit with Savage in New York City.*[2] *While Thurman continued to think about expanding "The Significance of Jesus" series, evidently nothing came of this, and he soon turned his attention to other book projects. Savage and Thurman remained in touch, with the former contacting Thurman in the spring of 1939 about publishing the "Mysticism and Social Change" series that had just been delivered in February.*[3] *This did not materialize, either, but Thurman's determination to publish a book only increased in the early 1940s. There are hints that he was working on a book about the personal struggles and spiritual lives of young people, drawn "from his years of work with thousands of students," perhaps something of an updating of his BD thesis on student sexual morality, though this project never got beyond the early talking stage.*[4] *Thurman contacted Savage again in early 1942, proposing to expand his 1935 essay "Good News for the Underprivileged"*[5] *to a book-length manuscript (this eventually became the 1949 book* Jesus and the Disinherited)[6] *as well as the publication of an illustrated series of Thurman's prose poems,*[7] *though once again these proposals were rejected.*

Professor Howard Thurman
Howard University
Washington, D.C.
Dear Professor Thurman:

We have been reading with considerable interest the multigraphed report of your addresses on "The Significance of Jesus," given at the Central Area Conference of the Student Christian Movement of Canada. There is no question in our mind but that these pages contain some excellent material. You sent them to us in response to our question whether you had a manuscript for publication. You asked whether we would recommend your rewriting this material with the idea of making a full book. It is difficult to answer this question because so much depends on just how you do it. Of course, the subject has been worked over frequently by so many people. When one speaks, presentation from the platform makes a great deal of difference, and of course a writer is not able to place emphasis in the way that a speaker can. While this is good material, we question our interest in a book, which would be merely an expansion. I wish you would let us know when you have anything else in mind, and I would be glad to have a talk with you any time you are going through New York, for we are interested in your work.

Sincerely yours,
[*signed*] W. L. Savage
WLS:klw
P.S. We are sending your material on to you at Howard University.

TLS. HTC-MBU: Box 19.

1. William L. Savage (1898–1990) was the longtime religion editor at Charles Scribner's Sons.

2. To W. L. Savage, 25 February 1938, HTC-MBU: Box 19.

3. From W. L. Savage, 13 April 1939, HTC-MBU: Box 19.

4. Harold B. Ingalls, "Howard Thurman: Being a Few Highlights of an Interesting Life," *Intercollegian*, April 1941, 137–38.

5. Printed in volume 1.

6. HT, *Jesus and the Disinherited* (New York: Abingdon-Cokesbury, 1949).

7. To W. L. Savage, 21 January 1942; From W. L. Savage, 29 January 1942, HTC-MBU: Box 20. Savage's response was again negative.

To Channing H. Tobias

21 February 1938
Washington, D.C.

The World's Alliance of YMCAs, hoping to reverse what President John R. Mott[1] *would call in a letter to Thurman the "Anglo-Saxon" bias in its official representatives, is interested in recruiting Thurman for a six-month stint as adviser and lecturer that would include a tour of Europe and Africa.*[2] *In this letter, written to his friend Channing Tobias a day after a meeting between Thurman, Mott, Benjamin Mays, and Mordecai Wyatt Johnson, Thurman emphasizes his doubts about the project's uncertain finances and the "makeshift" nature of his proposed participation. Thurman considered the proposal for several months before finally declining the offer.*

My dear Dr. Tobias:

The notice from the Religious Activities Committee has not reached me yet, but it evidently is on the way. I do not see any reason why I should not serve.

I had the conference with Dr. Mott, Dean Mays, and President Johnson yesterday. I am frank to say to you that the case as made to me is not very convincing. Frankly, it seems to me that I am really wanted as an acceptable substitute to hold the thing together until it is possible for Dean Mays to get released. It is not because of what I may be able to contribute in my own right that my services are desired, but there would be least objection to my coming in to do this than if someone else were asked. I wonder if I am making myself clear to you. There is an opportunity, to be sure, but it is the kind of opportunity that an acting dean has as compared with a person who is the dean in the situation.

The concrete proposal is that I give to the World Committee six months of my time and take the other six months to carry out my own personal plans. This makes very little appeal to me. I do not know what Sue will think about it when I see her March 1st. I may be all wrong about my impression of the thing, but at the present moment it does not look very good. The question of finance was gone into a little. Dr. Mott made a special point of emphasis that he would like to get my decision as early as possible because he would have to raise the money covering the cost of travel and salary. He also makes a case for my accepting the University's allowance for Sabbatical and letting whatever comes to me from the Committee be extra. You see, the whole thing, Dr. ~~Mott~~ {Tobias}, seems to me to be a makeshift arrangement. And, frankly, I am not impressed with it at all. I do not want to dismiss it, however, until I hear from you and have more time to deliberate over it and to confer with Sue. It may be that all these mechanical difficulties and emotional limitations should not be permitted to interfere with the overwhelming opportunity of which this is capable. Dr. Mott feels that it is an act of Providence that you and Benny[3] thought of me as the person without conferring with each other. He says that a cable from Mr. Strong[4] in Geneva accepts the suggestion with enthusiasm. My final word is that I feel no call to do this particular job, and it may be that the explanation that I have given above, as partial~~ly~~ as it is, is not related to why I do not feel the call. Perhaps I do not know why. I shall continue in my meditation upon it and it may be that the light of God will make clear to me what is the path to take.

Sincerely yours,
[*signed*] Howard Thurman
Dr. Channing H. Tobias
347 Madison Avenue
New York, New York

TLc. HTC-MBU: Box 21.

1. John Raleigh Mott (1865–1955) was a longtime leader of the YMCA and advocate of foreign missions and ecumenism. From 1915 to 1928, he was general secretary of the International Committee of the YMCA, and from 1926 to 1937, he was president of the World's Alliance of YMCAs. He remained active in international Christian organizations thereafter. In 1946 he was awarded the Nobel Peace Prize.

2. From John R. Mott, 24 February 1938, HTC-MBU: Box 21.

3. Benjamin Mays.

4. Tracy Strong (1887–1968) began his work with the YMCA in Seattle, Washington, in 1925 and became general secretary of the World's Alliance of YMCAs in 1937, remaining in that position until 1953. During World War II, he was active in protecting prisoners of war and interned persons in many combatant nations.

To John R. Mott

15 MARCH 1938
WASHINGTON, D.C.

Thurman comes close to accepting the offer to spend a year working and traveling for the YMCA. His interest in going overseas and having the chance to visit Africa was balanced by lingering doubts about appearing under the auspices of the YMCA.

My dear Dr. Mott:

I am in receipt of your letter under date of February 24th.[1] In outlining the proposal on behalf of the World's Committee, you have made the position quite clear and to the point.

I was not convinced after our conference that you were interested in whatever contribution I might be able to make resulting from the experience of God which has been vouchsafed to me through the struggles of my own life, but rather you seemed at that time to be interested in the perfecting and the carrying through of a plan with my fitting into the picture as one link therein. In your letter, however, you have clear{e}d that up to my satisfaction.

Mrs. Thurman and I, after careful and prayerful meditation, feel inclined to accept the invitation. Somewhere in my own mind and spirit there are misgivings that continue to escape me for analysis. I am not quite committed in the way that I was before going to India. I hesitate always to move without profound inner assurance that it is The thing for me to do. Perhaps the time element is lacking, and the privilege of withdrawing myself from activities for several days to give my mind and heart over exclusively to reflection upon the proposal. I do not know what it is. But in fairness to you, I am saying that my mind is in a tentative state yet. It is reasonable to assume that after I go more deeply into a thoughtful analysis of the possible significance of the proposal, I shall find the leading that I seek. Very often in my life it is that way. I am, therefore, giving you my word of affirmation.

With reference to the length of time, Mrs. Thurman and I are agreed that it is much better if we consider the proposal on the basis of twelve months rather than six. This would give us the opportunity to establish our family at one place, say Geneva, and the children may have a full school year without moving. In the second place, it would make the whole experience more leisurely and, other things being equal, more effective. In the event that we did go for a year it would mean a commitment from September, 1938, to September, 1939, with a month's vacation, perhaps coming in August of 1939. This would mean that Dean Mays could begin in September, 1939. Rochester is willing to extend certain professorial courtesies to me for one semester, but this is not very acceptable to me because of the uncertain nature of the family location, namely six months in America and six months in Europe. If our children were older it would be very much simpler. I suppose that the proportionate distribution of my time would be about the same for twelve months as was suggested for six. It would mean, perhaps, spending three months in Geneva, and then three months in intermittent travel; then one long journey into Africa and perhaps the last two months in Geneva.

If I went for the year it would mean canceling my preaching and lecturing schedule that is already being set up for next year, a schedule that takes me into the colleges and universities in various sections of the country. If I were remaining at Rochester I could carry on.

I was particularly pleased by the next to the final paragraph in your letter, in which you expressed your willingness to have me associated with the staff, giving my energies to the interpretation of religion from my own background and meditation and leading. Frankly, I have had very little interest in the machinery and the organization of our institutions. It is not that I do not recognize the profound importance of and necessity for having at the core of a dynamic movement a sound closely integrated organization, but this is not my interest nor my emphasis. I would be very much happier and very much more useful if I am relieved of the responsibility of dealing very much with the framework of the Association. Whatever contribution God enables me to make, I think it will be in another area. What I shall do in the event that our plans are consummated, I would much prefer discovering as I move into the experience. It would be a joy, I am sure, to work with the Committee in Geneva on the whole comprehensive plan and even some of the details of its ramification. I simply assume that whatever my particular responsibility is this would be included.

With reference to the salary, I think that whatever arrangement the Committee makes with Dean Mays for the two years for which he is invited should obtain for the one year covered by my invitation. If this were done, I think it would meet the total situation. With reference to my Sabbatical, when my work started with the Committee the University would be relieved of any responsibility.

Please accept my personal thanks for the kind letter which you sent and be assured of my profound interest in the far-reaching significance of this new step on the part of the Committee, even though it may not be possible for me to participate in it actively.

Faithfully yours,
[*signed*] Howard Thurman
Dr. John R. Mott
230 Park Avenue
New York, New York

TLS. HTC-MBU: Box 12.

1. From John R. Mott, 24 February 1938, HTC-MBU: Box 12.

To Richard R. Wright Jr.
31 March 1938
Washington, D.C.

Thurman writes Bishop Richard R. Wright[1] *of his interest in visiting South Africa in the near future and his possible intention to do so.*

My dear Bishop Wright:

It was certainly a significant evening for me to be present with you and Mrs. Wright at the home of President Nelson.[2] You gave to me a fresh and powerful interpretation of much that I have felt about Africa and our relationship to it. May God bless you in the work to which He has committed your effective hands.

I am not certain as to my next year's plans, but in the event that I go to work for the World's Committee in Geneva, I shall certainly see to it that my assignment will take me to South Africa. Please let me have your address there.

My warmest personal greetings to you.

Sincerely yours,
[*signed*] Howard Thurman
Bishop R. R. Wright, Jr.
Wilberforce, Ohio

TLS. HTC-MBU: Box 21.

1. Richard Robert Wright Jr. (1878–1967) was a sociologist, social worker, educator, and minister who served as the African Methodist Episcopal Church bishop in South Africa (1936–40). He was also president of Wilberforce College twice (1932–36 and 1941–42). Wright was the son of prominent educator Richard R. Wright Sr., who was the first principal of the Georgia State Industrial College for Colored Youth (Savannah State University). In 1898 the younger Wright earned the first baccalaureate degree awarded by the college. He went on to earn a bachelor of divinity degree, the equivalent of a master of divinity, and a master in biblical languages from the University of Chicago. It was during Wright's years at Chicago that he developed close ties with George Edmund Haynes, a cofounder of the Urban League, and he worked with Jane Addams and many of the people involved in the settlement movement. He later became the first black to receive a PhD in sociology from the University of Pennsylvania, and his dissertation was published as *The Negro in Pennsylvania; A Study in Economic History* (Philadelphia: A. M. E. Book Concern, 1912). Wright also wrote *87 Years behind the Black Curtain: An Autobiography* (Philadelphia: Rare Book Company, 1965).

2. William Stuart Nelson.

To John R. Mott
4 April 1938
Washington, D.C.

After much deliberation Thurman decides to reject the one-year position with the World's Alliance of YMCAs.

My dear Dr. Mott:

I promised Dr. Tobias on Friday that I would send you a letter within the next two or three days giving my final decision.

After thinking the whole matter through with very great care and making it of central significance in my own meditation, I am not able to bring myself to a clear leading that this is the Thing for me to do. I am, therefore, sending this formal statement declining your invitation to associate myself with the World's Committee of the Y.M.C.A. for next year. I could offer as possible reasons the fact that I am still recovering from the terrible toll of India and my physical condition is far from satisfactory; or I could say that the unsettled conditions in Europe at this moment make it unwise to transport my family there. But as important as these considerations are, as well as several others I might mention, I do not offer them as my reason for declining your invitation. I have one basic reason, namely, it does not appeal to me as the thing that I ought to do.

I want you to know how much I appreciate your interest in my consideration, and it is my desire that a satisfactory arrangement may be worked out whereby it will be possible for the situation to be held together until Dean Mays is free to carry on. I am genuinely sorry that it does not seem to me to be the things for me to do, but with my judgment as it is I am left with no choice except the one that I am taking.

With every kind and warm regard, I am

Sincerely yours,
[*signed*] Howard Thurman
Dr. John R. Mott
235 Park Avenue
New York, New York

TLS. HTC-MBU: Box 12.

"The Integration of the Ethical, Social, and Educational Program"

28–30 April 1938
Raleigh, N.C.

Thurman delivered this talk to educators at the fourth annual meeting of the National Association of Personnel Deans and Advisers of Men in Negro Educational Institutions at Shaw University in Raleigh, North Carolina, held 28–30 April. The talk was transcribed and edited by apparently not published. A copy survives in Thurman's papers.

Thurman spoke several times in 1938 on the situation and problems of black education.[1] *The 1930s were a time of transition and challenges for many black colleges. By 1930 the principle of black leadership at black institutions of higher learning had been firmly established. Secondary and vocational programs were rapidly being eliminated, and many black colleges were seeking and obtaining accreditation for the first time. Enrollment was rapidly expanding.*[2] *At the same time, there were contrary trends. Public colleges for blacks in the South, while gaining new respectability and accreditation, depended on southern legislatures for their financing and were usually very cautious in challenging the status quo. Private colleges, meanwhile, were increasingly funded not by their founding denominational organizations but by conservative philanthropies such as the General Education Board. This practice spawned concerns that black colleges would produce a generation of leadership that, in the words of historian James Anderson, "would cooperate with instead of challenge the Jim Crow system."*[3]

Thurman's lecture reflects a common strain of complaint among black intellectuals in the 1930s, critiquing black institutions of higher education for their narrowness and their intellectual rigidity.[4] *He builds on his earlier works and similar arguments in "Higher Education and Religion" and "The Task of the Negro Ministry" on the limitation of higher education in black college.*[5] *The purpose of education in contemporary America, Thurman argues, is to guarantee and to perpetuate the established order, and black colleges do this in insidious ways, by conferring on their graduates an elite status and then not honestly confronting their severely limited vocational opportunities. As a result there is a tendency for black graduates to become "over-individualized" and to separate their fates from the rest of the black community.*

The topic as you see on the program is "The Integration of the Ethical, Social, and Educational Program." The topic presupposes the actual existence of an ethical, social, and educational program in the college. It is an assumption that I do not make because in my opinion the facts do not warrant it, but I shall talk about it, as if such an assumption were real.

As a preliminary statement, I want to point out something of which you are all conscious, and something that has been discussed in some of the previous topics; namely, there is a basic and apparently fundamental lack of confidence and commonness of spiritual unity and aim that exists between the faculty, the administration,—those who carefully formulate policies for the majority of the institutions—and those people who are more or less on the receiving end of the faculty and administration—the students. It is not a new thing that I am pointing out, but there is a lack of confidence because of an interpretative difference in aims. It is hard to interfere with student activities without meddling or making them feel that one is being dictatorial.

Functional Significance

But I want you to think a little while about the functional significance of an ethical program. We shall assume for the present that an ethical program would be organized so as to influence the behavior, and more potently, the choices of the students in a direction of higher values and ideals.

Such a program would point out the moral responsibility that goes with the freedom of learning; the moral responsibilities that are involved when persons are permitted to withdraw themselves from society—such as students are permitted to do—in order that they might become odd and different; the responsibility that will provide opportunities for discipline, such as integrity—a very simple moral task but very important—and moral discipline, such as honesty in the preparation of lessons and examinations. This is an assumption that it is a very simple thing, but it is very hard to get because college life for us, as for other people in the country is two or three steps removed from much of the traffic of the world. There tends to be something very artificial, unnatural, and sterile about the atmosphere of the institutions of learning; things always seem to be operating in a vacuum, until they are seen as a part of life. The emphasis is on tomorrow. I am just a student now; I am just a student.

In a small college town, when celebrating an event, the students went to a theatre and threw eggs and tomatoes and sent everybody home slightly embarrassed and slightly uncomfortable, and when they were reported, the authorities said, they are really just students,—you know.

There is probably something unreal about the very atmosphere in which the true nature of the ethical ideal is to be determined. In a college the true nature of ideas can be determined; while in a community of another type the survival value of ideas can be determined. To illustrate, a man takes a course in European History. Unless the teaching is very good, the student cannot take any more interest in the newspapers than he previously did. The history was just another course. That tends to be true in all institutions of learning. How much more true is it of Negro institutions. When a student of a certain class gets in college, he is just one, two, three, four, five, six, seven steps removed from the rest of his kind. Do you see what I mean?

I think that there should be given a definite place in the curriculum for philosophy. I do not mean merely Ethics taught as a glorified Sunday School class. I went to a class in Ethics, as an undergraduate and it was a nice reminiscent class where we could occasionally get fragments of insight—which was just like the Saturday night Sunday School class.

There should be a definite place for philosophy in the curriculum of a college. Very little emphasis is given to philosophy now.[6]

Secondly, I think that there should be occasions during the school year when the group behavior of the college can be interpreted in terms of some high creative moral pattern. In other words, I think that the same should be done for the behavior of the group, as for the individual. Here is a boy who needs guidance: We say to him, at the rate you are going, life will look like this for you. The same thing that we do for individuals who need encouragement, or who need critical guidance, the same thing can be done for the group unit that makes up the college life. And at special moments in the year, attention should be called to the ethical significance of the seemingly dramatic moments in the lives of national or international figures. We should capitalize on that so that when society "dishes" up a very good character to be taken apart, our students will have an understanding.

For instance, Ramsey McDonald who became the first Labor Prime Minister of England had certain far-reaching ideas, and there came a time when he had to make a choice between the integration of his position as a labor leader and the saving of the British Empire as he thought of it. It was a moral issue. McDonald went up to his native heath, then returned to Downing Street and renounced his past and became the spearhead of a coalition cabinet; that was a moral decision in itself.[7]

The Social Program

The functional significance of the social program should be to develop students along two lines: The first is in regard to recreation. The college has a very definite responsibility in guiding, in teaching students how to recreate themselves, improve themselves physically and mentally, and at the same time, have a good time.

The second has to do with increasing a social conscience with regard to the world. I think that this is very important. It is important because of the very nature of the dilemma, the psychological dilemma, that an underprivileged man faces when he becomes educated. When he is educated, he is apt to become over-individualized so that it is very difficult for him to see himself in relation to a wider social responsibility. In order to achieve what he has, it is necessary for him to shoot out of the mass of his kind to become unusual and different. It takes time for a man to do this, and we actually think that he is different from the rest. The logic of this whole matter is that the gulf between the masses of the people and the privileged, educated members of society will become wider and deeper as the educative program demands more highly specialized individuals; unless the college does something, the average college students will look upon the mass of Negroes in the same critical, hostile manner that people who are on the outside regard them. That seems to be inevitable because of the vary nature of the educational enterprise in society. But suffice it to say that a social conscience needs to be encouraged and developed in the social program of the curriculum; and that needs to be done in a lot of ways. It can be done in the Social Sciences and in certain other courses. It can be done by the exercise of a positive social attitude by the privileged children, members of the college community.

Educational Significance

The functional significance of an educational program is to lay the foundation for a broad, comprehensive education so that individuals will be at home in the world. The college can be a great inspirational agency to those individuals who are prepared by its teachings, and traditions to "walk through the traffic of life with the dignity of solitude."

I am not an Educator. I speak as a layman, but I will tell you what I think. The purpose of education in our democracy, as it is now constituted, is to guarantee and to perpetuate the established order. And any institution of learning that varies noticeably from that fundamental position cannot hope to live. The price that the institution must pay for survival in society is to leave, to subsequent generations, its framework. If it does not do that, it cannot survive.

A Negro student whether educated in the North or South, in segregated or mixed schools has the same general social attitude that a white student has. He has the point of view of the privileged and the controllers of society. But when he gets out he must function as a member of an under-privileged minority. For this reason I have never seen an educated Negro who was not discouraged in a very definite sense. He stands ever in the presence of an overwhelming frustration. We do not wonder at Dr. Wilson's reference to the significance of the "Big Apple."[8]

For the most part, our schools are busily engaged in keeping alive—meeting objective standards set up by people who have everything at stake in preserving the framework of social relations as they are. This educational program must be coordinated and unified on the basis of a creative synthesis which will enable the members of the college community to work out their own destiny.

Detachment, objectivity, and power should be possessed so that students can be seen as individuals.

> To suffer woes which hope thinks infinite;
> To forgive wrongs darker than death or night,
> To defy power which seems omnipotent;
> To love and bear; to hope till hope creates,
> From its own wreck the thing it contemplates;
> . . . Neither to change, nor falter, nor repent;
> This like thy glory, Titan, is to be
> Good, great and joyous, beautiful and free;
> This is alone Life, Joy, Empire, and Victory![9]

That seems to me to be the thing towards which the college should send those who come within its walls on their educational sojourn.*

TD. HTC-MBU: Box 193.

1. See the "Commencement Address Delivered at the Tennessee A & I State College" and "The Contribution of Baptist Church Schools to Negro Youth," published in the current volume.

*Editor's Note: Presented above is a summary of Dr. Thurman's address as taken from stenographic notes.

2. For a contemporary overview, see Buell G. Gallagher, *American Caste and the Negro College* (New York: Columbia University Press, 1938).

3. James D. Anderson, *The Education of Blacks in the South, 1860–1935* (Chapel Hill: University of North Carolina Press, 1988), 276. See also Raymond Wolters, *The New Negro on Campus: Black College Rebellions of the 1920s* (Princeton, N.J.: Princeton University Press, 1975).

4. For typical critiques see W. E. B. Du Bois, "Education and Work," *Journal of Negro Education* 1 (April 1932): 60–74, and Carter G. Woodson, *The Mis-Education of the Negro* (Washington, D.C.: Associated Press, 1933).

5. Both are printed in volume 1.

6. Thurman later argued that the absence of philosophy in black colleges was deliberate: "In the missionary colleges of the South, few (if any) courses were offered in the formal study of philosophy. I believe that the shapers of our minds, with clear but limited insight into the nature of our struggle for survival and development in American life, particularly in the South, recognized the real possibility that to be disciplined in the origins and development of ideas would ultimately bring under critical judgment the society and our predicament in it. This, in turn, would contribute to our unease and restlessness, which would be disastrous, they felt, for us and for our people." *WHAH*, 43.

7. James Ramsay MacDonald (1866–1937) was twice prime minister of Great Britain (1923–24, 1929–35), and the first leader of the Labour Party to hold that position. In 1931 a crisis brought about by the Depression led to MacDonald breaking with the Labour Party and heading a national unity government dominated by the Conservative Party.

8. "Dr. Wilson" was presumably Frank Wilson, who was Thurman's good friend and at the time dean of religion at Lincoln University in Pennsylvania. The big apple was an African American social dance that probably started in Columbia, South Carolina, in the early 1930s. It had affinities to the exuberant steps and jumps associated with the Lindy hop, and the big apple craze was at its peak around the time of Thurman's talk. It is likely the dance, rather than the nickname for New York City (not commonly used in the late 1930s), to which Thurman was referring.

9. The closing lines of Percy Bysshe Shelley's *Prometheus Unbound* (1820), spoken by Demogorgon, who overthrows his father, Jupiter.

To Prentice Thomas

23 May 1938
Washington, D.C.

Prentice Thomas is an obscure figure today, but he was a significant figure in the struggle for racial equality in the late 1930s and 1940s.[1] *His career represents an early example of Thurman's role as a presence and inspiration for the direction of the nascent civil rights movement. Born and raised in Texas, Thomas majored in religion at Howard and stayed on for a law degree.*

In 1937 Thurman recommended him as a staff person for Sherwood Eddy's interracial cooperative farm in the Mississippi Delta, describing Thomas as a "Negro whose intelligence and academic background was equal to any of the white people on the Farm."[2] *Thurman wrote the letter printed here to Thomas while Thomas was in retreat at Pendle Hill, the well-known Quaker study center in Pennsylvania. He was a conscientious objector during World War II and from 1942 to 1943 worked in New York City on the NAACP legal staff with Thurgood Marshall, pursuing a variety of antidiscrimination cases.*[3] *Thomas epitomized many of Thurman's most cherished ideals in the late 1930s: a person of deep religious commitment who used his connection to God as a means to try to change the world and an educated African American who had not forgotten how to speak to, and for, the poor. He wrote Sherwood Eddy in 1937, "Prentice Thomas will be heard from some day as a lawyer and a champion of the rise of the disinherited."*[4]

My dear Prentice

I was very happy to get your letter and I am sorry that I must write to you in formal terms but there is not time to take my pen in hand.

I think you have a point about the camps[5] and Negroes. It is very difficult for Negroes to get into those places that require self-sustenance in the summer time. There are those who can afford to attend them but they do not know anything about them. I wish that the same sort of effort that is put forth in interesting white people in the project would be put forth with reference to Negroes. Perhaps another year I can do something about this. I am sure that we ought to be able to send someone into a camp another year. It is too late to do anything about it now.

I think that it is all right for you to be quiet on the labor front for a little while until you pass your examination. I would like to see you try to pass the Bar in Nashville. Maybe Mr. Napier would be helpful to you in some way.[6] He is one of the Trustees of the University.

I am getting the group interested in doing something for the agricultural workers next winter. You will keep in touch with me so that the plans they work out can have the most important meaning for the cause to which we are both dedicated.

It was good to see you the other day and I hope sometime before the summer is over we shall have a chance to get together again.

Sincerely yours,
[*signed*] Howard Thurman
Mr. Prentice Thomas
Pendle Hill
Wallingford, Pennsylvania

TLS. HTC-MBU: Box 21.

1. Prentice Thomas, a native of Texas, graduated from the Howard School of Law in 1937, after previously studying with Thurman at the School of Religion. He later worked

as a lawyer for the Southern Tenants Farmer's Union and as a lawyer in Nashville and Louisville.

2. Thurman thought it a serious problem in interracial organizing that less educated blacks often deferred to the judgments of whites (or better-educated whites thought blacks should defer to their judgment). To Sherwood Eddy, 26 May 1937, HTC-MBU: Box 6.

3. Thomas left the NAACP after sharp criticism from Thurgood Marshall and Walter White, over Thomas's interest in extending the organization's ambit to organizing sharecroppers, what Risa Golobuff has called his "more left-leaning and agricultural bias," Risa L. Goluboff, *The Lost Promise of the Civil Rights* (Cambridge, Mass.: Harvard University Press, 2007), 183–184.

4. To Sherwood Eddy, 26 May 1937, HTC-MBU: Box 6.

5. Probably a reference to the summer programs, camps, and retreats sponsored by liberal Christian organizations.

6. James C. Napier (1845–1940), free born in Nashville, was for many decades the most prominent black politician in Nashville and was a close associate of Booker T. Washington. From 1911 to 1913 he was register of the Treasury in the Taft administration. An 1872 graduate of Howard University School of Law, he was a member of the board of trustees at both Fisk and Howard universities.

"Commencement Address Delivered at the Tennessee A & I State College"
3 June 1938
Nashville, Tenn.

On the occasion of this commencement address, the Pittsburgh Courier *described Thurman as "an idol at Tennessee State College, where he has been heard on several occasions." (He shared the podium with the young Adam Clayton Powell Jr., who the previous year had succeeded his father as pastor of Abyssinian Baptist Church in Harlem.)*[1] *Thurman's address was one of several related talks that he delivered in 1938 on specifically black themes addressed to black audiences, and it can be viewed as part of a trend among black intellectuals in the 1930s to criticize the limitations of black colleges.*[2] *As background Thurman notes the growing gap between the rich and the poor at home, and between the richer and poorer nations, and he argues that imperialism is parasitic upon the inherent vitality of both these poorer nations and underprivileged races. He warns that education too easily can become a tool that reinforces the position of those in power and regrets that black colleges often have functioned in this role. Thurman also observes that black college graduates, as underprivileged persons, often find themselves recapitulating existing power relations, to their personal and collective disadvantage. Finally he emphasizes the accumulated weight of the African American past and the responsibility of the current generation to redress historic injustices.*

"We Die, But You Who Live Must
Do a Harder Thing Than Dying is,
For You Must Think, and Ghosts Shall
Drive You On."[3]

The college might say to those young men and women who come to it for the first time what a contemporary writer puts upon the lips of a young mother. "My son, may you seek after the truth. If anything I teach you be false, may you throw it from you and go on to deeper knowledge and richer truth than I have ever known. If you become a man of thought and learning, may you never fail to turn down with your right hand what your left hand has brought up through thought and study if you see it at last not to be what it is. As you become an artist, may you never paint any picture other than as you see it. As you become a politician, may no success for your party or even love of your country ever lead you to tamper with reality and to play a derogatory part. In all of the circumstances of life, my son, present yourself intent on the truth and cling to that as a drowning man flings himself on a plank and clings to it knowing that whether he sinks or swims with it, it is the best that he has. Die poor, unknown, unloved, a failure perhaps, but shut your eyes to anything that seems to them to be the truth."[4]

I want you to think for a little while this morning about the past, and I am using as the words which come to us from the past, particularly from the past that we know, from the people that we represent, from the past of the Negroes—words that have been put on the lips of some other people and these are the words, and these words are my subject, "We die, but you who live must do a harder thing than die, for you must think and ghosts shall drive you on."

We die, but you who live must do a harder thing than dying is, for you must think, think, think, and ghosts shall drive you on. I came over to this building early this morning, looking around, and I saw the picture somewhere, a drawing of Rodin's "Thinker"—the man buried in thought, they say.[5] And it carried me back to my childhood, because when I was quite a boy someone gave me that picture and I used it as a model and it was my favorite pose. (It was something like this): And I was worried like this all of the time because I didn't have anything to worry about. My brows furrowed and I had everything about the pose. One day my mother sent for me to put some wood in the wood box. I was in character and I told my sister to tell my mother I was thinking. Well, I did not repeat that.

What do you think of the people in the past? the Negroes in the past? what do you think they meant by these words that I am saying this morning—"We die, but you who live must do a harder thing for you must think." Well, I want to talk a little about what I think they had in mind and about two or three ghosts that were not ghosts in their time but may be ghosts in our time that are hounding us and driving us on; filling us sometimes with panic, sometimes with despair, often with great inspiration.

There is a ghost of insistent confidence in one's own mind and one's own ability, and one's own group. It seems extraordinarily significant to me that after the years that have passed we are threatened with a profound loss of [confidence] in our own minds and in our own abilities because we have been so consistently despised we have at last begun despising ourselves.[6]

I was walking through a part of Atlanta, Georgia, called, "Slide," a slide just below the bottom of the campuses of Morehouse and Spelman. It was on Thanksgiving night and there were some men sitting around a fire talking about the loss of jobs. It was before we had heard about a depression in 1922. Finally, after discussing what they should do at Christmas time with money, one young fellow got up and went walking off humming a song to the tune of a blues—I don't remember the song but the words were, "Been down so long, down don't worry me."[7] And there you are. So heartily, so thoroughly, so completely despised that at last we are beginning to despise ourselves. And men cannot live without hope; men cannot live without confidence in themselves; and it is this first thing that we gather from the past for it was in the far-off time when environment was completely organized against people who were slaves, in the midst of those limitations, deserving as they were, people growing up who had amazing confidence in the peculiar quality of their own minds to transcend the limitations of their environments and establish for themselves a place of security and strength in the midst of their hostile environments. That is some of the past. Down in Alcorn, Mississippi there is a state college for Negroes. When you go to Alcorn you see two dormitories, a chapel, a president's house, all of which were built more than seventy-five years ago by men who themselves were slaves, who did not have any say so over their own bodies, but who, in the midst of that kind of situation plod over it with such creative minds and spirits, that they[8] were able to abstract things which could be used and build institutions for themselves. All of the work was done by men who did not own their bodies.[9] That is one of the ghosts that shall drive the young Negro on. And those men said unto us, "We die, but you who live must do a harder thing than dying is, for you must think." That is the first kind of ghost—confidence in your own mind, in your own abilities, the kind of moral power that makes it possible for an individual to be himself over and against the combined testimony of his environment; and to affirm his integrity as to his mind and as to his ability.

The second one: a confidence that in the last analysis life can be trusted. Now this is very difficult for me to make clear. Confidence that life is dependable; that life is its own restraint; that as Tennyson suggested, "That nothing walks with aimless faith;"[10] that everything that there is in one's world has possibilities of significance and usefulness. That life can be depended upon. Now, that expressed itself in the past and in an occasion in the present in two very important ways that I want to point out. First, vitality is given to people who believe in life. Vitality is given to people who live close to the primary and elemental expressions of life. We hear quite a bit about imperialism, about how people are being ground into so much powder; how people of the earth are being ground into the earth. We hear a bit about colonization, about what is being done in Africa and in Germany. But back of imperialism is not so much the hunger for bread, but back of imperialism there is this deeper light—hunger on the part of men who have become powerful and as a result of their power have been cut off from the roots of life, who are now trying to find those masses of people in the world who are close to life, who are elemental, who are simple, who have vitality. And they are laying hold on those people and sucking the life out of them. That is the psychology of imperialism. It is not because one man wants to kill another man so much, but because people who have grown up as powerful people in the world have grown mean and emaciated and sterile, and they are looking around for a luscious people of the earth and laying on them to suck their strength.

It gives you an interesting confidence in life. That is why, in the past, Negro slaves (and I want you to hear this), that is why Negro slaves could not be killed. He couldn't be killed because he laid hold on life, elemental life, with such an abiding enthusiasm that the only way you can destroy him was to destroy life. It taught him how to laugh. Now I want you to understand that. Not how to be a fool. Now how to clown, but that it taught him how to live because he saw clearly that the world only opposes men, whether their hearts beyond turn ashes and vanish as the snows upon the sandy dessert path. And as he saw men take themselves so seriously, he laughed. It was the laughter of the vital man, the laughter of the strong man who struggles up out of defeat to live again. He saw the meaning of this little analogy. Some ants spend a lifetime building an ant mound, an ant heap. It happened that the ant heap was about complete but for one spot, and one ant was coming up bringing the necessary grain of sand for that little incomplete spot. As he deposited it he lifted himself upon his haunches and said, "My, my, my! My ant hill that I have built, my world, my need." And the wind began stirring and carried the ant to destruction, but the ant mound remained. That is what the people of our past saw. And when you see that release with all your mind, it releases your tension and releases in you a vitality that gives you not only insight and courage, but power to achieve.

The second practical thing is in the sense of community, of oneness, this faith in life that is the people. The sort of thing that was true in the past and is not so true now. We are beginning to pick up the threads of it, but that ghost is holding us now and then—in our colleges and universities we see evidences of it. The way in which those people in the past saw—saw very clearly, that the fate of the least advantage, the fate of the least privileged was tied up fundamentally with the most privileged and the most advantaged.

I was having a discussion group and some young college students were talking about what we can do for the masses. It was a very interesting discussion and one boy said, "I don't know who the masses are because," he said, "My mother is a cook, my father drives for the city." There were about six other fellows who were sitting in the room and their mothers and fathers were doing the same things and the masses of the people do the work and he said, "We must be talking about ourselves." An idea that had never occurred to these boys who in the midst of their learning had forgotten that there is a primary relationship between the front and the back which could not be separated. The turtle may advance his front feet from beneath his shell, but he cannot move his body until he pulls up his back feet. The great battle cry of all of us who are privileged to get learning and all of the other advantages to the people who are part of the great mass of the underprivileged in America—your slogan—my slogan must be always, "Bring up the rear." And the day that we forget to bring up the rear there isn't any front. Now, that is what we learn from the past.

Now, there are one or two other things to be said about it. This means that of all the learning that we get, of all the every single idea that we get, must somehow work its way down into our minds until we see how that idea is related to the needs of the group of which we are a part. . . . Now let me make an illustration. What is the functional significance of education? What is it? I am not an educator and I don't know anything about the theories of education except what I have heard, but I know this, Whatever the theory is, the fact is that the functional significance of education in our democracy is to guarantee and perpetuate things as they are now. Where does that leave you and me? The need of education is to guarantee, perpetuate and establish order. That is true regardless to what is your strife, whether you were taught in the North or South, whether you are taught by Negroes or white people, regardless to where you are and what you do and under what conditions you will stay.

If you are staying in our democracy you are being fed only the education upon which democracy says it can perpetuate itself. Now, when we learn that it means that we come out into the world with the ideas, with social attitudes, with the particular philosophy of education that may be in vogue at the time, but with all the equipment that belongs to the people who stand in control of our system, but when we function we function as a minority, not as people who are in control of society and individuals. I have never in my life seen an educated Negro who was not discouraged unless I am looking at someone this morning. Because of the complications that arise between the skills, and particularly the social attitudes that we have and the place that we must fill when we go out in our communities and in our work. If you don't believe that this is true, examine the attitudes that many of our students take toward the masses of the people. What is the attitude taken toward them. You know what it is. We try to get as far away from them as we can. Try to have as little to do with them as possible and think of them as a great weight holding us down. If it were not for them, we could take wings and soar. Yes, we could. That does not come out of the past. That is not the voice of those saying, "We die, but you who live must do a harder thing than dying is." That comes out of the present, and if those of us who are privileged to think, those of us who are privileged to be students, those who are privileged to withdraw from activity four, five or six years and work at social objectives, if we are not able to see that while there is a lower class, I am of it; while there is a man in jail, I am not free.[11] If we do not see that, then it is better if we were never born. "We die, but you who live must do a harder thing, for you must think." You must relate everything you learn to the needs of the masses of which you are a part, and if that is not done, then of what use is it?

And then, finally, the third ghost has to do with confidence in God. I have often wondered and doubtless you have wondered too, why it was that my forebears and your forebears became Christians? I have often wondered about that—an unprecedented phenomena. Here were these people who took over and embraced the religion of the men and women and of the civilization primarily that had victimized them. I do [not] know the answer. I have two suggestions.

First, that they saw in the genius of religion of Jesus Christ, a messenger and a signal for the underprivileged and dispossessed that perhaps cannot be seen by people who stand in a position of power and control. And the second is, that as a result of a great creative, spiritual inspiration to go beyond themselves gratuitously for the redemption of the religion that had been disgraced in their midst. And that ghost comes to us from the past. Confidence in God. Faith in religion. It is rather possible now to be cynical about religion, rather possible to be at least agnostic or to pretend to be indifferent. It is a sign of intellect, maturity, I understand. I was talking with a freshman once, years ago, at the University of Rochester. He was delightful boy, and he was for a discussion on religion. If there was a lull, he would aim forth with some new-old question. I was reminded of the mother who prayed that she would die before her daughter discovered that her radical questions were old to her. Well, when we finished the boy asked if he might walk across the campus with me to my room. We began talking and, not to disappoint him, I talked about religion. He said my mother and father are A. M. E.'s and I asked, "Well, what about you," and he said, "Well, I am inclined to be a little atheistic" (Bless his little heart). He was about sixteen and had just finished his first course in Biology, had been reading about twelve years, and he was at that moment of complete darkness before the first finger of dawn appears at the East describing the color of the sunset. Well, you see, that is what I mean so that when you go back into your community, you have heard of this music, the organ, solos and orations as to procedure, and then you will go back home and you will be bored to death because your mother and father sent you to school and you don't want to hurt their feelings, and you will get up on Sunday morning and go to church, but you know there isn't anything for you. So you would like to be placed somewhere else. I don't think you would like to go home because your ideas of religion are not the same. They simply couldn't understand how wise you are, how you have changed, how much you understand about these things, you know. Well, don't be fooled and don't be a fool.

One of my high school teachers in the class of Geometry asked a very hard question one day, and I answered it. As soon as I finished, he said, "Howard Thurman, I want you to come by the desk" and I could hardly wait. I knew if I kept on going, someday I would be a great creative mathematician. And when I walked up to his desk, he looked at me a long time and then said, "I want you to learn this—you must always do your own thinking, but remember, wisdom was not born with you."

Now, that is what your father will tell you, if you crowd him, but he is going to have respect for you, but that is what he is thinking. So I am speaking for him, now.

There is something in the background of religion that we have distilled out of our experience that you had better get your hands on. Because there is nothing in the modern world, nothing that can speak to your deep material needs, my friend, that you will face; there is nothing that can do it; no philosophy that can do it. There is something out of the past, however, that will give you insight as to procedure in the present—not bound to it, but there is a strength and a vitality there that you will need.

The ghost then, is a confidence of God that belongs very essentially to the hearts and minds of the people. Without that, you would not have peace. I have discovered one important thing, and I hope you will discover it before you die—there is only one kind of man who is safe in the world. One, and that is the man who can stand anything that can happen to him. Everybody else is under the hammer. When you can absorb, make room for your spirit, squeeze all of the violence out of all the things that meet you, it is then you are a master of life. And if you can't do that you will be a slave of life. Now, that is a confidence in God stated in simple language. That is the great ghost that drives you on. Drives me on, drives you on; and everything you touch, everything, if it is to have meaning, must be summarized in terms of some kind of absolute meaning—it must have some kind of guarantee of all the meanings of value to life, and if you don't have that, then you are but a jangling echo among the empty hills of the barren world. "We die, but you who live must do a harder thing than dying is, for you must think." Think, and the ghosts will drive you on.

Give me the courage to live
Really live not merely exist
Live dangerously, scorning the risks
Live honestly, daring the truth,
particularly the truth of myself
Live relentlessly, everything
changing, everything growing,
everything adapting
Enduring the pain of change as
though it were the pain of birth
Give me the courage to live
Give me the strength to be free
And endure the burden of freedom
and the loneliness of those without chains
Let me not be trapped by success
Nor by failure or pleasure or grief
Nor by malice or praise or remorse
Give me the courage to go on facing all that waits
Go eagerly, joyously on and seeing my way as I go
Without anger, or fear, or regret
Taking whatever life gives
Spending myself to the fullest
Head high, spirit winged.

Till the shadows draw close
Then evening with darkness shuts down
Naked and blind
And I go out alone as I came
Even then, Oh gracious God, hear my prayer
Give me the courage to live[10]

"We die, but you who live must do a harder thing than dying is, for you must think and ghosts will drive you on."

The Bulletin: *Tennessee Agricultural and Industrial State College*, 26, no. 9 (June 1938): 1, 4–7.

1. "A. C. Powell Jr., Howard W. Thurman to Be Heard by 165 A-I Seniors," *Pittsburgh Courier*, 24 May 1938.

2. See "The Integration of the Ethical, Social, and Educational Program," printed in the current volume.

3. Thurman had used this text in his unpublished eulogy for Juliette Derricotte in 1931. The verse is from "The Boy in Armor" by poet, novelist, and historian Hermann Hagedorn (1882–1964); see Hagedorn's *Ladders through the Blue: A Book of Lyrics* (Garden City, N.Y.:

Doubleday, Page, 1925), 59–61. "The Boy in Armor" is an antiwar poem, spoken by a dead soldier.

4. Olive Schreiner, *From Man to Man; or Perhaps Only . . .* (New York: Harper, 1927), 158; reprinted in HT, ed., *A Track to the Water's Edge*, 153.

5. The French sculptor Auguste Rodin (1840–1917) made his first version of *The Thinker* in the 1880s, and made a number of larger versions in the early twentieth century.

6. See the use of the same anecdote in "'Relaxation' and Race Conflict," printed in volume 1.

7. Alcorn Agricultural and Mechanical College, now Alcorn State University, in Claiborne County, Mississippi, was founded in 1871 on the site of Oakland College, a white Presbyterian college that closed shortly after the Civil War. Several antebellum buildings from Oakland College became part of the Alcorn campus, of which the most notable is the stately Greek Revival–style Oakland Memorial Chapel, completed in 1851. The slave artisans who built the Oakland Memorial Chapel, Thurman is arguing, could not have imagined that within a generation it would be used to educate freed slaves.

8. Thurman misquotes Tennyson, "In Memoriam," stanza 54, "That nothing walks with aimless feet."

9. From Eugene V. Debs, "Social Reform," in *Labor and Freedom: The Voice and Pen of Eugene V. Debs*, ed. Phil Wagner (St. Louis: Wagner, 1916), 89.

10. Margaret Stanton, "A Prayer," included in one of Thurman's poetry scrapbooks, HTPP: Blue Poetry Notebook.

From Clarence J. Gresham

16 June 1938
Atlanta, Ga.

After Morehouse president Samuel Archer announced his retirement in 1937, Thurman received considerable correspondence from friends, colleagues, and even the retiring president himself, apprizing him of the status of the search, soliciting his opinions, and in some instances trying to persuade him to make himself available for the position. Here Clarence Gresham,[1] a fellow Morehouse alum and longtime friend, writes a gossipy letter to Thurman speculating on the succession.

626 Beckwith St.
Atlanta, Ga.

Dear Howard,

Your letter came and I was glad to hear that all are well and that you are to be on leave next year. I hope you will have a chance to get plenty of rest.

The World[2] carried Watson's[3] picture & a statement of the fact that you were to be away & he would fill your place. I wish for him success in his work there next fall.

Dr. E. R. Carter[4] was telling me this week that the Trustees of Morehouse are to select a new president this summer. Mr. Archer has consented to be president emeritus. Mrs. Archer asked to be permitted to live in the dean's home, the one Hubert[5] now has. The Board hasn't acted on that as yet. I saw a letter from Geo. Cohen of Washington suggesting Jim Adams'[6] name. I was told sometime back that Albert Dent[7] was looking forward to that job. Well! I hope enough of Morehouse {men} who have influence will see to it that Morehouse gets some one who knows about educating Negroes. And I hope the Board will not make the mistake of selecting Hubert or any body else of his type. Morehouse is too fine a school to be left to die. Hubert and Brazael[8] have done enough harm already. Several of the students have been by and told me how unpopular Brazael and Williams are and he said nobody has any confidence in Hubert.

What would be fine, and I mentioned it to Rev. Carter, if you could spend the year here, instead of going to Rochester. Of course Miss Read & Mr. Hubert would die.[9]

I am taking my vacation in August and hope to motor to New York City. Shall see you in Washington when I pass thru, if you are home.

Love to family.

Sincerely,

[*signed*] C. Gresham

ALS. HTC-MBU: Box 8.

1. Clarence James Gresham, who graduated from Morehouse in 1923, was the pastor of Ebenezer Baptist Church of Athens, Georgia. For additional information about Gresham, see the biographical footnote in volume 1.

2. "Lucius Jones, "Thurman's Sub: Atlantan Fills Thurman's Post This September," *Atlanta Daily World*," 15 June 1938.

3. Melvin Watson.

4. Edward Randolph Carter (1858–1944) finished in the first graduating class of Atlanta Baptist Seminary (now Morehouse College) in 1884. He served as the pastor of Friendship Baptist Church in Atlanta from 1882 to 1944. Under his leadership Friendship established a home for senior citizens, which bore his name. Carter was also instrumental in establishing Spelman College, and in 1894 he wrote *The Black Side*, a book about the contributions and accomplishments of black Atlantans.

5. Charles Dubois Hubert (ca. 1890–1944) served as acting president of Morehouse College from 1937 to 1940. He earned his bachelor of divinity degree at the Rochester Theological Seminary after completing his studies at Atlanta Baptist Seminary in 1909. In 1914 John Hope brought Hubert back to Morehouse as a professor of religion, paying him a higher salary than Hope himself earned. In his autobiography Thurman called Hubert "a solid, pervasive influence on the life of all the [Morehouse] college men of my generation" (*WHAH*, 46). See also Edward Allen Jones, *A Candle in the Dark; A History of Morehouse College* (Valley Forge, Pa.: Judson, 1967).

6. James B. Adams was a member of the Morehouse College and Atlanta University Boards of Trustees from 1933 to 1936.

7. Albert W. Dent (1904–84), a 1926 graduate of Morehouse, was superintendent of Flint-Goodridge Hospital at Dillard University from 1935 to 1941, when he was appointed president of Dillard, serving in that capacity until 1969.

8. Brailsford Reese Brazeal (1903–81), a Dublin, Georgia, native, graduated with honors from Morehouse in 1927. He was hired as an economics instructor at Morehouse soon after he graduated. Later he was appointed professor of economics and head of the Department of Economics and Business Administration. In 1941 Benjamin Mays, president of Morehouse, appointed Brazeal the college's first dean of academics, assigned to raise the academic standards of the institution. Brazeal earned his doctoral degree in economics from Columbia University. He is the author of *The Brotherhood of the Sleeping Car Porters, Its Origin and Development* (New York: Harper, 1946).

9. Gresham is referring to the strained relationship between Thurman and Florence Read, president of Spelman College, dating back to his tenure at that institution (1929–32). Read wielded considerable power as the treasurer of Morehouse College during the Archer and Hubert administrations; no purchase at Morehouse could be made without her approval. See Jones, *Candle in the Dark*, 129–30.

To Kendall Weisiger

21 June 1938
Washington, D.C.

Writing to Morehouse trustee Kendall Weisiger,[1] *Thurman outlines in detail the five ideal attributes of a new president. Thurman asserts that the institution's most defining value of "self-respect" must not be lost amid its current financial crisis.*

My dear Mr. Weisiger:

I am taking this occasion to write you as an alumnus of Morehouse College. I have been informed that Mr. Archer has been made president emeritus and that his successor is being sought.

I am writing to say that I hope the Trustees will take the time to select the best available man in the United States for this job. I do not presume to dictate to you, or to any other member of the Board, as to just who should be chosen. I have no candidate in behalf of whom I am writing. I trust that the Committee will bear in mind the following things:

1. The man should be well educated. That is, he should be a man who has not only thorough formal training, but one who has breadth of culture and refinement with perspective and masculinity; for Morehouse fundamentally is a men's college.
2. He should be a man with enough of youth in him to understand sympathetically the needs and the problems of youth, and to be able to plan a comprehensive program for the meeting of those needs.
3. The tradition favoring a layman as president should be given careful consideration. In my opinion the new president should be a religious man,

but I am not inclined to favor his being a preacher. The reasons for this are obvious.[2]

4. He should be a man of courage, integrity, and balance. These are very critical days in which we are living, and it takes an intellectual and moral and spiritual maturity to provide healthful leadership to young Negro men.
5. And finally, he should be a creative thinker in the matters which have to do with education and the development of youth.

In the past Morehouse has made a very important contribution to Negro education. It has always had limited resources, but its men have been free. The College is face to face now with the psychological handicap of feeling itself to be disadvantaged as contrasted with the economic security of the other institutions in the Affiliation.[3] This must be overcome. The total effect both on faculty and students is definitely demoralizing. Morehouse College is in danger of loosing its self-respect, the one thing that has made it an outstanding institution throughout the years. It is for this additional reason that I write you. It is my prayer that the accurate guidance of the living God will attend all of the deliberations of the Committee so that the choice of a man will be along the lines of the fulfillment of a definite purpose.

Sincerely,
[*signed*] Howard Thurman
Mr. Kendall Weisiger
Morehouse College
Atlanta, Georgia

TLS. HTC-MBU: Box 191.

1. Kendall Weisiger (1903–90), an official of Southern Bell and Telegraph Company in Atlanta, was a longtime member of the Morehouse College Board of Trustees. See Edward Allen Jones, *A Candle in the Dark*, 104.

2. Thurman is alluding to his views on institutionalized religion, particularly his objection to denominational influence on the educational programs of colleges and universities.

3. In 1929 Atlanta University and Morehouse and Spelman colleges agreed to a formal affiliation, creating the Atlanta University System.

"Kingdom of God"

26 June 1938
Northfield, Mass.

Thurman's address at the annual Northfield Conference[1] gives insights into his understanding of the "Kingdom of God," a key topic in debates within interwar liberal Protestantism.[2] Thurman defines the Kingdom of God as a commitment by an individual to become a living instrument of God. He provides a catalog of the world's horrors in the late 1930s, but while he encourages involvement with the world, he warns against reducing the Kingdom of God to the realization of "one particular thing" and argues that "only infinite energy is able to meet infinite need." As in many writings of the period, Thurman was deeply concerned about ways to develop inner spiritual resources to balance and address the era's external challenges.

Instead of the subject that is announced on the calendar of the Conference, I am preaching this morning about the Kingdom of God. In connection with what I have to say, I would like you to hold in your minds an excerpt of a letter written to Muriel Lester by Mahatma Gandhi:

> "Speak the truth without fear and without exaggeration, and see everyone whose work is relative to your purpose. You are on God's work so you need not fear men's scorn. If they listen to your requests and grant them, you will be satisfied. If they reject them, then you must make their rejection your strength."[3]

As to text, I am using three words from the Lord's Prayer and the last half of a sentence of St. Augustine. "Thy kingdom come," these are the words from the Lord's Prayer. The sentence from Augustine is this: "Lord, make me a pure man,—but not yet." The part I am using for my text is, "but not yet."[4] The reconstructed text then reads: "Thy kingdom come, but not yet."

There are many attitudes that Religion may take towards Society. Religion may ignore the social order; it may act as if it lives in a vacuum. It may withdraw from society, seeking refuge and redemption in flight. Or, it may acknowledge the presence of society but refuse to be touched by it. It may be in itself a striking interpretation of those words,—"Be ye in the world but not of the world." It may live in the midst of society, if it has to, but it may steadily refuse to be contaminated by society. It may assume that society in all of its ramifications is not a concern to it. Or, again, it may look upon some particular diseased spot in society and say that this is a goal to salvation and, therefore, it may become a special pleader for some particular kind of reform and, on the basis of this agitation, it may seek to bring in a new order; it may seek to fulfill the demand of the Kingdom of God.

That is always the problem of reformation: To put all of one's emphasis upon one particular thing and when that thing is achieved and the Kingdom of God has not come, then the reformer sits in the twilight of his idols or may decide that some particular thing, some single aspect of life is the raw material out of which the goodness and the fullness of experience can be realized. Thus it will be seen that the good and the evil in life will be worked through and upon until the evil disappears more and more and the good increases, finally to displace all flaws and error. This seems to me to be at least a part of the hope and aspiration of those who pray "Thy kingdom come."

When we examine these words of Jesus, one of the first things that strikes our attention is the fact that Jesus said that we must pray, "Thy kingdom come," with emphasis on the word "thy." The use of the word "thy" there points out the fact that there was present in Jesus' mind a realization that there are other kingdoms in the world, so that he instructs us to be very definitive in our requests, very discriminating in our requests so that out of the many kingdoms of the world, we may pray for a particular kingdom—"Thy kingdom come." There are many kingdoms competing for the loyalty of men, many kingdoms that have established squatters' rights in the lives and in the minds of men. These kingdoms move sometimes with great rapidity until at last they seem to dominate us completely so that always when we pray "Thy kingdom come" there is floating through the hallways of our spirits the piercing echo that arises from other kingdoms within us "but not yet." Always as we see the Christian pray "Thy kingdom come" we see one who also is conscious of some part of him that has not yielded to the rule of God; conscious of the fact that there is some part of him that insists upon saying,—"but not yet, Lord, not yet."

When the prayer of this prayer looks at the world without blinkers and he sees how hard life is in many ways, his first great temptation is to stop with indignation and to cry out with disgust as to the terribleness of things; the temptation to stop there. When we read in the papers that thousands and thousands of defenseless men, women, and children—particularly women and children—are dying because of pellets of destruction that drop from engines of warfare flying through the breezes in Europe and China[5] and Peshawar[6] we read about the fate of the share-croppers in Mississippi and Arkansas,[7] it is terrible—horrible. What a nightmare life must be for those who live always on the threshold of some thing of terror; but the temptation is to stop with our being outraged, the depths of our minds being stirred but, if we are not careful, we will discover that in our outcry and in our anxious indignation we have merely sublimated our impulses to help—hence it is less and less likely that we shall go beyond outrage and beyond crying out loud.

It is like a young tree that makes the mistake of pouring all its life into the first bloom of Spring—all of its life goes into the blossoms and then when the fruit time comes it has no strength. It is like two young apple trees that shrivelled up one spring. They died from too much blossoming!

And then the Christian protects himself by seeking sometimes to reduce the exposure to pain; to reduce his exposure to the horrible side of life by keeping himself from direct contact with it. It is all right to read about it. It is all right to hear some one who has come from the place where crosses break in the streets. It is all right to listen to him; but no one likes to be exposed to terror, to the faults and the facts of the ugliness of life. It is perfectly natural that men should shrink from allowing themselves to be exposed to the continuous and persistent pull of misery and squalor and pain. Perfectly! But from a conscience deep within us, from a commitment which we have, and sometimes stumblingly and sometimes plainly, and here a little and there a little, we seek—each in his own way and to the limit of his strength—to make it possible for others to go to heal,—to give the cup of water to parched lips. We send others to administer in a primary fashion to need, and this is good and this is right. It is the soul of much that has made this world a good place in which to live. But always I must be careful lest I become merely aware of the world and its need without being affected by the needs of the world.

The Christian is dedicated to God's kingdom. He must bring his methods as well as his heart under God's scrutiny. When he carries out the command of the gospel, in his anxiety to help he is often tempted to use artificial and ineffective methods. He neglects to bring the methods that he seeks to use to redeem the world under the scrutiny of God. He neglects to make of the methods that he seeks to use the same kind of absolute demands to which his heart is trued and to which his own dedication is given. He is sure of his commitment. He desires to give his life to God; his heart to God; and to say, "Here I am Lord, use me," but often he neglects to bring with him the methods that he is going to use in order to make the desire of the heart a fact in experience.

Therefore, the heart of what I have to say is this: When we pray "Thy kingdom come" it means that we are asking that our hearts and lives be used for God's kingdom. Therefore, it is imperative that we who pray the prayer become channels—literally channels—through which the knowledge, the courageousness, the power, the love, the endurance needful to meet the infinite needs of the world may flow. For only infinite energy is able to meet infinite need, and we who pray this prayer become channels through which God's life of healing and redemption may flow. We must search more and more creatively how to devise methods by which good may supplant evil, by which the hearts of men may be redeemed, and by which the world in which those hearts must function may be redeemed.

More and more then the demand of God lays hold not only upon my heart, but it lays hold upon my mind, upon my body, upon my dreams, upon my hopes, upon my aspirations. It lays hold upon the remotest detail of my life and my character, and it will not rest in me until all of me can pray "Thy," "Thy kingdom come," and the last echo in my spirit that says, "Not yet Lord, there are some things I would do; there are some things I must do, wait a little while. I may give a part of me, but I cannot give all of me now," has gone. When we really pray that prayer it will mean that the last echo which says "not yet" will fade away and we shall present ourselves in the world as the living instruments of God by which and through which He seeks to bring His kingdom in the world so that wherever we are there the Kingdom of God is at hand. But, if that is not our consummate desire as we pray, the prayer is but an act of the grossest, basest sacrilege.

> "Life does not grow more simple with the passing years, but its deeper needs are unchanging. The secret of peace is not to be sought at the end of the road, but in the spirit in which we journey. It is to be sought in the consciousness of the sustaining love of God who is committed to a real participation in all our strife; who does not set us free from the possibility of pain and tears, but who feels the hurt of our wounds, the salt bitterness of our sorrow; who spends Himself, not only with us, but for us, and in the travail of redemptive passion anticipates the victories of the spirit. And, finally, whatever pilgrimage we under take must be undertaken, in spite of the interior loneliness of all great spiritual processes, in the comradeship of our kind and all well-being must always be our goal. We are never to forget that we are so tied up in one bundle that peace and reconciliations in which others are not involved are quite impossible. The note of service must be deepened and in our care for those who lie wounded and broken along the road we shall forget our own wounds and our own weariness. So conceived, so reenforced, life is never impossible, but does indeed become, so these books and leaders teach us, an adventure whose greatness is its own justification and whose difficulties may become for the faithful and discerning but stairs to radiant and triumphant regions."[8]

"Thy kingdom come, but not yet."

1. Founded by the prominent evangelist Dwight L. Moody (1837–1899) in 1886.

2. A stenographic transcription of this sermon was made at the time it was delivered. Thurman received a copy in April 1939. From Raina Kurtz, 19 April 1939, HTC-MBU: Box 11.

3. Muriel Lester, *My Host the Hindu* (London: Williams & Norgate, 1931), 15.

4. Augustine, *Confessions*, 8.7. This is usually translated, "Grant me chastity and continence, but not yet."

5. During the Spanish Civil War the Nazis employed aerial bombardment on a large scale, most famously in the raid on Guernica on 26 April 1937. In their war against China, which started after the Marco Polo Bridge incident on 7 July 1937, the Japanese regularly used aerial bombardment against military and civilian targets.

6. There was frequent tension in the North-West Frontier region of India (now in Pakistan) between British forces and local Muslim tribal groups, and to quell the insurgents the

British in the 1930s made use of aerial bombardments. A few months before Thurman visited Peshawar in February 1936 the Royal Air Force (RAF) bombed some local tribes, and the *New York Times* reported the day before Thurman's talk of subsequent RAF bombings in Waziristan in the vicinity of Peshawar ("British Bare Plot for Afghan Coup," *New York Times*, 25 June 1938).

7. Beyond the general hardship of southern sharecroppers, Thurman is referring to the well-publicized confrontations of the Southern Tenant Farmers' Union with authorities in Arkansas and Mississippi in the late 1930s.

8. This is the concluding paragraph of Gaius Glenn Atkins, *Pilgrims of the Lonely Road* (New York: Revell, 1913), 338–39. Thurman modified the first part of the third sentence from the original: "It is to be sought in the consciousness of the sustaining love of a God who is committed, by the very nature of His Godhead, to a real participation in all our strife; who does not release us from the battle, but who shares the fight. . . ."

To Herbert King

7 July 1938
Washington, D.C.

This short letter to Thurman's good friend Herbert King conveys his glee at boxer Joe Louis's quick knockout of Max Schmeling at Yankee Stadium, a contest that had been freighted with political overtones of a fight against Nazism and its theories of racial superiority. By 1938 Louis was probably the best-known African American overseas; already in 1936 Thurman noted how much interest there was among Indians about Louis, and the prevalence of Negro stereotypes in common depictions of the boxer.[1]

Louis and Thurman died within days of each other in April 1981. Vernon Jordan observed shortly after their deaths that both men had overcome the challenges of being "born into the deepest poverty of the Black South" and that "each in his own way stood for an entire body of Black achievement, as inspiration to countless Black people who drew sustenance from the deeds of one and the message of the other."[2]

My dear Mr. King:

Just a hurried note to say that the letter which you sent is an historical document. It advised me of the passing of one more upward thrust of white Nordic Arian supremacy at the hands of an humble son of the soil whose name is Joe Louis.[3]

I shall be away in the South most of the month of July, but sometime in early August I would like to come up to spend a couple of days doing nothing but visiting with you and taking in a show or two. I have a lot of talk for you and I know you have a lot of talk for me. I got a good letter from Herb[4] mailed aboard ship.

Will see you soon.
Sincerely,
[*signed*] Howard Thurman
Mr. William H. King
2816 Eighth Avenue
New York, New York

TLS. HTC-MBU: Box 10.

1. See "What We May Learn From India," Fluker and Tumber, *A Strange Freedom*, 209.

2. Vernon Jordan, "Our Fallen Heroes: Thurman and Louis," *Los Angeles Sentinel*, 30 April 1981.

3. The German boxer Max Schmeling (1905–2005) upset heavyweight contender Joe Louis (1914–81) at Yankee Stadium on 19 June 1936, knocking him out in twelve rounds, Louis's only knockout defeat during his prime. Louis was the reigning heavyweight champion at the time of their rematch on 22 June 1938, also at Yankee Stadium, and he won in the first round at 2:04, having knocked down Schmeling three times.

4. Reference unknown.

From Samuel H. Archer

19 July 1938
Atlanta, Ga.

Samuel Archer informs Thurman about the arrangements for his impending retirement, talks about its financial strains, and concludes with a thinly veiled attempt to recruit him for the position of president.

Dear Mr. Thurman:

I must first thank you for the copy of the address which you sent me. From my point of view not a word was said amiss.

Under separate cover I am returning the detective stories which you sent me. The books were well written. The plots so interesting that a second reading was worthwhile.[1]

Mr. Weisiger came to see me a few days ago bringing your letter with him. I, of course, heard it for the "first" time as he read and praised the letter and your clear and complete blue print of the needed man.[2] If some man {a minister} has the qualifications which you named, Mr. Weisiger would not object to a <u>minister.</u>

On October first I go into what is called retirement. The college has done all that it could do to supply retirement allowance. A form was given me so that additional money will be applied for from the Ministers and Missionary Benefit Board of the Northern Baptist Convention.[3] I have every reason to believe that the sum asked for will be granted.

Mr. Weisiger feels that some man should be taken from his job and take up the work here at once. On the other hand I have a feeling that Mr. Hubert should serve for at least one more year. I say this without losing sight of the fact that we are to raise a large sum of money. Some of the burden of raising money should be assumed by our trustees and I would like to see them take an active interest in planning the financial campaign. My other reasons I shall not mention.

I heard Mrs. Thurman with much interest and profit Monday evening but did not get an opportunity to contribute to the scholarship fund.[4] There may not be much money in the Archer till but we are never too poor to give to a good cause.

The chief thing that I have in mind is left unsaid with reference to the next president of Morehouse. You might not agree with me. I need your cooperation.
Sincerely Yours,
[*signed*] S. H. Archer

TLS. HTC-MBU: Box 1.

1. Thurman was an inveterate reader of detective stories, though he rarely if ever wrote about them. This was noted by his friend Harold B. "Pete" Ingalls in a 1941 article: "He has never been known to travel without two things—a volume of detective stories and a book of poems. He is an authority on both types of literature, although he keeps the former as completely absent from his conversation as he most richly interjects the latter into sermons and discussions." Harold B. Ingalls, "Howard Thurman: Being a Few Highlights of an Interesting Life," *Intercollegian,* April 1941, 137–38.

2. See To Kendall Weisiger, 21 June 1938, printed in the current volume.

3. The Ministers and Missionaries Benefit Board of the Northern Baptist Convention was founded in 1913 to meet medical, insurance, and pension needs of ordained and lay church workers. See "American Baptist: A Brief History," http://www.abc-usa.org/resources/history.pdf.

4. The Juliette Derricotte Scholarship Fund.

To Roy Norris

23 July 1938
Washington, D.C.

Thurman responds to a prospective student who is undecided about whether he should attend Howard or Yale. While acknowledging that Yale would offer more educational resources and better facilities, at Howard he would not be lacking in inspiration nor would he be subject to "questions of race."

My dear Norris:[1]

When your letter came I was in Georgia and Florida and I have just returned to the office today.

I am herewith trying to do an impossible thing, namely, answer your letter. I am writing you very confidentially, saying to you what I would say to myself if I were facing the same problem. In the first place, I cannot answer the question for you. I can only give you advice. There are two or three things which you ought to take into consideration, first, you ought to see your way clear to get most of the $160 that you need before getting out on the limb at Yale. It is quite all right to have remunerative employment, but to be up there without money in a rigorous climate, cutting down on diet and the like, is decidedly bad. I do not wish to frighten you but almost every other year some Negro student dies from tuberculosis contracted under the circumstances I am describing.

In the second place, you will get some things at Yale which you cannot get here. We may just as well be honest about it. There is a better theological library immediately available to you, larger faculty, larger contacts with more able students who will give to your own mind the exercise and the discipline that it needs. Again, I doubt whether there is as much inspiration for you, a Negro, at Yale, as there is at Howard. Then, inasmuch as all of the academic contacts you have had have been in a Negro college it may be to your advantage to spend some time in a white institution. You will get at Howard University a good course, restricted because of our facilities, but comprehensive, and you will not have to be bothered with the questions of race and the like.

I have not answered your questions and this is not a good letter, but in a very unorganized way I have tried to point out some of the possibilities.

With reference to your helping me in connection with the Chapel, that could not become effective until the year after next now anyway, and I would not let it enter into my decision. I had not heard about the World Student Conference[2] for next year in Europe.

Let me know what you decide because I am interested. If we could talk there are many things that I would say to you, but I do not wish to be mistaken and therefore I will not write them.

Sincerely yours,
[*signed*] Howard Thurman

TLS. HTC-MBU: Box 14.

1. Roy Norris (?–1985) attended Yale Divinity School before contracting tuberculosis in the early 1940s. (Thurman's worries were prescient.) After regaining his health, he earned his PhD at Columbia Divinity School. Norris went on to work for the National Council of Christians and Jews and the Urban League.

2. Thurman is probably referring to the World Conference of Christian Youth, held in Amsterdam from 26 July to 3 August 1939, with approximately 1,500 delegates in attendance.

To Samuel H. Archer

26 July 1938
Washington, D.C.

While Thurman offers effusive praise to Archer for accomplishments in his decades at Morehouse, he rejects Archer's not-so-subtle hints about recruiting him as his replacement, saying he is not interested in the presidency, while holding out the possibility that he might, after prayer and reflection, change his mind.

My dear President Archer:

I am sending this letter first of all to thank you for the books which you returned. If you would like to have another set I would be very happy to send them to you.

A letter from Brezeal[1] says that he did not have room to print excerpts from the address that I gave, and it is well. He also asked for a rather complete statement of my itinerary for next winter, which thing I shall send to him sometime in the near future.

I am deeply sobered by the thought of your retirement and yet I know that it is the best possible thing for your own wellbeing. I hope that your income will be supplemented by a grant from the Benefit Board of the Convention and that you will have all that you need to make life comfortable and complete for yourself and family. It is my deep desire also that you be able to continue to live on the campus so that through the years the richness of your experience and like will be available to the generations of students and teachers that will be privileged to know you. You have done a full day's work. Morehouse College owes more to your genius, your patience and ability, than to any person who has been connected with it.[2] As I have said so many times to other people about you, you are one person who fits the description that William James uses about Emerson, you are a "once born soul."[3] I do not think that you would knowingly do harm to any living person. It is difficult for me to put into words my own deep regard for your life and character.

In my informal reply to Mr. Weisiger's letter, I too suggested that it would be very difficult and perhaps unwise to select a man who would be ready to begin work when the College opened in the fall. It would be a much wiser procedure to select the person and give him time to prepare himself psychologically and in other ways for the tremendous responsibility involved in the presidency of Morehouse. He would need time for this. What you say about the Trustees taking the responsibility for raising money is of primary importance. What Morehouse needs is a man who will work internally in the life of the College, leaving the Trustees with the major responsibility for raising the needed funds. This is as it should be.

This sentence in your letter is very disturbing: "The chief thing that I have in mind is left unsaid with reference to the next president of Morehouse. You might not agree with me. I need your cooperation." I wish you would say quite frankly what you have in mind. Judging from the remark plus one other that you made when we talked two weeks ago, I presume that what you have to say is with reference to me. I think you know me well enough to know that my own life is full with the things to which I am committed in my commitment to religion. I am extremely happy in doing what I am doing now. Where I work is not of primary importance, so long as I am doing the job that I feel I can best do. I have no ambition to become the president of Morehouse College. This, I think, you can take from me. I know many of the problems of Morehouse. I am confident that I know what it needs now. I have thought long and hard on ways by which these needs can be met because I love the College and I feel the weight of its opportunity.

If you want me to be your successor I would consider it a rare and holy honor. But I am not at all sure that such a thing would be in keeping with the will of God, for my own life. To me that fact is of primary importance. I am writing you frankly as I feel. I know there are many people whose word would have great weight who would not be interested in having a man with my kind of ideas at the head of the College. That fact would disturb me if I were ambitious for the place. I felt free to write Mr. Weisiger[4] as I did because I had no interest in trying to get the job for myself. If the opportunity is presented to me I would make it a matter of careful meditation, analysis, and prayer, and if, at the end of a period of such reflection I felt that it was The Thing for me to do, I would say yes. If, at the end I felt that it was not the thing I would say no. It would be a source of deep humiliation to me if anyone thought that my interest in the College and my activities with reference to it during the past months have been dominated by a kind of personal ambition. You will pardon my burdening you by writing so fully and at such length, but I wanted you to know how I feel, and I wish that you would express yourself to me in the same frank manner.

I hope that you will continue improving and that at your leisure I will hear from you.

Sincerely yours,
[*signed*] Howard Thurman

TLS. HTC-MBU: Box 1.

1. Brailsford Brazeal.

2. As Thurman recalls in his autobiography, "The men of the college honored and liked President Hope. They revered and loved Dean Archer." *WHAH*, 38.

3. For William James "once-born souls" were exemplars of the "religion of healthy-mindedness." Lectures 4 and 5, *The Varieties of Religious Experience* (London: Longmans, Green, 1902), 78–123.

4. To Kendall Weisiger, 21 June 1938, printed in the current volume.

To Melvin Watson
26 July 1938
Washington, D.C.

In this letter Thurman commends his friend Melvin Watson for choosing to join the faculty of Dillard University in New Orleans, even though it means he will not be able to fill in for Thurman while he is on sabbatical from Howard. In addition to assessing the academic environment Watson will find at Dillard, Thurman advises him to have plenty of good reading material, join a book club, and find himself "an intelligent, keen young lady" for companionship.

My dear Dean Watson:

You have already received my telegram advising your release from Howard University. We were all very loath to give you up because we had looked forward to your being here and to your work with us. We are planning to divide the work between two of our more recent graduates, giving to them an opportunity which ought to mean a great deal.

I think that you are making a very wise choice in going to Dillard. In the first place, President Nelson is a very good man with whom to work. He has a deep interest in religion and in problems of personnel, and will give you every possible encouragement. In the second place, Dillard has no traditions because it is a new institution. You have a chance to do significant experimentation in the field of personnel adjustment and in creative religious experiences for undergraduates. Again, your faculty are comparatively young and very well prepared for the most part. They will provide constant incentive and stimulation to you to bring to your tasks each day the cream of your mind and spirit.

Of course, the place is isolated. You will find great difficulty in keeping the springs of your life flowing so that one of your first jobs must be to seek new ways for recreating your own mind through wider and deeper reading, and by taking advantage of certain cultural things that you have not been particularly concerned about up to this time. If I may be bold enough to suggest certain things: First, you ought to subscribe to a very liberal list of good magazines, not all of them serious. Your list should include a magazine like "The New Yorker," for instance. Second, you ought to be in one good book club. Third, you ought to have a good radio with electric phonographic section and little by little you ought to begin building up a library of fine canned music. Fourth, you should look the city of New Orleans over very carefully, beginning at Dillard and moving out, to find you an intelligent, keen young lady who is not a student for the purpose of providing you with really stimulating feminine companionship. You do not need to waste your time with a child, or with someone who will consider you a good grab off the tree. Remember, you are a good prospect, you are unmarried and you have never been married. You are young, you have a good job and a car. What more does the heart of the climber wish? I think that if you do some of these things and several others that you might think of, you will be on your way more definitely than ever before to fulfill your own destiny.

Sue wants to know if you can drive up here this weekend and take her to New Rochelle, New York, where she is having her show.[1] She is due there Monday night, August 1st. It would mean being out from summer school from Saturday to Tuesday. Let her know at once, please.

When you come up I shall see you to talk.

Sincerely yours,
[*signed*] Howard Thurman
Dean of the Chapel
Dean Melvin H. Watson
Shaw University
Raleigh, North Carolina

TLS. HTC-MBU: Box 21.

1. One of Sue Bailey Thurman's lecture demonstrations of the arts and music of India, staged to raise money for the Juliette Derricotte Scholarship Fund.

To Russell C. Barbour

28 July 1938
Washington, D.C.

The Sixth Baptist World Congress, hailed as one of the greatest Baptist events of the period, was scheduled to occur in Atlanta, Georgia, during the summer of 1939. More than sixty thousand white and black Baptists from around the world attended the gathering. A year before the event, Thurman shares the skepticism of the National Baptist Voice *editor Russell C. Barbour*[1] *concerning the availability of adequate accommodations for black delegates to the congress in the Jim Crow South.*

My dear Russell:

I am sending you a copy of the address that I gave in Milwaukee before the Northern Baptist Convention,[2] this in accordance with my promise.[3]

I like very much the things that you are permitting to {be} said about the World's Baptist Alliance in Atlanta.[4] I do not believe that it will be possible for satisfactory arrangements to be made for colored people who are attending the convention. Through your office I wish you would circularize a large number of Negro ministers to see what their particular attitude is towards this question. I think this would be very wise if you can get in writing beforehand the precise nature of the arrangements provided by the local committee. The Idea is to submit on to whom you send a circular letter asking for their reaction. Then these reactions should be compiled and submitted to the Executive Committee of the World's Baptist Alliance. I realize that it may not be possible for you to do this without creating an embarrassing situation for yourself. You are the best judge.

I am so involved here that it is not possible for me to get away to join you in a slow motor trip through Texas, but if you can arrange for us to bunk together at St. Louis I think it is possible for me to come by there for several days on my way to Los Angeles. The last part of September I am opening the Los Angeles Sunday Evening Club series,[5] and from their I go up to the Northwest. Let me get some word on this as soon as possible.

Sue sends greetings to you and family.

Sincerely yours,
[*signed*] Howard Thurman
Enclosure
Reverend Russell C. Barbour
National Baptist Voice[6]
Nashville, Tennessee

TLS. HTC-MBU: Box 2.

1. Russell C. Barbour (1897–1944) earned a BA from Morehouse College, an MA in religion and philosophy from Colgate University, and a JD from Bishop College (1944). He became a civic leader in his hometown of Galveston, Texas, where he edited the *Colored American* newspaper and served as pastor of Macedonia Baptist Church (1921–29). In 1929 Barbour became pastor of the First Baptist Church in Nashville, Tennessee, and the following year he was elected editor of the *National Baptist Voice;* he retained both positions until his death.

2. The Northern Baptist Convention was established in Washington, D.C., in 1907, and one of its major purposes was to establish cooperation between several Baptist missionary societies. The organization's name was changed to American Baptist Convention in 1950, and in 1972 it became the American Baptist Churches in the USA.

3. "The Contributions of Baptist Church Schools to Negro Youth," published in the current volume.

4. The Baptist World Alliance (BWA) was formed in London in 1905 to foster cooperation among Baptists of all cultures, races, and nationalities. Members of the BWA meet every five years, and the organization's Sixth Baptist World Congress was being planned for Atlanta in July 1939.

5. Thurman spoke on 25 September 1938 at the First Congregational Church in Los Angeles under the auspices of the Los Angeles Sunday Evening Club, a devotional lecture series generally broadcast on radio and patterned after the Chicago Sunday Evening Club.

6. The *National Baptist Voice* is a publication of the National Baptist Convention, an organization of African American Baptists founded in 1895.

FROM SAMUEL H. ARCHER
3 AUGUST 1938
ATLANTA, GA.

In a continuation of their summer correspondence, Archer explains why he suggested Thurman's name to the trustees as his choice for the next president of Morehouse.

Dr. Howard Thurman,
Washington, D.C.
Dear Friend:

It was very cheering to receive your letter[1] with its good words for me and your willingness to consider any offer of the presidency of Morehouse College that may be presented to you.

I used the term any offer because the salary is not as large as it should be. The perquisites almost equal the salary.

On the basis of your letter I presented your name to Mr. Weisiger as my one and only choice for the presidency of Morehouse College.

Mr. Hubert is sincere when he says he does not want the presidency. His wife does not want him to be president of Morehouse. That settles the matter.

There are some fine things just around the corner for Morehouse in Mr. Hubert's field.

The Baptist of the northern section of Georgia will rally about Morehouse if our plans include a Theological school with some training for Christian workers.

Remember me kindly to Mrs. Thurman. I like her social grace and charms. But do not tell her I said it, if you think she objects.

Sincerely yours—
[*signed*] S. H. Archer

ALS. HTC-MBU: Box 1.

1. To Samuel H. Archer, 26 July 1938, printed in the current volume.

"THE CONTRIBUTION OF BAPTIST CHURCH SCHOOLS TO NEGRO YOUTH"
6 AUGUST 1938

This talk, delivered before in the annual meeting of the Northern Baptist Convention in Milwaukee at the end of May 1938, was the third address Thurman gave in 1938 on the subject of blacks and higher education.[1] It is related to his talk "The Integration of the Ethical, Social, and Educational Program" and his commencement address at Tennessee A & I and includes some of the same material. Thurman discusses how, historically, church schools were important for fighting illiteracy and teaching basic skills so blacks could read the Bible and come to understand the "genius" of Christianity and its promise of "redemption." Thurman also examines how the traditional role of Christian schools is changing, as southern states take over more of the responsibility for primary and secondary education for blacks and as the interest of Christian philanthropies in black education wanes. While he acknowledges that church schools will have to redefine their role, Thurman believes their independence and their institutional freedom will be of continuing importance.

I want you to think with me this afternoon about certain aspects of the contribution of Baptist church schools to Negro education. It only happens that the qualification "Baptists" is placed in this subject because the fundamental contribution of missionary education to Negro youth is essentially the same regardless to the particular denomination or affiliation. With the possible exception of the Quakers, the attitude of the American Protestant Church towards the freedmen and subsequently towards their posterity, has been more benevolent, benign, and missionary than an expression of simple brotherhood and kinship.

At the close of the Civil War there were two fundamental problems facing the freedmen. One was economic and social, while the other was largely psychological and spiritual. The masses of the Negro freedmen had lived within the rigid imitation of a slave economy and had developed no sense, therefore, of responsibility for the future. They had no need to be concerned about guaranteeing themselves economically against days of leanness and hunger. For because they were slaves it meant that the economic responsibility for their subsistence belonged to the master. The result of all this was that when slavery was abolished these people were released on the labor market to compete with individuals who themselves had developed more skills pointing towards economic survival because of the necessitous nature of their circumstances and experiences. The story of the scramble and the fight for economic survival is one of the most fascinating and heartbreaking in all the annals surrounding the life of the Negro in the world. But it is not our purpose to deal with it this afternoon.

The second problem was more difficult and more subtle. It has to do with a slave mentality that had become the guardian of the minds of these people through the long years of their enslavement. It is no accident that one of the interesting New Testament transactions[2] of the word "sona,"[3] which ordinarily means body, or slave. That is to say, a thing that eats, sleeps, breeds, dies, but has none of the more subtle and far-reaching significance ordinarily attached to personality. Men cannot be slaves for three hundred years in a system which ruthlessly eliminated all opponents to it without finally developing a way of looking out on a world that belongs essentially to the beaten and the chained. Because they lived in a world in which they were constantly despised, they began to despise themselves.

Christian education of necessity had to address itself to this need and to this demand, and whatever has been the nature of its contribution it is best revealed in this area. What then is the contribution of the church school to Negro education? In the first place, the first contribution was made to the freedmen in terms of bringing him to the Christian religion. I have never quite understood why the Negro freedman became a Christian unless it was due to the fact that he saw in the message of Jesus Christ something which was deeper and more profound than what he was taught about the meaning of that message. Let me illustrate what I mean by a personal experience.[4] Two years and a half ago, when we were beginning our Pilgrimage of Friendship to the students of India, Burma, and Ceylon, our schedule called for ten days in Colombo. On the second or third day I was invited to speak before the Law College of the University on "Civil Disabilities Under States Rights in the United States of America." At the end of the lecture there were questions, and then I was invited downstairs to have a cup of coffee in private with the President of the club. As soon as we had finished our coffee he said to me, "I had not planned to ask you a question like this, but after listening to you upstairs I am inclined to think that you are an intelligent man." And then his question was this: "What are you doing over here?" He said, "I know what the publicity says about your making a pilgrimage of friendship from the students of America to the students of India, Burma, and Ceylon, but that does not answer my question. What are you doing here." "This is what I mean," he said. "Slightly more than three hundred years ago your forefathers were brought from the West Coast of Africa as slaves in the holds of slave vessels owned and controlled by European Christians." In fact, said he, "the name of one of the slave ships was 'Jesus.' One of your great Christian hymn writers, John Newton, was a dealer in the slave traffic. You remember him. He wrote the hymn 'How Sweet the Name of Jesus Sounds to a Believer's Ear,' and published 'Glad Tydings.'" "You were sold," continued he, "in the new world to other people who were Christians. For three hundred years the sanction of religion was given to the system of slavery and Christian ministers, quoting the Apostle Paul and the Old Testament, gave moral and religious justification of its continuance. Slightly more than seventy years ago you were freed by a man who was not a member of any church, but a man who was the spearhead of certain social, economic, and political forces, the significance of which he himself scarcely understood. And since that time you have suffered in ways that defy any formula of expression at the hands of Christians in a Christian land." "And now," said he, "here you are over here talking to us as an interpreter of the Christian religion and I cannot understand it." "I do not wish to be rude to you, but I think you are a traitor to all the darker people of the earth and I wonder what you can say in defense of your position. You, an intelligent man." Now this experience points out what I mean.

The first contribution of the church school to Negroes was in terms of a dramatic and far-reaching effort to redeem their spirits in the name of Jesus Christ. And the most obvious approach to the redemption of their spirits was through the vehicle of learning, giving to their minds the simple skills and tools of learning so that they could read the Scriptures for themselves and walk in the way of life. It wasn't long, then, before the mind and heart of the ex-slave penetrated to the genius of the religion of Jesus and saw in it the redemption of the dispossed and the disinherited. Perhaps this is the reason that the Christian religion was seized upon with such amazing avidity.

The second contribution was in the nature of a secondary resultant from the emphasis upon the saving of the souls of the ex-slaves. I refer to the profound attack that a church school made on illiteracy. In the early days of Reconstruction, there was practically no free education. The people early recognized that the simple rudiments of education were necessary in order that the freedmen may be able to survive in their new relationships and at the same time to improve themselves and to themselves a sense of emotional security. As worthy as this ideal was, it was too low, for the pioneers in Negro education, those early consecrated men and women, wanted to give to the freedmen the type of education that they themselves had experienced and enjoyed. This is responsible for the early designation of the schools, academies, colleges and universities.

It is also responsible in part for the emphasis upon the classics. The unique thing about this education was not its attack on illiteracy, with the concomitant result heightened self-respect. It was not its emphasis upon the classics,—and it was this that many people condemned—but it was the fact that it was purposeful education. It had at its center an emphasis upon character and upon service. These early teachers had made many sacrifices. They had left the protection of their homes and their communities in the East, in the North. Many of them had refused opportunities for more profitable and perhaps more socially rewarding vocations; many of them in high devotion had turned their backs forever on the possibilities of marriage and the normal life of a home. Forsaking everything, they came to the South on a great moral adventure. There were some who came for the love of adventure; there were some who came because they loved a cause; there were some who came because they loved the Negro; and there were some who came because they wanted their lives to atone for the brutality and the ravages and the rape of slavery which their kind had heaped upon the black man. It was a goodly company and the schools they established were causes and commitments and purposes as well as institutions of learning.

The result was that the boys and girls and young men and young women who came under the influence were caught by the flame of their spirits and were sent into every section of the Southland dominated by a desire to serve their fellows. If I were to dramatize in a figure their message to the youth it was this:

However far ahead of his body a turtle may extend his two front feet, he cannot move his body until he brings up his hind legs. Their motto was "Bring up the rear! Bring up the rear! Bring up the rear!" Long before I heard of Eugene Debbs I knew the meaning of his famous trilogy: "While there is a lower class I am in it; while there is a criminal element I am of it; while there is a man in jail I am not free."[4] This then is the second great contribution of the church schools to Negro life.

The third contribution of church schools has to do with the present time. It is to provide a wise, intelligent, courageous, religious leadership for Negro life in the present tremulous times and for the extremely difficult days ahead. I shall ask you to bear with me while I point out the necessity for this emphasis in Negro education. During the last quarter of a century changes have taken place in Negro education. The needs have demanded adjustment in approaches and methodology at certain points. The southern states took over first the teaching of the rudiments of learning and made it a function of the state worked out in the free schools. Gradually the state has taken over almost all secondary education and latterly, through the stupendous development of land grant colleges, the state has occupied a large area of collegiate and technical training. In the very nature of the case, this has made for the secularization of education.

Again, due to the relaxation of interest in the profoundest welfare of Negroes, because their development has made it more and more difficult for the American white man to refuse to give to them the courtesies extended to equals, there has been a falling away of interest in Negro education on the part of American white Christians who are in large measure the controllers of the economic wealth of the country. As long as the reaction to the needs of Negroes were largely emotional and sentimental, funds were easier to secure. There is little of the obviously heroic that can be made as the basis of appeal for continual support of institutions like Shaw, Morehouse, Spelman and the like.

The second observation in this connection is that as Negroes themselves became a trifle more affluent and economically secure, the general feeling has been that they should take over in toto the support of their own education.[5] I may say in reply to this suggestion, just in passing, that Negroes as a group are poverty-stricken and there are fewer opportunities for them to earn a living available at this amount than at any time since the beginning of our century. This fact is true. The depression or recession and the increase in the population to the contrary, notwithstanding.

The third fact that belongs in this part of the picture has to do with the way in which in recent years philanthropy has been formally organized in foundation or trusts and funds, and churches feel less responsible for expressing their Christian testimony in terms of gifts that are within the limitations of their resources. The distinctive Christian influence in education has gradually and quietly receded into the background and the field has been left in large part to the state and to foundations. Teachers are no longer enlisted in an adventure that belongs peculiarly to these times, but are hired on the basis of salary and merely academic equipment their proficiencies.[6]

There are many other factors that enter into this situation that I do not have time to enumerate. It is true that what has been happening to Negro education has been happening to a large degree to education in general, and the emphasis that Negro colleges need at the moment is an emphasis needed by other colleges in our democracy. Wise and intelligent interest on the part of the church is the only thing that can give to normal, formal, education a religious emphasis that is not smug, unrealistic, but open, courageous, challenging. The church school, then, ought to be a school that stands in the field of education uniquely for character and the religious point of view. In order to do this its academic standards must be as high as the highest, its equipment must be first rate, its students must be carefully chosen, and with all of this it must be a place that provides the opportunity for young people to develop a thoughtful consecrated outlook on the world. From its walls must come young men and young women into our democracy who will place their trained minds and their lives at the disposal of the profoundest needs of our community life.

For Negroes this is most important. Our leadership has a far harder job, for it must be realistic, it must recognize that the Negro is an underprivileged, disinherited minority in American life, surrounded by a dominant controlling majority. I must face the tragedy and the demoralizing effects of segregation and discrimination within the church and within the social order. It must guide its youth though the experience of education that has its purpose filling their mind with ways of thinking about society that will dedicate them to social change, that will provide it its effectiveness, a better place for them. This is hard to do in state controlled institutions. It is apt not to be done in church controlled institutions. But the genius of the religion of Jesus, to which the church is officially dedicated, is the lever and dynamic available in the very assumptions upon which the church school is built.

At this moment then, in the year of our Lord, 1938, in keeping with the past contribution of our churches to Negro education, namely, the presenting of the message of Jesus and the teaching of skills of knowledge and the inspiring of the service motive, there is this present challenge to have a large share in the training of wise; intelligent, courageous, religious leadership for these tremulous times and for the terrible days ahead. As the accidental custodians of economic advantages and privileges, to do less than this is to profane and blaspheme the name "Christian," which is our calling and our commitment.

National Baptist Voice 22 (25) (6 August 1938): 4–5.

1. For the background to this lecture, see HT to Russell Barbour 28 July 1938, printed in this volume.

2. Thurman presumably meant *translations* here.

3. *Soma* (not *sona*) means body in ancient Greek, and is not commonly used to describe slaves, for which the standard term is *doulos.*

4. For an annotated version of this meeting, see "India Report," printed in the current volume.

5. This is the general theme of Carter G. Woodson, *The Mis-Education of the Negro* (1933; repr., Trenton, N.J.: Africa World, 1990), 26–32.

6. See James D. Anderson, *The Education of Blacks in the South, 1860–1935* (Chapel Hill: University of North Carolina Press, 1988), 238–78.

To Mordecai Wyatt Johnson

13 August 1938
Washington, D.C.

Howard president Mordecai Wyatt Johnson's refusal to provide university funds for Thurman to travel to Poughkeepsie to attend the World Youth Congress speaks to a growing estrangement between Johnson and his onetime protégé.

My dear President Johnson:

I am very sorry that you could not see your way clear to approve the request relative to the Second World Youth Congress.[1] I had gone into the matter very carefully and thoroughly, and it was my considered judgment that there ought to be representation there and that such representation would establish for Howard University some exceptionally fine contacts for the future. So sure was I in my conviction about this that I paid my own money, five dollars, as an advanced registration fee, which amount I shall not get back. I would spend my own money to go but I do not think that it is worthwhile to put any more of my personal money in trying to develop my work here.

My travel budget could have very easily absorbed the cost without working any hardship on the limited amount of money the University allocated for travel. I do not understand, therefore, how it could possibly affect the total budget of the University, inasmuch as the amount allocated for travel in my own budget has already been set up and passed upon. As the conference opens Monday, August 15th, I do not see that anything can be done about it. All of this I regret profoundly.

Sincerely yours,
[*signed*] Howard Thurman
Dean of the Chapel
President Mordecai W. Johnson
Howard University

TLS. HTC-MBU: Box 24.

1. 1 The Second World Youth Congress was held at Vassar College from 15 August to 24 August under the auspices of organizations dedicated to promoting international peace and cooperation. More than five hundred delegates from more than fifty countries attended.

FROM BENJAMIN E. MAYS
11 SEPTEMBER 1938
WASHINGTON, D.C.

Thurman and Mays are promoting each other for the presidency of Morehouse. Mays, writing while Thurman was on a West Coast speaking tour, expresses a diffidence to the outcome of the search, and he assumes that Thurman, as a Morehouse graduate, would be the better candidate and would have an inside track for the position.

Dear Howard:

Thanks for your letter. You type so much better than you write. I guess you say the same about my writing and that I should be typing instead of scribbling. But you type so much better than I do—so I am writing. I write much better than I type.

It was kind of you to mention me to Mr. Wesiger.[1] On the other hand, I had & have just about assumed that a Morehouse person would be considered, since there are a few very able Morehouse men. I say few because for that particular position, they are few. In talking with a number of people, I have said that it ~~was~~ would be impossible for them not to consider you for the position and I am quite sincere in this. With the possible exception of President Johnson, you are the most widely known Morehouse graduate and certainly you have done and are doing a unique work—It wouldn't surprise me at all if the mantle fell on your own shoulders.

With respect to positions of that kind, I have taken about the same position you have taken—let things take their normal course. As far as I am concerned, the School of Religion here is sufficient to keep me for the next twenty five years.

I said to you some time ago when Bond[2] was here that I would be willing to push you for the position and still am. Suppose we discuss the whole affair when you come here. Frankly, I think I would hardly be acceptable to them.

The fellows seem to enjoy your house—have heard no complaints at all. The enrollment is much larger. We have 36 degree students & two auditors total 38 probably 40 before the end of this week.

I know you have had a rich experience & that you have, as usual, performed well.

With kindest regards

I am

yours truly

[*signed*] Benj E. Mays

N.B. I got your address from Miss Butts. I hope you get this.

B. E. M.

TLS. HTC-MBU: Box 191.

1. Kendall Weisiger.

2. Horace Mann Bond (1904–72), an educator who served as president of Fort Valley State College (1939–45) and Lincoln University (1945–57). Bond authored several books, including *The Education of the Negro in the American Social Order* (New York: Prentice-Hall, 1934).

From Howard H. Brinton

2 February 1939

Wallingford, Penn.

Howard Brinton[1] responds to Thurman's request for a copy of his essay titled "Mysticism and Social Change." Thurman's lectures with the same title were already prepared prior to receiving Brinton's letter.

Dear Howard Thurman,

I'm going over a file of my letters. I was surprised and much grieved to find that yours of the 16th of December (!) had not been answered. This was due to carelessness of my secretary who put the letter in the wrong file. Is it too late to send you the essay on Mysticism and Social Change? Probably so, but I think I shall send it to you any how as you may be interested in its contents although I do not think it is of any great value. Your lectures are probably already written.

I am sending you also two essays of mine which have some bearing on this subject.

Please forgive this inexcusable delay. If your lectures are published may we have a copy as this is a subject with which we are constantly dealing in our efforts to make Quakerism socially effective and to coordinate the inner and the outer life.

Sincerely yours

[*unsigned*]

Howard H. Brinton

1. Howard H. Brinton (1884–1973) was the codirector (along with his wife, Anna) of Pendle Hill, a Quaker religious education institution outside Philadelphia. In addition to writing more than a dozen pamphlets on Quaker belief and practice, Brinton is also known for his work on conscientious objectors during both world wars.

"Mysticism and Social Change"

13–16 February 1939

St. Louis, Mo.

In the fall of 1938, Thurman was invited to give a series of lectures at Eden Theological Seminary, near St. Louis, for its spring convocation.[1] *Its sponsors were amenable to either of the two suggested topics by Thurman: "Message of the Religion of Jesus to the Disinherited" (a subject he would return to) or "Mysticism and Social Change."*[2] *Thurman delivered his lectures on the latter topic on four consecutive days, 13–16 February 1939, and they were published in the* Eden Theological Seminary Bulletin *in spring 1939. Despite some contemporary interest in publishing a revised form of the lectures, they were never reprinted.*[3]

These talks as a unit represent the culmination of many years of thought by Thurman on the religious and social significance of mysticism, a project that he had been considering at least since his study, a decade before, with Rufus Jones at Haverford College. "Mysticism and Social Change" also shows Thurman at his most scholarly. These are lectures, not sermons. There is little here that is autobiographical, although he asserts at the beginning that only someone who has some acquaintance with mystical experience is qualified to write about it. A poem of his composition provides the sole, tantalizing glimpse of his inner spiritual life.

The opening essay is one of Thurman's most extended efforts to provide a philosophical basis for mystical experiences. He makes a distinction between rational, or reflective, knowledge and intuitive knowledge. If rational knowledge is based on chains of deduction, intuitive knowledge bypasses logical inference to arrive directly at its conclusions. The mystical experience is a form of intuition; it comes "with overwhelming conviction and certainty, with the immediacy of an experience." This connects the mystic to the "common ground of unity or being," of which particular experiences are separate manifestations. Mysticism, Thurman argues, is "monistic-dualistic," at once providing a sense of the unity of all nature with God, as well as the sense of the separateness of God.

The second essay discusses the nature of mystical symbolism, broadly following the schema outlined by Mary Ann Ewer in her study of the topic. Thurman argues that mystical symbols are not real, and in his mysticism Jesus provides "the fullest expression" of what is disclosed to the mystic in the moment of illumination, which for Thurman, as he mentions here, was largely derived from his contemplation of the works of nature.

The third essay examines the relationship between mysticism and ethics. Thurman argues that though the mystic quest is necessarily solitary and often involves asceticism, the vision of unity that is the goal of this quest involves all of creation and all of life, including the degraded and imperfect social world in which we live. The value of mysticism is in the experience of the unity of all being. The ethical challenge comes from the obligation both to be true to one's mystical vision and to "achieve the good which in some profound sense is given in the moment of vision."

It is only the final lecture that speaks directly to the question of mysticism and social change. In this talk, which has strong similarities to themes in the 1937 series "The Significance of Jesus," Thurman develops Rufus Jones's notion of "affirmation mystics," those "who are concerned with working out in a social frame of reference the realism of their mystic experience." Thurman places the obligations of affirmation mystics to seek social justice in a socialist context, in keeping with his other writings on social justice in the late 1930s. People face "a life and death struggle for bare security" in large part because a few persons have possession "of the means of production and are in a position to control for their own interests" the well-being and personhood of all humanity. Thurman concludes that the oppressed, if they remember the necessary role of God and a united humanity to achieve social transformation, will avoid acts of violent coercion.

In reprinting "Mysticism and Social Change," the original notes have been maintained as footnotes.

I. "Mysticism—An Interpretation"

In the *Function of Criticism*, T. S. Eliot suggests, with reference to literary criticism, that the only critic who is qualified to interpret another's writing, is one who in some sense stands in the same stream of fact.[4] It seems to me that this position applies very definitely to an interpretation of mystical insight. I do not claim to have scaled the heights of rarefied illumination so vivid to the mystic in his moments of clarity, but I have lived for a long time in the stream of the mystic's experience and am convinced that there is available to me some significant and relevant clues as to his interpretation.

In addition to all of this it has been necessary for me to participate both passively and actively in what is generally known as the social struggle forcing me always to test at long last the validity of the mystic insight in terms that always include the empirical. Nevertheless I do not speak as an expert in either but always as a seeker after the truth, after a deeper insight and a greater knowledge.

It is my purpose in these four lectures to discuss in broad outline the fundamental meaning of mysticism, and what mysticism seems to me to suggest as to the meaning of life and the nature of reality. And in the second place to examine the symbolism of mysticism to see if it does not offer an important means

Thurman (fourth from right) with Howard University students. Morehouse College Archives.

Olive and Anne Spencer Thurman, circa 1937. (Olive above, Anne below). Courtesy of the Thurman Family and Arleigh Prelow/Howard Thurman Film Project.

Thurman (center) and unidentified men. Courtesy of Olive Thurman Wong and Arleigh Prelow/Howard Thurman Film Project.

Thurman with Howard University ushers. Arleigh Prelow/Howard Thurman Film Project.

for disclosing the genius of Christian mysticism. And in the third place, with these two things having been done, to examine the direct or implied relationship between Christian mysticism as reflected in its peculiar symbolism and Christian ethics. And finally, to discuss the contribution that mysticism thus delineated makes to social change.

No one who is even casually acquainted with the general field of mysticism can escape the conviction that voices are many and the confusion wide spread and rampant as to what is meant by mystical experience. There is the distinction between Eastern and Western mysticism, Oriental and Occidental; and the distinction between Catholic and Protestant mysticism.

Fundamentally, the mystic rests his case upon the meaning of a primary contactual experience of God. It is first hand. He considers himself as standing within the experience itself. Usually the experience is located in a framework of practices or disciplines conceived as being in some sense preparatory in their nature. The pattern is logical and arises out of a basic assumption about the nature of reality. To use a figure, there is in the life of man an "apex," "an uncreated element,"[5] "a door that cannot be shut,"[6] that is the point of synthesis for the finite and the Infinite, the nexus of man and God. This is not to suggest that there is some peculiar organ resident in man by which the mystic experience is made possible for him. The language is rather descriptive of what the mystic means in his interpretation of his experience. The assumption is that the finite and the Infinite are not two fundamentally separate universes of discourse but that they are grounded in a transcendent unity.

The Russian theologian, Berdyaev,[7] takes the position that there is a fundamental distinction between spirit and nature. I think he is right in recognizing the dualism but when he makes it a thoroughgoing and exhaustive dualism he is in error. It seems to me fundamentally false to insist upon the denial of interaction between the spirit and the natural world. Man is in himself both of these. It is not either-or, but a both-and, relationship. There are moods of the human spirit. The scientific mood by which the natural world is apprehended and interpreted is but one of the moods of the human spirit. Those moods which have to do with appreciation, with value judgments are also fundamental moods common to the life of man. The scientist, for instance, knows "too well that behind the symbols of Mathematics, and the formulae of Chemistry and Physics and the rigid generalizations of Psychology and Social Science, lie the unexplained mysteries of twilight and music, of autumn lights fringed with silver, of human fortitude and idealism."*

The experience of the mystic and its assumption provide a world-view that gives rational validity to the experience itself. One of the insistent qualities

*Cf. Nicolas Berdyaev, *Freedom and the Spirit*, 9, 17.

of mind is the tendency to reduce all phenomena of experience to manageable units—to work over the conglomerates of experience until they yield intelligibility. In other words, even experience, that phenomenon of which the conscious experience itself is but one aspect, must be in some sense rational, comprehensible to the mind of the subject. Even the profoundest judgments of agnosticism are but attempts to maintain sanity and rationality in the presence of overwhelming imponderables. The same is true of the mystic when he tries to imprison or isolate in a single word or concept or phrase, the vision of the Ultimate. Such expressions as the "Unknown Unknowable," or the "Nameless Nothing" are cases in point.

It is quite important to raise the question as to whether the mystic's experience can be interpreted as a form of knowledge. The primary question is, are there in fact different kinds of knowledge fundamentally or merely different manifestations of knowledge arising out of a common ground of unity?

Principal Hughes has given a very significant discussion of the ground of Mysticism in his volume, *The Philosophic Basis of Mysticism.*[8] In my subsequent discussion as to whether the mystic's experience may be interpreted as a form of knowledge, I am following somewhat in detail, Principal Hughes' chapter, "Are There Different Kinds of Knowledge?"* He begins with the fundamental proposition that truth in its finality is a unity.[9] There is basic to all formal quests for knowledge the assumption, yea, the conviction that all conditions as seen in the various fields of knowledge are resolved in a higher synthesis which is made possible because of the ground of unity out of which all knowledge arises.

After a rather cursory discussion of the theory of knowledge of Plato, Aristotle, Spinoza, and Bergson, he reaches the conclusion that no knowledge is possible to man except on the basis of reason, for even the barest sensation involves "awareness" as an element of consciousness and this involves reason, though it may not involve reasoning.[10] Knowledge arrived at by reasoning involves certain principles and laws of thought. It is formal, discursive, proceeding according to logical pattern from one point to another. The process of reasoning is a formulation of the mind as a result of reflection upon the action of the mind as it functions in acquiring knowledge. They are at least implied in the very act of reflection itself. Now, on the other hand, knowledge that is intuitive seems to short-circuit the process, to dispense with the formalities. This fact really means that life itself is deeper than thought about life.[11] The point of difference then between rational knowledge or reasoning and intuitive knowledge or reason is that the former is inferential throughout and its course can be adequately charted; while the latter is an immediate experience making its own case directly.

*T. H. Hughes, *The Philosophic Basis of Mysticism,* Chapter 4.

The second difference is that the conviction that arises as a result of logic is one of which we, ourselves, are conscious of arriving at, whereas in an intuition it seems to be forced upon us from without—it seems that reality has made an impact upon us. Of course, this element is always present in the moment when the mind grasps a totality and it is implied in the logical steps through which the mind passes in its quest.

To elucidate the meaning, suppose we consider what really happens when someone answers a question that we ask about the meaning of an idea. When we ask a question it is scarcely ever asked about the thing that we wish to know. In the moment that our question is answered and we say—I see—in that moment of perception it is as if our mind and the truth we seek were alone existent in the universe. Reflective thinking may in a sense be regarded as the process by which the mind in its own initiative removes barriers which obscure the truth until at last by relentless pursuit there is nothing left to obscure the vision and we say therefore.[12] Thus, even in discursive reasoning there is a leaping quality in the mental process. In the moment of intuition the mind leaves behind the process and its grasp of knowledge is immediate and comprehensive. If the knowledge arrived at has come at the end of a formal process, there is a sense of intellectual security present because one knows that what one has grasped can be made available to anyone else whose mind can follow through the same way. Logic provides a road map that can be reproduced indefinitely and made available to all intelligent travelers.

With intuitive knowledge the picture seems much more complicated for in the moment of realization we are not conscious of process, of steps, we are only conscious of the "isness" quality of the knowledge. There have not been those attendant states of consciousness as we eliminated things which obscured our vision making for an increasing crystallization of convictions. We cannot escape the lingering suspicion that deception has not been entirely eliminated. But with intuitive knowledge there is something which seems to be final, complete, exhaustive. The element of deep feeling seems to be more convincing in intuitive knowledge. Logic rules out feeling—or at least feeling is at a discount and this means that one of the most important elements in personality is eliminated.[13]

The late Professor James Ward[14] bases his whole treatment of Psychology on the assumption that conscious life begins in a vague *feeling-continuum* and that intelligence and conation develop by differentiation of functions within this continuum at the call of the pressing needs of life. The primal fact is the feeling-continuum, and in that sense it is the stuff out of which reason and volition and their subsequent activities grow. Attention which is the primal mode of conation is thus dependent on feeling. Further, it is through attention and the effort to guide it in more intense and concentrated directions, that the differentiation of reason appears and subsequently grows.[15]

It would seem, therefore, that in intuitive knowledge more of man's personality is involved than in more rational knowledge. It is more personal.[16] It is reasonable to suggest then that such knowledge is essentially more real and it touches and partakes of reality at a deeper point than the knowledge attained by the processes of discursive logic.[17]

The profound contention of the mystic with reference to his deepest religious experience is not unlike at every point the knowledge of intuition. It comes to him with overwhelming conviction and certainty, with the immediacy of an experience. It strikes him with the vividness and clarity of a sensation.[18] He sees the vision; for the vision breaks in on him when he is ready to receive it.[19] All of his disciplines are preparatory to his moment of vision. Eckhart suggests that when the soul is emptied of creatureliness, God has no choice but to come in. Their deepest and richest knowledge comes to them in a state of passivity. What they really mean by passivity is an openness and a receptivity, a laying of one's self bare to God.[20] They are receptive, God is disclosive.[21] It is only when the mystic begins the work of interpreting the core of his experience in terms of the world of thought and doctrine in which he has been reared that we come upon the differences in the types of religious mysticism. The experience itself is identical at *basis* but it falls upon a background of thought and tradition which is different.[22] As I have suggested, we shall discuss this more at length in our next lecture on Symbolism.

If it is true that there is a predominately feeling element in the mystic's experience and that the total personality is more deeply implicated than may be involved in the process of intellection, we can understand the meaning of the mystic's claim to knowledge of ultimate reality. It will help us also in understanding the case for the validity of such knowledge. Personal knowledge differs from impersonal knowledge in the fact that it bears within itself a greater and more determinative element of feeling.[23] It is a fact of simple experience that we can come to a real knowledge of a person only by the pathway of feeling. On the basis of isolated facts we may learn various things about a person. But we do not feel that we know the person until we have had a primary give and take exposure to him. When there has been an interaction of personalities, when we have shared in another's secrets with the kind of creative interpenetration of spirit, which we call love, it is then that we are prepared to say that in some real sense we have knowledge of the person. We can only know another as a personality in the deepest and most intimate reaches of his being as we love him and he loves us, in that two-fold act of self giving and self receiving. By philosophy and rigidly scientific discipline we cannot come to a knowledge of persons in any profound sense. We cannot expect to find the meaning of another person at the end of a syllogism. We cannot expect to find God at the end of a syllogism. Knowledge about God given to us by philosophy and science may help us to supply content for our primary experience. We may understand something about His workings and the method of His activity in the world and in history. We may even obtain some understanding of His character and His nature but if we are to know God in the sense of knowing Him personally, with intimacy and warmth, we can only do so through the knowledge of love. We must approach Him along the same avenue by which we seek a deeper knowledge of each other's personality. Religious truth then acquired in the experience of fellowship with God and through His self-disclosure is valid. Attempts to describe it break down but do not relieve the mystic of the obligation to continue the attempts. The mystics agree, for the most part, that ultimate reality is personal and that He can best be known by love. This is not to insist that mystic experience yields only truth about reality, for the basis element is an immediate contact with reality, but there comes through it an enrichment of mind, an added power and range of apprehension, a deeper insight and an enlarged outlook upon life accompanied by an intensification of spiritual energy and a heightened sense of personal life in Union with God.

With this argument of Prof. Hughes' which I have gone to some length to outline and at points to elaborate, I am in substantial agreement.

What then is the significance of the experience of unity with God that the mystic realizes? If there is a common ground of unity or being of which particular forms of consciousness are manifestations, then the difference between manifestations has to do with form of differentiation and the attendant level of consciousness achieved rather than a more absolute difference. Mystical experience then may be characterized as being monistic-dualistic. A very excellent art form expressive of my idea is to be found in Rodin's Hand of God—A large hand with palm exposed yet with the fingers extended so as to form a balanced boundary for what the artist conceives as protruding creatively from the life of God. The fingers may be thought of as the boundaries of finitude; within the hand there is a conglomerate of chaotic stuff of life and coming up out of it with increasing differentiation are the shapes of human beings. Thus it is seen that there is no thoroughgoing dichotomy between the created forms themselves and between the created forms and the creative manifestations of the Creator.

It is obvious that the general flavor of the ground of the mystic's experience is pantheistic and on its lowest level can scarcely be distinguished from a vague glowy feeling about the world of nature and of man. I shall discuss this more at length under Symbolism but it is necessary to make a few comments relative to it at this point. If it remained on that level it would be the merest sentimentality devoid of any profoundly significant ethical quality and certainly devoid of moral tensions. This is true because there is no sharp transcendency but rather a diffused transcendency. The religious mystic and certainly the Christian mystic in his experience of intentness, intensity, ineffability and passivity, is conscious of being grasped by a reality that is focal and fontal. All incipient experiences of unity in which the whole realm of nature participates are but intimations of what is achieved in the personal experience of the mystic, himself. It is not a denial of the presence of negations, of tensions, of evil, but it is rather a triumphant achievement of the human spirit. It carries with it in its wake a subsequent, meaningful increment moral in quality, spiritual in tone. In the mystic's experience we see the ultimate meaning of all religious experience.[24] "With (most of) us there is only a spark, whilst with them it is a long flame; but in us and in them, alike, the same fire burns."* It seems to me then that religion generally always awakens and stimulates this kind of consciousness. As Principal Caird says, "Religion teaches us to recognize that ultimate reality which knowledge seeks beyond the vale of phenomena lies in a Being who speaks not only to us but in us; and on the other hand that the realization of the highest in our will is possible only as that will becomes the organ and vehicle of a divine purpose which is realizing itself in the world."[25]

The problem then for the mystic is to carry the reality of his vision which is monistic in its very nature into the ordinary commonplace experience of life. He has to utilize what has been referred to as the principle of alternation. The meaning of this and its implication must be worked out in our discussion on Mysticism and Ethics.

We are now prepared to examine the significance of symbolism in an effort to understand the peculiar characteristics of Christian mysticism as they have revealed themselves in the explanation that the mystic has given of the forms through which his experiences come and the attendant validity that they have guaranteed.

II: "Mysticism and Symbolism"

In this discussion I am following the sub-divisions suggested by the nature of the inner stimuli of mystical experience as outlined by Mary Ewer in her volume, *A Survey of Mystical Symbolism.*[26] She suggests that these subdivisions fall logically into four great types. First, there are the momentary inner stimuli or brief experiences such as those upon which poets occasionally build lyrics. The characteristic quality is brevity. They come like a flash of blinding light completely obscuring everything else. Second, there are the complex stimuli of long duration which cause introspective persons looking back over their own inner development to compare it to a never ending quest, to a weary and bitter warfare or to a peaceful growth. Third, there are the dim but powerful inner urges which so unite with certain external stimuli, the sight of the sunrise or a flight

*Quoted by Kirk, *Vision of God*, p. 534.

of wild birds or of the priest at the altar—that these are evaluated as of infinitely greater significance than can be any inner stimulus divorced from external counterparts. Fourth, there is the steady inner equilibrium which in its height is the goal of all the other types—the experience of a self *unified* not only within itself but also with the Infinite, relationship to which such inner stimuli reveal. It would be instructive to examine Symbolism under the four main subdivisions: the symbolism of the momentary mystic experience, of mystic growth and development, of the divine order and of the abiding mystic experience.

It is important first, however, to examine the nature of symbolism itself. What is symbolism? Are symbols things in themselves? Do they stand for something other than themselves? Is there any relationship between the form of the symbol and the thing of which it is a presentation?

Perhaps the most persistent quality of mind is that which makes it demand that the conglomerates of experience yield a rationality of meaning. This must be reduced to manageable units of perception or there can be no meaning. Knowledge comes to the mind as immediate or mediate. It is the essence of the mystic's position, as we pointed out in our last lecture, that his knowledge of reality is *immediate.* The mystic experience is *primary* for the human spirit and it is only when it is broken down into manageable units of intellection that it becomes a part of the sequential totality of experience. The meaning that the mystic derives from his immediate knowledge of God becomes for him the key to his interpretation of the manifestations or symbols of reality. In a sense, concepts themselves are symbols of ideas. To illustrate what I mean: If we thought for a moment of meaning as an apperceptive mass inarticulate and in a sense chaotic; concepts, images, logical patterns of thought, are instruments for imprisoning bits of meaning. The content of a particular meaning has a signification for the mind that cannot be separated from the symbol used to express the meaning. In other words, the meaning of symbols is in the symbol itself as well as that of which it is a manifestation. Sometimes a group of symbols in a certain relationship communicates meaning that cannot be contained in any one of the symbols. Again long association with a certain symbol like a word, may cause the definitive nature of the symbol to become increasingly blurred and meaningless. If we may think of symbols as a wooden frame placed against a background of meaning giving particular content to the meaning; the much handling of the frame causes it to be loose in its joints, the nails become old and the frame is wobbly. The result is meaning leaks through the cracks and crevices of the joints and ceases to be clear cut. The use of the word "love" in religion is a case in point. It becomes necessary to devise a new symbol or at any rate to get a new frame to communicate the specific nature of the concept or word.

With this digression, let us come back to the basic idea that the mystic uses as his clue to the interpretation of symbolic manifestations of reality, the essence of his immediate experience of reality arising out of his mystic insight. He is always looking for one symbol that is sufficiently inclusive of meaning so that to use it as a channel of mediation of reality is the most direct route to a mediate experience of God. The Christian mystic finds that symbol in a person, Jesus Christ.

For many Christian mystics Jesus Christ evaporates as a symbol and becomes reality itself. He is the object of their devotion. He is the God of Religion, the ineffable One Whom to know is life. This is the predominant pattern of Roman Catholic mysticism. It must never be forgotten that the mystic must use as his frame of symbolic reference that body of doctrine, religious faith and tradition with which he is familiar and in which he has developed. One can understand then how Jesus Christ becomes not merely a manifestation of God but God, Himself, in the frame of reference of the Roman Catholic mystic. The sacraments of the church, particularly the Eucharist and Baptism, are therefore the truest, most logical and inescapable symbols of God. They become the point at which mediate experience of God lays hold upon the spirit of man.

I appreciate this position even though for me it leaves much to be desired.

But there is another kind of Christian mystic for whom Jesus Christ remains an inclusive symbol of God. He sees in Jesus the fullest expression in time of what is disclosed to him in his own moment of illumination. He is the classic example of the "as above, so below," criterion of mysticism. The meaning of this is profound for the ethical insights that arise in the mystic's experience. This position is only different from the dominant one of Roman Catholicism in the way in which Jesus is viewed as a categorical symbol of reality rather than as a *temporary symbol of reality.*

We are now prepared to examine the language of mystical symbolism on the basis of the subdivisions as set forth by Miss Ewer. First, the analogies which she uses in an effort to give meaning to "momentary inner expressions:"[27]

> "I journeyed to a hill top at close of day
> Darkness stole upon the valley beneath as sleep on a tired brow.
> Silence pursued me all the day
> Won at last—
> Exhausted I lay at his feet . . .
> No sense of senses, time—space all
> Awareness of self spread out till I and all
> Around me run together
> In one expansive, streaming, liquid quiet,

Suddenly with a start—time begins
The heavy cares of the years seemed lighter now—
God so near
I was radiant
With holy light."*

Or in the vision of Isaiah: "In the year that King Uzziah died, I saw the Lord."[28]

Mystical literature is full of references to light which seems to correspond to an inner stimulus and to be most accurately expressive of it. The momentary experience of the mystic is analogously expressed in terms of physical sensations, such as seeing, hearing, tasting, smelling, touching. But sight remains as one of the important analogies because it is expressive of light which is always contrasted with darkness. It is a figure that implies more of the quality of the intellectual than the emotional. When I say, "I see," it means that obscurities, limitations, darkness have all been blotted out. It is the crowning moment for the mind when truth lays hold on it with a compelling mediacy. In the *Paradiso*, Dante depicts the beatific vision in classic words that literally groan under the weight of transcendant beauty:

> "And all their faces were of living flame, and of gold their wings; and for the rest they were all white beyond the whiteness of snow. . . . This realm of security and joy, peopled by folk alike of old time and of new, centered its looks and its love upon one mark alone. Oh, three fold light, whose bright radiance shed in a single beam upon their eyes doth so content them, look hither down upon our storm-tossed lives."[29]

When such symbolism is used of the momentary mystical experience, the mystic is trying to express what is essentially personal and beyond verification.— To him it is a flash of blinding light but here *again* his words are misleading for a flash of blinding light simply means that all differentiation and articulation are blotted out.

The language of hearing is often used in an effort to throw light on the meaning of his momentary experience. Even the most superficial acquaintance with the Hebraic prophets reveals the meaning of this type of symbolism. Here we have to do with a quality that is much more emotional and which has more of the definitively ethical content than in the vision. I am mindful, however, of the fact that the same quality may be present in the vision as in the experience of Isaiah in the temple. Against the darkness of the age I can see the illumined finger of God guiding me in the way that I should go, so that high above the clash of arms in the conflict for position, for rights, for status, for place, for

*The Lecturer.

priority, I can hear speaking distinctly and clearly to my own spirit the still small voice of God without which nothing has meaning, quite, with which all the rest of the journey, however difficult, however painful, however devastating will be filled with a music all its own and even the stars in their courses and all the wooded world of nature participate in the triumphant music of my heart.

When the mystic uses language symbolic of seeing and hearing, touching, etc., he is seizing upon the best possible analogy for which exact terminology is non-existent.

In the language of spiritual progress, we come upon another use of symbolism to express a qualitative experience. Many times we encounter expressions that have to do with the voyage of the soul, the ascent of the spirit. The mystic way has been symbolically classified, emphasizing three aspects, namely, the *via purgativa*, the *via illuminativa*, the *via unitiva.* The three realms of Dante's journey correspond with these three ways. Eckhart discusses under appropriate language the same fundamental idea. In Frances Thompson's classic, "The Hound of Heaven,"[30] we see illustrated the symbolism of the pursuit of the soul by God. Here man is not seeking God but God is seeking man.

The symbolism of progress has to do often with that which has taken place in the total experience of the individual when he has undergone a profound re-centering of his personality. A change has taken place. Call it conversion, call it regeneration, but the individual lives a new life. He has become a new creature. Such a transformation of centering is often the result of excruciating agony of spirit and mind and at the end he does not ever escape the penetrating rays of his vision. The symbolism of growth is encountered many, many times. The whole language of the lover and the way in which he becomes more and more at one with the beloved belongs here. This type of symbolism seems to me to reveal one aspect of the paradox that there is in the mystic's experience. In his moment of vision he seems to be caught up into a totality like the silence of absolute motion in which all the dross and impurities of his character are destroyed. And yet when it passes, he is seen to be to himself a man in whom the dross and the impurities hang like a poisonous cloud in the inmost reaches of his spiritual life.

Under the third type of symbolism, we encounter those types most expressive of the world of nature. I need only to mention the place that solar and phallic symbolism have played in the whole language and literature of religion. My own earliest experiences of religion are tied up with my reaction to the sun as it passed through its various phases; and particularly the sea. The coming of spring after winter snows have passed; falling leaves and fading flowers of autumn days; the lightning, the thunder, all these manifestations of nature have somehow united with certain powerful inner urges of the human spirit causing them to be evaluated in particular terms. The continuity of life expressing itself in cycles has somehow found an inner counterpart in the experience of the individual with meanings in his world. It is not an accident that men have found themselves unable to resist the effort to probe into the world of nature for meanings which they have often dimly sensed within. This is very well dramatized in the works of the nature poets.

But the Christian mystic goes beyond mere pantheistic insight. He sees the pain, the struggle, the frustration that there is in the world of nature and it becomes a symbol of the moral struggle of human life. He agrees with the prophet who identifies the moral and spiritual triumph of God in the life of man as a part and parcel of the triumph of the will of God in the world of nature. When men are able to beat their swords into plow shares and their spears into pruning hooks, then the wolf and the lamb shall lie down together; the goat and the leopard's cub shall rest in the leopard's lair, the wolf and lion shall graze side by side, herded by a little child; the cow and the bear shall be friends and the little child shall play on the hole of an asp and the babies feed in the nest of a viper and there shall be no injury and there shall be no killing. All of the world of nature shall be a sacred hill because, says the prophet, the land shall be as full of the knowledge of the eternal as the bed of the ocean is full of water.

And here we come upon the fundamental symbolic significance of initiation ceremonies that have loomed so large in the life of all religion. "There is an effort to convey to the individual such a share in the organic life of his race as will persist even in death." It is aside from my purpose to discuss the significance of these in terms of salvation.

The final type of symbolism that the mystic uses throws light on all the other symbolism; namely, it is an effort to reduce to symbolic communicability the central experience of mysticism—a self fulfilled, unified within; unified with but not dissolved in God. Much of the language of mystical union has to do with analogies drawn from the union that arises under certain circumstances between inanimate objects. The way that wood or fuel is consumed by fire or analogies drawn from rivers and their relationship to the sea. It is very striking to me that there is a fundamental paradoxical relationship between the waters of the land and the sea. All the waters of all the lands are fed by the sea and all the waters of all the lands go back to the sea. The goal and the source of the river are the same. The symbolism that is most striking to me of what the Christian mystic achieves in his union is that of the gulf stream moving through the waters of the sea, a part of it in a sense unified with the sea, participating in all of the basic manifestations of the sea but in a sense, it remains the gulf stream. The analogy, of course, is not complete, but very suggestive.

The symbolism of the union between man and woman in the relationship of love is a very old one in the language of mystical union. It is not to be wondered at that when the mystic tries to express what it is that he has experienced he comes again and again to such figures as the bride, father, mother, the spouse, the beloved wife, the fair maiden. Augustine has a great passage in the confessions. He says, "What is it then, that I love when I love my God? What is He whom my soul feels above itself? I have tried to grasp in my own intelligence, above all images of things; but at the moment when I reach that state of being I cannot fix my gaze and I fall back helpless into the common thoughts. I have carried away nothing from this vision but a memory full of love and, as it were, a regretful longing for things whose perfume is felt but which are out of reach. What is it then, that I love, oh, my God, when, I love you? It is not beauty of body, nor the glory which passes, nor the light which our eyes love; it is not the varied harmony of sweet songs, nor the aroma of perfumes and sweet flowers nor the voluptuous joys of carnal embraces. No, it is none of these when I love my God; and yet, in this love I find a light, an inner voice, a perfume, a savor, an embrace of a kind which does not leave the inmost of my self. . . . Sometimes, oh God, You create a state of soul in me so extraordinary, and You fill me with so intimate a joy, that it if lasted, all life would be different. . . . Who shall understand, who shall express God?"[31]

I cannot close our consideration of mysticism and symbolism without giving some attention at least to silence which is for me the symbol par excellence of the mystic experience. To me it is capable of sacramental significance partaking sometimes of the very essence of a means of grace. It does not mean inactivity but rather, the process by which the soul of man can plunge beneath the surface self to the very ground of his being and there become a part of a unity that gives meaning to the life of activity and function.

Words are important symbols of communication under certain circumstances. In order for men to reveal themselves to each other in casual relationships and intercourse, to blossom into speech was necessary. But it is strikingly significant to me that when meanings become vast and communication between the human spirits has to do with the deepest understandings, speech, vocal speech, is singularly inadequate. I venture to say that no one understands the meaning of friendship who has not reached a point in his relationship with another in which one felt one's way subtly but definitely into the life of another and achieved a sense of vitality and quickening with another life that transcended words, however genuinely uttered, and profoundly spoken. Therefore, it seems that in the mystic's reach for unity that can give a guarantor to all of the details of his life and living, he resorts to quiet meditation in which he is not passive in any quietistic sense but rather, he experiences an interpenetration of his spirit with the spirit of God that has channeled itself through the silence. In an appendix to *The Idea of the Holy* Otto[32] says, "Devotional silence has a three fold character. The numinous silence of sacrament, silence of waiting and the silence of union or fellowship. The numinous silence of sacrament is the culminating point in worship."* When I was a boy I was always driven to worship when I saw a storm come up on the shores of the Atlantic Ocean on the Florida coast. A stillness pervaded everything. The tall sea grass stood at attention. As far out as my eyes could go the surface of the sea was untroubled, quiet, but expectant. I could almost hear the pounding of my own heart against my ribs. Then, as if by magic, there came a stirring of the wind, increasing in intensity and expansiveness until the sea grass, the loose dry sand, the surface of the ocean were all caught up in an increasingly maddening fury—the storm had come. Otto says that such an analogous silence in worship is the last act before the worshipper is conscious of the coming of God. The second type of silence is the silence of waiting. It is preparatory in its nature leading to the third form of silence. It is apt to be what I characterize as noisy silence. There is the calming down of the spirit, the settling of the mind and the focusing of one's self upon the act of worship. It is in this connection that I have found the reading of devotional literature of primary importance.

I was told the other day, by a friend, that very often Thomas Aquinas, when working on heavy theological matters, if he discovered his mind wandering or unable to grasp in any satisfying sense the metaphysical concepts that he sought would stop his work and read some devotional literature in order to bring all of his powers to a point of worshipful focus. In public address, I have often found it useful to read something aloud to the hearers for the purpose of getting them to settle their minds for the message and then giving what was in my mind and heart to give. It is in this area that much of the tortures of the soul in prayer is located.

The third type of silence is the completion of the waiting and sacramental silence. It is the act of consummation. It is the awareness of God in communion. It is the climax of the mystic act of worship. It is an achieved fellowship with God in its very essence and affirmation of the solidarity and the unity of life. At long last, the human spirit gets some indication of its ultimate possibility and meaning. What the mystic has found true for himself, he quite reasonably assumes to be worthfully significant for every other human being and to that end he dedicates his days and his labors. It is from his experience of fellowship with God on the pinnacle of ineffable experience that is at once the mainspring of his ethics and key to his participation in the ethical struggles of his kind.

*Rudolf Otto, *Idea of the Holy*, pp. 216ff.

III. "Mysticism and Ethics"

Many thinkers are of the opinion that mysticism makes no contribution to ethical theory in general and social ethical theory in particular. Bertrand Russell[33] says, "What is in all cases ethically characteristic of mysticism is absence of indignation or protest, *acceptance* with *joy*, disbelief in the ultimate truth of the division into two hostile camps, the good and the bad. This attitude is a direct outcome of the nature of the mystical experience; with its sense of unity is associated a feeling of infinite peace."* What this point of view and similar ones overlook is the fact of the reality of evil and sin as the mystic discovers it first in his own spirit and then in the world of men. The life of the mystic is worked out in the world of men and things. There *is* an element of the solitariness in his experience. Perhaps it is the solitariness of life that makes it move with such ruggedness. All life is one and yet life seems to move in such intimate circles of awful individuality. The power of life is in its aloneness but this is a paradox of paradoxes. There are thresholds before which all men stop and only God may tread and even He in disguise. Each soul must learn, so the mystic thinks, to stand up in its own right and live. How blissful to lean on another, to seek a sense of the everlasting arm expressed in the presence of a friend. We walk a part of the way together but on the upper reaches of life each path takes itself away to the heights alone. Ultimately, I am alone, so vastly alone that in my aloneness is all the life of the universe. In such moments of profound awareness, I seem to be all that there is in the world and all that there is seems to be I. It seems to be true then that in the mystic's moments of highest spiritual experience (of manifestations) all divisions, all tensions are resolved—only the vision, the experience itself seems to be the real but this is not for long. He knows that he cannot escape the fundamental problem of ethics as it works itself out in his time-space relationships, namely, what is the true end of man and how may that end influence the conduct of his life.

The goal of the mystic, therefore, is to know God in a comprehensive sense; for God is grasped by the whole self or the whole self is laid hold upon by God—the vision of God is realized inclusively. To illustrate precisely what I mean, let me quote an extract from the life of Tolstoy. It is the same quotation used in this connection by Dr. Hocking: "When I saw the head separate from the body and how they both thumped into the box at the moment, I understood, not with my mind, but with my whole being, that no theory of the reasonableness of any present progress can justify this deed; and that though everybody from the creation of the world, on whatever theory had held it to be necessary, I knew it to be unnecessary and bad."[34]

*B. Russell, *Mysticism and Logic*, p. 11.

The mystic experiences unity, not identity, but it is a unity that penetrates through all the levels of consciousness and fills him with a sense of the Other. He uses symbolism to help him keep alive this sense of presence. He discovers, however, that it is not possible to keep the consciousness of the presence of God alive at a high point in his experience over long time intervals. The most natural thing for him to do is try to recall by memory what has been experienced. But this, too, fades away even though it leaves a deposit in his personality. The glow that was cast on all of life is apt to be dimmed as he becomes more and more involved in the many. He comes upon the fact that deep within the structure of his own personality and life are the things which obscure and blot out his vision. In other words, the struggle with impulses, with inner divisions, unworthy desires, purely self-regarding tactics including the whole world of egocentric manifestations, all these are regarded by him as an indispensable part of the defect of his vision.

Discipline of some sort becomes necessary and inevitable. The details of his life among the many must be brought into line with the fullness of his vision. The disciplines have tended to center around the struggles of the flesh. Much of the psychopathology of mysticism has to do with this phase of it. To give only one instance of extreme practices, we may refer to Suso's early life as reported by Principal Hughes.[35] From his 18th year on for twenty-two years, he sought to break his wild spirit and his pampered body by a series of painful practices. For the first ten years he shut himself up in absolute seclusion in his cloister. . . . For a long time he wore a hair shirt and an iron chain, later a hair undershirt with nails, which pierced his flesh at every motion and whenever he lay down. In order not to be able to avoid the bites of vermin (for he did not bathe during the twenty-two years), he put his hands in slings during the night. He bore a cross, a span long with thirty nails and seven needles bound upon his bare back; every day he lay down upon it or threw himself upon it. For a long time a door was his bed. The pains of cold, hunger, thirst and the bloody flagellation he inflicted upon himself for so long a time and with such severity that he came near dying. Reference need only be made to the far reaching significance of this tendency in the very warp and woof of monasticism. The fundamental point, however, is that in ascetism and its discipline is a recognition of the reality of evil and the profound conviction that it can be overcome. No one who studies the disciplinary practices of heroic Christian mysticism can hold as tenable the theory that mysticism regards evil merely as illusion. In the extreme forms of asceticism there is that which is profoundly revolting and sadistic but there is the bold recognition of the fact that nothing not even one's physical well-being and life is quite worthy of obscuring the vision of God. In my opinion this insight represents religion at its best and it lifts the moral dignity of the life of man to a high and holy level.

Suppose we approach the problem from another angle? From the earliest moments of conscious life there is a tendency towards a developing self-consciousness or differentiation and uniqueness within the stream of consciousness itself. The babe usually discovers its separateness from others—from its mother, for instance, who stops feeding him sometimes even as he wishes her to continue. In some strange way separateness and divisibility dawn in his mind as a way of thinking about the world. He is beginning to locate himself in a series of other-than-self relationships. He discovers that he cannot control completely the other-than-self's to which he must adjust himself and by which he is surrounded. Various techniques of adjustment and control are developed, such as crying, laughing at the right moment, etc. It must be a great moment in the life of a baby when, acting reflectively upon his experience, he discovers for the first time that often it is the crying baby that gets rocked. Then a moment comes when he can hold his own bottle so as to release the mother or the nurse. From his point of view, that is not the purpose of the act. It is a primary act of self-extension and is the beginning of a social process of cooperation purely in self-interest, that is implied in all of the humanitarian impulses that later as an adult may develop in him.

Another day comes. It is the greatest and most prophetic moment in the life of the child. Struggling along, held almost horizontal to the floor by nature and by his own undeveloped self-consciousness, he staggers unsteadily to an upright position on his feet—miracle of miracles, there he is, suspended between the ceiling and the floor with his little feet touching, he stands alone. His act says: *I did it.* In that moment of deepest awareness his knees give way and the floor rises up to meet him. But always with his environment the struggle goes on apace—the struggle to achieve individuality, to discover a practical reinforcement of the self so he can act as an individual, as a person, as a unit, as a whole.

He carries his struggle for selfhood into his relationships with the world of nature and with the social order. It is the way of growth. The story is essentially the same for all human beings. It is a unity that is developed and perhaps brought into being by the vicissitudes of life and experience. The ground of personal morality and ethics is in this struggle. Things become immoral that defeat this achieving individuality. To be sure it is a morality on the lower level waiting for a higher touch, a higher synthesis.

What is true of human life in general and of the developing of self-consciousness of man in particular, is also true of the mystic in worship. In his act of worship the mystic achieves a transcending unity. His self-centeredness is resolved in a higher synthesis. God possesses him. Something new enters the picture, it is a new value judgment. Now things are not ethical or unethical merely because they aid or take away from his achieving individuality but because they are now viewed as ways that lead to the mount of vision or away from the mount of vision. The meaning of life is for him summarized in the vision of the good which he has thoroughly experienced. The vision makes mandatory that he *be* good so as to stand ever in immediate candidacy for the reception of God.

This is a most radical experience. It involves a judgment of the will with reference to the ends which one has sought in living and achieving the self. The judgment of God now stands where the judgment of the self stood before. Things are no longer merely ethical or unethical, they are sinful or righteous—a religious quality has appeared in morality. Now the moment that the religious quality appears, the stage is set for withdrawal from social intercourse and in a sense a withdrawal of the self from nature. Hence the struggle with the flesh—in short, asceticism.

But this is only one aspect of the logic of the result. As a result of his vision, the former tensions are not resolved in function. He has to go through the whole process of the achieving of individuality with God as the new center of reference. It requires a very stern exercise of the will because a new orientation has taken place. In a sense he is becoming a new creature, a qualitative urgency is at the focal point of his consciousness. I venture to say that every new synthesis of the individual around a fresh goal on whatever level of experience it may take place, is but an implied reference to the ultimate goal of human life, namely, to know God, in some exhaustive and completely thoroughgoing sense.[36] When Commodore Perry suggests that for twelve years he was ill at ease until he planted the stars and stripes over the North Pole;[37] when a music critic says of Roland Hayes[38] that he sings because he must sing; when a news reporter suggests that Walter Hampden had to stop playing in a contemporary drama to play the role of Shylock in order to keep a contract with his soul;[39] when the Apostle Paul says, "woe is me if I preach not the Gospel"[40] or when he exclaims to Agrippa, "I was not disobedient to the heavenly vision";[41] or when Jesus says, "the spirit of the Lord is upon me, for He has anointed me to preach the Gospel to the poor, to open the eyes of the blind, to unstop the ears of the deaf, to release the captive, to announce the accepted year of the Lord"[42] these fundamentally are in the same frame of reference.

It is this inner equilibrium that must be maintained at all costs so that the person will stand ever in immediate candidacy for the direct visitation of God. This is the heart of the meaning of discipline in the religion of the mystic.—All the negative things are present in the discipline, yes, this cannot be denied; the highly abnormal aberrations of mind are present, oftentimes, to be sure. But there is something more, there is strength, power released in the life of man here, a kind of concomitant overflowing of creative energies which demand that he *true* himself by the highest. This he seeks to do through discipline with unrelenting austerity; he must bring himself, his will, his feelings, his very thoughts and impulses under the synthesizing scrutiny of God. All else is trivial and in a sense irrelevant. The greatest mystic-ascetics in the Christian tradition have turned the whole stream of Christian thought and achievement into new and powerful channels of practical living.

The flesh does fight against the spirit. In Jesus Christ as symbol, temporary or permanent, the Christian mystic sees the meaning of the triumph of the spirit over the body; the transcending and triumphant power of God over the most relentless pressure and persistence of things that divide and destroy. To know Him in the fellowship of His suffering seemed to the Christian mystic the key to his victory. In this the mystic proves himself a man of rarest insight and power. In this insight the mystic anticipates the needs of all men. We want deliverance from things which divide, which bind and render us impotent and purposeless. We want to find a controlling purpose for our living and for our lives. With relentlessness and fever we seek always to find meaning, in some ultimate sense, for our lives so that we may be able to live with dignity and courage in our world. This the mystic achieves by what to him is an experience of an absolute good and his ethical task is to retain that good in the "*for instances*" of experience.

What Professor Hocking[43] has called the principle of alternation is in the very structure of all experience. The mystic discovers this in a most extraordinary fashion. He is a man—he is a part and parcel of all the world of nature—he has warring impulses within and participates in strife without. He sees that the world of things and men does not conform to the unity which he has experienced in his vision. Was his vision false? Was his experience genuine or was it merely an illusion? He finds that the two worlds must in some sense be one because he participates actively in both at the same moment but he is convinced that the meaning of the below is in the above.

With such a conviction, ascetism no longer means withdrawal from men but rather it means a steady insistence that one's human relations conform more and more to the transparency of one's inner graces, one's inner equilibrium in which is his consciousness of the active presence of God. Humanity is viewed as a unit within which are particular individuals all of which must be yielded to the control of God. This calls for the highest possible ethical demands for one's own conduct, for one's outgoing relation. Often it leads one to cut right across all social forms, all social behavior patterns, all conventions. There is a profound element of anarchy in all spiritually motivated behavior. The temptations to pride, arrogance, self-righteousness, are ever present but the risk has to be run and the only safeguard is the recurring vision in the acts of worship themselves. And insistently the significance of the acts of worship must be tested by the degree to which they remain living channels for the direct release of God into the life of the worshipper. When they become institutionalized they are apt to become dead so that the mystic seems always to be the foe of institutional religion. He is very sensitive to the crystallizing of acts of worship into dead forms. It is profoundly true that he does not stand in need of the institution or the institutional forms as such. Even in Catholicism any careful reading of the testimony of the mystics convinces one that the church has no real friend in the mystic.

In addition to the scrutiny of the mystic's personal relations as far as what he will do or will not do in a given situation, there is a whole question of the quality of service the mystic must render to his fellowmen.

Canon Kirk has a most illuminating discussion on this point in his *Vision of God.** He insists that the concept of service has two profoundly different elements in it—one is the service of humility, and the other is the service of patronage.[44] Only the former is Christian. It is his opinion that only worship guarantees to service the quality of humility that makes it really Christian—really good. There is no gratuitous quality when it springs from patronage. It is the attitude of condescension, of arrogance, the "holier than thou" manifestation much of which I have experienced in missions and observed on the mission field. It says, I am better than you, poor devil, I am really a very different order of being and out of my plenty, out of my advantage over you, I deign to come to your rescue. You ought to be grateful to me. In fact your gratitude must have in it a certain abjectness in order that my own position and ego may be rendered even more immune to attacks of unity.

Humility cannot be acquired in that way. It comes only when a man looks at himself, what he is, in the quiet but penetrating glow of his vision of God. Without this he cannot maintain the necessary increment of humility at the very center of his good deeds. He has been loved by God, he has received the blessing of the presence of God as an act of grace and he must salute the good that there is in the other by the quality of humility present in his deeds for the other. It was in speaking of Jesus that Simkovitch says, "Humility can never be humiliated."[45] If that quality is present, then to have one's deeds gratefully received, to be thanked, even to be appreciated is beside the point. If what is done is applauded or not applauded, if it is known by others or unknown to others, it is irrelevant. If one is persecuted by the very individual whom one serves, that, too, is beside the point. It is only in the presence of God, in the moment when one is caught up in an all embracing unity that this new way of seeing one's self in one's relations is achieved. Kirk says, "Disinterested service is the only service that is serviceable."[46]

The concept of service as a means of acquiring merit has never been without its witnesses. The highest mystics insist that the essence of right acting is that it should be performed without regard to merit, to reward or punishment. Only

*K. E. Kirk, *Vision of God*, pp. 445ff.

the rare spirit achieves this as a rule of life but it is to be noted that whenever men love each other, action for the beloved takes on this quality of disinterestedness. The implications of behavior of this kind derived from the mystic's insight has far reaching and revolutionary significance for social change.

IV. "Mysticism and Social Change"

I come now to the last and, in some ways, the most fundamentally crucial lecture of the series. We shall begin with the proposition with which we closed our last lecture. The basic ethical significance of mysticism is individualistic; this cannot be successfully refuted but it has also been pointed out that even in the moment of vision there is a sense of community—a unity not only with God but a unity with all of life, particularly with human life. It is in the moment of vision that the mystic discovers that (his) "private values are undergirded and determined by a structure which far transcends the limits of one's individual self." The good which is given him must somehow be achieved in a framework of experiences native to his own life which his life "for instances" in a rich variety of details. The ascetic impulse having as its purpose individual purification and living brings the realistic mystic face to face with the society in which he functions as a person. He discovers that he is a person and a personality in a profound sense can only be achieved in a milieu of human relations. Personality is something more than mere individuality—it is a fulfillment of the logic of individuality in community.

Rufus Jones uses the term, *affirmation mystics,* to apply to those who are concerned with working out in a social frame of reference the realism of their mystic experience.[47] He says that the mystic is always more than any finite task declares, and "yet he accepts this task because he has discovered that only through the finite is the Infinite to be found."[48] Now the mystic is compelled to deal with social relations for two reasons. First, because much of the limitations and corruption of his own life of which he seeks to rid himself through discipline and rigorism is due to the fact of his belonging to a community of men and interest which foster the very things he discovers beclouding his vision. In the second place, in his effort to achieve the good, he finds that he must be responsive to human needs by which his life is surrounded. We shall discuss each of these in its order.

1. Isaiah saw the Lord—when he was dropped back into the stream of his conscious life he saw himself to be a man of unclean lips dwelling among people of unclean lips. The two facts are not different facts, they are essentially the same fact. It is basic to the Christian tradition that social sin and personal sin are bound up together in an inexorable relationship so that it is literally true that no man can expect to have his soul saved alone. The affirmation mystic is driven then, in the very nature of the case, in the very interests of the fulfillment of his

mystical vision to a grave concern in the state of the soul of other men. The crudest and barest individualistic ethic, realistically considered would guarantee this. Many a monastic ascetic, fleeing from the world to the wilderness discovered that in the barren wastes of his own solitariness were present all the things from which he had fled. What lesson is more clearly evident than this in the temptation story of Jesus, the basic issues inherent in the political framework of the Roman Empire, the problems of a suppressed minority, all these and many others were with Him. In the lonely night watches they were among the other wild beasts from the world of nature which kept the vigil with the Son of Man. It is not only the socialist but also the affirmation mystic or the man seeking the fullness of the vision of God who must say truly, "While there is a lower class, I am in it. While there is a criminal element, I am of it. While there is a man in jail, I am not free."[49] The distinction between personal selfishness and social selfishness, between personal religion and social religion which we are wont to make, must forever remain artificial and unrealistic.

The mystic, under obligation to achieve the good which in some profound sense is given in the moment of vision and which he already possesses, is concerned about the sins of human life. He discovers that they fall roughly into two general classifications—those that are in some sense personal and private because they concern certain manifestations of the ego, that are unrestrained, undisciplined, chaotic—what is ordinarily thought of as the sins of the flesh. His first move, therefore, is to conquer these, to reduce them to a manageable unit, to bring them under the central domination of a will that is committed to ends of purity and holiness. His second concern must be with those that spring from the collective unrestraint of his fellows, the social chaos which results from dominant forms of economic and political organization. The personal question, what makes it difficult and well nigh impossible for me as a person to achieve the good in my own life leads inevitably to the question, what makes it so difficult for my society to achieve the good? He may limit the questions to those aspects of his society that are united on the basis of a common goal inspired by a collective vision of God such as a church or Order but the problem fundamentally remains the same. For even if it is achieved in a selective group this group bears a fundamental relationship with all others and their achievement stands ever under attack until it is universal.

He sees that the root of many of his own difficulties is located in the fact of his own personal economic insecurity. He must earn a living, under conditions that are not responsive to his master concern, namely, the achieving of the good in his life. It is the merest romanticism to assume that because God is the Creator of human life and human nature and the world of nature that He is also in control of the network of social relationships by which men are bound to each other in ways other than a common ground of being. The freedom of the will of man is always the instrument that is apt to make for chaos in the social relations of men. The problems of human relations can never be solved merely by the radical transformation of individuals in society. Therefore, there are certain basic fears that never leave the mystic, fears that are rooted for instance in the threat of insecurity and all that goes with it. He cannot achieve the good even in his simplest relations with his fellows because of the difficulties involved in establishing a basis of trust between him and them that will not victimize him in his effort to maintain himself in the world. This is true because each man is an actual threat or may easily become an actual threat to his security. The tendency is to let the ethical insight of love remain transcendent in his relationships but never imminent in them.

The risk of annihilation is too great. Now the Catholic mystic who identified himself with some order in the church short-circuited this whole problem on the economic side because the church guaranteed to him his economic needs and released him from direct responsibility for them. It simply put the whole problem one or two steps back in the process but did not solve it. We shall have occasion to refer to the bearing of this fact on service a littler later in our discussion.

Or again when he tries to achieve the good in his political relations he is brought sharp up against the fact that these relationships are characterized by methods of control in the State which give the advantage to one class as over against another class—that justice is robbed of its moral quality and is merely a state of equilibrium which represents a truce between the exploiters and exploited with the weight of the decision always on the side of privilege and power. The problems seem so hopeless that there is ever present the temptation to flee from the world and attempt to settle the problem of achieving the good along lines true to the very nature of asceticism.

2. The mystic is forced to deal with social relations in the second place because in his effort to achieve the good he finds that he must be responsive to human need by which he is surrounded, particularly the kind of human need in which the sufferers are victims of circumstances over which, as individuals, they have no control, circumstances that are not responsive to the exercise of an individual will however good and however perfect. This brings up for discussion once again the question of service. May I remind you of Kirk's quotation that "Disinterested service is the only service that is serviceable." Now, precisely what is disinterested service? In an appendix to *The Vision of God*, Canon Kirk has a most illuminating analysis of the concept. He defines selfishness "as a lack of due regard for the well-being of others," and "unselfishness . . . is the payment of due regard to the well-being of others."[50] It would seem to me that disinterested service is a kind of service that has no narrow ulterior motive at work, a kind of service in which the person served is not a means to some end in which he does not share and participate directly. There are at least two levels of

disinterestedness—one, in which the individual is free from exploiting the need of others for purely narrow interest or gratification. An American novelist of the last century put it this way,[51] "No man may say I have smiled on him in order to use him or call him my friend that I may make him do for me the work of a servant."* There is a second level of service, in which the individual is interested in relieving human need because he sees it as in some definite sense crowding out of the life of others the possibility of developing those qualities of interior graces that will bring him into immediate candidacy for the vision of God. It is in this latter sense that we come upon the mandatory raison d'etre of the affirmation mystic's interest in social change and in social action. He is not interested in social action because of any particular political or economic theory; he is not interested in social action primarily from the point of view of humanitarianism or humanism—as important as these emphases are, but he is interested in social action because society as he knows it to be ensnares the human spirit in a maze of particulars so that the One cannot be sensed nor the good realized. He is not deluded into thinking that once men are freed from carking care, from anxiety due to poverty or riches, from misery due to greed and exploitation, they will automatically be in immediate candidacy for the perfectionism of the spirit. He sees, however, that with these situations relieved there is available a psychological climate in which men may ascend the mount of vision with freedom and abandonment. This can only be done when individuals become persons; they cannot become persons in a society in which the majority of mankind is involved in a life and death struggle for bare security. In this struggle a comparatively small number have arisen above the line of bare security and have established themselves in such a strong position of control of the total economic life of man that they may be regarded as the very custodians of the lifeline of the masses of their fellows. They have possession of the means of production and are in a position to control for their own interests and the perpetuation of their kind the natural resources that are the main bases of supply for the masses of the people, all of this without a sense responsibility to the people. In the absence of this responsibility to the people there is very little hope that the individuals who make up the rank and file of mankind can become persons. Social power in society as we know it is inevitable. The problem is to place dynamic and effective inner moral and external social checks upon the centers of social power. This can only be done by broadening the basis of social responsibility on the part of social control until it includes all of the individuals in society and by injecting a sense of high morality in the persons who emerge as a result of the radical alteration in the structure of social relationships which is involved. The guaranty of the basic economic needs of the persons will be located in the collective will of

*Allen, *The Choir Invisible.*

the body politic and with reference to the struggle for bread the imperialistic will of persons can be relaxed. When this happens the insight of the mystic as to the ultimate meaning of human life will have practical relevancy without seeming to be unrealistic, romantic or sentimental.

Between the present order of society and that order of society which we have described is a perilous way but it is a way in which the affirmation mystic must chart his course. What then is his course of action? Let me gather up the threads of my position to this point: the affirmation mystic interprets the meaning of man's life in terms of an experienced unity with God in a conscious sense. "To know that our being has been taken up and made an organic part of His very self, because He wills and because we will it, is the end of true mysticism."[52] What he experiences he is under obligation to achieve in experience. In his effort to achieve this in experience he is brought face to face with evil in his own life and in the lives of others and the reflection of this evil in the relationship by which he is bound to his fellows and his fellows are bound to him. He cannot escape the responsibility of working out the good in a manifold of inner and outer relations. He knows that he cannot escape in mere asceticism even as he recognizes its merits he must embrace the social whole and seek to achieve empirically the good which has possessed him in his moment of profoundest insight. In his effort to do this, he constantly checks his action by his insight. It keeps his insight true and his action valid.

Now we are prepared to point out certain things with reference to the way he charts his course. First, he must bring his own spirit, those stubborn and recalcitrant aspects of it, under the domination of the God whom he has known in his mystical union. This, alone, is often the quest of a lifetime. His inmost desires must be checked by his new will. In this he does not ever struggle alone, God is his strength. In the second place, he must be as charitable towards the weaknesses of others as he is towards the weaknesses of himself for he knows through bitter experience that much has flown from his own life into the lives of others that was unworthy and that it is mandatory that he look with understanding compassion upon others as that which is unworthy flows from them to him. Further, his inner purity demands that he must not condemn in society what he does not condemn himself. These considerations belong primarily in the realm of personal piety. There can be no substitute for personal piety for he cannot be a liar to himself. In the third place, he sees that he shares consciously or unconsciously in the collective guilt of his age, of his society, of his race, and his problem is how to work out an atonement for this guilt in ways that would be redemptive and not make this action the goal of life. The obvious thing for him to attempt is some form of moral appeal to his fellows that will make them acutely aware of the nature of sin and to bring them to judgment. If he is dealing with persons who share with him in some collective manner, a conscious sense of the ultimate meaning of human life, his basis of appeal is comparatively simple. It remains to point out to them in a wide variety of ways how their collective action vitiates the possibility of achieving the good in experience. In the absence of such unanimity on the part of the controllers of society his problem is to bring such persons to a mount of vision in which they themselves stand in immediate candidacy to be laid hold on by God. Activity of this sort is apt to be futile for reasons that are obvious. Therefore, the affirmation mystic has to deal with them in the areas of their activities. Preaching to such persons, in my opinion, is apt to be a waste of effort and is a blind alley. Some method must be achieved by which the sufferers in the situation can act so as to shock the oppressor into a state of upheaval and insecurity. This is possible only when the oppressed individuals can become persons in a social classification and a basis of equality can accordingly be established between them and the oppressor. It is for this reason that I do not see any substitute for the emergence of a conscious sense of community among the masses of men which will provide a dignity and a worthfulness characteristic of persons on the basis of which equality between them and the oppressor can be established. The moment this is done the ground is prepared for pointing up to them the ultimate significance of life. It is in moral and spiritual leadership of this quality that the affirmation mystic comes into his own. Resistance to any efforts pointing towards community among the masses is the inevitable reaction of the controllers of society. By threats, coercion, overt violence, depending upon the desperateness of the situation, they will seek to hold the masses in a state of depersonalized individualism and because they dominate the political life of the society the State will be called upon to sanction the measures that are taken. The final question then is, can the affirmation mystic give his approval to coercion? The logic of his ethical insight says "no," for he understands that violence hardens the egocentric will of men and gives to unrestrained self-regarding impulses the widest possible range with the nullification of all inhibiting moral sanctions and impulses.

He, therefore, refuses to reach the conclusion that violent coercion is the ultimate means by which a community of men can be achieved in which individuals may emerge as persons standing in immediate candidacy for the vision of God. At long last it may be true that life is its own restraint, that the seeds of destruction are inherent in the nature of evil and what one individual grasps as the ultimate end of life is somehow even now being worked out through long weary stages in the revelation of God in the progress of history. It is this faith and this confidence that makes the affirmation mystic see that working and waiting are two separate activities of the human spirit but he who works for the new day in that act waits for its coming which can be achieved by God and God, alone.

Eden Seminary Bulletin, Spring 1939, 3–31.

1. Eden Theological Seminary was founded in 1850 and moved to its current home in Webster Groves, Missouri in 1924. Originally a seminary for the Evangelical Synod of America, it is now associated with its successor denomination, the United Church of Christ. One of its best-known graduates, Reinhold Niebuhr, a good friend of Thurman's, was on the board of the seminary in 1939 and very likely played a behind-the-scenes role in the initial offer to Thurman for the lecture series. The first black student entered Eden Theological Seminary in 1933.

2. From Harold Pflug, 28 October 1938, HTC-MBU: Box 17.

3. For contemporary publishing interest in the lectures, see From William L. Savage, 13 April 1939, HTC-MBU: Box 19. A portion of the lecture series was reprinted in Walter Earl Fluker and Catherine Tumber, eds., *A Strange Freedom: The Best of Howard Thurman on Religious Experience and Public Life* (Boston: Beacon, 1998), 108–23.

4. Thurman slightly misstates Eliot's comment in "The Function of Criticism" (1923): "At one time I was inclined to take the extreme position that the *only* critics worth reading were the critics who practised, and practised well, the art of which they wrote." The main qualification Eliot offers "is that a critic must have a very highly developed sense of fact," which is reflected in Thurman's paraphrase. T. S. Eliot, *Selected Essays* (New York: Harcourt, Brace, 1950), 19.

5. A common phrase of German mystic Meister Eckhart (ca. 1260–1327).

6. Perhaps a reference to Revelation 3:8.

7. Nikolai Berdiaev (1874–1947) was a Russian émigré theologian. Among his many books was (with the author listed as Nicholas Berdyaev) *Freedom and the Spirit* (New York: Scribners, 1935).

8. Thomas Hywel Hughes (1875–1945), a Welsh theologian, authored several books on the psychology of religious experience. As Thurman indicates, he is closely following "Are There Different Kinds of Knowledge?" chapter 4 in Hughes's *The Philosophic Basis of Mysticism* (Edinburgh: Clark, 1937), 110–46. Instances where Thurman directly quotes or closely paraphrases Hughes are indicated below.

9. "Truth is, in the final analysis, a unity." Hughes, *Philosophic Basis,* 110.

10. "No knowledge of any kind is possible to man except on the basis of reason, for even the barest sensation involves 'awareness' as an element of consciousness, and this involves reason, though it may not involve reasoning." Hughes, *Philosophic Basis,* 117.

11. "Life is deeper than, and prior to, thought. Experience is antecedent to reflection." Hughes, *Philosophic Basis,* 119.

12. Thurman had long been interested in reflective thinking; see his essay in volume 1, "Can It Be Truly Said That the Existence of a Supreme Spirit Is a Scientific Hypothesis?"

13. "In the sphere of science, therefore, feeling is at a discount, and emotion is suspect. But to discount feeling is in reality to rule out an essential and basic element in human personality." Hughes, *Philosophic Basis,* 121.

14. James Ward (1843–1925) was an English psychologist, whose article "Psychology" in the ninth edition of the *EncyclopÊdia Britannica* (1875) was an important critique of the dominant school of associationist psychology. Ward argued for a more active model of the mind's attention and interaction with the external world. His fuller treatment of the subject is found in his *Psychological Principles* (Cambridge: Cambridge University Press, 1918).

15. "The late Professor James Ward, in his notable essay on 'Psychology' in the *EncyclopÊdia Britannica* bases his whole treatment on the assumption that conscious life begins in a vague *feeling-continuum*, and that intelligence and conation develop by differentiation of functions within this *continuum* at the call of the pressing needs of life. The primal fact, however, is this *feeling-continuum*, and in a sense it is the stuff out of which reason and volition, in their subsequent activities, grow. . . . Attention, which is the primal mode of conation, is thus dependent on feeling. Further, it is through attention, and the effort to guide it in more intense and concentrated directions, that the differentiation of reason appears and subsequently grows." Hughes, *Philosophic Basis,* 121.

16. "In intuitive knowledge, as distinct from rational knowledge, more of man's personality is involved. It is, in a word, more personal." Hughes, *Philosophic Basis,* 123.

17. "May we not also say that such [intuitive] knowledge has more of the essentially real in it, that it touches and partakes of reality at a deeper point than the knowledge attained by the processes of discursive reasoning?" Hughes, *Philosophic Basis,* 124.

18. "When . . . we consider the knowledge which the mystics enjoy in their deepest religious experience, we discover that it resembles at every point the knowledge of intuition. We have seen that it comes to them with overwhelming conviction and certainty, having the immediacy of an experience. It strikes them with the vividness and clarity of a sensation." Hughes, *Philosophic Basis,* 124.

19. "It breaks in on the soul when it is in a fit state to receive it." Hughes, *Philosophic Basis,* 124.

20. "What they really mean by 'passivity.'" Hughes, *Philosophic Basis,* 125.

21. "They are receptive, God is disclosive." Hughes, *Philosophic Basis,* 125.

22. "Whilst the experience itself in all these [different religious traditions of mysticism] may be, at basis, the same, it falls on a background of thought and tradition which is different." Hughes, *Philosophic Basis,* 126.

23. "We may state the position tentatively by saying that it is along the line of feeling that we attain to the most real and intimate knowledge of a person; that personal knowledge differs from impersonal knowledge in the fact that it bears within itself a greater and more determinative element of feeling." Hughes, *Philosophic Basis,* 137.

24. The following quotation is from Kenneth E. Kirk, *The Vision of God: The Christian Doctrine of the Summum Bonum* (London: Longmans, Green, 1931), 534, quoting Henri Bremond, *Introduction à la philosophie de la prière* (1929).

25. Edward Caird (1835–1908) was a British idealist philosopher, master of Balliol College, Oxford, from 1893 to 1907, and the author of numerous works on religion and philosophy. The quotation is from Caird's *The Evolution of Theology in the Greek Philosophers* (Glasgow: MacLehose, 1904), 2:3–4.

26. Mary Anita Ewer, *A Survey of Mystical Symbolism* (London: Society for Promoting Christian Knowledge, 1933), 22, passin. Ewer (1892–1961) was a writer on theosophy and other religious topics. Thurman's October 1934 *Journal of Religion* review of Ewer's book is printed in volume 1.

27. These examples were written by Thurman himself, and likely provide a tantalizing glimpse of a mystical experience, poetically rendered.

28. Isaiah 6:1.

29. Dante, *Paradiso,* canto 31, lines 15–18, 28–30.

30. The most famous poem of the English Catholic writer Francis Thompson (1859–1907), and a favorite poem of Thurman's.

31. Augustine, *Confessions*, X, 6 (8).

32. Rudolf Otto (1869–1937), German theologian, whose best-known work is *The Idea of the Holy: An Inquiry into the Non-Rational Factor in the Idea of the Divine and Its Relation to the Rational* (London: Oxford University Press, 1923).

33. Bertrand Russell was a noted British philosopher and the author of numerous books; for additional information about him, see the biographical footnote in volume 1. This quotation is from his *Mysticism and Logic* (London: Allen & Unwin, 1917).

34. From Leo Tolstoy's *My Confession and the Spirit of Christ's Teaching* (1887), quoted in William Ernest Hocking, *The Meaning of God in Human Experience: A Philosophic Study of Religion* (New Haven, Conn.: Yale University Press, 1912), 466.

35. Hughes, *The Philosophic Basis of Mysticism*, 380. Henry or Heinrich Suso (ca. 1300–1366), a student of Meister Eckhart, was a prominent German mystic.

36. Thurman offered a similar catalog, with most of the same people, in his 1927 essay "Finding God," printed in volume 1.

37. Thurman confuses the explorer Robert Peary (1856–1920), the leader of the 1909 expedition that was probably the first one to reach the North Pole, with Commodore Matthew C. Perry (1794–1858), whose expedition "opened" Japan to the West in the 1850s. Peary, like Perry, was an American naval officer, rising to the rank of rear admiral.

38. Roland Hayes (1887–1997) was an African American concert tenor and a friend of Thurman's.

39. In "Finding God" Thurman offers the same anecdote about Hampden and Hamlet, though Thurman's confusion is perhaps understandable, since Hampden appeared on Broadway in *Hamlet* and *The Merchant of Venice* in consecutive runs from October 1925 through February 1926, and Thurman probably saw both productions. *WHAH*, 53.

40. 1 Corinthians 9:16.

41. Acts 26:19.

42. Luke 4:18.

43. William Hocking's "principle of alternation" held that "God and the world . . . must be worked in with one another forever: forever they must be pursued in alternation," so that the mystic and religious seeker will be able to combine "the peace of the hermit" with "the variety and stress of life." *Meaning of God*, 407, 427.

44. Kirk discusses this in a subchapter headed "Is 'Worship' a Higher Ideal than 'Service'?" *Vision of God*, 445–51.

45. Vladimir G. Simkhovitch, *Toward the Understanding of Jesus and Other Historical Studies* (New York: Macmillan, 1921), 60.

46. Kirk, *The Vision of God*, 451.

47. In a series of works, beginning with *Social Law in the Spiritual World: Studies in Human and Divine Inter-Relationship* (Philadelphia: Winston, 1904), Rufus M. Jones championed the distinction between "negation mystics," who are otherworldly contemplatives, and "affirmation mystics," who have been champions of great reforms and moral crusades.

48. Jones, *Social Law*, 154.

49. A favorite quotation of Thurman from Eugene V. Debs.

50. Kirk, *Vision of God*, 553.

51. James Lane Allen (1849–1925), a Kentuckian who often used his native state as the setting for his fiction, wrote these lines in *The Choir Invisible* (New York: Macmillan, 1897), 359.

52. Jones, *Social Law,* 155.

"A VISION OF GOD AND HUMAN NATURE"

6–10 MARCH 1939

TORONTO, ONT.

Under the auspices of the Student Christian Movement of Canada, Thurman delivered a series of sermons at the University of Toronto's Wycliffe College in March 1939. In the first lecture, not printed here, Thurman argued that knowledge "must have a frame of reference that gives to it its particular validity and meaning" and explains that he could not "live meaningfully without establishing a frame of reference in which the details of my living will find significance and fruitfulness and creativeness." He concluded by leaving the audience with two questions, which he resumes discussing here. Thurman's reflections in this essay emphasize that those who glimpse a "vision of God" must make a commitment to remake not only their own world, but also their relation to nature and to the social world and its ills. This cannot be done as a lone individual, but only as one who is part of a community of like-minded individuals. The argument in "A Vision of God and Human Nature" is similar to Thurman's two other extended works of this period, "The Significance of Jesus" and "Mysticism and Social Change."

DR. THURMAN'S ADDRESS—TUESDAY

Life is hard, brutal, unjust often immoral. It is the courage you bring to life that matters, not life. You will stand once more in the sunshine once you have the strength to say that.

We shall continue our discussion of yesterday afternoon by giving some attention to the two questions with which we ended our thought together. What demands am I as a Christian to make upon myself? What methods shall I employ to secure the triumph of these demands over the complex unruliness of my own spirit? {(} What demands am I as a Christian to make upon myself? What methods shall I employ to secure the triumph of these demands over the complex unruliness of my own spirit?{)} All of this in an effort to establish a frame of reference in the light of which I may charter my course through the world, with assurance and with conviction and with dignity. Now it seems to me that the first thing that I must do is this: I must embrace as a self-conscious act of will on my part the interpretation of the destiny of man on the earth as Jesus dreamed it. {(} I must embrace as a self-conscious act of will on my own part the destiny of man on the earth as Jesus dreamed it.{)} For looking at the earthly career of Jesus we see Him as a Jewish teacher with a mystic sense of His almighty commitment making it mandatory for Him to proclaim universal love as the means of life abundant.

Within the confines of that ~~formation~~ a spirit which was to Him so fully giving that it penetrated all his consciousness. He lived gently but ardently, gently but firmly, with vision proclaiming that life as he (defined) {envisioned} it is available to all people, rich, poor, secure, insecure, privileged, underprivileged, saints, sinners. Valuable as a practical "for-instance" of living to all people at whatever cultural level or whatever degree of material or spiritual degradation they may find themselves. Not only did he live this vision ardently, gently, persistently but he died terribly as a supreme exemplification of his own teaching. Therefore when men contemplate his amazing career they are driven to say that whatever else God may be like he must be like this. It is small wonder then that a New Testament scholar said that man may come to knowledge of God through every good man, but that he who seeks God with all his heart will some day on his way meet Jesus.

I must embrace as a self-conscious act of will on my part the interpretation of the destiny of man on the earth as Jesus dreamed it. Ye have been told he said, that you shall not commit adultery; but I say that the thought of lust in the human heart is in every sense as bad as the overt act of adultery, in that it exists in the human impulse of life. You have been told an eye for an eye, a tooth for a tooth; but I say, if you do not relax the very impulse of retaliation you give yourself over to a destiny of evil. You have been told that you should love your neighbour and hate your enemy; but I say that you must move out on the highway of your life with an all embracing impulse of redemptive love and creative goodwill, even towards him who seeks the very destruction of your life, if you want to be a son of God.[1]

But I must not stop there. By a disciplined use of my imagination I must definitely give meaning to my commitment with reference to my innermost self and with reference to the physical environment, and with reference to my social environment.

The Fallacy of the Fool—And God saw everything that he had made and beheld that it was very bad and on the seventh day therefore he could not rest. In the morning and the evening he visited himself with terrible [word missing] and on the seventh day he finished that which is of [word missing] of the sea and the lights of the firmament and he gave it imagination because it was made in his own image and those unto whom it is given shall see God.

By a disciplined use of my imagination, I must give meaning to my commitment, with reference to my inmost self, my physical environment and my social environment. Jesus insists upon a certain childlike quality of self-projection, if the realm of God is to enter into us, or if we are to enter into the realm of God.

e.g. I was visiting at the home of a friend and a young boy entered the room with his kiddy car and said "Mr. Thurman, will you help me change a tire? I have had a blow-out." We changed the tire; and still it would not go. The boy said that it must be out of gas, and went into the other room and returned with a glass of water. He got on his kiddy car, drank the glass of water, and was off. A sense of penetrating realistic self-projection without which the vision of God cannot be translated in living for-instances.

Now let us analyze this just a little more. First I must embrace as a self-conscious act of will on my part the destiny of man on the earth as Jesus dreamed it; then I must by a disciplined use of my imagination give meaning to that commitment which rules my inmost self. With reference to my inner self, I must achieve an inner harmony. There must be some control over my impulses, over my desires and appetites, which impulses, which desires and appetites at some earlier stage in the life of man were for guidance or for physical survival in the world. But I must bring under the control of a central commitment all the unrestrained impulses of my life. The first self-regarding impulse that befell the life of man was to guarantee survival against enemies; but I must bring it under control in the interest of an inner harmony that is the expression of my commitment, which commitment is a self-conscious act of will on my part. I must not merely be content with being a son of nature, I must achieve the right to call myself a son of God. As a son of nature many of these impulses move without restriction; but as a son of God I must bring a new orientation to the sense of my being, and to the sense of my self-conscious thought of willing and acting.

For some this means going through a great emotional or a great psychological upheaval that results in establishing a new behaviour pattern. When I come through that experience all of life takes on a new meaning. We can understand what George James[2] says when he came past the angel with the fiery sword, "All the world had a new smell." I think the modern age is apt to be superficial in its rejection of the significance of such catastrophic transformations.

I must embrace as a self-conscious act of will on my part the destiny of man on the earth as Jesus dreamed it. That inner harmony is achieved often as a result of a great cataclysmic upheaval that sends me in a new direction, in spite of all of the subtle pullings of my personality to go back in the old direction. For some others it means a slow growth of progressive control, a gradual re-commitment of all the behaviour patterns of life; slowly but little by little transforming areas of my life and character that are not under the central focus of my commitment; a gradual development of the processes, making gains and experiencing losses, but always pursuing the impulse of my life like a nemesis. "Yet all experience," Tennyson makes Ulysses say, "is but an arch wherethro' gleams that untraveled world whose margin fades forever and forever as as I move."[3] I am on my way to achieve it. I have not arrived. He guides me, and I shall arrive in His good time.

For others it means a natural unfolding of the life, a transparent quality. They are what William James call "once-born" souls.[4]—Story of a man who could do nothing but good.

However I go at it, whatever may be the destiny for me as a result of how I am put together, it seems to me that I do not escape the inexorable demand that I bring myself under the persistent and constant scrutiny of the judgment of God with reference to the details of my character; and in the light of this commitment I am able to achieve an inner harmony that makes me anticipate in myself the very kingdom of God, even while it is yet a dream of my imagination. If I do this I find that God is not unrelated to the whole process but that God becomes a much more direct need to my spirit. Thomas Aquinas, when at work on problems and finding his mind wandering, took up devotional literature which rested his mind, and then he was able to turn back to metaphysics with less confusion.

Poem:—Give me courage to live, really live, not merely exist, give me the strength to be free and give me the courage to go on, taking what life gives, spending myself to the full, head high, spirit winged like a god till the shadows draw close. Even then gracious God hear my prayer, give me courage to live.

Dr. Thurman's Address—Wednesday

We shall begin this afternoon where we stopped yesterday afternoon. By the use of my imagination I must seek the points at which it is possible for me to bring the impulses of my inmost self under the control of my central commitment.

To-day I must seek to bring my physical environment under the control of my central commitment to God, as envisioned and as dreamed of and as lived by Jesus Christ.

In the first place, it seems to me then; I must achieve harmony with the world of nature so that my fear of life will be relaxed, and not only relaxed, but so that my fear of life will be transformed to love of life which makes me dedicate my particular life to high and holy ends. We shall examine the bearings of that proposition as a part of what we have to say this afternoon.

Man is surrounded by the impersonal world of nature. Much of the effort of human life is spent in an attempt to reduce the world of nature to a series of manageable units of understanding and control. Man is not satisfied until somehow he is able to put the face of a man upon the world of nature. In the evolution of man in the world there came a time, it seems, when the mind of man did not have to be held down by the functioning of certain impulses towards survival, when the energy of the human animal was not all consumed in the effort to guarantee and protect itself against a hostile environment. Man came down from the trees and lived in a hole in the rocks, and it must have been a great moment in the life of man when he was able to close that hole up against prowling animals of prey. There was a great difference between the peace and relaxation of that first night in the ground as over against the last night in the tree. There was time for man to dream about other days in the past and to play with guesses about to-morrow and to-morrow and to-morrow. Now this developing rational process in man caused him, it seems to me, to support himself in the world of nature so that more and more he seemed to himself to be something apart from the world of nature. He looked upon nature with increasing objectivity, and religion has helped him. Thought about the gods and the meaning of life helped him further to hold himself separate from the world of nature. As his consciousness of values increased, he became aware of the sea that exists between himself and the world of nature, and the world of nature became something that was evil and sinful, something that was always working against his spirit. The god of nature or nature itself seemed more and more to be man's enemy, and his experience of the world of nature tended to verify and validate that judgment; for somehow it seems even to us that there is a great gulf between the uncharitable workings of the world of nature and the private world of desertions and hopes and fears and longings of the human spirit.

I was in a flood once and there is something uncanny about the way the water gradually rises and rises; and despite the fear of man or despite the prayers that leap out of the desperateness of the plight of man, the waters rise. So man has sought to protect himself from nature. He has elevated himself to a high position over against the world of nature, so that he wants to think of himself as being in some sense equal to a more intelligent than whatever controls the world of nature. I am the captain of my soul, the master of my fate. Henley called that poem "Invictus": "Victus" is the real truth of the matter.[5] Therefore man said,—I must put myself over against the world of nature and elevate myself so that I shall be wiser and more intelligent than the blind forces; for you see, they are blind, because they do not penetrate my private secrets and desires and fulfill my private needs.

Story of a man whose child was killed by his neighbour's dog, and who at first desired revenge on the owner of the dog, and refused to give him seed to plant his field. But he came to realize that man must be wiser than the blind forces of nature. I must plant my field with grain because I am wiser than nature; I must plant my enemy's field with grain so between me and him God may exist, so that God may become a reality in a relationship where he has not hitherto found existence. My defense against nature as an enemy tends to make man do this.

Or I may decide that nature is vindictive, that it is trying to pursue me in a relentless fashion, and that I must fight it, not merely control and resist it. I must defy it. It is my enemy and it is personal. Man laughed and shouted "I will beat the god of nature yet," and he ploughed his fields over again after there had been a continued loss of crops.

Eventually the mind of man discovers that nature is not trying to do something to him, but that nature is ignoring him; and that is worst of all. We cannot stand being ignored even by nature because it takes away from us the important grounds of self estimate. Ex. a child fighting an older person who does not resist. "Why don't you fight me back. Don't ignore me," is her cry. Crush me, if you will, but I shall take comfort in the fact, even as I go to destruction, that you have used all the powers of your mind and spirit to crush me; and the measure of the weapon that you use is the measure of my significance.

But man has not stopped there. One of the important contributions of psychology, biology, physiology, etc. to religion, is precisely at the point that they have insisted that the gulf that man has made between nature and himself must be brought closer together. There is something deep within him that always wants to take wings and fly. When man thinks like that about nature he begins to discover that the harmony that he seeks within himself, the harmony that he is trying to achieve under the aegus and domination of an overmastering commitment to the highest and holiest ends of life, that there are surrounding him in nature aspects of that harmony of which he himself as a child of nature is essentially a part. And the task of man with reference to the world of nature is to seek fresh ways by which he can guarantee an identity of the harmony within and the harmony that he sees at large in the world of nature, a harmony that seems to be impersonal in some of its aspects. Commander Byrd in his book "Alone" at the end of the Chapter entitled "God" says that as he stood outside his dugout looking over the broad expanse of the polar seas he became objectively aware of the harmony in the realm of the world of nature; and he knew through all the levels of his consciousness that the world of nature is a cosmos rather than a chaos, and that if he could reach within himself the harmony that is within nature then he could understand nature and perhaps be understood by it.[6] It is like the second temptation of Christ in the wilderness, when the devil tempted Christ to hurl himself down from the temple. "The world of nature is not fundamentally harmony; it is not fundamentally orderly; it is capricious, and if you have the formula you can do what you want to do." Christ replies that one can't go against the law of nature because the world of nature <u>is</u> orderly, and anyone who goes against these laws tempts God to destroy.

Let us pursue it one more step. It seems to me then that harmony, law, order, resourcefulness, are there in the world of nature and must be made to serve the ends of the Christian commitment rather than made to serve the ends of selfishness and greed and baseness. It is not a paradox to me that in the material world at the very time when the mind of man is most far reaching, devising ways and means to bring nature under control, at this moment the mind of man has lost confidence in the very integrity of human life. They do not believe that the mind of man can devise methods by which it is possible for men to live together on the same planet in groups without blowing each other's brains out, and that conviction seems to be increasingly rife at this moment. It seems to me that this is because the world of nature, the physical environment of man, has not been brought under the persistent domination of the central commitment of the will of man to the way of life as for-instanced in Jesus Christ. Men have studied chemistry; and one of the crowning acts of their attainment is to devise a form of poison gas for which there may not quickly be found an antidote. Chemical elements, neutral in themselves, and a manifestation of the harmony of a world of nature, man seizes and transforms into sprays of death, because the physical environment of man has not been brought under a central dedication to its self-conscious end to which I think Jesus Christ calls the human spirit. It is for this reason that the prophet Isaiah said there shall come a time when men shall beat their swords into ploughshares, and their spears into pruning-hooks, and the lion and the lamb shall lie down together; the little child shall play on the hole of the asp, and the child shall play in a nest of vipers and not be poisoned: For the knowledge of God shall at last have penetrated all the levels of consciousness on the planet. And that, it seems to me, is the great and central challenge of the Christian religion:—to make the physical environment become the very agency of self-conscious creative material and spiritual ends. And it is to that end that we, as members of the University, are called in our time.

DR. THURMAN'S ADDRESS—THURSDAY

What demands am I as a Christian to make upon myself, what methods shall I employ to secure the triumph of these demands over the complex unruliness of my own spirit? I must embrace as a self-conscious act of will on my own part the destiny of man upon the earth as Jesus envisioned it. By a disciplined use of my imagination I must constantly give meaning to that commitment with reference to my inner self, by bringing into line the impulses in me, however unruly they may be, so that there will be in my life an inner harmony based upon a profound consecration to God. I must also constantly give meaning to that commitment with reference to the world of nature, with reference to our physical environment, so that the resourcefulness and the harmony and beauty and richness of nature can somehow be made subservient to, or part of, a useful, deep, ~~or~~ and central commitment of my life, based upon this profound consecration.

Now this afternoon I must deal with the third thing. Not only must I constantly give meaning to my commitment with reference to myself and to my natural environment but I must do the same thing with reference to my social environment, ~~and~~ To-morrow we shall deal with the spiritual resources that are available in the tradition of our faith for those who would live a life after this fashion.

I must constantly give meaning to my commitment with reference to my social environment. "Behold I send you out as lambs among wolves." "You must be as wise as serpents and as harmless as doves." "Rejoice when you are being persecuted falsely for my sake." "And then the tempter carried him to a high place and showed him all the kingdoms of the world, and he said 'I will give all those to you, if you worship me. For even though you may not think so, the kingdoms of this world belong to me, and if you are planning to make a conquest of the kingdoms of this world in the interest of the kingdom of God, you must do so with my leave.'" We shall hold these things in the background of our mind, and one other: it is a picture from the Prophet Jeremiah, a curse upon him who relies upon man, who depends upon mere human aid . . . but happy is he who relies on God. He has no fear of scourge, hurting his life he goes on peering through when all around him have turned, and he looks out on the world with quiet eyes.

Man is surrounded by an impersonal social order. He is a part of the social order, he is a part of society but at the same time he is, if he be thoughtful, conscious of the fact that there is something radically impersonal about the social order. Like nature it will not take into account his private desires and his hopes and fears. Example: Eggs cost twenty-five cents one day and the next day the same eggs through no fault of your own cost three cents more. There is something very impersonal about ~~the~~ a social order that will not take into account the fact that I have private ambitions, desires and fears. Society impinges upon me at every point and it does not ask me any questions. It dictates what clothes I wear, and my diet. It has something it calls etiquette by which it places restrictions on behaviour and it does not ask me any questions about it. Only the most romantic person can say that the social environment, this impersonal aspect of society, is under the control even of a very high type of morality, not to speak of a great Christian commitment. If I have embraced as a self-conscious act of will the interpretation of the destiny of man on the earth as Jesus dreamed it; if on the basis of that commitment I have surrendered my life to a profound consecration and I seek to give that kind of testimony in my society; and if I seek to bring those aspects of my social environment with which I have to do under the control of that central commitment and of that deep consecration; if I try to do that, certain definite things must follow.

In the first place I can not remain silent in the presence of evil and injustice. I must cry out. It is mandatory that I cry out. I must protest. Now my protest, my crying out will be righteous. It is what they call "righteous indignation," but in there is often a conspicuous absence of penitence. A deep and profound penitence is needed. For if I recognize that I myself am a part of my social environment, and if I see manifestations of evil and injustice that are not under the control of the will and the purpose of God, but represent the unrestrained manifestations of creative egoistic impulse in man, if I am conscious of that, I must see that I participate in the injustice that I condemn by virtue of my membership in the society that is doing the injustice that caused me to cry out. Even if in my personal relationships no man may say that I have smiled on him in order to use him, or that I have called him my friend to make him do the work of a servant, even if in my personal relationship I have been able to carry out the details of my commitment, yet I am a part of my social environment and I participate in the order and disorder of that environment. All because of the deadness in my own spirit, because of the way in which I have not been able to bring my own self under the guidance of my central commitment, the way in which I have compromised this commitment, the way in which I have refused to apply it, in all of these ways I have contributed to my amoral insensitiveness in the world. If I am insensitive to evil, it means that the moral appeal to evil is very difficult. I can not continually restrain myself in the presence of the challenge to do good and to be good without paying for it in terms of moral and spiritual disintegration. ~~and~~ Much of the cynicism of modern life hinges upon the fact that moral man has not been willing to recognize the relationship that exists between the amount of moral and spiritual atrophe in his own spirit and the things that he is willing to do from day to day.

In the second place I must deliberately widen the area of my exposure to injustice with a view to helping and healing. We shrink from exposing ourselves to suffering and misery, and say that it is not our fault if we can't stand it because we did not make ~~myself~~ ourselves. I can't expose myself to evil and suffering and poverty because my nervous organizm is too delicately put together, so I shall hire somebody to do that for me who can stand it. God made him that way, he shall be my representative. If I am to be instrumental at all in bringing my social environment under the scrutiny and the dream of Jesus Christ and according to the will of God, I must be aware of injustice. I must deliberately widen my sensitiveness to injustice. I must see that while there is a lower class I am in it, where there is a criminal element I am of it, while there is a man in jail I am not free.

Thirdly, I must be persistent in my search for a technique and for methods by which the insights of my commitment can be implemented in practical terms of social transformation. I must take my mind with all of its creative powers, and my spirit, and try and search, always seeing if somehow I can implement my spiritual insight so as to make it effectual in the world that stands over and against the purpose and will of God. I am living in a society based largely upon violence. I must try and understand what it is. Violence is a very efficient and effective method by which men are able to effect justice in social relationships. The civilized man is one who is willing to make violence ultra-ratio,—rather than primo-ratio. A civilized man is one who is able to use all other methods before violence is used. A threat of violence is just as direct and effective. But he learns that violence hardens the will of man so that it outrages the dignity of human life. He discovers that hate is the handmade of violence. But he must look at it carefully. Hate very often performs a social function. When man finds himself in the presence of overwhelming and overmastering frustration, and he cannot cry aloud, the only thing left for him is to crystallize himself into a hard granite defiance of hate against the destroyer. But hate burns up the moral and spiritual bearings of the hater and leaves him a stranded corpse on the shores of his desolate experience. Therefore, if he is willing to give his testimony in the way of which I am talking, he must be opposed to it. It leaves then only one creative method that is not in disharmony with the central commitment of his life to God universal true. And here again he swings back to what Jesus proclaimed and of which his life became the for-instance . . .

Such a person in an impersonal lifeless, social environment moves into its midst as the ambulating epitomy of love, conscious that in the very nature of his commitment he has to prepare himself to enter into the heart of the meaning of the cross. Such a person as that says, I shall die perhaps, but that is all that I shall do for death. Death has important business in all parts of the world but I will not help him to destruction. I am not on death's pay-roll. I shall die, but that is all that I shall do for death. I shall not take him to any man's door. I am not on death's pay-roll.[7] And then I shall know what is meant by "My God, my God, why hast thou forsaken me?"

ADDRESS OF DR. THURMAN—FRIDAY

Bernard Shaw's Preface to "On the Rocks"[8] says, speaking to Pilate—"Cast out fear."

We come now to the last of our series together, and I want you to think of all the things we have been saying as a general background to the problem and the source of power and strength for one who undertakes to live in the world on the basis of the kind of commitment about which we have been thinking together.

There is the strength, of course, that comes from a great cause and a personal loyalty to that cause. The strength that comes from a central dominant commitment that somehow gives to a man's life a more-than-ordinary and commonplace significance. It seems to me that a great commitment gathers together the rather fragmentary aspects of living and focuses them toward the centre of one's concern and interest and meaning. It integrates those things that stand on the fringes of one's life that may not directly be related to his central commitment. It always strikes me with new power when I read those words of Jesus about the pearl of great price, about the man who ploughed in the field and discovered a treasure, and he sold everything he had in order to purchase it. But the cause must be one that makes an inexorable demand upon the life; a cause too great and compelling that in the very nature of the case it hardly seems possible that the individual will be able to fulfill it in a lifetime. The cause it seems to me which was the central concern of Jesus was the realization of a kingdom of friendly men upon the earth. A kingdom of friendly men in which the security of one man is guaranteed by all men. It seems to me that at every point Jesus was vitally concerned about a radical alteration of the framework of relationships of men so that any individual man would feel free to relax his tension and fear of insecurity and even of death. It is extraordinary to me, and it becomes more utterly amazing, that most human beings live their lives in the world from behind the barricades of their ghetto. They look out on the world and other people and have a profound mistrust of anything that will destroy these barricades. There is a great famine of trust in the world. And if men are haunted by the fear of hunger and poverty, if men are haunted by the fear that when they are old they will be destitute and stranded; that their children will grow up in a world without security; then each man at whom he looks seems to him to be a potential threat to his own life, and to relax his self-regarding impulse is to commit suicide. The way of life that facilitates a friendly kingdom in which trust is possible and in which love is practised is so staggering that it can only be the dream of God, and one who commits himself to such a cause pays the highest possible tribute to the dignity and the significance of man.

Now that is one source of power. But that is not enough. The life and the career of Jesus Christ most specifically is a source of power for the individual thus committed. For Jesus has identified himself primarily with the best that the mind of man can dream of as man contemplates the good life for himself, and for his age, and for his generation. So miraculous, it seems to me, is the fact that Jesus has identified himself primarily with the very best conception that man's mind can generate of the meaning of the good life in the world, that he constantly seems to be appealing not to any one age, or to any one race, or to any particular period of history, but he seems to be the for-instance of the good life for all ages and for all periods. It is not to suggest that he exhausts the possibilities of the revelation of God; but as far as my mind can grasp the meaning of life in the world, it seems to me that his insights are valid for establishing squatters rights, so that when I think about the ultimate possibilities of life I find myself thinking about it in some such terms as he has pictured it. So that I am driven to study his life, to examine his teaching, to lay myself bare to the persistent quality of his influence. Yes, it seems that I have no choice but to do that. And he becomes then a source of power for me as I try to live this kind of life. But after all, that becomes in a sense personal and private, and in some ways it is mystical, and I find myself driven to another source of power, the power that comes from the fellowship of men and women who themselves are committed to this end; And here I think we come to an important fact about the whole career of Jesus. Jesus had disciples not because he had profound misgivings as to whether or not his teaching would be perpetuated, not because he wanted to pass on to other generations his profound utterances. I think his faith in God and his amazing grasp of life would not let him be too deeply concerned at that point. But I think his disciples served as a kind of community. By the practical significance of his religious insight, and standing within the fellowship of his disciples, he projected himself into the Greco-Roman world and was able to carry on proclaiming eternal life. And his message of the kingdom of God he proclaimed against the unanimous testimony of his environment, always having available for himself, primarily, an intimate human fellowship in the midst of which he could find an other-than-self reference for his religious insights. This community of disciples gave to him the status of being a religious person in the world, rather than a religious individual in the world. For it is against a framework of the community that an individual emerges to the status of a person; and he can project himself functionally as a person in society because his roots are fashioned in an other-than-self reference that gives to him meaning. So it seems to me that some kind of fellowship is mandatory; and as far as the function of religion is concerned, the degree to which the Church provides that fellowship, that kind of community, that will give to the individuals in society the status and the dignity of persons against this frame work, against this background of social reference. To that degree will it be able to inspire in man a loyalty that transcends the loyalty to the class, that transcends the loyalty to the state, that transcends every other loyalty in the world, and to that degree it will always be an actual threat to any other organization of society that insists on demanding of men a greater loyalty. So that a fellowship of that sort becomes a source of power for the individual who moves out from it functionally in society, and whatever such a person does goes shock free with great glory. A background of intimate fellowship that has the significance of community for him, that gives to him the status of persons rather than individuals.

But all of these are not quite enough.

I need the power that comes from a great central commitment in life, and the great power that comes to me from meditating upon the life of Jesus Christ, and then the strength that comes out of that fellowship of men and women of a common dedication around a great purpose. But the ultimate source of power is God.

Somehow I must have a vital relationship with someone who can absorb all of the limitations of myself, all of the limitations of my personality, all of the limitations of my actions, and who in the absorption of these limitations will become for me the ultimate and absolute guarantor of all my meaning, of all my world of values, of all I envision when my mind and spirit are most lucid and clear. And the method by which I become increasingly aware of this powerful person, this source of utter strength and assurance, is worship, mediation and prayer. I do not become aware of him at the end of a silogism, or at the end of any logical pattern, helpful as those things may be. It is in prayer, in worship of that quality that I become fully conscious of the ultimate source of power. Prayer, then, it seems to me, grows first of all out of an imperative agency of trust which impels me to keep afresh in my spirit the very dedication to which my life is given. In moments of quiet I am able to touch at the centre of my spiritual focus the cause to which my life is dedicated. It is only worship that keeps at the centre of service humility, so that the worshipper of God, who serves his fellow men does not have contempt for the weakness, the limitations, the sordid aspects of the lives to whom he gives himself. Gratitude, appreciation, all of those things, are to him at long last irrelevant. It seems to him that worship provides a sense of power that makes courage and purposefulness possible even for one with limitations. It gives openness of joy because it destroys fears which are always present, fear of failure, fear that I shall live for a cause and find that it is wrong in the end. Without God nothing has meaning. I know for myself what it is to which my life is given, and I cannot know it for another. Strength, then, that grows by persistence, power that is born with purpose, a better understanding, a better insight, a clear love. The world shall grow by your striving; life and the world are advancing. You shall know that for yourself in the language of your own spirit, and in the imagery of your own mind, and after the fashion of your own reflective processes.

TD. HTC-MBU: Box 191.

1. Thurman's paraphrase of Matthew 5:27–48.

2. Thurman meant to ascribe the quote to George Fox, the founder of the Quakers. He gets the attribution right in HT, *Disciplines of the Spirit* (New York: Harper & Row, 1963), 24.

3. Alfred Lord Tennyson, "Ulysses," Stanza 2, l.14–15.

4. William James, *The Varieties of Religious Experience: A Study in Human Nature* (London: Longmans, 1905), 80–83.

5. William Ernest Henley (1849–1903), an English poet whose best-known poem is "Invictus," Latin for *unconquered.*

6. Admiral Richard Evelyn Byrd (1888–1957) was the first person to fly over the North and South Poles. In "The God of 2.5" Byrd writes, pondering the ice and the sky in Antarctica, writes "the day was dying, the night being born–but with great peace. Here were the imponderable processes and forces of the cosmos, harmonious and soundless . . . It was enough to catch that rhythm, momentarily to be myself a part of it. In that instant I could feel no doubt of man's oneness with the universe. The conviction came that that rhythm was too orderly, too harmonious, to perfect to be a product of blind chance—that therefore there must be purpose in the whole and that man was just a part of that whole and not an accidental offshoot. It was a feeling that transcended reason; that went to the heart of man's despair and found it groundless. The universe was a cosmos, not a chaos; man was

rightfully a part of that cosmos as were the day and night," Richard E. Byrd, *Alone* (New York: Putnam: 1938), 85.

7. Edna St. Vincent Millay, "Conscientious Objector" (1931).

8. In the preface to "On the Rocks," a political comedy, set in the present , completed in 1933, Shaw included a dialogue between Jesus and Pilate, with the following speech by Jesus. "I say to you Cast out fear. Speak no more vain things to me about the greatness of Rome. The greatness of Rome, as you call it, is nothing but fear: fear of the past and fear of the future, fear of the poor, fear of the rich, fear of the High Priests, fear of the Jews and Greeks who are learned, fear of the Gauls and Goths and Huns who are barbarians, fear of the Carthage you destroyed to save you from your fear of it and now fear worse than ever, fear of imperial Caesar, the idol you yourself have created and fear of me, the penniless vagrant, buffeted and mocked, fear of everything except the rule of God: faith in nothing but blood and iron and gold. You, standing for Rome, are the universal coward: I, standing for the kingdom of God, have braved everything, lost everything, and won an eternal crown," George Bernard Shaw, *Too True to be Good, Village Wooing, and On the Rocks. Three Plays* (New York: Dodd, Mead: 1934), 228.

FROM ALLAN A. HUNTER

27 MARCH 1939
LOS ANGELES, CALIF.

Allan A. Hunter,[1] *the pastor of Mt. Hollywood Congregational Church in Los Angeles, shares with Thurman his wish that a spokesperson for the Jewish people would respond to Nazism with a call for peace as Thurman and a few other prominent non-Jewish speakers have done. As the country gears up for World War II, Hunter also asks Thurman to guide their mutual friend, U.S. Congressman Jerry Voorhis, back on the path of pacifism.*

Dear [H]oward:

This being Monday morning, and a meadow lark being in full swing all drunk with spring outside the window, I find myself naturally wanting to salute you and wish you and Sue and the two daughters the kind of sunlight that is now streaming into this room. From time to time we hear of you and often we recall some of your insights,—scattered through note books and reemerging into consciousness. Often we recall what you said to Connie, the girl engaged to a communist who kept pushing you after church in the manse on the issue of what a Jew should do about the Nazis. What you suggested there,—that one can somehow maintain the integrity of one's spirit on the third level of refusing to hate,—lingers with us. It doesn't seem to be haunting many in the world, though. If only some Jew could become the triumph of Zion and clearly say what you say, and what Jesus made plain. But no voice somehow rises above the clamor, no Jewish voice. Perhaps we shall be hearing one soon. Einstein, if he could just have stuck to the idea during his personal crisis when the shoe began to pinch his toes, would have done something more significant perhaps than relating magnetic fields to one another.[2] But we have no right to insist that the Jewish race keep on producing prophets in the line of the Greater Isaiah, have we?

Yesterday for the last ten minutes of[3] Fosdick's sermon as guests at lunch we heard the kind of appeal not to join the devil in fighting the devil, not to try to cast out Satan with Satan's technique. And it was splendid. But it wasn't a Jew who was saying it.

Our Muriel Lester group every morning is supposed to pray "Show us what we can do today to prevent hatred of Germans, Jews and Japanese"—and one adds "gentile" if one likes. I am coming to think that we have somehow to demonstrate to the world that the technique when one sees a child bitten by a rattlesnake of shouting "We've got to do something we've got to do something I'll get a shotgun" is not so practical or relevant as the technique of unhysterically tieing one's handkerchief above the bite, accurately with a razor blade cutting an ex where the fangs went in and one self sucking out the poison. Incidetenally, if one is fit, one can swallow enough of the venom to kill two or three children with no bad results. Of course if there is a careless canker in the mouth from too much eating of cake, the poison may be deadly.

I used to think it was a race between the two techniques and that maybe technique Number one would win. Now I begin to see that irrespective of time, one uses if one is trained Technique No. 2. It's in the nature of things and what is called success is not the point. After all, what does it matter if the rattlesnake does get away while you're sucking out the poison and perhaps saving the child's life? Those who rush for the shotguns generally find their target elsewhere when they get back with their weapons anyway. Of if they shoot in the direction of the disappearing snake they only fill the child with buckshot. But of course this is carrying the analogy too far.

Harold Laski[4] spoke at UCLA a few days ago. "If it comes to a choice, bending the knee to Hitler—or the battlefield, I choose the battlefield" and about everybody I was told applauded, some wildly. And we taxpayers are subsidizing that sort of thing.

Well it's some comfort to know that you and few others who have been pounding away on a more effective climax than that are not yet silenced. To me it's rather stirring the way old Kirby[5] and others ring a bell on every campus they go to.

By the way Howard have you had the chance to get Jerry Voorhis[6] in contact with any small intimate group in Washington. He desperately needs to be exposed to your insights. It would be worth quite a good deal of time, if you by hook or by crook, could arrange contact with Jerry. Just a few more months of what he is exposed to {in the house} might discolor his mind permanently. But I don't think his voice for the bigger and more threatening navy is the whole story. He would like to dedicate his political force in the right direction. Only he needs friends who will remind him of what the right direction is. And it looks as if you and possibly you alone could do that for Jerry. The New York FOR people are too far away and maybe one or two have a little alienate{d} Jerry.

Chet Williams[1] has pretty well gone over. He probably has to go through the valley and nothing much can be done about it, I suspect. But I do wish somebody could keep in touch with him and with Elizabeth and the boy.

As for Martha,—but why burden you more?

Our love to you four. All goes well out here, in the personal sense that is.

Sincerely
[*signed*] Allan

TLS. HTC-MBU: Box 9.

1. Probably Chester Sidney Williams (1907–1992), a graduate of the University of California, Los Angeles.

2. For additional information about Hunter, see the biographical footnote in volume 1.

3. Albert Einstein (1879–1955), a vocal pacifist during World War I, renounced his German citizenship and left Germany in 1933 soon after Adolf Hitler became chancellor. To the chagrin of his pacifist associates, Einstein was so convinced that Nazi Germany was preparing for war that he urged free Europe to ready itself for war. Einstein wrote a letter to President Franklin D. Roosevelt urging "watchfulness and, if necessary, quick action" on the part of the United States in atomic-bomb research which led to the Manhattan Project. Albert Einstein to Franklin D. Roosevelt, 2 August 1939, http://www.atomicarchive.com/Docs/Begin/Einstein.shtml.

4. Harry Emerson Fosdick, pastor of Riverside Church in New York City. For additional information about him, see the biographical footnote in volume 1.

5. Harold J. Laski (1893–1950) was born in Manchester, England. He graduated from New College at Oxford, and he lectured at McGill (1914–16), Harvard (1916–20), and Yale (1919–20). In 1920 he joined the London School of Economics, where he taught until 1950. His publications include *Authority in the Modern State* (New Haven, Conn.: Yale University Press, 1919); *A Grammar of Politics* (New Haven, Conn.: Yale University Press, 1925); and *Liberty in the Modern State* (London: Faber & Faber, 1930). Laski was a committed socialist and leader of the Labour Party.

6. Kirby Page, a leader of the Fellowship of Reconciliation. For additional information about him, see the biographical footnote in volume 1.

7. Horace Jeremiah "Jerry" Voorhis (1901–84) served in Congress as the representative of California's Twelfth District from 1937 to 1947. He challenged Christians to take up the burden of witness for their faith by approaching politics as a Christian vocation. Voorhis believed the major responsibility of government was to create opportunities for the people to work at the solutions of their problems through the applications of the basic Christian principles of mutual aid. He lost the 1946 election to Richard M. Nixon. Later he was executive secretary of the Cooperative League of the U.S.A. He was also the executive secretary of the Cooperative Health Federation of America, and among many activities served as a member of the division of Christian Life and Work of the National Council of Churches.

Sue Bailey Thurman (right) with Mary McLeod Bethune (center) and unidentified woman. Courtesy of the Thurman Family and Arleigh Prelow/Howard Thurman Film Project.

FROM MARY MCLEOD BETHUNE
13 NOVEMBER 1939
WASHINGTON, D.C.

Mary McLeod Bethune,[1] *Thurman's lifelong friend, was appointed director of the National Youth Administration's Division of Negro Affairs in 1936, making her the most visible and arguably the most influential of African Americans in the so-called Black Cabinet of the Roosevelt administration. On 29 November 1939, Bethune appeared on the National Broadcasting Company's radio program* America's Town Meeting of the Air[2] *to present on the topic of the meaning of democracy. Here she asks for Thurman's views on the subject so that she could incorporate them into the speech.*

My dear Dr. Thurman:

I am to make a five minute speech on "What Does American Democracy Mean to Me."

I shall be speaking in the name of our entire group and I am desirous of a cross-section of opinions for inclusion in my thoughts. Will you send me a statement at once giving me your views. This is a coast-to-coast broadcast and it must be right.

Sincerely yours,
[*signed*] Mary McLeod Bethune
Mary McLeod Bethune
Director, Division of Negro Affairs

TLS. HTC-MBU: Box 2.

1. Mary McLeod Bethune (1875–1955) was a prominent African American educator and racial leader. For her friendship with the young Thurman, see account in Volume I.

2. *America's Town Meeting of the Air* was a current affairs program on the NBC Blue Network (after 1943, the American Broadcasting System), hosted from its beginning to 1952 by George V. Denny Jr. (1899–1959). Its period of greatest influence was in the late 1930s and early 1940s. In the program on 29 November Bethune gave an impassioned defense of the role of blacks in American society and the war effort, and the need for full civic equality, saying in part, "Democracy is for me, and for 12 million black Americans, a goal towards which our nation is marching. It is a dream and an ideal in whose ultimate realization we have a deep and abiding faith. We have fought for America with all her imperfections, not so much for what she is, but for what we know she can be." htpp://soundlearning.publicradio.org/subject/history__civics/say_it_plain/Profile Trasnscript_%20mary%Mcleod%208.pdf

To John Nevin Sayre

15 December 1939
Washington, D.C.

Thurman writes a recommendation letter for a job with the Fellowship of Reconciliation (FOR) on behalf of James Farmer, a student at Howard University. It is while working as a part-time student secretary within this pacifist organization that Farmer's own ideas about nonviolence as a strategy for social change coalesce. He went on to be one of the founders of the Congress of Racial Equality (CORE). It was Thurman who originally introduced Farmer to the study of Gandhi and encouraged the young scholar's analysis of the historical relationship between religion and racism.[1]

My dear Nevin:

One of the graduate students in the School of Religion, a Mr. J. Leonard Farmer, Jr.,[2] informs me that there is a possibility of his being chosen to do some field work in behalf of peace for the F.O.R. I wish to second this move with complete enthusiasm, because Mr. Farmer is not only an able student with a dynamic personality, but is one who has a deep concern for peace. As a young man of many contacts his influence in this direction would be wide and varied. I have very great confidence in his sincerity and his intelligence. I commend him to you without reservation.

I hope your health is bearing up lustily under the strain of these terrifying days.

Sincerely,
[*signed*] Howard Thurman
Dean
Dr. John Nevin Sayre
Fellowship of Reconciliation
2929 Broadway
New York, New York

TLS. HTC-MBU: Box 20.

1. James Farmer, *Lay Bare the Heart: An Autobiography of the Civil Rights Movement* (New York: New American Library, 1985), 142.

2. James Leonard Farmer, Jr. (1920–1999), a native of Texas, graduated from Wiley College in 1938, where his father was professor of theology, before obtaining a Bachelor of Divinity from Howard University School of Religion in 1941. Following Thurman's recommendation, he started working for FOR in 1941, and in that capacity in 1942 was a founder of the Committee (later the Congress) of Racial Equality, which split off from the parent organization. He led CORE until 1946. After working as a labor organizer, he returned to CORE in 1961 as its director, leading it through the heyday of the civil rights movement until leaving in 1966. He served as assistant secretary of the department of Health, Education, and Welfare from 1969 to 1971. See James Farmer, *Lay Bare the Heart: An Autobiography of the Civil Rights Movement* (New York: Plume Books, 1985).

Hymn: "God I Need Thee"

1940

"God I Need Thee" is probably Thurman's most popular poem. Its first appearance was likely in the Intercollegian and Far Horizons *in April 1935. The poem was immediately popular, and numerous church organizations requested the right to reprint it, which Thurman always granted. Despite its appearance in print in 1935, Thurman had not finished tinkering with the poem, and it would take a few years for the standard version to appear. The later version of the poem altered some wording, standardized the length of the stanzas, and was more formal and hymnlike, with the addition of the vocative "O," greater capitalization of nouns, and the replacement of the poem's* yours *with* Thys. *In 1940 Thurman collaborated with the distinguished African American composer John W. Work in setting the poem to music.*[1] *Two versions of the poem follow, the initial 1935 version and the standard version.*

"God I Need Thee"

God I need thee
When morning crowds the night away,
And the tasks of waking seize my mind
I need your poise.

God I need thee
When clashes come with those
Who walk the way with me,
I need your smile.

God I need thee
When love is hard to see
Amid ugliness and slime,
I need your eyes.

God I need thee
When the path to take before me lies,
I need your faith.

God I need thee
When the day's work is done,
I need your rest.

Intercollegian and Far Horizons, April 1935, 170.

"God I Need Thee"

O God I Need Thee
When morning crowds the night away
And the tasks of waking seize my mind—
I Need Thy Poise.

O God I Need Thee
When clashes come with those
Who walk the way with me
I need Thy Smile

O God I need thee
When love is hard to see
Amid the ugliness and slime
I need Thy Eyes

O God I need Thee
When the path to take before me lies

I see it—courage flees
I need Thy faith.

O God I Need Thee
When the day's work is done
Tired, discouraged—wasted
I need Thy Rest.

Kirby Page, ed., *Living Prayerfully: How to Experience Life's Deepest Satisfactions and Serve Mankind Most Effectively* (New York: Farrar & Rinehart, 1941), 463.

1. Howard Thurman and John W. Work, "God I Need Thee" (New York: Galaxy Press, 1949). John Wesley Work III (1901–67) was a distinguished music educator, composer, and ethnomusicologist who spent most of his career at Fisk University, with more than one hundred compositions to his credit, primarily for chorus. He was the author and compiler of *American Negro Songs and Spirituals: A Comprehensive Collection of 230 Folk Songs, Religious and Secular* (New York: Bonanza, 1940).

FROM HOWARD A. KESTER
11 JANUARY 1940
INDIANAPOLIS, IND.

Howard "Buck" Kester[1] *writes Thurman of his plans to try to get the federal government to take action against Klan violence in South Carolina.*

Dear Howard & Sue:

I promised to let you know when next I planned to come to Washington. I am bringing a group of folk from South Carolina to see Department of Justice officials about the Klan situation in South Carolina.[2] We expect to leave Greenville on January 28th, Sunday and barring road trouble we should arrive about noon Monday. We will be in Washington thru Tuesday or Tuesday evening as some of the folk may have to get back to work by the 31st.

Could you secure places for four or five persons—so far all men—upstanding gentlemen from South Carolina while we are there? Meals won't matter—just beds. If you can do this it would be highly appreciated for which I'll speak for you.

The situation in S. Car. grows steadily worse and it is important that we keep the identity of these people I bring secret as well as our mission. If words get back "home" that they are up in Washington it may not do them any good. At any rate we have decided to let them, that is, the members of the delegation, decide whether they want to see any reporters, speak publicly, etc.

If we can get the Depart of Justice to crack down it will be a good days work.

Please write me in Black Mountain if you can help us—and write if you can't. I'm having to write on the fly but will be in B. M. a couple of days next week to get my mail, etc—

Love to both of you always.

[*signed*] "Buck" Kester

ALS. HTC-MBU: Box 10.

1. For additional information see biographical note on Howard Kester in volume I.

2. The Ku Klux Klan underwent a revival in South Carolina in 1939 and 1940, intimidating efforts at voter registration in Greenville, arresting NAACP officials on spurious grounds, and terrorizing segregated National Youth Administration camps in Simpsonville and Fountain Inn. Although there were demands by Thurgood Marshall and others that the federal government step into the situation, and despite statements by Attorney General Robert H. Jackson and Deputy Attorney General O. John Rogge promising that the Justice Department would investigate, evidently no indictments were ever returned. "Ask U.S. to Intervene in S.C. Vote Case," *Chicago Defender*, 9 September 1939; "Intimidations Herald Revival of S.C. Kluxers," *Chicago Defender*, 21 October 1939; "G-Men Probe Klan Activities in S.C.," *Chicago Defender*, 28 October 1939; "Urge Klan Probe; Aged N.A.A.C.P Head Arrested," *Chicago Defender*, 23 December 1939.

To Henry Noble MacCracken

22 January 1940

Washington, D.C.

In 1940 Vassar College in Poughkeepsie, New York, became the last of the Seven Sister colleges to admit black students, and this letter reflects part of Thurman's efforts to assist in its integration.[1] *Thurman in 1928 became the first African American to preach at the Vassar chapel,*[2] *and he was a friend of longtime Vassar president Henry Noble MacCracken.*[3] *(Thurman returned to Vassar frequently, with ten appearances there between 1928 and 1941.) Thurman rarely commented on what must have been one of the most striking features of his increasingly public ministry in the 1930s and early 1940s—many of the white colleges that invited him to speak had few if any black students—but the contradiction between MacCracken's liberalism and his personal commitment to interracialism and Vassar's racially exclusive campus had long been a sore spot among civil rights activists.*[4]

Thurman sought to address the integration question through personal contacts and an exchange of students. Bolstered by knowledge of a student committee and some faculty support for bringing Negro students to Vassar,[5] *Thurman's first step had been to invite President MacCracken to speak at Rankin Chapel the previous year. Following up on conversations during that visit, Thurman here suggests Dorothy Walker, a sociology major, as a good candidate to be the first identifiably black student at Vassar (though Walker ultimately never attended the school).*[6] *Thurman's daughter Olive graduated from Vassar in 1948.*

My dear President MacCracken:

At last I think I have found the kind of young lady who will do the thing that we both had in mind in our conversation when you were down here. I refer to Miss Dorothy Walker of this university. You may possibly recall the young lady who sat at dinner with us. She has most of the qualities that would make adjustment for her comparatively easy there. She is a junior in college, and, of course, would have to take a year longer for graduation. She is not an "A" student; her academic average to the end of this semester will be about a "B." I can verify this and send you a transcript at the end of the semester. Her major is sociology.

She is a person of real leadership. At the present time she is the chairman of our Student Fellowship Council which is the most comprehensive and influential undergraduate organization for men and women in the university; she is also the chairman of the Tri-State Area Council for the Student Christian Movement, this council is made up of students from all of the Negro and white colleges in the District, Maryland and Delaware; and she is also a member of the National Student Council of the Student Christian Movement. With reference to her finances, her family are just able to support her at Howard University. If she should be accepted there it would mean a substantial scholarship of some sort. From my own point of view I regret this fact very much because the girl who comes in at this time should be self supporting. It would make many things easier in my opinion. My only misgiving about her is the fact that her academic record to date is not as high as in my opinion such a record ought to be. I am sure that she has ability and the rest of it, but the fact is it would be a double tragedy if for any reason she would not make the academic grade at Vassar.[7] If after you see her record and you are interested in pursuing the matter further, I would be very glad to send her up to see you for a conference at my expense.

Warmest greetings to you and Mrs. MacCracken.

Sincerely yours,
[*signed*] Howard Thurman,
Dean
President Henry Noble MacCracken
Vassar College
Poughkeepsie, New York

TLS. HTC-MBU: Box 191.

1. Vassar was established in 1865 with an endowment from Matthew Vassar, a wealthy brewer. Although two students of African American heritage had previously graduated—

Anita Florence Hemings, class of 1893, and her daughter Ellen Parker Love, both descendants of Sally Hemmings and Thomas Jefferson—they had passed for white.

2. M. Perkins, "The African American Female Elite: The Early History of African American Women in Seven Sister Colleges, 1880–1960," *Harvard Educational Review* 67 (Winter 1997): 17.

3. For a review of Thurman's 1928 talk at Vassar, see Lester A. Walton, "Negro Minister Fills Pulpit at Vassar," printed in volume 1.

4. For biographical information about MacCracken, see volume 1.

5. Perkins, "African American Female Elite," 17.

6. *WHAH*, 98–99.

7. Beatrix McCleary, the daughter of an African American New York physician, was the first African American woman to attend Vassar openly. She later became the first African American woman to graduate from the Yale University School of Medicine, and she became a psychiatrist.

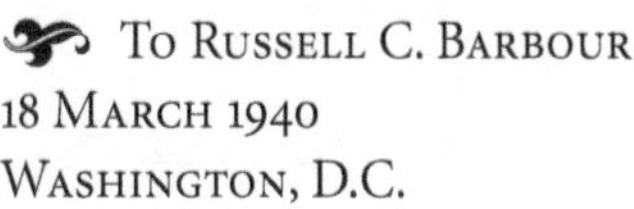

To Russell C. Barbour
18 March 1940
Washington, D.C.

With the outbreak of World War II in Europe in September 1939, there was renewed discussion of reinstituting military conscription in the United States. Thurman, a stalwart pacifist, writes his friend Russell Barbour, editor of the National Baptist Voice, *to appeal to National Baptist Convention president L. K. Williams*[1] *to clarify the convention's policy on conscientious objection. He also wants the convention to take a public stance on the possibility of American involvement in the war and its implication for African Americans.*

My dear Russell:

I have been planning since my visit to Nashville to get a letter to you but there has not been very much time in which to correspond. You promised to put me back on the mailing list of the voice which has not been done. I wanted very much to know what you said in the voice about the Christian Mission. It is the first time that one of our religious editors have had a chance to study the Mission at close range. Please send me the back copies if such is possible. I want to express my deep appreciation for all the courtesies which you and my friend Maxwell extended to me during my stay in Nashville. I am very sorry that I did not have a chance to see Mrs. Barbour.

Did you confer with Dr. Williams about providing some opportunity for the members of the National Baptist Convention, who may be conscientious objectors, to register the fact with the State Department through the office of the Convention? From my point of view, this is a matter of transcendent importance and I trust that something can be done about it.

Where is the National Convention this year? I certainly think that the whole implication of religion and peace and the fate of minorities ought to be presented before the whole Convention. I hope you know me well enough to know that this is not a veiled suggestion that I be asked to do it. I am exceedingly anxious, however, that it should be done and if I knew Dr. Williams intimately, I would make the direct suggestion to him to be passed on to the program committee. You follow my point, I am sure.

Let me get some word from you soon.

Sincerely,
[*signed*] Howard Thurman
Dean
Reverend Russell C. Barbour
The National Baptist Voice
412 Fourth Avenue N.
Nashville, Tennessee

TLS. HTC-MBU: Box 2.

1. Lacey Kirk Williams (1871–1940) served as president of the National Baptist Convention, U.S.A., from 1922 to 1940. He was also pastor of Chicago's Olivet Baptist Church (1916–22).

"A 'Native Son' Speaks"

17 May 1940
Chicago, Ill.

Thurman generally avoided giving talks that focused on race relations, especially before racially mixed audiences. This, he felt, took him out of his strengths as a speaker and thinker, beside which he found the assumption behind such invitations faintly patronizing—as if the only topic whites thought blacks fit to speak upon was some aspect of the "Negro Problem." As he wrote to B. F. Lamb of the Ohio Council of Churches in the spring of 1940, "I am not sure that I am the man to bring the message on race relations. I very rarely ever make addresses directly in this field except as my basic concern about religion leads me to."[1] But at the very time he wrote this letter, he had just made one of his most striking exceptions to this policy in his address to the Chicago Roundtable of the National Conference on Christians and Jews on 11 April 1940. His comments were subsequently printed in the Advocate, *a Jewish newsweekly published in Chicago.[2] The reason why Thurman chose to deviate from his standard practice is not clear, but "A 'Native Son' Speaks" stands apart from the vast majority of his mature writings.*

Thurman focuses here on the Great Migration of southern blacks to Chicago and other northern cities in the years after World War I, the most significant social transformation among African Americans in the first half of the twentieth century. Thurman concludes that in some respects the Great Migration left African Americans worse off, leading to the loss of many vital resources—family, church, and the support of neighbors—that were available to them in the South. Discrimination in housing and employment, competition against better situated immigrants, as well as the lack of political connections, adequate support networks, and social services, left the migrants largely to fend for themselves. Moreover the newcomers to northern cities found themselves shunned by the established black elites and relegated to worship in storefront churches. Thurman's arguments that the Great Migration led to a decline of black social structure and his caustic comments on the "black bourgeoisie" resemble those advanced by his Howard colleague, E. Franklin Frazier, in The Negro Family in Chicago *(1932) and elsewhere.*[3]

Nonetheless Thurman allows that for all his negative comments on the consequences of the Great Migration, the Negro "has found more democracy in the city than from the area from which he came." With this has come the discovery "of a new kind of individuality," and with that a new sense of anger against discrimination and second-class status. For whether Negroes lived in the North or the South, he argues, there has been little change to the grim reality that "generally speaking the Negro is not a citizen." With another war on the horizon, Thurman points out that it was only during the Great War, when the "dominant social group," requiring the cooperation of Negroes, conferred upon them a measure of citizenship and personality. The emptiness of this promise was revealed after the war, which led to the anger and rage of the Red Summer of 1919—a "cry of pain" that was also a sign of life.

Thurman concludes that the only way forward was for the dominant institutions in society to "guarantee the Negro's right as a citizen to belong and to participate in the common life." He looks with particular interest at interracial unionism as a strategy for racial advancement, an approach strongly advocated by Thurman's good friend and Howard colleague Ralph Bunche. Through a genuine embrace of interracialism, perhaps even the church, "disgraced and prostituted in a new world," could find its redemption.

According to the census of 1930 between the years 1920–30, the number of Negroes living in the North and born in tire South increased from 737,423 to 1,355,789. More than 58% of the Negroes living in the North were born in the South while less than 1% of those living in the South were born outside of the south. 40% of the total Negro population lived in the five southern states of

Georgia, Mississippi, Alabama, North Carolina and Texas; while 70.7% of the total population came from the remaining southern states.[4] This means that almost 3/4 of the total population of Negroes was in the south in 1930. And most of those who were living in the south were in the rural areas. Therefore, any discussion of the Negro in the City must of necessity mean the northern city and to a very great extent Negroes who themselves, though living in the north were born in the south. This limits our area for consideration quite decidedly.

The fundamental thesis of my paper is that the Negro in the northern city is not a citizen and his position is a perpetual threat and constant disgrace to democracy.[5] In the first place, Negroes have come into certain northern cities in very large numbers. They are in a real sense, late arrivals, as city migrants. As late arrivals, they are forced to be marginal dwellers. They are on the fringes of the economic life of the urban community. The present problem for them is one of crass, elemental, physical survival. They have no money, hence they must live in the worse possible neighborhoods, the more crowded tenement areas and in fire-traps, where they become easy victims to disease, crime and exploitation. The housing problem of Negroes in cities smells to high heaven; this is beyond debate! If I might quote from a Negro authority in this field who resides in Chicago, "Negro communities have never been absorbed completely even into the better economic group of Negroes. It is my knowledge that the high murder rate, death rate, crime in general, particularly with regard to juvenile delinquency, are peculiar to these slum areas, irrespective to what race is living there in any particular period. It has been proved in Chicago that the crime rate of Negroes living in these blighted areas is no higher now than 45 to 50 years ago when other racial groups lived in them. The difference is, however, that other groups remained in these areas only until the second generation, when through Americanization processes, better chances at getting ahead in earning a living, they were able to move on into the next highest strata, while the Negro, because of high visibility has not been able to escape from these areas, even when a small proportion of them do move into better residential districts there is always another wave of them coming in to fill the place."[6]

In the second place, their social life is uprooted; in the city he has to give up his sense of community and the security that came there from which obtained in the south. He is depersonalized. His status is not fixed by the previous generation but is part at least by his own efforts and good fortune. In the south he was in a fixed status, in a mold that was set by the fact of 300 years of slavery and its concomitant resultants in the mores subsequent to the Civil War. He had a place. To be true, he was always a victim, always the goat but within the zones of agreement he had the status of person. The southern white man lynched him, tortured him, intimidated him in many cruel ways, but for the most part he was never permitted to go hungry. However degenerate and amoral a southern white man may have been in his total dealings with the Negro in the south, almost with unerring insight he saw to it that he was fed.

On coming to the City the personal life of the Negro was disorganized and his status was uprooted. This total situation caused the development of a sense of being always at loose ends.

It is important at this point to raise the question as to what kind of environment he found in the city. In the first place he came into an environment that was highly competitive. He met many other immigrants from various parts of the world. He was almost immediately regarded as a threat to the economic security that they themselves were building up. The environment of the northern city had prepared these new comers from the old world quite definitely with specific content for their attitude towards the Negro. One of the most significant and damaging indictments of the white man in the northern city in this regard is the fact that he passed on to the European immigrant both by discriminatory treatment, by words and deeds, his prejudices against the Negro. The northern white man demonstrates at once to the immigrant though he has not yet learned to speak English, that his place insecure as it is more secure than that of the Negro who has been here since the country started. In jobs he is preferred—in hotels he is accommodated—in public places he has relative immunity from discrimination because he is white.

In the second place, life found that opportunities for earning a legitimate livelihood were highly restricted but the one place in which he could muscle in was in the rackets of one kind or another. So that the white immigrant who controls the rackets largely, looked upon him as a tool that could be used in bringing fresh monies into his coffers. But here again he was penalized because he was late coming and because of his marked visibility. His activities had to be confined to less conspicuous areas that almost always were petty and segregated among his own people. Here the Negro became a front or contact person to deal with other Negroes. The same general technique is used in more respectable businesses such as theaters and eating houses in Negro districts.

In the third place, he found scarcely no organized religious life willing to welcome him. Some of the Negroes who had lived in the north for generations belonged to white churches. The migrant from the south for various reasons was not welcomed very often to worship in the northern Negro churches. I am within the mark when I say that Christianity in the north was much more kindly disposed to the Negro while he lived in the south than it was towards him as a neighbor in the north. It was easy to love the Negro at a distance than to welcome him as a brother. This is one of the paradoxes of American history that the Negro has maintained an interest in Christianity through the years. It sometimes seems to me that for some inexplicable reason he has taken upon himself the redemption of a religion that has been disgraced and prostituted in a new world.

The Negro in the city has sought to establish himself in this area of this life by building his own little church and importing his leadership from the south. Hence, the store-front church and the cast off synagogue.

In the fourth place, despite all that I have said he has found more democracy in the city than from the area from which he came. One of the significant psychological results of his uprooting has been a discovering of a new kind of individuality. When a man becomes an individual he becomes conscious of himself. He also becomes conscious of discrimination against himself. As he becomes conscious of himself he also seeks alignments that will give to him a new basis of security. One of the obvious possibilities close at hand is politics. In the city the Negro is discovering political power and the vast significance of the force of numbers. So that in the city his chances for becoming a citizen are greatly enhanced.

It is important to point out in this connection that generally speaking the Negro is not a citizen. He is several steps removed from active participation in those social, economic, political arrangements by which our common body politic is controlled. The character of a democracy and the character of those who live in it is determined by the amount of active responsibility felt by and is possible for the individual. When responsibility is withdrawn from the individual or not permitted him, then democracy is imperiled. The shame of American democracy and those who are its custodians in church, school and state is the systematic way in which minorities in general and Negroes in particular, have nothing to do with its functioning outside the market place. Responsibility, a free initiative, the sense of the future, these are the things that make for civic character, that make real citizens. These are denied the Negro.

It was not until the last war that the Negro became aware to some degree, of his citizenship. Persona was conferred upon him by the dominant social group—he was made to feel that he counted—that the future of democracy was dependant upon him. For one breathless, swirling moment he became conscious of being a part and parcel of the very core of the nation. During the excitement of war and the releases incident thereto, he was not immediately conscious of the bearings of this new experience upon his common life. True, there were few voices calling attention to the fact that things after the war would be or not be as they were before. But when the troops were mustered out and like a tremendous octopus, American society sought to place the Negro back into his position of anonymity—there was wild resentment expressing itself in rioting, etc., in northern cities. This rioting was a sign of life, of an awakening citizenship. I read in a magazine several years ago a story told by a lady who was a patient of Dr. Locke,[7] famous Canadian physician. She said that in the chair just ahead of her and before the doctor sat a crippled girl. After a few deft manipulations of the little girl's foot by the doctor she gave a sharp, piercing cry of great pain. The waiting patients were stunned. In the afternoon some one offered sympathy to the father. He appreciated it and said, "When our daughter first came, the doctor could do anything to her foot and she would not feel it, so today when I heard her scream, I said, thank God, life is in the foot as last."

The practical problem is then, how can American democracy confer upon the Negro persona which means the status of an individual with a sense of social responsibility and worth? An individual has persona or personhood conferred upon him by a social group that has definite statues to which he belongs and of which he is an extension. So that he is himself plus the group or, groups that guarantee him. He is therefore, never dealt with merely as an individual because those who do it know that at long last they are held responsible for what happens to him by the group that guarantees persona. This fact creates quite a problem for the Negro because his whole group as a group lives on the periphery of the national life—as a group it may scarcely be said to have status hence the kind of social units that can best confer persona upon the Negro are those social units that are bi-racial in character. One of the most interesting happenings in this connection is the way that being a member of a union immediately states the Negro in the labor world and to some extent controls this regard. In my opinion, not until churches, schools, governing boards of all kinds, political, secular and religious, guarantee the Negroes' right as a citizen to belong and to participate in the common life will he ease to be merely an individual, eating, occasionally, sleeping, breathing but remaining the perpetual threat and condemnation of democracy. He must be given responsibility and the incentive to exercise a free initiative if life ultimately is to be sane and secure for us all.

The Advocate, 17 May 1940.

1. To B. F. Lamb, 16 May 1940, HTC-MBU: Box 12.

2. The text exists in two versions, identical in their texts except for one difference, noted below. There is an undated typescript from Thurman's Howard years, "The Negro in the City," HTC-MBU: Box 107, which was probably Thurman's preferred title for the essay; the *Advocate*'s title reflected the widespread interest in the recent publication of Richard Wright's novel *Native Son*, set in Chicago, the first book by a black author to be a Book-of-the-Month Club selection. The *Advocate* version includes subheads, extensive italics, and paragraph breaks probably not original to Thurman, and with one exception they have been eliminated.

3. E. Franklin Frazier, *The Negro Family in Chicago* (Chicago: University of Chicago Press, 1932).

4. In 1930 the black population in the South (defined as all of the states in which slavery was legal in 1860, plus the District of Columbia and Oklahoma) was 9,585,417, or about 80.6 percent of the total black population of the United States.

5. At this point "The Negro in the City" adds "Responsibility for this rests on the shoulders of those who control schools, churches and the state." HTC-MBU: Box 107.

6. Paragraph break as in "A 'Native Son' Reports."

7. Mahlon William Locke (1880–1942) was a Canadian physician whose unorthodox method of treating arthritis through foot manipulation received a good deal of attention in the 1930s. Many medical authorities in the United States and Canada doubted the efficacy of his treatment methods. See Barbara Clow, "Mahlon William Locke: 'Toe-Twister,'" *Canadian Bulletin of Medical History* 9 (1992): 17–35.

To Russell C. Barbour

31 May 1940
Washington, D.C.

Written amid the news of the devastating rout of France during the Nazi offensive in 1940, Thurman, worried about the heightened preparations for war in the United States, expresses interest in addressing delegates at the upcoming National Baptist Convention in Birmingham, Alabama, and again encourages the National Baptist Voice *editor Barbour to push for the denomination to take a stance on conscientious objection to war.*

My dear Russell:

The delay in answering your good letter[1] is very long, but I have thought of you many times.

I cannot write at length as I would like to, because I am still pushed for time. My engagements in summer conferences and colleges take me through the entire month of June, hence it will not be possible for me to come down to Nashville at the time you mentioned. I shall keep it in mind and plan to do it at the first possible break in my schedule.

I was in Memphis at LeMoyne College for commencement. I saw my father in spirit, Sam Owen.[2] He said that he was going to talk with you about the possibility of having me give the address in Birmingham, Friday, September 6th. He said that the brethren ought to have a wider acquaintance with me. I told him at the time that the first part of that week I would have to be up at Keuka Lake, New York, but that I am definitely interested.[3]

I do hope that you have talked with the chief about the "Conscientious Objectors,"[4] we may be at war by September. I hope not!

It seems that Bennie Mays will be going to Morehouse.[5] They need a man there in the saddle.

Sue sends her greetings and do not let too many day pass before I hear from you or see you.

Sincerely,

[*signed*] Howard Thurman,

Dean

Mr. Russell C. Barbour

412 Fourth Avenue, North

Nashville, Tennessee

TLS. HTC-MBU: Box 2.

1. From Russsell C. Barbour, 20 March 1940, HTC-MBU: Box 2.

2. Samuel Augustus Owen, former pastor at Mt. Bethel Baptist Church in Daytona, Florida, had encouraged Thurman to attend his alma mater, Morehouse College. While Thurman was still a Morehouse student, he received his license to preach from Owen, and later, in the summer of 1925, Owen delivered Thurman's sermon of ordination (*WHAH*, 17, 57). For additional information about Owen, see the biographical footnote in volume 1.

3. There is no evidence that Thurman attended the meeting.

4. The "chief" was L. K. Williams, president of the National Baptist Convention, U.S.A. Thurman had asked Barbour to speak with Williams in his letter of 18 March (printed in the current volume), and Barbour quickly replied that he "had a long conference with Dr. Williams several weeks ago and I found him so absorbed in the effort to return the Republicans to power I could not impress upon him as I desired the importance of placing before our State Department the position of our conscientious objectors" (From Russell C. Barbour, 20 March 1940, HTC-MBU: Box 2). Thurman and Barbour may have had some influence, though, since Williams advocated that the convention recognize conscientious objection status in his annual address, "The Church and War" (*Proceedings of the Sixtieth Annual Session of the National Baptist Convention, U.S.A., Inc. held with the Baptist Churches of Birmingham, Alabama*, 9 September 1940, 71–72, HTPP—Subject files, "National Baptist Convention, U.S.A. Inc.").

5. Benjamin Mays took office as president of Morehouse College in 1940 and served in that capacity until 1967.

"The Light That Is Darkness"

June 1940

Thurman composed this sermon at the height of the Nazi expansion in Europe in 1940, when "the moral bankruptcy of our time seems only matched by the keenness and power of our knowledge." The war has made apparent both hypocrisies that had previously been hidden and the underlying dichotomy between power and wisdom that had plunged the world into war. It is unclear where he may have delivered the sermon; a typescript version, as well as later versions dated 1949 and 1958, survive among his personal papers.

"The eye is the lamp of the body—{so} if your eye is generous, the whole of your body will be illumined, but if your eye is selfish, the whole of your body will be darkened. And if your very light turns dark—then what a darkness it is!"[1]

There always seems to be a gulf, deep and turbulent, between the so-called theoretical and the practical; between the ideal and the real; between the dream and its fulfillment; between what a man will{s} to do and what at long last he is able to accomplish. The conflict is nevertheless real, even though it is quite possible to make no {definitive} distinction between theory and practice, between the ideal and the real. An idea or ideal held in mind may be maintained in a highly rarified and closed world without regard to those aspects of one's environment that would interfere with it and disturb it. It is because of the way in which ideas may be made to function entirely within the mind that they sometimes seem to be so very different from their concrete manifestation. It is of primary importance therefore to give strict attention to the quality and the kind of ideas which we embrace in order that the light that is within us be *light* rather than darkness.

It is a striking fact that precisely at the moment in human history when the mind of man has made the most far reaching discoveries in the world of nature; precisely at the moment when hitherto unexplored aspects of nature have been reduced to manageable units of understanding and usefulness and control, there seems to be lacking the moral quality necessary to guarantee that these discoveries, these useful increments of nature be used to bless and enrich human life. The moral bankruptcy of our time seems only matched by the keeness and power of our knowledge. Our knowledge has made a neighborhood out of the earth, but it has not taught us how to create neighborliness on the earth. At this moment much of the light that is in us is darkness! {—} deep tragic darkness!

The light that is in you—may it not become darkness—that is my wish for each of you this day.

The light that is in you becomes darkness when your knowledge alienates your affection from and stultifies you{r} appreciation of people.

It is true that the environment in which learning takes place is often artificial and one or two steps removed from the traffic of normal life. The environment is largely under control. A highly selective process has made possible your associates and {the} general atmosphere by which your life has been surrounded. These facts make those of us who live in the atmosphere of colleges and universities very susceptible to two very commonplace illusions. First, there is the illusion of Omniscience!

This illusion is apt to make us think that we know much more than we really do. Particularly are we tempted in this way when we are brought into immediate contact with old editions of learning such as our parents. It is a very sobering thought to realize that your most radical ideas are often old ideas to you{r} mothers and fathers.

Socrates suggested that he was the wisest man living because what he did not know, he did not think that he knew. The illusion {of Omniscience makes us fail to appreciate other people and what they know.}

{The second illusion} is that life will make an exception in your case. In a sense it is true that your advantages in this excellent college have marked you as persons of high privilege. But this fact merely increases the measure of your responsibility to life. It does not mean that the laws of life will not or do not apply to you. There is a deep inner logic in experience which makes for an element of what seems to be fatalism. Everything counts—as Tennyson suggests, Nothing walks with aimless feet.[2] You are what you are today because you are standing on the shoulders of an infinite series of yesterdays.

No individual, no nation, however powerful and mighty, can escape the relentless and inner logic of life. I must pay, you must pay; nations must pay—each for what he gets. If I am selfish, hardened as to my sympathies; insensitive to the needs of others, it is like these qualities I become. And more than that—that which at long befalls me is merely what I have been. I create my own judgment—the history of my life is my judgment.

If individuals can live recklessly and without a sense of moral responsibility and at the same time build a decent and healthy world—then the moral order itself is an illusion. If nations for hundreds of years can build their empires out of the blood and vitality of millions of defenseless and so-called backwards peoples, if they can exploit and abuse and torture human life and squander their resources until there is nothing left but a mockery of decency and self-respect—if nations can do this as they have done in Europe for several centuries and not be bathed in the blood they themselves have caused to flow upon the earth, then the moral order itself is an illusion. The history of a nation is the judgment of the nation.

Your light becomes darkness when it inspires skepticism, which may persist until it deadens faith and hardens into cynicism and a frozen sneer.

Skepticism is quite characteristic of any period of transition. We should not be unduly alarmed if as students making our adjustment in a world different from the coziness of our homes we are frosted over with varying kinds of skepticism. This simple fact is known to anyone who has watched generation after generation of students come and go. The attitude of negative self-assertion at first dominates the mind in the new surroundings and then, if things move along after a normal pattern, this attitude changes gradually to one of positive self-assertion. It is what some call adjustment.

Skepticism makes acute the sense of loneliness and personal isolation when life seems everywhere to be out of joint. When the contradictions of experience seem to be ultimate, skepticism follows for a season. Enraged power and madness seem at this moment to be sweeping over the world. But there is something about the human spirit that can never find skepticism as a final resting place for the mind. The spirit of man stubbornly refuses to accept the contradiction of experience as ultimate. Sometimes blindly, sometimes with little hope of vindication, often with wild irrationality, the spirit of man dares to affirm that the ultimate end of man is good. This is an important fact for you to remember, for it becomes the basis of hope in times of despair; the incentive for dreams of a better day when times are out of joint and men have lost their reason, and the ground of optimism when worlds crash and dreams whiten into ash! The light that is in you becomes darkness when through fear and a sense of isolation you permit your skepticism to devour your faith. The skeptic doubts knowledge, but he always has faith in his own. When a man denies one thing it is because it is inconsistent with something else which he {holds} as being valid. It is your responsibility to find a way of life that is worth following; a belief that can be honestly held even in moments of greatest personal or national agony, a social order in which the weakest individual can find shelter. This you must do lest your light turn to darkness.

Finally, you light turns to darkness when you lack the courage and the will to do what you know to be right. To see the right does not mean of necessity that we will do the right. The sin and sorrow and misery of human life are not all due to blindness. Much of it is due to the fact that we are not willing to do at a particular moment what we know we ought to do. Fear of criticism, fear of a loss of security or a loss of prestige, a thousand fears paralyze our action and render us impotent and vain. It is only the power of God that is able to change our wills with sufficient dynamics to do with increasing effectiveness the right that we see. All visions must be achieved in order to be effective. If I refuse to achieve my vision then the vision itself begins to grow dim until I become darkness.

Your light becomes darkness when you lack the courage and the will to do what you know to be right.

The new mother, when she looks at her child, whispers in her heart—my child may you seek after truth. If anything I teach you be false may you throw it from you and go on to deeper knowledge than I have ever known; if you become a person of thought and learning may you never fail to tear down with your right hand what your left hand has built up through years of thought and study if you see it at last not to be founded on that which is; if you become a politician may no success for your party or even love of your country ever lead you to tamper with reality and to play a diplomatic part; die poor, unknown, unloved, a failure—but shut your eyes to nothing that seems to them to be the truth.[3]

TD. HTC-MBU: Box 196.

1. Matt. 6:22–23.
2. Tennyson, "In Memoriam" stanza 54.
3. Olive Schreiner, *From Man to Man; or Perhaps Only . . .* (New York: Harper, 1927), 158; reprinted in Howard Thurman, ed., *A Track to the Water's Edge*, 153.

To Herbert King
3 June 1940
Washington, D.C.

King wrote Thurman on 31 May that "it is such a strain on my mind to realize that neither you nor Frank [Wilson] will be present at Talladega" and that with Thurman's absence, "I will be missing you, dear Brother, in so many ways that elude description."[1] As Thurman made clear in his response, this would be the first summer meeting of the Student Christian Movement that he would miss in fifteen years, in part because of his busy schedule and in part because of his misgivings about the direction of the movement, which involved the phasing out of the black conference at Eagles Mere, North Carolina, in favor of a new conference center at Talladega.[2] King suggested to Thurman that, if his "heart" and "mind" would permit it, "a letter to the Talladega men would be very much appreciated by the men as well as me." Although Thurman offered his personal support to King in whatever he chose to do, there is no indication that Thurman wrote the letter King requested, and his admonition, "the dream of a orderly, decent society is not your dream, it is God's and you must relax your tension about its ultimate outcome," was a gentle, very Thurmanesque criticism, suggesting to King that he ought not to get too closely tied to any one plan for advancing interracial cooperation. The letter is an indication of the growing estrangement between Thurman and the Student Christian Movement and of the tensions that led, within a few years, to King's own traumatic break with the movement.

My dear Herb:

I have waited to hear from you and your letter, which came this morning is so welcome that I am writing you right off the bat.

I do feel awkward because I am not at Talladega, and shall not be there. This is the first time in fifteen years almost that I have missed our student conference. I am not sure that I have done the wisest thing in choice, that I have made, but it seemed at the time to be the best. My interest is deep and vital in all and anything that concerns our students in general and with which you are connected in particular. Please do not think that my absence from the conference means that my interest is gone. I am sure that it would do you much good, and give to me much strength to be with you during these very trying days. Remember this, that any decision that you feel called upon to make in the interest of truth and the minority, you may depend upon my completest backing. I have never said this to anyone else. These are very hard times and everybody is jittery and afraid—those of us who are in a weaker position but must cope with people who are in a stronger position may expect to suffer, not for what we have done, but for what life is doing to those who are stronger. One thing you must keep clearly in mind, and that is, the dream of an orderly, decent society is not your dream, it is God's and you must relax your tension about its ultimate outcome.

The treasury of the Chapel and the Fellowship Council, and Howard Thurman is defunct. We shall have one person perhaps at Eagles Mere, but beyond that there will be no conference representatives.[3]

My schedule is as follows:

June 9th, Colby Junior College—baccalaureate
June 11th, Knoxville College—commencement
June 12–17, Lake Geneva Men's Conference
June 21–28, Northfield Preparatory School Conference.

I shall be in Washington on the 19th and hope that you can be here.

Monk,[4] Tommie[5] and I are planning to drive to Mexico for July.[6] I did not raise the question with you about going because in the Union Seminary Bulletin you are listed to teach in the Summer School. If this is not correct, it would be ground if you could join us. We are driving in Monk's car from New Orleans. There is much more to write about, but I shall save it until I see you.

Sincerely,
[*signed*] Howard Thurman
Dean

Mr. Herbert King
Talladega College
Talladega, Alabama

TLS. HTC-MBU: Box 11.

1. King expressed his own misgivings about the Talladega arrangements, writing to Thurman that two white southern leaders of the YMCA would be in attendance and that while "you don't know a lot about these gentlemen, but you can do a lot of accurate guessing, I am sure." From Herbert King, 31 May 1940, HTC-MBU: Box 11.

2. Ibid.

3. Thomas Hawkins attended the conference. Hawkins (1907–1985) was a graduate of Howard University, where he starred on the football team. He was assistant dean of students at Howard (1933–1946), and dean of students at Hampton Institute (1946–1975.)

4. Nickname for Melvin H. Watson.

5. Thomas Hawkins.

6. Thurman had long been interested in attending one of Hubert Herring's Mexican summer seminars (see To Hubert Herring, 10 November 1934, printed in volume 1) and

made tentative plans to attend the seminar in 1937 (where one of the attractions would have been a meeting with Leon Trotsky), but the plans fell through. From Hubert Herring, 5 May 1937, HTC-MBU: Box 9. In the spring of 1940, when Thurman was at a physical and mental nadir, he began again making plans to attend Herring's seminar. As he explained to Herring, "I am literally dead on my feet and I shall not be interested in much strenuous physical or even intellectual activity. I need most, a change of scenery and relaxation but I shall get as much out of the seminar as I feel able to attend," To Hubert Herring, 14 April 1940, HTC-MBU: Box 9; From Hubert Herring, 21 May 1940, HTC-MBU: Box 9. Thurman said much the same, in a more jocular tone, to Melvin Watson: "My mission in life is just to sit under a tree with somebody to scratch my back and pour cold lemonade down by throat. As a matter of fact, my dear Monk, that is why I am considering carrying you to Mexico at your expense." 16 May 1940, HTC-MBU: Box 40. And this is what Thurman did, traveling with Hawkins and Evelio Grillo, a Cuban American student the Thurmans had befriended in Washington, D.C., and who was then attending Xavier University in New Orleans. See Evelio Grillo, *Black Cuban, Black American: A Memoir* (Houston: Arte Público, 2000), 73–78, and To Melvin Watson, 16 May 1940, HTC-MBU: Box 40.

Review of Oswald McCall, *The Hand of God*

July 1940

Oswald McCall's The Hand of God[1] *contains brief meditations on religion and Christianity, which, as Thurman notes, he had already used in his services at Rankin Chapel and to which he frequently returned in his subsequent career. McCall's collection of short, nondogmatic reflections about the meaning of Christianity was a likely influence on some of Thurman's later publications in the same vein, such as* Meditations of the Heart.[2]

This is no ordinary series of meditations. They belong acutely to our age and are couched in the language of modern man. A spirit of deep mature warmth permeates them despite the often unconventional phraseology. I have used the volume experimentally both in private and in public worship; it meets a real need. The title comes from Rodin's sculpture, "The Hand of God"; the book is divided into three sections: "The Hand," "The Fingers," and "The Thumb." It is essentially Christological in its emphasis but sufficiently comprehensive in its subject matter and lyric passages to give a genuine lift even to those who may not find the author's assumptions about Christ congenial to their own spirits. The ideas and treatment of them reveal a mature piety affirming itself in a hard time.

Journal of Religion 40 (1940): 317.

1. Oswald W. S. McCall (1885–1959), born and raised in Australia, came to the United States in 1921 and served as minister for congregational churches in Berkeley, Chicago, and Vancouver. He authored several popular works of religious reflection, including *The Hand of God* (New York: Harper, 1939).

2. HT, *Meditations of the Heart* (New York: Harper, 1953).

FROM LANGSTON HUGHES
21 JULY 1940
CHICAGO, ILL.

During much of his career, writer and poet Langston Hughes[1] *supported himself by doing lecture tours at historically black colleges and universities. He writes to his friend Howard Thurman to find out if he would like him to do a lecture at Howard University in the fall, and he also mentions several mutual acquaintances from Sue Bailey Thurman's years in Harlem.*

Dear Howard,

An appearance in October for the Ohio Library Association's annual conference and one or two other important lectures have come up in the fall, delaying my departure for the coast until about Thanksgiving. I recall that you spoke to me about coming to Howard this season. I am wondering now if you would like to have me come sometime this fall? If so, please let me know soon so that I can fill in my schedule.

Tell Sue Louise[2] is here for her vacation, and Alta and Aaron Douglass[3] have come out for the Exposition. Be sure to see it if you come to Chicago. Parts of it are excellent.

My best to you both,
Sincerely,
[*signed*] Langston
P.S. My book, THE BIG SEA,[4] comes out August 5th with a chapter on Washington therein.

1. Langston Hughes (1902–1967), a poet, playwright, novelist, and essayist, was one of the most prominent African American literary figure of his time. See "Langston Hughes Morehouse Guest," *Atlanta World* 11 December 1931.

2. Louise Thompson Paterson (1901–1999), a native of Chicago and a 1923 graduate of the University of California at Berkeley, taught economics at the Hampton Institute in Virginia before moving to New York City in the late 1920s, where she became a well-known figure in Harlem Renaissance circles. In the 1930s she became a prominent African American Communist, and in 1940 married William Patterson, another prominent African American Communist in 1940. She would remain involved in black freedom struggle and left causes for the remainder of her life. While teaching at Hampton Institute, she became friends with Sue Bailey. Both left in 1927 after their active support of a student strike, and for a while she and Sue Bailey shared an apartment in Harlem.

3. Aaron Douglas (1899–1979), a native of Topeka, Kansas, became one of the best-known African American artists in New York City in the 1920s and 1930s. His murals and illustrations for books and magazines became iconic images of the Harlem Renaissance. In 1944 he became a professor of art at Fisk University. He married Alta Mae Sawyer, also a native of Topeka, in 1926. For many decades a prominent figure in Harlem social circles, she died in 1959.

4. Hughes refers to his autobiography *The Big Sea* published by Knopf in 1940. In the chapter titled "Washington Society," Hughes writes about the snobbery of the black elite in segregated Washington, D.C.

To Fellowship of Religious Workers
September 1940
Washington, D.C.

In early 1940 Thurman helped organize the short-lived Fellowship of Religious Workers in Negro Colleges and Universities, an organization composed of approximately twenty-five men devoted to addressing issues of concern to faculty, administrators, and students at historically black colleges and universities. Thurman asks for the Fellows' feedback on the accompanying letter of invitation to the Fellowship's second annual conference in Raleigh, North Carolina.

Dear Fellow:

I am enclosing a copy of the letter to be sent to college presidents relative to our conference in February.[1] Will you please list any comments you may have and return the letter with your comments and suggestions to Frank Wilson. The deadline for this is December 5th. We must have your cooperation.

Very sincerely,
[*signed*] Howard Thurman
Convener Secretary of the Conference

Dear President—

No group is more acutely aware of the perils confronting democracy today than college administrators and faculty members. The advance of military despotism in Europe and Asia, plus the subtle encroachments of the anti-democratic spirit in our own land, are sufficient causes for real concern about the preservation of essential human liberties and the protection of the integrity of human personality. All tyranny, subtle or overt, is a direct threat to the exercise of initiative, the right of self-direction, and the voluntary acceptance of responsibility by those whose effectual power is not measured in terms of military, economic, or political prominence.

In defense of those values which make life worthwhile, the duty of educational institutions is contained in their very history. The original purpose of the college was to equip young people so to understand the meaning of existence and so to prepare themselves for useful services in society as to aid in breaking the shackles of enslavement to ignorance, bigotry, disease, and poverty, and to assist in the elevation and enrichment of our common life. To this end the college proposed to provide physical facilities, a teaching staff, and an atmosphere appropriate to the proper development of persons who would become competent to fulfill the aforenamed functions.

From the very beginning, the college for Negroes has defined its function in terms of leadership. It has been assumed, correctly, that this objective would be achieved not merely through the medium of formal instruction but more significantly through the total impact of all the experiences within the college upon all the students who participated in its activities and who shared in the opportunities provided by the college.

A great part of the wholesome development of students resulted from fine associations with members of the faculty, for the most part informal and unofficial. At the present, a still greater influence is exerted by the organized campus activities through which special talents are exploited and special interests pursued. In these matters, varying degrees of autonomy have been granted to students in accordance with administrative policy and in proportion to supposed levels of capacity for self-direction. This increased partnership of students in the management of affairs has ranged all the way from the right to chew gum or use lipstick with impunity to the privilege of sitting in deliberative councils which deal with academic policy, the curriculum, housing of students, discipline, and student finance.

In all this, what have we learned about the democratic way of life? What evidence is there that we really believe in the democratic ideal? To what extent do attitudes and practices on the campus equip students to carry important responsibilities as members of a democratic society? What are the evidences of tyranny, despotism, and corruption in campus elections, in social affairs, and in methods of obtaining college degrees? To what extent are students loaded with excessive responsibilities prematurely, or relegated to unimportant chores in the interest of "safe and sound" adult control? Does the college confirm or negate one's confidence in the possibility of decency and justice in man's collective relationships?

At this crucial period in world history it is important that we take stock of so vital an enterprise as the college for Negroes in its attempt to provide guidance and opportunities for the emergence and development of a generation of young people who can function with intelligence and integrity in a country that still accords minorities the right to live.

The Fellowship of Religious Workers in Negro Colleges and Universities is calling a conference on the subject—"Student Leadership in the Negro College" to convene at Shaw University and Saint Augustine College, February 14 to 16, 1941. The approach to this subject will include the following:

An analysis of the stated purposes of colleges with reference to leadership development; especially in the light of the status of the Negro in American society.

An examination of the effects of organized campus life upon the development of the democratic principle in student affairs and in associations between faculty and students.

A sampling of experiments in shared responsibilities in the management of life on college campuses.

Interpretations of the special obligation of the Negro college in demonstrating the possibility of real democracy at work in a specific community.

Some indications of the connection between what happens to a student during his college days in matters of campus citizenship, and what is likely to happen to him in the exercise of citizenship after graduation.

Suggestions for future thought and action in terms of the larger demands for making our present experiences "proving grounds" for the ideas and ideals that we hold regarding fundamental decency and mutuality in human relationships.

Administrators, faculty and students from every Negro college in the United States are asked to be present and to join in the deliberations of this conference. More details will be coming later regarding the daily time schedule, leadership, expenses, etc. We welcome inquiries and suggestions.

Very sincerely yours,
[*signed*] Frank T. Wilson
Chairman of Planning Committee

[*signed*] Howard Thurman
Secretary-Convener of the Fellowship
Note: Please address all communications to Dean Frank Wilson, Lincoln University, Lincoln University, Pennsylvania.

TLc. HTC-MBU: Box 7.

1. The three-day conference occurred in February 1941 on the campuses of Shaw University and Saint Augustine College in Raleigh, North Carolina. The purpose of the conference was to analyze the historical role of the Negro college in developing African American leadership; examine the effectiveness of the systems of campus life in modeling and nurturing "democratic principles" among students, faculty, and administration; and showcase "experiments" in democratic interaction occurring at some institutions. See the program of the "Student Leadership in the Negro College" conference, the second conference sponsored by Religious Workers in Negro Colleges and Universities, Shaw University and Saint Augustine College, Raleigh, North Carolina, 14–16 February 1941, HTPP Subject Files.

FROM A. J. MUSTE
9 SEPTEMBER 1940
NEW YORK, N.Y.

A. J. Muste[1] *writes with news that Thurman was unanimously selected, in absentia, to be one of the three vice chairmen of the Fellowship of Reconciliation (FOR).*

Dear Howard Thurman:

We have just finished what was probably the greatest and most significant Annual Conference of the Fellowship of Reconciliation. There was a very large attendance at Chautauqua, and great and deep going enthusiasm and committment to the non-violent way of life.[2]

I am enclosing an advance copy of the message of the Council. There are some fairly important editorial revisions to be made, but in substance and in principle it expresses the mind of the Conference.

At the meetings of the Council held at Chautauqua, Nevin[3] and I were re-elected as co-secretaries, Kirby Page and Douglas Steere as vice-chairmen, and Professor Arthur Swift of Union was made chairman of the Fellowship. We had thought to make Douglas Steere chairman of the Council and Fellowship and Arthur Swift of the Executive Committee, but Douglas Steere is in Germany, and will not return for some months.

This left a vacancy in the vice-chairmanships, of which we have in recent years always had three. A number of names were considered for the position, all of whom are fully consecrated to the work of the Fellowship and to our principles, but when your name was suggested there was an immediate, unanimous and enthusiastic decision to ask you to take this post. You still have another year to serve as a member of the Council, so that there is no question of your first being elected or coopted to the Council involved.

I need not go into the reasons why we need to{\} have the full support and all possible help from all of our experienced people in these days. The fact that they are all tremendously busy at their own work does not alter that. It is precisely the busy people who are usually the best qualified to render additional service.

I hope that we may have an immediate and favorable reply to this call. If, however, there is any question about it, then I trust that you will not make a decision until Nevin or I have had a chance to confer with you further.

With all good wishes, I am,
Sincerely yours,
[*signed*] A. J. Muste
A. J. Muste
ajm/em
uopwa 1 16
enc.

TLS. HTC-MBU: Box 13.

1. Abraham Johannes Muste (1885–1967) was a minister, labor leader, socialist and Trotskyist, educator, and Christian pacifist. He was also executive director of the Fellowship of Reconciliation from 1940 to 1953.

2. The Annual National Council Meeting of the Fellowship of Reconciliation was held on 7 September 1940 in Chautauqua, New York. At that meeting the organization elected members of the FOR to various posts for the remainder of 1940 and through the year 1941. See Minutes of National Council Meeting of the Fellowship of Reconciliation, 7 September 1940, Swarthmore Peace Collection, Swarthmore College.

3. John Nevin Sayre, for additional information see biographical note on Sayre in volume I.

To A. J. Muste

20 September 1940
Washington, D.C.

Thurman accepts A. J. Muste's invitation to be a vice chairman of FOR[1] *but articulates the inherent conflicts that arise from being both a pacifist and an advocate for fair treatment of African Americans who join the military.*

My dear A. J. Muste:

I have hesitated a long time in answering your letter relative to my accepting the vice-chairmanship of the Fellowship of Reconciliation. The truth is, I have not yet seen my way clear to get the time to take any active responsibility in this regard. I know that everybody else is busy also, but my work makes such absolute demands on all of my time and energy that there simply is nothing left with which to do additional things, but I am willing to do what I can even though at the outset I must make it clear that it will be very little. I am doing two jobs in the university and serving a rather large constituency in different parts of the country in other ways. The crisis that is upon us simply deepens my responsibilities here in the university and elsewhere. Negro men and women need so much more counseling during these times than ordinarily. The complications of our social order make it very difficult to keep clear of critical conflicts. For instance, I am sure that the thousands of Negro men who will be taken into camp should not be deserted by other Negroes like me. Often our very presence will stay the hands of brutality and cruelty on the part of white men who are in position of authority over them and whose normally weak scruples as to treatment are almost thoroughly routed by the customary moral disintegration opened by war.[2] And yet I know that war is not only futile but is thoroughly and completely evil and diabolical.

What my duty is as a Christian is sometimes very obscure. All of this is to suggest to you that all of my surplus energy, if there be any, is taken up in specific problems having to do with the decisions which hundreds of our fellows who think as I think are forced to make. At any rate, I shall do what I can. I shall try to come to an occasional New York meeting.

With every kind regard, I am

Sincerely,
[*signed*] Howard Thurman
Dean
Mr. A. J. Muste
The Fellowship of Reconciliation
2929 Broadway
New York City

TLS. HTC-MBU: Box 13.

1. See From A. J. Muste, 9 September 1940, printed in the current volume.

To Ruth Gildersleeve

23 October 1940
Washington, D.C.

Thurman writes a thoughtful response to a letter from a young woman at Marietta College in Ohio who is confused about what she sees as a contradiction between the scientific theory of evolution and the biblical story of creation.

My dear Ruth:[1]

I am afraid that merely writing a letter to you about the theory of evolution will be of no definite value. I am glad that you are mixed up and confused, because it means that your thinking is being aroused. Do not be uneasy, it will not last always. The important thing is that you must not become emotionally disturbed by it. If you have in your library Tyler's "The Coming of Man," you will find this to be of help to you.[2] It is important to remember that the theory of evolution, as all scientific theories do not explain, but merely describes what is happening. It seems to me that as resourceful and as creative as I think God is, it is not important what method he chose to use in building a world. The important thing to remember is that however the thing got started God is the origin of life. This is what religion says. Now you may go to science to find out how he did it.

It is quite exciting that you are at Marietta. I hope you will have a good year and if I am ever through that section this winter I shall look you up. Let me hear from you again sometime.

Sincerely,
[*signed*] Howard Thurman
Dean
Miss Ruth Gildersleeve
313 Third Street
Marietta, Ohio

TLc. HTC-MBU: Box 8.

1. Ruth Gildersleeve attended Marietta College from 18 September 1940 to the spring of 1942. She attempted a degree in the sciences but did not graduate from the college, according to the Marietta College Records Office.

2. John Mason Tyler (1851–1929) was the author of many works on religion, among them *The Coming of Man* (Boston: Jones, 1923).

To Mordecai Wyatt Johnson
26 October 1940
Washington, D.C.

In 1938 Thurman had permitted the establishment at Howard of a student ministry called the Wesley Foundation associated with the Methodist Church of America, but he had expressly forbade them from meeting on campus.[1] *The organization violated Thurman's instructions, and he writes Johnson that a "dangerous precedent" would be established if this practice is allowed to continue.*

My dear Mr. President:

I am writing this letter to call your attention to the fact that the Wesley Foundation, which is the name of the student organization of the Methodist Church of America, holds its regular meetings in a building on the campus. Inasmuch as this is a sectarian organization, I am wondering whether or not it is a dangerous precedent to be established. In a comparatively short time, my guess is that other religious groups will be desirous of having their meetings on the campus.

I do not think this is in keeping with the policy of the university as I have understood it. The meetings are being held in the school of religion.
Sincerely yours,
[*signed*] Howard Thurman
Dean
Dr. Mordecai W. Johnson
President
Howard University

TLS. HTC-MBU: Box 23.

1. See To H. D. Bollinger, 19 January 1938, printed in the current volume.

FROM NATHAN W. COLLIER
9 DECEMBER 1940
ST. AUGUSTINE, FLA.

Thurman had long retained an affection for Nathan Collier,[1] *the president of his high school alma mater, Florida Normal and Industrial Institute, which had since become a four-year college.*[2] *Collier, now ailing, asks Thurman to replace him, along with making a blunt assessment of Florida's black youth.*

Dear Dr. Thurman:

As I told you when you were in St. Augustine I am anxious to have you succeed me as President of Florida Baptist College. This letter is strictly personal and confidential. Please do not discuss it with anyone who will let it get to the press for publication, or with anyone who will start it out on the rounds of the Negro "grapevine telegraph line."

There is not, as you know, a single four year accredited Negro Christian College in the State of Florida. As one of the nation's most gifted sons, and a native son of Florida, as well as one of Florida Normal's most distinguished graduates, I want you to return to Florida and build on our campus here the greatest four year Christian College in the State of Florida. There are nearly one-half million Negro youth in the State of Florida fondant[3] under the strains of the rag-time music, rushing pell-mell into the jaws of hell through the doors of Florida's jungles of ball rooms and jooks, and no one has yet appeared on the scene with sufficient personal magnetism and oratorical ability to claim their attention causing them to leave the broad and popular dance highways to hell and enter the narrow and less attractive, narrow way, at least the Christian way of service for the Master. Florida with its nearly one-half million Negro youth is issuing a call to leave their Macedonian cry to come over into Macedonia[4] and help save us from the death dealing gin-mills and hell bound dance halls. You can do this job. I want you to head up this four year Christian College in Florida, which now appears to be the only hope they have in sight. If you fail them, it now appears to me that the majority of them, if not all, will continue on their raging rampage leading into the gates of hell.

Having no endowment Florida Normal has to offer you to begin with a modest salary of $1,000 for the first year for ten months, and increase this pay just as soon as its income will warrant.

If you decide to come, and could come as early as January first, 1941 we would like to have you do so, heading up our million dollar endowment drive (five year plan) which if reasonably successful, could start you off at once with a larger salary than one above referred to. In which event, merely as a matter of routine you will use temporarily the title as "Dean of Religious Education." I think I can get the Southern Baptist Convention (white) to guarantee $50 per month on your salary.

About the middle of last June, because of a complete breakdown in health I entered the University of Georgia Hospital, Augusta, Georgia. The staff reported that unless I immediately relieved myself of the load of money raising and work at the Institution I could not survive. I have been here for treatment five and a half months, and it now appears that I have just as many more ahead of me here. In view of the foregoing facts I decided if you will take up the place and accept the presidency, I shall keep my connection as President emeritus to help where I can, but give you a free hand, helping out all I can upon your request. If you accept, you will have absolutely, complete control, no interference of any sort or kind from any source, not even I will have a word to say, except or unless you request my advice.

Anxiously awaiting a reply.

Yours for the salvation of Negro youth of Florida
[*signed*] N. W. Collier
NWC/F

P.S. We have ready for you and your family to live in a neat, five room cottage with all modern conveniences. Later on as funds come in and are available, a modern mansion can be erected as a home for President Thurman.

TLS. HTC-MBU: Box 4.

1. Nathan Collier was president at Florida Baptist Academy during Thurman's high school years. For additional information about Collier, see the biographical footnote in volume 1.

2. Thurman had often returned to Florida Normal. In 1931 he offered the Founder's Day address, telling the audience that "President Collier has been here in one place for 37

years, working, dreaming, suffering, and rejoicing sometimes, trying to make it possible for young people to carry forward the world's work satisfactorily, satisfied himself that they have seen the light—that they will be able to go where he will not be able to go and do what he cannot do." "Hold Founder's Day at Florida Normal," *Chicago Defender*, 25 April 1931.

3. Probably the French word for *melting*.

4. Acts 16:9.

To Nathan W. Collier

6 January 1941
Washington, D.C.

Thurman responds to Collier's plea that he consider the presidency of Florida Normal and Collegiate Institute.

My dear President Collier:

I have kept your letter[1] for almost a month trying to come to some kind of decision with reference to the challenge which it presents, and even at this writing I am unable to give you any kind of satisfactory answer. I know from your letter what the situation is, and I would like very much to be able to do the thing that you have so graciously asked of me. My situation, however, is so involved here that it is quite impossible for me to be relieved of it at this time. It happens that I am carrying one of the major responsibilities at Howard; as a matter of fact, the entire structure of the religious life of the university outside of the School of Religion rests formally on my shoulders. The things on which I have been working for during the past few years are just now beginning to show some signs of fruition. If I withdraw, they collapse. I find it almost impossible to justify this on moral grounds. I am gradually forming a proposal which I shall make to President Johnson when he returns to the city sometime this week.[2] What his reaction will be, I do not know, but as soon as he and I talk it through, I shall write you again. I have not talked with him before because I could not come to a clear position in my own thinking.

You have done a profoundly significant day's work there and have built a monument of service and inspiration to a great host of Negro youth. In your own character and devotion, and amazing intelligence and courage, you are a constant source of strength to all of us. My prayers and my deepest feeling go forth on your behalf that your health will be fully restored and that many years of vigor will continue to be yours.

I know this letter will doubtless be a disappointment to you, but believe me, it is the best that I can do now. I promise you, however, that I shall write again as soon as I confer with President Johnson. My warmest personal greetings to you.
Very sincerely,
[*signed*] Howard Thurman
Dean
President N. W. Collier
Florida Normal and Collegiate Institute
Saint Augustine, Florida

TLS. HTC-MBU: Box 4.

1. From Nathan Collier, 9 December 1940, printed in the current volume.
2. It is not clear what Thurman's proposal was or how Johnson may have responded to it.

To S. W. Smith

25 February 1941
Washington, D.C.

Following the death of L. K. Williams, pastor of Olivet Baptist Church and National Baptist Convention president, Thurman was contacted by a member of the pulpit committee to gauge his interest in standing for the pastoral position. In this letter to Dr. S. W. Smith,[1] Thurman confirms that he will preach one Sunday at Olivet[2] to test the waters but says that he is not interested in competing for the job.

My dear Doctor:

At last I have worked out a date on which it is possible for me to visit Olivet Church to preach at least, Sunday morning, if I find that I cannot stay any longer. The date is March 23rd. I would appreciate it if you could confirm this date by the end of the week so that I may complete arrangements for having someone preside in Chapel for me.

I am sure you understand the spirit in which I visit the church. I do not wish to be involved in competition, or any of the petty things which are apt to go on in connection with a vacancy. I am prepared, however, to consider prayerfully, and with as much judgment as is available to me, the challenge and the opportunity a fine church like Olivet offers. I am very well located here with an appointment for life. I feel that Mrs. Thurman and I are doing a good day's work on behalf of the cause of God in the life of the youth of this place and other places, but I cannot refrain from exposing myself to the possibility of another kind of opportunity where problems are different and the responsibility is of a more varied type. It is in this spirit that I visit the church.

Mrs. Thurman sends greetings to you and Mrs. Smith.

Sincerely yours,
[*signed*] Howard Thurman
Dean
Dr. S. W. Smith
4666 South State Street
Chicago, Illinois

TLS. HTC-MBU: Box 20.

1. S. W. Smith (1881–1964), a member of Olivet, was a leader of the search committee to find a new minister. The prominent Chicago physician once held the position of superintendent of the surgical staff at Wilson Hospital in Chicago and served as a surgeon in the Olivet Health Bureau. In 1943 he became the medical adviser for Victory Mutual Life Insurance Company, an African American–owned insurance company founded to create jobs and encourage saving for community betterment. Smith was born in North Carolina and graduated from Meharry Medical College in Nashville.

2. Olivet Baptist Church, founded in 1850 as Zenia Baptist Church, is the oldest black Baptist church in Chicago. Under the pastorship of Lacey Kirk Williams (1916–1940), Olivet grew in size and prominence, and in the 1920s had an estimated membership of over 10,000 persons. In recent decades it has struggled to regain its former influence.

From J. T. Brown

27 February 1941
Jacksonville, Fla.

Days after the funeral of Nathan Collier, president of Florida Normal and Collegiate Institute, J. T. Brown[1] *writes to implore Thurman to accept an appointment as president of the school. Brown tells Thurman that the Board of Trustees' decision to offer the position to him was unanimous because they believe that he is "the only man known to us who can do this work."*

Dr. Howard Thurman
Howard University
Washington, D.C.

My dear Dr. Thurman:

We buried our friend and brother, Dr. Collier, Tuesday afternoon on the campus of his beloved Florida Normal. The weather was propitious and the crowd was uncountable, the sorrow could be felt deeply and almost cut with the hand.

This great school is leaderless-fatherless.

I am asked to write, expressing to you the unanimous desire for you to assume the leadership of this school and complete this marvelous "unfinished task" of President Collier.

There is a deep, spiritual faith in you as the only man known to us who can do this work. Dr. Collier wished you as his successor, the people—everybody—wants you: Providence seems to have marked you out for the task by having you to come and look it over last year, preparatory to this call; it is the infant cradle in which your splendid talents had their intellectual rocking into consciousness; your name has been shown to so many as God's man in answer to prayer; in this materialistic age when God's Spirit is at a discount, among many in the placing of men in their fields of labor, God has revealed to other praying men in visions, the decision that you are the man "to come over into Macedonia and help us."[2] While the vision may not yet have come to you, it will surely come if you, like Paul, will ask and wait for direction.

There is a mammoth redemptive task which Florida Normal and Industrial Institute is intended and destined to fill in our beloved Southland for our race and the world for which God in His kindly providence has endowed, trained and fitted you, making you pre-eminently the man "who has come to the Kingdom for such a time as this."[3]

My dear Thurman, if you will read the history of your life, as directed by the providence of God, on your knees, I am sure, God will enable you to interpret this as His call to the task for which your entire previous life is a preparation.

This is not just a personal opinion expressed; but I am a trustee of the school, always have been; and was in the Trustee Meeting Tuesday morning held on the campus and am expressing the unanimous and prayerful desire of every member of the Board from the Chairman, Dr. Ford to the least member.

Miss Blocker, with her eyes suffused with tears, urged me to inform you of her desire to have you take over this divine work.

I shall leave Jacksonville for Nashville Monday morning, March 3rd.

You may address your reply to me at Fourth Avenue and Cedar Street, Nashville, Tennessee, or you may reply to Dr. J. E. Ford, Chairman, Board of Trustees, Jacksonville, Florida, c/o Bethel Baptist Church.

God bless you, Son; take your time; pray and let God decide for you; Do not decide yourself.

Yours sincerely,
[*signed*] J. T. Brown
Acting Secretary of Trustee Board
Florida Normal & Industrial Institute.
JTB/ebe

TLS. HTC-MBU: Box 2.

1. Jacob Tileston Brown (1860–1947), an 1891 graduate of the Hampton Institute, received BST and MA degrees from Lincoln University in Pennsylvania, and was a co-founder and first president of Florida Baptist Academy in Live Oak, Florida in 1892. He subsequently served as pastor in many prominent congregations, including the Mount Zion Baptist Church (Miami), Spruce Street Baptist Church (Nashville), the Metropolitan Baptist Church (Memphis), and the Dexter Avenue Baptist Church (Montgomery). For many decades he was editor in chief of the Sunday School Publishing Board of the National Baptist Convention, and was the editor and author of many works in the field of theological education.

2. Acts 16:9.

3. Esther 4:14.

From A. J. Muste
14 March 1941
New York, N.Y.

Muste asked Thurman to spend a week in Detroit on behalf of FOR to help a local minister teach the techniques of nonviolence to workers who were attempting to unionize the Ford Motor Company. Muste feared that violence would erupt if workers decided to strike and that Ford would try to use race to drive a wedge between black and white employees.[1]

Dear Thurman:

You will realize at once how tremendously important is the situation described in Owen Ge{e}r's[2] letter, of which I am enclosing a copy. I have written Jim Farmer. I suppose the chances of Jim's being able to get away just at this stage in his seminary year are pretty slim. Unfortunately, I have got myself so heavily booked up that it may be six weeks before I can possibly put in more than a couple of days in Detroit, without having to cancel a score of pretty important engagements and throwing a lot of things out of gear. I have written Owen the situation, and asked just when things are likely to break.

Would there be a possibility of your going to Detroit to work for a week or so, or even for a couple of days, on this matter? I am not at all sure that it doesn't require a mature person rather than Jim, excellent as would be some of the contributions that Jim could make. If you cannot go, is there anyone else with whom I could take this matter up? Are there people in Detroit whom we ought to put Owen in touch with? Are there people working in Washington with the N.L.R.B.,[3] etcetera, who ought to be approached, and who might be helpful?

I'm just shooting out questions, trying to think of resources in this difficult and crucial situation. If you can let me have a line from you immediately, I'll appreciate it a lot.
Faithfully yours,
[*signed*] A. J.
enc.
copy

1. The United Automobile Workers Union (UAW) began its battle to unionize Ford Motor Company as early as 1937. Ford was the last of the big three automakers to be unionized (the other two major automakers were General Motors and Chrysler). After Ford fired several union organizers and workers in spring 1941, a spontaneous walkout occurred. Ultimately unionization came in large measure because of successful organizing by workers in the African American community.

2. Owen Meredith Geer (1898–1971) was minister of the Mount Olivet Community Methodist Church in Dearborn, Michigan, from 1935 to 1947. After 1947 he was a minister in Los Angeles, where he chaired a minister's group concerned with farm unionization, and in 1948 his activism in the labor movement resulted in his being summoned before the State Senate Un-American Activities Committee. His writings include *Christ's Pathway to Power: A Book of Personal Devotion and Evangelism* (Chicago: Epworth League and Young People's Work, 1936).

3. National Labor Relations Board.

[Enclosure: Owen Geer to A. J. Muste]

13 March
292 Broadway
New York City

Dear A. J.:

It is going to be impossible for me to attend the meeting of the Council on March 27–28, much as I regret it! I accepted, some months ago, an invitation it go to the University of Wisconsin on that date to speak at a state conference of youth. I wish there were some way of changing the set-up so I could come, for there are maters on which I greatly need help.

Some time ago you asked me about the situation at the Ford plant, wanting to know if there is anything that can be done by the F.O.R. I have pondered the problem, and have a suggestion or two to make. The situation is bad here. As you know, the CIO[1] has asked for an election, and has filed strike notices with the

Labor Board and the State Labor Mediation Board. They are hoping that a strike will not be necessary, but are in doubt as to the possibility of the matter being settled without it. The outlook is good for an early election. These strike notices seem to have stepped up government attention to the matter, and Dewey[2] has been here of late. All sentiment expressed here indicates that the CIO will win an election. A foreman told me the other day that there is no doubt in his mind that the CIO has more than a majority of the employees signed up now. Ben Allen, who investigated the plant under the Senate Committee on Civil Liberties some two years ago, and is here now helping to organize the CIO, says he has no doubt of them winning an election.

The problem is: Will Ford sign a contract, even if they do win an election? The union is in doubt of it, and therefore plan to strike in order to show their power to compel bargaining. A strike will probably mean bloodshed, for the Service Men are headed by a ruthless leader in Bennett.[3]

Even though the company has posted notices that men are free to join the union, there is a systematic program of beating taking place throughout the plant now. A group of men will come through and attack a man at work who is wearing a union pin, and then he is fired for fighting back. This is done in order to intimidate, and also to incite a race riot. Ford employs many Negroes, and Bennett has brought pressure on them thru their pastors and otherwise to keep them from joining up. Also he hopes to precipitate trouble between the races, which will give him a chance to discharge on masse a number of the men who are in the union.

The tension between the races is growing, and there is need for work to be done here at once with the whites and colored, and especially the pastors. Detroit and vicinity have many southerners who have strong anti-Negro feelings, and there is going to be terrible trouble if the situation gets out of hand.

I have made some suggestions to the Dearborn preachers, but for the most part get little response. They are so accustomed to keeping silent on the issues at the plant, that I rather doubt if they will have the courage to do much, unless they can get some real help.

I talked recently with one of the CIO men who's working in the situation, and who is also a member of my church. He feels that the situation is very dangerous, and wants us to do what we can to help meet it. Here is my proposal:

Can you and Jim Farmer get away, and plan to spend a week or two here, working with the ministers, the CIO, and the general public? We have an entree through the union which will assure us of fine cooperation from them. The newspapers will handle the matter fairly well, I think. And the Detroit Council of Churches, as well as the Michigan Council of Churches, will do their bit. I have just been asked to serve as the Chairman of the Committee on Industrial Relations for the State Council of Churches, and that will help in my work.

I think we could do at least three things:

1. Help educate the unions in the techniques of non-violence.
There is real need, and little is being done, save by the leaders themselves. The FOR has a message for such situations, and with our literature we could do a good job of educating them. The meetings of the union will be open to us, I am sure.
2. Reach the Ford workers, colored and white, through their churches and other organizations.
The Negro minister is a significant factor in this situation, and Bennett well knows it. He is under rather heavy pressure at the present time from the company, and they have been making it possible for certain preachers to hand out jobs to men, in order to get their support for the anti-union program. We can call to their attention the dangers inherent in racial discord, and urge them to have nothing to do with these racial fights.
3. Inform the general public.
Of course little gets into the public press, and there is general ignorance of the true situation. We should have a committee with will make an impartial study of the situation, and wherever it finds violence and coercion, bring it to light. The union is being charged with coercion, and of course there is bound to be a certain amount of it in any union drive. But there is nothing to compare with the coercion and intimidation which is being handed out from the company.

Now I know that you are terribly busy, and you have a heavy speaking schedule, but two or three weeks spent here this spring could well save some lives, and might become an outstanding example of the thing that the FOR can do in an industrial conflict. I shall be glad to work with you, and to help set up a local committee. Jim could do effective work with the colored people as well as the white, as could you.

I think your letter to Kerrison[4] was splendid. We'll make contact with him.

Faithfully yours,
[*unsigned*]
OWEN (GEER)

TLc. HTC-MBU: Box 13.

1. The Congress of Industrial Organizations (CIO) was a federation of unions that organized workers in industrial unions in the Unites States and Canada. Created in 1935 as the Conference of Industrial Organizations within the American Federation of Labor (AFL), it became a separate labor federation in 1936, merging with the AFL in 1955 to form the AFL-CIO.

2. Charles Manuel Dewey (1922–92) was a militant labor activist in Detroit who supported the UAW's organizing efforts in that city. See the Charles M. Dewey Collection, Archives of Labor and Urban Affairs, Reuther Library, Wayne State University.

3. Harry Bennett (1892–1979) headed Ford's Service Department, or internal security. A former boxer and ex–Navy sailor, Bennett was hired by Ford in 1916 and swiftly became Henry Ford's right-hand man. By the early 1940s, Bennett supervised a cadre of three thousand men, who used threats, intimidation, and violence to fight unionization. After Henry Ford's grandson Henry Ford II became president of the company in 1945, he fired Bennett.

4. Irvine "Irv" Kerrison (1916–96) earned a bachelor's degree from Albion College in Michigan in 1938 and a master's degree from Wayne State University in 1941. At this time Kerrison was beginning his career as a labor educator in Detroit, and in 1947 he became director of the Rutgers Institute of Labor and Management Relations. He earned his PhD from Columbia University in 1951.

To A. J. Muste
19 March 1941
Washington, D.C.

Thurman informs Muste that he is too busy to do the work that is needed in Detroit to unionize the Ford Motor Company. He assures Muste, though, that on his next trip there he will meet with Owen Geer, a local minister involved in the labor crisis, to map out an effective strategy. Thurman also discusses the difficulty he anticipates in convincing black workers that they would be better off siding with the union than with Ford.

My dear A. J.:

I have been greatly concerned about your letter[1] and I am desirous of doing something about it. My own work is so involved and packed with commitments that I cannot take any time out. Personally I do not think that any real good can be accomplished, unless some one person could work with the Detroit situation over a period of weeks. I go to Detroit every year, and shall be there for two or three days at Easter time. The problem is very complexed, and I am not sure that any one has the answer. The only thing that I can do is to arrange to have a long talk with Owen Geer when I am out there and see if some of the people whom I know very well are willing to meet with him to review the whole problem and to think in terms of a constructive strategy. As far as the Negroes are concerned, many of them are convinced that Ford's past attitude toward them in terms of employment as contrasted with other groups in Detroit was so superior that they find it hard to be convinced that their fate is not more definitely tied up with Ford's with fewer risks than with other groups, however powerful. The group has been exploited in so many ways that it is hard for them to believe in anybody under any circumstances. Least of all, any group bearing a union label. So much education has to be done to overcome this handicap. I shall drop Owen

Geer a note and make an appointment with him for the day I shall be in Detroit. Out of our conversation and discussion something might be evolved.
Sincerely,
[*signed*] Howard Thurman
Dean
Mr. A. J. Muste
The Fellowship of Reconciliation
2929 Broadway
New York, New York

TLS. HTC-MBU: Box 7.

1. From A. J. Muste, 14 March 1941, printed in the current volume.

From Marshall A. Talley
21 March 1941
Nashville, Tenn.

On 12 February, 1941, Thurman spoke before a meeting of the International Council of Religious Education,[1] *an association representing over forty religious denominations.*[2] *The crowd was enthusiastic. Among those in attendance was Marshall Talley,*[3] *director of the Sunday School Congress for the National Baptist Convention, who wrote him a month later, telling him that "numbers of white persons were almost thrown into hysterics as they commented with me upon your marvelous delivery and the profound philosophy of your utterances." Asking if he could publish the talk, Talley's letter went on to mention an incident several weeks after the talk in Chicago, when at a meeting of the International Council of Religious Education in Cincinnati, black attendees had not been treated with respect. Thurman wrote back, agreeing to Talley's request for publishing his talk, adding that most white Christians "have never made up their minds to try the gospel out. Indeed, I don't suppose any of us have. We must keep on working, and keep on blasting. In my opinion we have compromised and soft-pedalled so long that the truth always seems radical and terrifying."*[4] *The February Thurman's talk was published in the* Sunday School Informer *under the title, "Our Underlying Spiritual Unities."*[5]

My dear Dr Thurman: I have had much to say and to write concerning your great message before the International Council of Religious Education in Chicago during the month of February. I am writing to thank you sincerely for this marvelously informative and spirited message. Perhaps you will never know the extent of the results of your deliverances at this time. Numbers of white people were almost thrown into hysterics as they commented with me upon your marvelous delivery and the profound philosophy of your utterances. I wish you would permit me to publish this message in full in our sunday school informer for May. I further desire to have a good photograph of yourself from which I desire to make a cut to run on the cover page of the informer.

Since leaving Chicago many of the executives of Negro denominations have discovered a change of attitude on the part of the executives of the International Council affecting the social relations we have hitherto enjoyed with the Council. At a recent meeting in Cincinnati where the executives of all of the denominational groups of the constituent units of the Council were called in session, we were most grievously humiliated. It seems that the total aspect of our social fellowship with the executives of the Council has been changed since our meeting in February. It seems that the masses of the people were with you almost in hysterical terms but that the Pharisaical or executive group has seen reason to change their attitude since that time. We felt the impact of the same 30 days later at Cincinnati. The stinging challenge as I saw it came from your utterance concerning the effort of teaching love behind walls of segregation and separation. I am not quite sure that the Cincinnati meeting on March 10, 11, in which the Negro denominational executives were barred and humiliated, was a result but we do know that it was the ordinary comment that a black man had come to the Council and "stolen the show." We are praising God for your great interpretation of the problems of our times. We propose to investigate to the depths as to whether the Council executives agree or disagree with your challenge regarding the walls of separation. Again, I wish to thank you sincerely for this marvelous message, one of the greatest to which I have ever listened, and permit me to beg of you that I may have the privilege of publishing this message in the May issue of the sunday school informer as referred to above.

With sentiments of most exalted esteem.

I am fraternally yours,

Marshall A. Talley

[*signed*]

Marshall A. Talley

TLS. HTC-MBU: Box 21.

1. The International Council of Religious Education was founded in Kansas City, Missouri in 1922, through the merger of the International Sunday School Association and the Sunday School Council of Evangelical Organizations, consisting of the religious education boards of forty denominations. In 1950, with several other ecumenical organizations, including the Federal Council of Churches, it merged to form the National Council of Churches.

2. Rev. John Evans, "Tells Religion Teachers They Must Believe," Feb 13, 1941, *Chicago Daily Tribune.*

3. Marshall A. Talley (1877–1953) served as director of the Sunday School Congress of the National Baptist Convention, dean of religious education for the National Baptist Sunday

School Union, and editor of the *Sunday School Informer.* Born near Concord, North Carolina, he graduated from Johnson C. Smith University (1904) and was ordained as a Baptist minister in 1905. He also studied at the University of Pittsburgh and the Union Theological Seminary. In 1936 Talley, a Democrat, won a seat as a state representative for Marion County in the Indiana General Assembly, and he additionally formed the Negro Welfare Committee in Indiana. In 1939 he became pastor of New Era Baptist Church in Indianapolis. When New Era united with Northside Baptist Church in 1945, he was elected pastor. Talley also coauthored with C. C. Adams *Negro Baptists and Foreign Missions* (Philadelphia: Foreign Mission Board of the National Baptist Convention, U.S.A., 1944).

4. 28 March 1941 To Marshall Talley, HTC-MBU: Box 21.
5. Published in the current volume.

To S. W. Smith
26 March 1941
Washington, D.C.

After Thurman's 23 March visit to Olivet Baptist Church to deliver a sermon, he tactfully informs Smith that he is open to the possibility of becoming pastor.

My dear Doctor Smith:

I am sending this letter to you before my recent experience is covered over by the responsibilities here and certain things might not stand out clearly in my mind a week from now, as they do at this moment.

First of all let me express my deep appreciation to you and Mrs. Smith for the gracious way in which, as always, you extended your fellowship and hospitality to me. It is difficult for you to realize, I am sure the place that you two occupy in the thoughts and feelings of the Thurmans. Through the years you have been gracious hosts to us, so that we feel perfectly free to call your home our home when we are in Chicago.

There is not much in detail that I need say about my experience at Olivet last Sunday. I was profoundly moved by the response of the rank and file of the people. You see, I believe that what our people need is to have the religion of Jesus taught to them in order that they may understand what it is that is required of them. I took a text that belongs to the 'war horses' and the 'whoopers,' but I wanted to appeal to the minds of the people, being confident that the feelings would take care of themselves. This, I think, was demonstrated on Sunday.

I was impressed also with the tremendous responsibility which leadership in the church must carry. In order for a man to do a constructive job in Christian leadership there, he would have to have the confidence and the backing of all the people and the intelligent counsel of the wisest and most consecrated members of the church. The thought of an opportunity that a church such as Olivet has in the city of Chicago is completely devastating.

I am sure you would want to know what my attitude toward the church is. I am giving it in a sentence: I was not prepared for a completely positive impression that the experience made upon me. If the officers are interested in approaching me with reference to the pastorate of the church, I wish they would give me the opportunity to discuss the whole question with them as a group of officers before any recommendation were made to the church. I would be willing to come out to Chicago for an evening in order to do this. I shall be preaching during Easter week in Detroit, and if I could meet with them sometime during the day on Easter Monday, it could be done with a minimum of expense to myself.

Please do not misunderstand me at this point. I am not trying to force any kind of decision, but the demands that are made upon me are so heavy that I cannot make any sudden changes without throwing a lot of things out of gear and causing very much embarrassment. Already my preaching engagements for next winter carry me to the University of Chicago, University of Iowa, Chicago Sunday Evening Club,[1] Vassar College, Wheaton College, Northfield Seminary, Mount Holyoke College, Phillips Academy in Massachusetts, and this is March.

Whatever happens, please know that my experience last Sunday was one that I shall always remember. If it is not a part of the plan of God that I shall leave academic work and go into the pastorate at this time, it will be made abundantly clear to all concerned.[2] With reference to this, I have no fear and no uneasiness.

My warmest personal greetings to you and to Mrs. Smith.

Sincerely,
[*signed*] Howard Thurman
Dean

{N.B. I am writing in this same general spirit to Mr. King but to no one else. Several people tried to get comments out of me while there but I let them talk.}

Dr. S. W. Smith
4666 South State Street
Chicago, Illinois

TLS. HTC-MBU: Box 20.

1. The Chicago Sunday Evening Club was organized in 1908 by Clifford Barnes, director of the Religious Education Association. Initially it was planned as an organization of Christian business leaders who would get together weekly to hear ecumenical sermons and discuss ways to address the city's social problems. Today it produces a weekly television show with subscriber stations nationwide. See Steven P. Vitrano, *An Hour of Good News: The Chicago Sunday Evening Club, a Unique Preaching Ministry* (Chicago: Chicago Sunday Evening Club, 1974).

2. Later that year Olivet appointed Joseph Harrison Jackson (1900–1990) as the new minister remaining in the position until his death. He was president of the National Baptist Convention from 1952 to 1982. He is best remembered as a fierce conservative opponent of Martin Luther King Jr. and the civil rights movement.

❧ TO JOHN E. FORD
28 MARCH 1941
WASHINGTON, D.C.

Thurman turns down the offer of the presidency of Florida Normal and Industrial Institute, citing his commitment "to the interpretation of religion" and a lack of interest in taking on the responsibilities of a top administrator in an educational institution. Despite the crisis in leadership, the college survived, and Nathan Collier's vision of a four-year college was realized.[1]

My dear Doctor Ford:[2]

I hardly know how to answer your letter because at the present moment my commitments are such that it is not possible for me to give the kind of unbiased thought to you implied suggestion. I steadily refuse to go into the administrative end of education because my mind is not fundamentally interested in that aspect of the responsibility. All my life I have given my energies and my time to the interpretation of religion. For me to become an administrator in an institution means in a sense turning my back on most of my past. This is not a light thing to do. I have no interest in going up and down the country raising money and securing funds with which to carry on a program, which in the very nature of the case, I myself would not have time to execute.

I would not like to stand in any one's way, so that, if I am forced to make a decision by April 15th, the answer has to be no. As I have intimated, I am considering one or two things, all of which must be weighted in the light of what seems to me to be the will of God for my own life.

I do appreciate the courtesy which you have shown me in your very gracious letter, and I am sorry that I cannot be of more service in my reply.

Very sincerely yours,
[*signed*] Howard Thurman
Dean

Dr. John E. Ford
Florida N. and C. Institute
Saint Augustine Florida

TLS. HTC-MBU: Box 7.

1. Florida Normal and Industrial College awarded its first baccalaureate degrees in 1945. It changed its name to Florida Memorial College in 1963, and moved to a new campus in Miami in 1968, where it has been known as Florida Memorial University since 2005.

2. John E. Ford, who served as pastor of the Bethel Baptist Church in Jacksonville from 1907 until his death in 1943, was a long time civic leader in Jacksonville, and dean of Florida Normal and Industrial Institute's School of Theology.

To John T. Stocking

9 April 1941
Washington, D.C.

In this letter Thurman thanks his old friend Dr. John Stocking[1] *for looking after his ailing mother in Daytona.*

My dear Friend:

I have been planning for several weeks to send you a letter of appreciation for your willingness to take up the care of mama. From the first time that you came back a different note entered her letters. She has the most enthusiastic things to say about you, because you are the only doctor in whom she really believes. Several years ago when she was up here, and Dr. Carson operated on her, she was not willing for the operation until I told her I was sure that it was the sort of thing of which you would approve.

I am looking forward to coming home for several days this summer so that you and I can fish to our hearts content and solve all the problems of the Negro and the white man. I want you to know what a source of personal inspiration you have been to me through all the years since I was a boy. Time and time again I go back to some experience which I had with you, some bit of counsel which you gave me, and find strength and inspiration, and all of this is on the level.

My warmest personal regards to Mrs. Stockings.[2]

Sincerely,
[*signed*] Howard Thurman
Dean
Dr. John D. Stockings
Second Avenue Midway
Daytona Beach, Florida

TLc. HTC-MBU: Box 20.

1. John T. Stocking (1888–1965) was Thurman's family physician in Daytona and one of young Howard's two "masculine idols" in his early life (the other was a cousin). Stocking offered to pay for Thurman's education if he had chosen medical school. "Dr. Stockings showed an interest in me from the beginning. . . . He had little regard for the ministry and was genuinely distressed that I would waste my intellectual gifts on such a vocation. . . . All through the years, until his death in 1963, I visited him whenever I went home." *WHAH*, 21–23. Thurman, who misstated the year of his friend's death in his autobiography—but probably not the year of their last visit—for some reason consistently misspelled Stocking as "Stockings."

2. Daisy Hardy Stocking (1888–1968) was active in local civic affairs, and In 1964 the National Council of Negro Women named her woman of the year.

"Our Underlying Spiritual Unities"

May 1941
Chicago, Ill.

"Our Underlying Spiritual Unities," originally given as a talk before a predominantly white ecumenical conference in Chicago, was published in The Sunday School Informer, a monthly publication of the National Baptist Convention.[1] *The varied audiences of the talk were an important indication of Thurman's growing reputation. The short talk was about the "common desire which we share for a better world" and the difficulties of achieving it in a world in which this common desire was either reduced to the level of a banal "truism" or belied by the evidence of world torn to tatters by war. The essential paradox of modern life was that despite the advances made in science, in psychology, and other spheres, "we have less confidence than ever in the ability of the mind of man to administer to those deeper needs of the human spirit for faith in each other, for hope, for growth, and security. We have reduced the world to a neighborhood without being able to achieve neighborliness. "At such times, the "spirit of man" had to affirm that life could be bettered, than apparent contradictions were not final and could be transcended, and we needed to affirm "sometimes blindly, sometimes with little hope of vindication," that "the ultimate end of man is good." To achieve this would require "singleness of purpose" and "the basic dependability of the Spirit of the living God to fill us with the power to do his will, if with all our hearts, we seek him" germinating and sprouting within us like a seed shooting for the sun. The talk closed with a fierce paragraph that he would reproduce verbatim, two years later, in "The Will to Segregation," opening with the question "how dare we undertake to teach reverence to children when we ourselves do not believe in reverence for life in general," concluding, in a critique of racial separation in worship, "can we expect more of the state, of the body politic, of industry than we expect of the church? How can we teach love from behind great high walls of separateness?"*[2]

He continued that "all human living and human action" was based upon one of two assumptions about the nature of life. Either our lives are "capable of change and alteration" or not. If change is possible, then we must live from the assumption that "all of the contradictions of human experience are not in a profound sense, ultimate." The fact that we are united by a common desire for a better world "is a truism." And in the world in 1941, "precisely at the moment when the mind of modern man has made the most far-reaching intellectual advance in the matter of exploring and exploiting the world of nature, plumbing the depths of the human mind and spirit with the tools of the analysts and the psychologists, precisely at the moment which we have achieved a greater mastery over disease than any time in human history—we have less confidence than ever in the ability of the mind to administer to those deeper needs of the human spirit for faith in each other, for hope, for growth, and security. We have reduced the world to a neighborhood without being able to achieve neighborliness."

Men and women who deal with the materials of religious experience and who undertake to guide the development of religious life of youth, must themselves become increasingly righteous and holy, or they must become increasingly suave, clever, oily hypocrites. We must immunize ourselves against the effects of our own insights, or be profoundly effected by them or, admit that they have no genuine significance for us, or for any one else. It is, therefore, most appropriate for us to examine the underlying spiritual unities or assumptions which guarantee the validity of our insights and our techniques. There are three assumptions which are basic for our work as teachers of religion. First, there is the common desire which we share for a better world, both with reference to the climate in which we function and the character of the individuals in the world. In the second place, the degree to which this desire expresses itself in singleness of purpose shared by us all, and in the third place, the basic dependability of the Spirit of the living God to fill us with the power to do his will, if with all our hearts, we seek him.

In the first place, then, there is a common desire for a better world. All human living and human action are based upon one of two assumptions about the nature of life. Either the stuff of life including the life of man, is manageable, capable of change and alteration, or it is not manageable, not capable of being changed and altered. If the latter is true, then it is merely an illusion to assume that any basic structural change in the life of man is possible. For it would then follow that all of the contradictions of human experiences are not in a profound sense, ultimate. Man is therefore, caught within the grip of forces within and without over which he cannot exercise any control whatsoever, nor can he basically desire to do so. The logic of this means that man cannot elect ends nor determine purposes even within zones of agreement established by the length and breadth of a single life.

But a close scrutiny of human life reveals that this assumption is not true. There is a deep bias in the human spirit that insists that the contradictions of human experiences are not ultimate, that social change is possible, yea, that even purposes can be altered, and the fate of any individual is in some sense, in his own hands. The spirit of man stubbornly refuses to accept the contradictions of experiences as ultimate. Sometimes blindly, sometimes with little hope of vindication, often with wild irrationality, the spirit of man dares to affirm that the ultimate end of man is good. This is an important fact, because it becomes a basis of hope in times of despair, the incentive of dreams of a better day when the times are out of joint and men have lost their reason and the ground of optimism when worlds crash and dreams whiten into ash.

It is a truism then that we are united by a common desire for a better world. For a world in which it is a rational hope that men may live together in peace and in fellowship. It is a matter of profound consideration to realize that precisely at the moment when the mind of modern man has made the most far-reaching intellectual advance in the matter of exploring and exploiting the world of nature, plumbing the depths of the human mind and spirit with the tools of the analysts and the psychologists, precisely at the moment which we have achieved a greater mastery over disease than at any other time in human history we have less confidence than ever in the ability of the mind of man to administer to those deeper needs of the human spirit for faith in each other, for hope, for growth, and security. We have reduced the world to a neighborhood without being able to achieve neighborliness. And yet, we continue to hope for a better world. **I think this fact continues to be true because of the nature of the spirit of man rather than because of the ethical quality of the life of man.** In the second place, the degree to which this desire for a better world takes the shape of singleness of purpose determines the quality of our power to achieve that which we seek. We have scarcely touched the possibilities of achievement vouchsafed to us because of the very nature of life. It is to be noted that in the world of nature that wherever the conditions for growth are met then growth is automatic. When a seed is planted and the conditions are right as to moisture, temperature and the like, the growth of the seed is automatic. It seems as if the limitless resources of nature are brought to a point of focus and release the moment the conditions are met. The same is true when an individual elects a single end and devotes all of his powers to the fulfillment of that end, he becomes a man of power and fulfillment. It is this very profound principle that Jesus enunciates in his statement "that God sends his sun to shine on the good man and the bad man."[3]

How dare we undertake to teach reverence to children when we ourselves do not believe in reverence for life in general or life in particular as a valid concept in our kind of world? Shall we teach lies to children? How dare we proclaim sincerity and genuineness as essential qualities for healthy living if in our innermost selves we do not have confidence in the survival value of such ideals of living. Can we teach trust when we are bound by a vast network of impersonal social relations which create the kind of climate in which trust cannot possibly thrive? Or can we teach trust even as we confess how little trust we have in each other in our cause and in our God? I wonder. What do we mean when we teach the brotherhood of man? When over and over again we give the sanction of our religion and the weight of our practice to those subtle anti-Christian practices expressed in segregated churches even in segregated graveyards. Can we expect more of the state, of the body politic, of industry than we expect of the church? How can we teach love from behind great high walls of separateness?

"Our Underlying Spiritual Unities," Sunday School Informer 8, no. 5 (1941): 7.

1. For background on the talk, see 21 March From Marshall Talley, published in this volume.

2. "The Will to Segregation" published in this volume.

3. Thurman's paraphrase of Matthew 5:44–45.

FROM VIRGINIA CORWIN

25 SEPTEMBER 1941
CLEVELAND, OHIO

Virginia Corwin[1] asks Thurman to talk about the pitfalls of interracial marriage with one of her former students, a white woman, who plans to marry one of Thurman's former students.

Dear Howard:

I had hoped very much that you might get to the Week of Work, both because I would have enjoyed seeing you and because I have a problem which I want to put up to you.

You may have heard echoes of this, but in any case I will give you the facts as I know them. Elizabeth Downe,[2] a graduate of Smith of a few years ago, and one of my old students, told me this summer that she was engaged to Roy Norris, a young negro, whom by the way you may know, for I understand that he took some work at Howard. He has been for two years in a State Tubercular Sanitarium in New York, and was discharged this summer. She has a job now with the Y.W.C.A. in New Haven. Norris, whom I do not know, urged her to marry him this summer, but she was unwilling to do it. He has not yet finished his work at the Divinity School, and of course has no job. They are none the less determined to marry in the future.

I am very frank to say that I cannot believe that there is much chance for happiness in this particular marriage, and I believe both of them should consider the situation very seriously indeed before they take the step. I should be interested in your judgment on the matter. It seems to me that there is a lot of sentimentality about negroes in Miss Downe's mind, and that is a pretty weak ingredient in the mixture of motives. She is a nice girl, of plain background, very little sophistication and comparatively little experience with men. She is twenty-eight, and therefore reaching that period when there is an added factor, that of knowing that unless she marries soon she will not marry at all. There is an optimistic lack of realism, I believe, in facing the fact that an interracial marriage will enormously complicate Norris's chances of getting a job, let alone his health problem, which is in itself a very serious one. I am afraid that I cannot believe that these are the rare, strong individuals who can make a successful marriage under the kind of untoward circumstances that a negro-white marriage must face at the present time. However, your judgment might differ from mine, and I should welcome for Elizabeth the chance to talk with you. I told her that I would write and try to find out when you might come to New York, for she could readily go down to meet you. If they should go through with the marriage, she certainly needs far more realistic understanding than she has now.[3]

Incidentally, when are you coming to Cleveland? Is there any chance that you will be speaking here abouts this year? If you are, I shall want to see you, and I should be simply delighted if there were a chance of getting you to speak to the College and of having some of the faculty and students meet you.

My best to Sue. It has been a long time since I have seen you both.

Very sincerely yours,
[*signed*] Virginia
VC : M

TLS. HTC-MBU: Box 4.

1. Virginia Corwin (1901–96) received a BA from Wellesley College (1923), a BD from Union Theological Seminary (1929), and a PhD from Yale University (1937). She taught courses on religion and biblical literature at Smith College during the 1930s before moving on to the Flora Stone Mather College for women at Western Reserve University (1939–42). In addition to teaching there, she also served as an assistant dean (1940–41). Corwin subsequently returned to Smith College as an associate professor of religion (1942–53) and then professor of religion (1953–66). See the Virginia Corwin Papers, Smith College Archives, Northampton, Massachusetts.

2. Elizabeth Downe (1914–2003) earned an AB from Smith College (1936), a BD from Yale (1939), and an MLS from Columbia (1955). When this letter was written, she was the assistant residence director at the New Haven, Connecticut, YWCA (1940–42). She went on to become archivist and historian for the National Board of the YWCA. She edited and authored a number of publications for the organization, including *Feminine Figures: Selected Facts about American Women and Girls* (1968–72). See the Elizabeth Downe Norris Papers, Smith College Archives, Northampton, Massachusetts.

3. Downe and Norris married in 1942. Although they remained married until his death in 1985, they ceased living together in 1950 and were legally separated in 1974.

To Virginia Corwin

1 October 1941
Washington, D.C.

In his response to the letter from Virginia Corwin,[1] *Thurman agrees that a white wife would impede Norris's chances of success as a leader in the black church. He promises to stop in New Haven, Connecticut, during his travels to counsel the couple.*

My dear Virginia:

I was in Cleveland for a day in September but I actually didn't have time to get to a telephone. It was very good to hear from you.

Roy Norris is one of my old students. He came by to see me the other day when he passed through Washington. He asked me if I had heard from a friend of mine in Cleveland about a friend of his. He did not go into detail because there was no time to talk. I told him that I would see him during sometime in the winter, I hoped. I am not surprised that the problem has arisen. There isn't much to say about it in addition to the analysis which you, yourself, gave in the letter. My one important objection is that if he aspires to a place of religious leadership among Negroes, he will have great difficulty at the present time if his wife is a white woman. I have several friends, men and women, who have married inter-racially and on the whole, they are getting along about as happily as most conservative and conventional marriages. Much depends upon the type of work the man does, if any, and where the couple plan to live. I am glad you did not offer the age-old illusory argument that it isn't fair to the children.

My proposal is this; that I have an hour or two to talk with Roy and Elizabeth together. If you suggest to Elizabeth to write to me, I think, I can work out a possible date when I shall be passing through New Haven and can stop between trains to talk with them. I am not sure it would do any good but I have had to do this sort of thing so many times in the past ten years that I may be able to anticipate some of the arguments and help them both to be more objective in what they are undertaking.

I do not know when I shall be coming through Cleveland but it will be sometime during the winter. If I know far enough ahead of time, I shall certainly let you know. I will be happy to get some of the people out there but best of all, it will be very exciting to see you again. Sue sends greetings. She is busy editing her new magazine.[2] Greetings and salutations.

Sincerely yours,
[*signed*] Howard Thurman
Dean of the Chapel

TLc. HTC-MBU: Box 4.

1. From Virginia Corwin, 25 September 1941, printed in the current volume.

2. In 1940 Sue Bailey Thurman served as the founding editor of the *Aframerican Woman's Journal*, the official magazine of the National Council of Negro Women. She continued to edit the publication until 1944.

To Helen Buchalter
6 December 1941
Washington, D.C.

Thurman's experimentation with forms of creative worship at Rankin Chapel led to the annual staging of "Living Madonnas" during the Christmas season. In these presentations students in elaborate period costumes would pose to replicate famous paintings depicting the Virgin Mary and the Christ child. During the Christmas season of 1941, Thurman writes to a journalist with the Washington Daily News *to invite her to see the presentation and write a review for her publication.*

Dear Miss Buchalter:[1]

During the past two years, the Andrew Rankin Memorial Chapel of Howard University has presented on the first Sunday in December a series of presentations of Living Madonnas and Ave Marias in Music. The performance is one hour in length usually and is the product of the cooperation of several departments in the University. In the center of the platform, a large gilt frame, seven feet wide and eight feet high, is placed. In this frame the Madonna is posed with a suitable costume, etc. Under soft lights the figures give the general impression of wax. While the student holds the pose, an Ave Maria is sung, either by an individual or by a group. The participants are students in the University. This year we are doing the Madonna by Dolci,[2] The Virgin by Forli,[3] The Madonna of the Harpies by del Sarto,[4] Madonna and the Saints by Bellini.[5] There is one other in the basic Gothic style. The Ave Marias are Bach-Gounod,[6] Schubert[7] and three others by Kahn,[8], Luzzi,[9] Arcobelt.[10] The last is done by the Men's Glee Club.

This program is to be given tomorrow, Sunday, in the Chapel at five o'clock and again at seven o'clock in the evening. It is very late and perhaps irregular because of its lateness but I am very anxious to have you see the service and write any criticism there{of} for your column in the paper. Because of the size of the Chapel and the seating, the very best seating positions are to be found in the center aisle. We do not reserve seats for very obvious reasons but if you can find the time to come and will let me know by telephoning my secretary at Columbia 9003, I shall be glad to reserve a seat for you. Kindly indicate whether

you will be coming at five or at seven. If I do not hear from you, I shall assume that my invitation came too late. I am enclosing a copy of last year's program.
Sincerely yours,
[*signed*]
Howard Thurman
Dean of the Chapel
Miss Helen Buchalter
Washington Daily News
Washington, D.C.

TLS. HTC-MBU: Box 3.

1. Helen Buchalter (?–1978) was art critic for the *Washington Daily News* in the 1930s and 1940s. She often reviewed artistic presentations and literature by African Americans for her paper.
2. Carlo Dolci (1616–1686).
3. Melozzo de Forli (1438–1494).
4. Andrea del Sarto (1486–1530).
5. Giovanni Bellini (ca. 1430–1516).
6. Johann Sebastian Bach (1685–1750) and Charles Gounod (1818–1893).
7. Franz Schubert (1797–1828).
8. Percy Kahn (1880–1966).
9. Luigi Luzzi (1824–1876).
10. Jacques Arcadelt (ca. 1507–1568).

To John Nevin Sayre
29 December 1941
Washington, D.C.

Thurman tells Sayre that he cannot devote time and energy to the publication Fellowship *because he is preoccupied with addressing the plight of black people, which has become increasingly dire with the nation at war.*

My dear Nevin:

I have given your letter very careful consideration. My life is even more crowded than it was some time ago. I don't know how it is physically possible for me to be of service to you in the way that is rightfully required. Now that we are at war and the plight of Negroes becomes increasingly more tragic, in the army and out of the army, something like a great blight has settled upon us everywhere. Every waking moment, I am involved in this at one point or another. I would suggest therefore that you secure the services of someone else who would be in a position to carry some responsibility in connection with the FELLOWSHIP.

I would suggest Rev. Arthur Gray,[1] minister of the Plymouth Congregational Church, whose home address is 407 Hobart Place, N.W. If you cannot secure Arthur's cooperation, I would suggest Rev. Samuel W. Williams who can be reached by addressing him at Howard University. He is a graduate student in Philosophy here, and is Associate Minister in one of the large Baptist churches.

I hope that I shall see my way clear to revise my demands so as to be practically helpful in some official way.

Very sincerely yours,
[*signed*] Howard Thurman
Dean of the Chapel
Mr. John Nevin Sayre
Journal of the Fellowship of Reconciliation
2929 Broadway
New York, New York

TLS. HTC-MBU: Box 20.

1. Arthur D. Gray (1907–79), a graduate of Talladega College (1929) and Chicago Theological Seminary (1934), was a Congregational pastor, denominational leader, social activist, and education administrator. He was pastor of Plymouth Congregational Church in Washington, D.C., from 1934 to 1944, and then became pastor of Chicago's Good Shepherd Congregational Church, at the time the largest African American Congregational church in the country. In 1950 Gray became the first African American chairman of the Executive Committee of the General Council of Congregational Christian Churches. He also served as president of his alma mater, Talladega College, in Alabama (1952–64).

Morehouse College Seventy-fifth Anniversary Sermon
15 February 1942
Atlanta, Ga.

Thurman's anniversary sermon was part of a weeklong celebration, 13–18 February 1942, of the college's founding in 1867. Featured speakers included W.E.B. Du Bois, sociologist Ira de A. Reid (1901–1968), and Clarence Mason Gallup (1874–1947), recording secretary of the northern Baptist Convention who delivered the anniversary address. Prior to Thurman's sermon, he was introduced by Morehouse president Benjamin Mays as "one of the members of a brilliant class at the institution and one of the most impressive speakers on the American platform today." Martin Luther King, Sr. (1899–1984), a Morehouse graduate and pastor of Ebenezer Baptist Church, read the scriptures, and offered a prayer and benediction. (It seems likely that King's namesake and thirteen year old son would have been in attendance as well.)[1] *In this talk Thurman argues for the unity of all life against those ideologies, at home and abroad, that would divide humanity into mutually exclusive races, nations, or classes. The talk survives only in an imperfect transcription with occasional gaps.*

I want to take this opportunity to bring greetings to Morehouse College on this significant occasion not only from the Morehouse men, some forty-four of them in Washington, and not only from those particularly in connection with Howard University, but also from Howard University itself, the faculty and the students. It happens that next month Howard University will be observing its 75th Anniversary also. Both of these institutions came into being about the same time shaped by the same singular, creative purpose.

Another word, I want to say. Naturally on an occasion like this, a Morehouse man's mind thinks of at least two of the great figures from the past whose presence may be found wherever Morehouse men are found. (Seems to have become a fashion; then, of course, it is very difficult to get it in hand.) I am thinking of Mr. Hope and I am thinking of Mr. Archer.[2]

Two men, speaking personally, who meant two very distinct things to me. Mr. Hope always stimulated my mind. The most stirring moments through which my mind has passed are identified with this chapel, and one of the seats out here when Mr. Hope, layman though he was, unfolded to us on occasion, the meaning, or some profound insight either in the New Testament or from Homer's Illiad. And as I grow older I find that many of the things that he has said, filling my mind, are falling into place now in a manner that is almost uncanny. I shall never forget.

Mr. Archer always stimulated my spirit. Mr. Archer always made me want to be whole and good, decent. He is one of the two persons whom I have known in my lifetime who impressed me in a singular manner. Two persons, one of whom was Mr. Archer, impressed me as being individuals who themselves would not consciously do a wrong thing to anyone. The most accurate figure that comes to me is a figure in Bernard Shaw's "The Black Girl Seeking God." You remember, this girl finally attaches herself to this philosopher and one day she is talking about how she can find God. She has obeyed all rules and followed all the roads. The philosopher said that, "If you are working in your garden, sometimes as you dig along you will find that you are making a crooked road. God will nudge you on the elbow."[3]

I do not think that it is possible to say more.

Now, I want you to think for a little while with these words as a background: [*text missing*]

There is one other reference which must be made. In the 11th Chapter of Hebrews, the 39th and 40th verses, we find these lines: "and these all having obtained a good report through faith received (not) in the promise. God having provided some better things for us that they without us should not be made perfect [KJV]." You will remember that also from your knowledge of the Bible, and of the 11th chapter of Hebrews. It is a great passage. It tells particularly what faith is, what it has meant to people through many years. It brings up a real call of many of the significant figures in the Jewish tradition, figures who have moved mountains, as it were; and then it has a discussion, a very dramatic discussion of certain figures who under the pressure of the circumstances of the moment, did not have time to make themselves known in terms of identity, but who lived in caves and in hiding, who lived on the ground, in the woods, who were harrassed, and heckled, and despite all of that they died without saying anything about being troubled. And then this writer says we came along. We belong to that same and essential tradition, and what they did not see come to pass we are experiencing. Apart from us in the present those who belong to the past cannot only not find any perfection but can find really no meaning in what they did. So I venture to say that the past and the present are the same time intervals. As a matter of fact, the past and the present and the future are all one time interval. The thing that we call the present is merely a point at which the past and the future meet and salute each other. That is the idea; that apart from the present the past has no meaning; apart from the struggle and sacrifices of these early fathers, according to the testimony; and aside from what they did, what we do now has no meaning. Aside from what we do, what they did has no meaning. That is the idea, and it is about all I have to say. You can see the appropriateness of the idea for a 75th anniversary.

All life is one. The facts of the biological union of man (a fact that no sane individual disputes, the attitude of the American Red Cross Blood Bank to the contrary notwithstanding),[4] the fundamental economic unity of modern man is no longer a question of opinion, and one reason why we are in the midst of such a tragedy at this present moment in the modern world is due to the fact that we have stubbornly constructed political units, little political worlds, islands, little social islands, at the expense of the personal organismic union that guarantees the significance of life, and at the expense of a profound (?) economic unity. At the present moment we find ourselves in a life and death struggle.

It is a very interesting thing. On one side, as far as political theory is concerned you find Communism, feudalism, some other kind of "ism" characteristic of America. On the one hand [*missing text*], on the other, Fascism and a certain kind of fascistic feudalism. On one hand we find philosophic atheism, like the sort of thing that is found in Communistic Russia, and coupled with the prophet of Buddhism and the faith of all on one side with some [*missing word*] thrown in for good measure and some voodooism and Confucianism from China and that is opposing. It is hard to tell, you see. What does all of this mean? That we have made these artificial lines, calling them political, sometime social, sometime economic, which arrangements, which lines undertake to ignore the fundamental and basic economic and biological unity of life. It is that that the writer of Hebrews grasped at once the projected on a screen in terms of the fulfillment of the spiritual and social yearnings of a group of Christians in the Greco-Roman World who at that time—at that moment—were being persecuted. So we get this picture, namely, that we are part of the past and the past is a part of the present, that we in the present are reaching back to the past, seeking, if we can, to fulfill the idea that the present experience is that which was projected by the past so that the past will make sense and the present will have meaning.

Now I want to call your attention to three things that, it seems to me, belong to the mind of the past: 75 years ago Morehouse College was projected in the world in a mood that was profoundly religious and spiritual and at the heart of that mood were three things. There was a great faith, a great reverence and a great commitment. At the heart of the religious mood that projected Morehouse College 75 years ago were these three things, at least; a great faith, a great reverence, and a great commitment.

A great faith in life. Yes. That sometimes lights a faith in the guarantor of life, a faith in God. Nothing can deliver a man from making his act of faith towards life, towards God, and these men who belong to that period, moved out of the assumption that they were [*missing text*], that God is real, that God is present, that God is with them, not through some representative, but that God, the great God, himself, would be present in the midst of their effort and in the midst of their difficulty, and this faith was found, for instance, in the attitude which they took towards the freed men. These men and women had just been released from human slavery. I sometimes think that we have not felt their thoughts about this situation, that the amazing significance of this whole experience weakens in our minds. Here are people of 75 years ago acting on the basis of their faith in God, expressed in the freed men, who undertook to give to a man, who just yesterday was a slave, the tools of learning. And they insisted that the freed man was a child of God and as a child of God to say they had some particular word to say to him, namely, "Son of Man, stand on you feet. Stop groveling, crawling, hanging your head down. Lift up your head, stand on your feet, Son of Man. You can, you are really living, child of God." Now that was very interesting, for you see that the effect of that on the mind of these freed men was to give them confidence, that it would be possible for them to learn, for them to reduce the mystery of learning, the mystery of the world of nature, to manageable units of understanding and control. So a faith in learning was developed. It is very striking to see, I think, that the mind of man became a mind when that mind was released from needing to attend to protection of the body from wild animals and things of that sort. As long as the early man had to come through woods, he did not have time to think. He had to look. When I was a boy in Sunday School, my teacher asked me one day. "What did Daniel do in the Lion's den?" What did he do? I said I didn't know, but I think he spent his time trying to keep his eyes on the lion. There was not time for reflective thinking. As long as man had to spend his energy keeping himself aware of all of the things that might come to him from his environment, he could not develop his mind. Mind could not be born. There was a man who said that modern man suffers from astigmatism; eyes pulled out of focus because the muscles of the eye have atrophied from a lack of activity. For there was a time when man walked through the woods he had to look this way, that way, (etc.) all at one time, and his eye muscles developed a certain something that kept his eyes focused. But after his enemies began disappearing, it was not longer necessary to look this way, that way, (etc.). These muscles were thus undeveloped. This process atrophied them, pulled his eyes out of focus. So instead of glasses, exercises were prescribed.[5] When man was going through a period like that, it was not possible for him to have a mind.—The environment forced man to use every bit of his energy in the business of survival. So these people who projected this great creative moment insisted that when the freed man was relieved to some extent from the adversity from the great and eminent necessity that was upon him as a result of slavery, that there was now a surplus energy of mind available to him.

The first thing that must be done with this mind; it must be forced to work upon the raw materials of the environment, to work upon problems which men have already mastered so that guidance could be given them in the process of learning, and once that has happened the mind might become creative in the profound sense. Now I ask you whether or not this faith, as we look upon it from the point at which we stand, now, does that faith find itself in the present day? Can we maintain the kind of faith without which their faith could not be perfect? Can we maintain a faith in God?

It is utterly amazing that two of the greatest nations in the world have in the interest of the highest well being of the body politic, the highest welfare of the individual in their body politics. These two nations, greatest in the word, have embraced a way of life that directly, systematically, profoundly, repudiates the very conviction upon which Christianity rests. I want to linger on that for a second. Germany, Russia (feature that?) have undertaken in a sense the same goals as far as what should happen to the best interest of individuals, have undertaken the same goals that we have held to ourselves; and we have found, you see, all along that the Christian religion if it were implemented could bring these goals to pass in human life. In passing we call it the Kingdom of God. Two nations, as a result of their great trial by blood and fire, undertaking to do precisely that same thing which our people have been trying to do, as an act of deliberate judgement on their part, rejected the Christian religion saying that it can never bring that to pass. It is in that kind of world that Morehouse College is called upon to justify a faith that was projected 75 years ago.

Second—a great reverence: In thinking about the 75th anniversary, I re-read Mr. Brawley's History of Morehouse College and the one thing that impressed me very much was the fact that the men who were a part of that early experience were such extremely able men. One of the early presidents resigned the presidency of a college in Iowa in order to take the presidency of this struggling college in Atlanta. Another was a professor of languages in the University of Iowa. He resigned that to come down to teach men who did not know their ABC's, and they insisted that the very best that had come to them should also be made available to these men and women who were just out of slavery.[6] I think that may be responsible in part for the very complete (?) and ambitious names by which our schools have been designated: universities, colleges, academies, when what took place then did not justify that, but it was in anticipation of that which was not yet, but would be sometimes. Back of that was this great reverence, a reverence for the individuals who make up the rank and file of the [*missing text*]. A reverence for human life, it seems to me is built fundamentally upon the respect for personality and the respect for personality means essentially this: that you meet people where they are and you treat them where they are as if they are where they should be. I meet you where you are. They met those freed men where they were—slaves, ex-slaves, ill-treated, many of them fear-stricken, chronologically old, and they treated them there as if they were where they should be, where they were destined to be. By doing that, they buoyed them into the fulfillment of a possibility that staggered their imagination, by putting over them a crown that for the rest of their days they are trying to grow tall enough to wear. Can that fact of reverence be maintained by us now? Your reverence for each other. Will you ever find justification in the world in which we live in this particular moment—in a world that is callous, hard? In a newspaper you read that 20,000 people went down to the bottom of the Atlantic Ocean and you turn on over looking at the ads and the funny papers. It means nothing. You listen to the radio and a troop ship has been struck by a torpedo and it means nothing. Do you realize what has happened to us? Our very sensitiveness is being so completely outraged by the brutality of the moment that it is very difficult for us to have a reverent regard toward anybody, even ourselves. The things that hate does—we are making war. We are not supposed to be sentimental in this war. (Nobody knows yet just what it is.) We have got to develop [*missing text*]. We have got to develop the hate. Why? Because you have got to be able to give yourselves moral justification for doing what under normal circumstances your normal sensitiveness would not permit you to do. My sister was a girl who would not cry when my mama whipped her. She would just look. The longer my mother whipped her the funnier my mother seemed to her. If Henrietta looked long enough my mother would just disappear. But that was not so with me. I cried. I jumped and I did all of the things that one would do under the circumstances and, of course, my performance gave to my mother what. A great sense of worthwhileness. Her justification for punishing me for my departure from truth, or whatever caused the whipping, was to be found in the extent to which I cried aloud so that to whip me did not seem as if she had done something wrong. The more I cried, the more I gave her justification. But when my sister did not cry, she thought there must be something wrong with this. As soon as discipline becomes reflective, that is precisely the sort of thinking [*missing text*].

This great reverence was the life of the student of that period, the reverence that the students had for each other. If that reverence is to find justification in the present, it means that we must face the present with a kind of creative thinking, understanding and social intelligence that is about to be lacking. We must provide the atmosphere into which it is possible for the people who make up the college community to be rid of their fears. We must provide the atmosphere in which the people who make up the college community may trust each other and at the same time keep their sense of security and their self-respect. We must provide this to fulfill this great insight that has come from the past. We must provide an atmosphere in which it is possible for those who are in the college community to face a world (in which this assumption or reverence for long {garbled} since dispelled) and act in that world on the basis of the profound self respect which they have discovered for themselves in this environment.

Third—a great commitment. I wonder what it was like back there? Two weeks ago at Wellesley, a very old lady said to me, "I don't go out to church very often or anything of that sort—I am so old. But I saw in the paper that you are from Morehouse and our family grew up on the moral enthusiasm that it got from Dr. Robert who at one time was one of the presidents of Morehouse." A great commitment. Singleness of purpose. The thing that President Mays referred to—fast purpose. And they had it. Unless you are convinced that you can do something about life, that life represents essentially raw materials, and are malleable, that it can be shaped, that it can be ordered, that it changes, then something can be possible with reference to life. Or if you are profoundly convinced that life essentially cannot be altered, cannot be changed, and of course, if you are convinced that life by its very nature will not yield, is not manageable, then you cannot do anything about anything, and any kind of hope is an illusion. If you have no hope then [*missing text*]. If you are convinced that life is yielding, that you can work over it with creative minds and spirits until you fashion something that is like your heart's desire—if that can happen to you, than of course ideals [*missing text?*] are very rational things, not only rational but mandatory.

The final word about black men they say has not been said. For better or worse. In some little New England Village some [*missing word*] tall-minded individual said, "for better or for worse, I see myself as tied to the faith and destiny of the least privileged people in America. Therefore, I must turn my back on any opportunities at home, my back on marriage, and teach Morehouse students in a barren land in the midst of people who despise me, mistrust me, and bury my life into the ground of these least in our society." And nothing could stop these people for they admitted a fundamental discovery that we must make. They made a discovery that the limitless resources in life are always available to the individual who fulfills and who satisfied the requirements. Jesus gave expression to this: "God causes his face to shine on the good man and the bad man."[7] When conditions for growth and development have been met then growth follows. When conditions for fulfillment have been met, then the individual places upon the altar the [*missing text*]. Then he becomes a person of power. His strength becomes as is he [*missing text*] It is a miracle. Biological logic, by any kind of formal process.

The thing does not make sense but here it is; the implication of the limited possibilities and the limited opportunities has been so marked because of the nature of the concentration. Can we match that today? Can we give today something that reaches high into the fulfillment of that great commitment which they had back there? Can we do that? Is Morehouse College today a complete—it is reasonable that a college should be—a complete commitment, a creative purpose? So that men who are a part of it enlist in a creative venture on the basis of a profound commitment. It is reasonable? But I say unto you that unless something like that happens, increasingly this is true: our institutions will be plants, plants, buildings, equipment. They will not be addressed to the fundamental needs of our life and the human justification which they for existence [*missing text*] as they are in a democracy, would be lost. For if we do not have at the center of our hearts a great and profound commitment to put at the disposal of the least privileged in our community and in our environment the finest flowering of our minds and experiments so that when these least become articulate, they will make a new day, a new moment, a new life in which a concept, even figurative, on which we have been reared, building not only [*missing text*]. It is to that that we are calling. Tools, skills, we have those. But techniques, methodology, that is the way we must fulfill this great commitment from the past. I agree with Eugene Debs, a very great American. He says that while there is a lower class, while there is a criminal element, I am of it. While there is a man in jail, I am not free. The takes at the moment is, it seems, working for a social order in which the least can find religious leadership and significance. This, it seems to me is the only basis on which we can keep going and maintain a moral and spiritual self respect. If we do not go forth like that, then apart from us those who strove in the past will find no fulfillment.

TD. HTC-MBU: Box 196.

1. William A. Fowler, "Overflow Crowd Hears Dr. Thurman," *Atlanta Daily World*, 16 February 1942.

2. Former Morehouse presidents John Hope and Samuel Archer.

3. "God is at your elbow, and He has been there all the time; but in His divine mercy He has not revealed Himself to you lest too full a knowledge of Him should drive you mad. Make a little garden for yourself: dig and plant and weed and prune; and be content if He jogs your elbow when you are gardening unskilfully, and blesses you when you are gardening well." George Bernard Shaw, *The Adventures of the Black Girl in Her Search for God* (New York: Dodd, Mead, 1933), 54.

4. In 1940 Dr. Charles R. Drew (1904–50), professor of surgery at the Howard University College of Medicine and pioneer in the development of blood banking and transfusions, was asked to spearhead international efforts to provide blood for fallen soldiers in Europe. Drew accepted the position of medical director of the Blood for Britain Program, and after successfully establishing blood banks throughout England, he was appointed director of the American Red Cross Blood Bank Program. In 1941 the U.S. military established a segregated blood storage program and refused to use African American blood in transfusions for white servicemen. Drew's refusal to endorse the segregated program led to a call for his resignation, which he willingly obliged.

5. Thurman is referring to the eye exercises popularized by William Horatio Bates (1860–1931) in *The Cure of Imperfect Sight by Treatment without Glasses* (New York: Central Fixation, 1920) and other works. Although Bates was a trained opthamologist, most of his peers thought his eye exercises of little value.

6. The president of "a college in Iowa" and the "professor of languages in the University of Iowa" are the same person: Joseph Thomas Robert (1807–84), a native of Robertville, South Carolina. He graduated from Brown University in 1828 and was a resident graduate and medical student at Yale University from 1829 to 1830. Robert returned to his home state to complete his medical training at South Carolina Medical College, from which he graduated in 1831, and the following year he was licensed to preach by his home church in Robertville. He attended Furman Theological Seminary for two years until he was called to pastor the Baptist Church at Robertville. He subsequently served as pastor for Baptist churches in Covington, Kentucky, Savannah, Georgia, and Portsmouth, Ohio. He then taught mathematics and natural science at Burlington University in Iowa. In 1864 Robert went to Iowa State University as professor of languages, but he returned to Burlington as the school's president in 1869. Robert took over Augusta Institute in 1871 and remained with the school after it moved to Atlanta and became Atlanta Baptist College.

7. Matt. 5:45.

To Patricia Van Blarcom

17 April 1942
Washington, D.C.

Thurman's relation to the war effort was extremely complex and ambivalent. If he remained a committed pacifist, he also provided encouragement and support to his many friends and students in uniform and, as this letter indicates, vehemently denied any aspersion against their ability and valor. If he did not believe in the war, he did hope that the war would open possibilities for racial equality within the armed forces and in postwar America.

My dear Miss Van Blarcom:

I am sorry that I have delayed so long in replying to your letter of March 2nd. There are two or three corrections that I would like to make. In the first place, you misunderstood what I said about the Negro in the Army. There are at the present time, Negro Officers with every rank from one Brigadier General to the lowest Non-Commission Officer. There are more than a hundred officers in the Army who are graduates of Howard University alone. At the time of my address, the only rank for our men in the Navy was in connection with the Mess. They at that time could not enlist in the Navy except in this department.

I regret that it is necessary for me to deny categorically the statement of your friend, relative to the emotional instability of Negro men under fire at the front. Records are available at the War Department showing the valor and courage and the ability of Negro troops. Anyone who wishes to get evidence on this may do so with a minimum of difficulty.

Little by little, the significance of Negroes for the armed forces on sea, in the air and on land is being realized, and I dare say, that before the war is over they will be in all the armed forces. It is the only democratic thing to do.

The book to which you refer is, "The Hand of God" by Oswald McCall,[1] and is published by Harper's.

Sincerely yours,
[*signed*] Howard Thurman
Dean
Miss Patricia Van Blarcom
131 Church Street
Boonton, New Jersey

ALS. HTC-MBU: Box 21.

1. Oswald W. S. McCall, *The Hand of God* (New York: Harper, 1939).

❧ From Kenny Murase

20 April 1942
Berkeley, Calif.

Feeling the pressure of racism and possible internment as a result of the war, Kenny Murase,[1] a Japanese American YMCA student activist at the University of California, Berkeley, asks Thurman's assistance in acquiring admissions information from Howard University. Before he could make plans to attend Howard, though, Murase was interned in an evacuation camp.

Dear Sir,

The exigencies of an all-out, total war has made it necessary for me, an American-born Japanese, to withdraw from the University of California to enroll in an institution in the East.

Investigations into various colleges have thus far revealed very little difference in their respective curriculum, fees and living costs. No particular college seemed to offer anything distinguished or unique.

Recently, however, in an interview, Mr. Herbert King, national secretary of the Y.M.C.A. now on a survey of the Pacific Coast, in reply to suggestions for eastern schools warmly recommended Howard University. He said that Howard would be glad to receive me and that I would enjoy my stay there.

Mr. King's suggestion aroused my interest and so I inquired among some of the Negro acquaintances at the University Y.M.C.A. as to their opinions on the advisability of my attending Howard. All were in hearty accord, and expressed great enthusiasm for such a plan, urging me to proceed.

It may seem singularly odd that a Japanese student should be interested in attending a college primarily for Negroes, but a review of my past experiences should afford an understanding of my intentions. Belonging personally as an individual to a racial minority group presents one concrete basis for my ambitions, although it should be made emphatic that the socio-economic problems faced by the Japanese are hardly analogous in degree with those faced by the Negroes.

For the past two years, through the Y.M.C.A. Race Relations Executive Committee[2] and the Welfare Council of the Associated Students of the University of California, I have been closely identified with the youth movement for better race relations. During the course of my work, I have acquired a scant knowledge of the problems confronting the American Negro and have been impelled to pursue further my inquiries into the nature, causes and effects of racial differences upon minority groups.

Vocationally, my interest lies in the sphere of social welfare work, particularly as it relates to racial minorities. I have just completed my second year at the

University of California and have maintained a grade point average of two point plus, while working most of my way through.

I would appreciate immediately an application for admission so that I may send an official transcript for your consideration. I would also appreciate any information as to available scholarships, employment and living costs. At present, I have {enough} funds to cover all fees, although perhaps insufficient to include total living expenses.

Your prompt attention to this matter will be welcomed gratefully.

Sincerely yours,
[*signed*] Kenny Murase
Kenny Murase

TLS. HTC-MBU: Box 13.

1. Kenny Murase (b. 1920), a Japanese American from a Fresno, California, farm community, was a student at the University of California, Berkeley, at the time he wrote this letter to Thurman. Soon thereafter—in June or July 1942—he was among the hundreds of Japanese American evacuees shipped to the Poston Relocation Center in La Paz County, Arizona. Murase became a social worker after the war, and he earned a doctorate in that field from Columbia University in 1961.

2. The University of California, Berkeley, YMCA and YWCA created the Race Relations Group in February 1936 to improve interactions among people of diverse racial heritages. The group formed subcommittees on education, research, housing, social and recreation activities, minority grievances, and a speaker's bureau, and it is credited with having helped "change the racial mores of an immense university campus and influenced the surrounding community as well." During the war the University of California, Berkeley, YMCA and YWCA helped relocate several thousand Japanese American students to colleges and schools in the Midwest and East. See Galen Fisher, *Citadel of Democracy: The Story of the Public Affairs Record of Stiles Hall, the Young Men's Christian Association at the University of California, Berkeley* (Berkeley: University YMCA, 1955), 23.

FROM EDWARD CARROLL

22 JUNE 1942
SEATTLE, WASH.

Edward Carroll, one of Thurman's fellow delegates in the India delegation in 1935–36, was the chaplain in the U.S. Army's 95th Engineer Regiment during World War II. His was one of three black Army units that helped build the Alaska Canadian (Alcan) Highway over an eight-month period in 1942–43. Carroll inquires about the possibility of a job after the war as Thurman's assistant at Howard University and quite humbly asks Thurman's opinion of his preaching abilities.

Dear Howard,

I intended to write you a letter before we left the country. In fact I tried my best to slip over to Durham to see you on your recent mission to North Carolina State College.

I think of you a great deal and imagine how much more you would get out of this country than ourselves. It is enabling me to deepen my spiritual and intellectual life. I have oodles of time to read heavy books, study the bible, and scrutinize people. This is indeed God's world. His manifestations are infinite.

How would you like to be in close association with wolves and bears? Probably your complete identification with little brother wolf and bear would make St Francis look ashamed. Maybe I can get you a nice bear skin for your study retreat.

Phenola[1] sent me a copy of Pearl Buck's address.[2] If you weren't making strawberry jam on that occasion what do you think of her speech? Personally, I didn't react to it so favorably. I guess I'm counter to the opinion of Negro intelligentsia. Certainly she spoke courageously. But she doesn't seem to grasp fully the real life and thinking of Negroes. She doesn't know that Negro soldiers are thinking broadly concerning enslaved peoples all over the world. Of course, I can't fully explain my position because of censorship. But I think your keen mind can discern my meaning. Please write me a good letter on this. I'm starving for such expressions.

A word about the future. It seems to me that you ought to be needing a capable assistant in your religious duties at Howard. If so, I'm making my application now. Of course, I don't know what you think of my ability. Obviously, you didn't feel my preaching was either ripe or mature enough for your University Congregation.[3] Whatever you think of my ability even if it is negative can be taken by me without destroying our friendship. For, I would love you even if you should hurt me. Our trip together in India increased my admiration and understanding of you. But frankly, if and when this war is over, I will be needing employment. I'm not going back to Morgan.[4] Seabrooke is doing what I wanted to do. I have received my Masters in Christian Education from Columbia-Union. And my experience in the Army is enabling me to put into practice the great principles of counseling and preaching both of which I enjoy. The Army is also teaching me good administrative methods and practice. I've had three years experience in the church, travel, and five years teaching. I will get my PhD if necessary as soon as this affair is over. Are there any prospects for me at Howard? If not, where should I be looking for a position?

Sincerely,

[*signed*] Eddie

P.S. I am now a Captain. No special achievement. It is almost automatic.

Please let me know where I can get some good records of choral singing—such as great hymns and anthems.

ALS. HTC-MBU: Box 3.

1. Edward's wife, Phenola V.Carroll.

2. Pearl Comfort Sydenstricker Buck (1892–1973), winner of the Nobel Prize for Literature in 1938, best-known for her novels set in China, was also a civil rights and women's rights activist. She published essays in both the NAACP's magazine *Crisis* and the Urban League's *Opportunity,* and she served on the Board of Trustees at Howard University for twenty years beginning in the early 1940s. In her speech to graduates at Howard on 5 June 1942, Buck urged her audience to understand the meaning of World War II and the global scale of the fight for democracy and equality. She told them to battle against racism in America, declaring that "discrimination in our country must go, because until it does, we will not have won the war." She insisted, though, that American blacks must see the conflict for racial equality in a broader international context: "If I have a criticism to make of the colored people of our country it is that they have been too selfish in their interest in equality. They have thought too often of equality only for themselves in this one country—and by so doing they have limited their own struggle and robbed it of size and force and meaning for the whole human race. You are not simply a group of people in one country—you are part of the great war of the peoples for freedom. . . . Be ready to speak for Africa at the peace table, and to speak for Korea. Make yourselves a part of America to whom these peoples turn for understanding." Pearl S. Buck, "Breaking the Barriers of Race Prejudice," *Journal of Negro Education* 11 (1942): 448, 452–53.

3. Presumably Carroll was upset that Thurman never invited him to be a guest preacher at Howard.

4. Before the war Carroll had taught at Morgan State College (later Morgan State University) in Baltimore.

To Raymond F. Harvey

29 July 1942
Washington, D.C.

Thurman was deeply concerned about the internment and maltreatment of Pacific coast Japanese following President Roosevelt's issuing of executive order 9066 in February 1942. In addition to visiting the temporary camp mentioned here, probably the requisitioned Santa Anita racetrack—Thurman calls it uneuphemistically a "concentration center"—he almost certainly visited the Amache Relocation Facility (also known as the Granada Relocation Facility) in Colorado the following June.[1] *The Fellowship Church, located in an area of San Francisco that had a large prewar Japanese population, made outreach to and reintegration of the local Japanese population one of its chief missions.*

To The Junior Member of the House of Harvey[2]

Greetings and salutations:

This is duly to inform you that I have made the round of the Pacific Coast and find the country in fairly good shape except a bad case of jitters. I saw some of the concentration centers for the Japanese. They are behind eight feet of barbed wire with the outside patrolled day and night with United States soldiers with machine guns. The point that I saw was a former racetrack and houses about 26,000 Japanese.[3] The horse stalls have been renovated, but I understand they still smell horsey. I preached the gospel, and wherever the gospel was not heard, I shook the dust off my feet and journeyed to the next institute.[4] I am glad you have carried out your decision and that Hempstead is still on the map. I am very proud of the way you carried through on this and shall have much to say about it during the winter.

I am leaving in a few days for Cornell, but will be back on, or before the fifteenth of August. I have several additional ideas that I want to talk through with you before school opens. I hope you can get down for Freshmen Week it will give us time for some preliminary working together. It seems as if it will not be possible for us to get the downstairs straightened out, but that is not final yet. There are many more things that I need to say, but it is too hot in Washington, and I have too much to do. Take care of yourself and remember me to your mother whom I have not met. Let me hear from you before the summer is over.

Yours for Democratic Order,
[*signed*] Howard Thurman
Dean
Mr. Raymond F. Harvey
73 South Franklin Street
Hempstead, New York

TLS. HTC-MBU: Box 22.

1. In spring 1943 Thurman received a letter from Emiko Hinoki, interned at Amache, asking if Thurman could pay a visit, "for you no doubt have a great and inspiring message to give to the minority group such as the Japanese Americans" (From Emiko Hinoki, 4 April 1943, HTC-MBU: Box 9). Thurman responded to another group of Amache internees shortly afterward that "I shall be operating on a very close margin of time, but be assured that if it is in range of human possibility for me, I shall certainly do this [visit Amache]." To Russia Piccinini Luca, 15 April 1943, HTC-MBU: Box 29. See also To Emiko Hinoki, 31 May 1943, HTC-MBU: Box 9.

2. Raymond Francis Harveym (1918–1992), a student at the School of Religion, assisted Thurman in services at Rankin Chapel, and would be the longtime minister at Greenwood Baptist Church in Tuskegee, Alabama.

3. Temporary detention centers for Japanese Americans were used from March 1942 through October 1942, when internees were moved to ten more permanent internment camps scattered in remote inland locations primarily in the western United States. There were more than a dozen temporary sites, usually located on large fairgrounds or racetracks; most were in California, but there were also camps in Washington, Oregon, and Arizona. It is not clear which facility Thurman is describing here. It might have been the racetrack at Santa Anita, California, which had a peak total of 18,719 detainees, or perhaps the Tanforan Racetrack in San Bruno, California, which had a peak population of 7,816. See the Civil Liberties Public Education Fund Web site, http://www.momomedia.com/CLPEF/camps.html.

4. Thurman's visit to the Japanese detention camp was probably one of a series of lecture/sermons he did during the summer of 1942 at five international institutes for the American Friends Service Committee. In a letter to Wilbur Woodson in June, he noted that the lecture tour would take him as far west as Los Angeles and as far east as Cornell University. To Wilbur Woodson, 5 June 1942, HTC-MBU: Box 22.

To Edward Carroll

31 July 1942
Washington, D.C.

Thurman responds to the letter from Edward Carroll, agreeing that Pearl Buck's address at the Howard University commencement missed the mark. He tells his friend that he would love for him to come to Howard University, but he cannot promise him a position because he is uncertain about his own situation there.

My dear Eddie:

Your letter came to me while I was in Portland. It was certainly good to hear from you and to know that you are carrying on under circumstances unlike which you had dreamed previously. On my way to the coast I visit{ed} the 9th and 10th Cavalry up at Funston. One of my boys is a Chaplain up there.[1]

I quite agree with much you have to say about Pearl Buck's address. I think her point of view is largely governed by the fact that she approaches the problem of Negroes from her background of work with the Chinese. This has its limitations and its handicaps. Some of the things which she said were quite extraordinary even for her.[2]

I saw Phenola the other day just for a little while. She ran into the house in passing. Sue and the whole family have been out of town all summer. I lectured in four International Institutes out on the coast. Sue joined me in Los Angeles, and we came back to Chicago in a day coach.

I am glad you are looking forward to what will happen after the war. Personally, I think that after the war, and your experiences, working on a college campus may be pretty tame. But, I am sure of one thing, nothing would make me happier than to have you associated with me in student work if I am still at Howard, and I am permitted to have an associate. I would be very happy to have you. I cannot ever feel right going to Morgan to speak after the dirty deal they gave you. I don't know who was responsible for it, but I feel very certain that it was wrong. I will keep my eyes open, so that if there seems to be a better opportunity somewhere else, I can advise you in due time.

I do hope that out of the rich experiences which are yours, you will be able to garner the kind of insight that we shall all need for the trying days of reconstruction ahead.

Maynard Catchings[3] has become associated with Herb King in the Student Movement. The Eagles Mere Conference was transferred to another place because of the bathing facilities for Negroes.[4] Charlie Wesley[5] has become president of Wilberforce. Richard McKinney got his PhD from Yale in June. That is about all the news. Please let me hear again soon.

Sincerely,
[*signed*] Howard Thurman
Dean

Chaplain Edward Carroll
95th Engineer Regiment (G.S.)
A.P.O. 998
Seattle, Washington

TLS. HTC-MBU: Box 3.

1. In 1941 the Ninth and Tenth Cavalry regiments—known as the Buffalo Soldiers—were formed into the Fourth Cavalry Brigade, commanded by General Benjamin O. Davis Sr. at Camp Funston, Kansas.

2. Thurman's difficulty with Buck's address is somewhat unclear. Perhaps, like Edward Carroll, he felt it was somewhat patronizing to be urged to embrace an international view of the race question when many African American intellectuals (such as Thurman and Carroll) had been making this precise argument for many years and most blacks saw the war as part of an international struggle against racism.

3. For biographical information on Lincoln Maynard Catchings (1914–84), see To L. Maynard Catchings, 29 April 1943, printed in the current volume.

4. For more information on the Eagles Mere Conference, see volume 1.

5. Charles Wesley (1891–1987) was a historian, educator, and AME minister. Wesley served on the Howard University faculty (1913–42) before becoming president of Wilberforce University (1942–47), and he became president of Central State University in 1947. He earned a BA from Fisk University in 1911, an MA in economics at Yale University in 1913, and a PhD from Harvard University in 1925—only the third doctorate awarded by Harvard to an African American.

❧ To Arthur L. James
15 August 1942
Washington, D.C.

Thurman writes a chatty and reminiscing letter to Arthur L. James,[1] *who mentored Thurman during his summers at First Baptist Church in Roanoke, Virginia, in 1924 and 1925.*

My dear Cousin Arthur:

Your letter came while I was away at Cornell University and I am hastening to send you an immediate reply. I think of you and the church very often, because the two summers I spent there were without doubt the most critically important summers of my entire life. I am sure that you can scarcely realize what it meant to me, a student, to have been surrounded by the wisdom and the kindness that you were able to provide. Again and again I go back to the nights on the front porch when you opened up your heart to me about many many things, and shared with me your hopes, your dreams and your experiences. The fact that "Miss Ada" took me in as her son and was always patient and kind and gracious to me went a long ways toward guaranteeing a full and fruitful future. The church people were my friends inspiring me to do my best and showing in so many ways through their prayers and kind words that they were backing me. I do not wish to have this letter prove embarrassing to you, but I wanted you to know that these things were true.

I am enclosing a photograph on the back of which, are the dates that I was there. October is a very busy month because it is the first full month of the school year. I would like to come down if just for a day. A week-end is out of the question, but perhaps a day during the week will be possible. I have just noted in your letter that I might make a short sentence about the church. Would you be willing to take whatever you want from this letter and put it in the booklet, or would you prefer having me write something else? I cannot be too exhaustive in my genuine feeling about the church and the work there.

I have been lecturing all summer in International Institutes on the Pacific Coast and at Cornell. I am back home now until after Labor Day, when I go down to see Mama for a few days. She continues to hold her own. Sue and the children will be home next week. Olive is going to school at the Northfield

Seminary in Massachusetts. She has two more years up there, and is developing nicely. Please give my love to everybody, and thank you with all my heart for all that you mean to me.

Sincerely,
[*signed*] Howard Thurman
Dean

The Reverend A. L. James
208 Patton Avenue, N.W.
Roanoke, Virginia

ALS. HTC-MBU: Box 10.

1. Arthur Leonard James (1877–1968) was a Baptist minister and civic leader. Born in Florida, James's father was a Reconstruction politician who was murdered as a result of his political activity. James was pastor of several churches around the state, including Bethel Baptist Church in Daytona, where he became closely acquainted with the Thurman family. From 1920 to 1958 he was the pastor of First Baptist Church, Roanoke, Virginia. See Arthur Leonard James, *Sketches of My Life and Ministry* (Roanoke, Va.: First Baptist Church, 1958).

To William Stuart Nelson
19 August 1942
Washington, D.C.

Thurman writes to the dean of the School of Religion at Howard, William Stuart Nelson, about his plans for meditation services at the Howard University Chapel. He also informs Nelson of his decision to register as a conscientious objector, though there is no indication that this had any change in his status at Howard.

My dear Stuart:

Yours was a good letter my dear brother, and I am sending this note to you to tell you to enjoy every minute of it.

There are several matters that I wanted to mention to you. First, my questionnaire came the other day, and in filling it out I signed the Conscientious Objector blank. I do not know whether anything will happen because of it, but we can talk about it when you return.[1] The prospects for next year certainly seem good indeed. I have not been able to put a single thought on the courses that I am to offer. I am waiting for you to return to give me the notes on what I said I would do. This would help me and bring it back to mind. Now Stuart, I thought we had a clear understanding that I would ring off on this worship proposition after doing them last year. I have so many demands made upon me, that I do not see how on earth I can prepare these three devotional talks. I am preaching more times in Chapel, and I plan some other things for the fall quarter, all of which will be quite exhausting. Have a heart brother, have a heart.

I am turning over in my mind the possibility of developing a weekly meditation service in the little Chapel. It turns on two things; whether or not I can do it so that it will not conflict with any plans which you may have for the Chapel (I am assuming that it will be all right with you as far as the use of the place is concerned); and whether it will be possible for me to find some one to play the organ for the service. It occurs to me as I write, that perhaps Miss Mayle can do this. The plan is to have a thirty minute service with readings, music and meditation. I am hoping to work out an arrangement for mimeographing the things that I read making them available for all who attend. There may be five people, ten, or fifty, I do not know, but we shall see. I would give it wide publicity, trying to interest any people on the campus who might wish to spend a quiet time.[2]

Inasmuch as Herb King is preaching in Chapel on Sunday, November 1st, it will be possible for you to use his services, if you drop him a note and tie the dates up now, even though, you do not know specifically what you want him to do. He leaves New York on the 26th, and will not be back for two weeks. I like the subject for the Convocation, and would suggest that you certainly include Ralph Harlow in the lectures. Not only do I suggest this because he has a very pointed contribution to make, but also because he does not appear on my preaching list for the first time in ten years, and he feels disappointed about not coming back to Howard, although he understands about the Sunday.

Sue and the children came yesterday, and we are here until fall. I shall see you when you are in the office in September. Warmest regards to you and Mrs. Nelson.

Sincerely,
[*signed*] Howard Thurman
Dean
Dr. William Stuart Nelson
Silver Bay Association
Silver Bay, New York

TLS. HTC-MBU: Box 15.

1. Under the terms of the Selective Service Act of 1940, by 1942 all men aged eighteen to forty-five were eligible for military service. Thurman could have registered under a IV-D deferment, available to ministers of religion or divinity students, but like some other pacifists who qualified for clerical deferments, he evidently felt that to employ this exemption would have been an evasion of his personal responsibility. Approximately fifty thousand men registered as conscientious objectors during World War II, half of them from traditional "peace churches," the Quakers, the Mennonites, and the Church of the Brethren, the remainder from other denominations (most prominently the Jehovah's Witnesses) or without formal religious affiliation. About thirty-three thousand of these men agreed to serve as noncombatants in the armed forces, primarily as medics. Roughly seventeen thousand persons refused to serve the military in any capacity, but twelve thousand of them served in the Civilian Public Service (see To Kay H. Beach, 4 September 1942, printed in the current volume). About five thousand conscientious objectors refused any sort of

cooperation with selective service and were sent to prison. What sort of conscientious objector status Thurman contemplated for himself is unclear. There was considerable pressure on those eligible for ministerial deferments to accept them rather than registering as conscientious objectors. For an example of this, see James Farmer, *Lay Bare the Heart: An Autobiography of the Civil Rights Movement* (New York: New American Library, 1985), 81–83.

2. While Thurman apparently never started regular meditation services while at Rankin Chapel, but would do so while at the Fellowship Church.

To Kay H. Beach
4 September 1942
Washington, D.C.

Kay H. Beach was a conscientious objector, spending the war years at the Larch Mountain Civilian Public Service camp in Corbett, Oregon.[1] *Beach had written to Thurman on July 29 about the case of Odell Waller, a Virginia sharecropper who killed a farmer in 1940 during an altercation over his family's right to the crop they had farmed. Waller was convicted of murder, and despite an extensive campaign to save his life by A. Philip Randolph, Eleanor Roosevelt, Pauli Murray, and many others, he was executed on July 2.*[2] *Beach worried what would happen if the protests over the execution turned violent. Although he was "greatly encouraged by signs of cooperation among the negro* [sic] *people in making a stand against such injustices," he was "unshakably committed to the belief that violent methods tend to jeopardize the chance of permanent progress." He added that "considering the highly emotional state of the general population at this time, a violent flare-up might be the starting point for that open conflict, which some have feared might come. I cannot help but feel that open interracial hostilities would postpone true equality for the negro* [sic] *for at least a generation."*[3] *Thurman appreciates Beach's sentiments, condemns violence, and is in favor of nonviolent protests, though he emphasizes that the goal of nonviolent protest was to not to avoid necessary confrontation.*

My dear Mr. Beach:[4]

I was very glad to receive your letter under date of July 29th.[5] I am very sorry that when I was in Portland it was not possible for me to make a visit to Corbett.

The question which you raise in your letter is one of very great concern to me, naturally. I am profoundly convinced that violent methods tend inevitably to inspire violent reactions. On the other hand, it is exceedingly difficult to draw the line between non-violent pressure and pressure that fulfills itself in some form of non-violent action. I am profoundly convinced that non-cooperation, for instance, is certainly a form of pressure, which form of pressure may be more devastating than the drastic and radical taking of life.

For many years Negroes for various reasons have tended to be far too docile. Their docility has been confused with an alleged meekness and cowardliness. Of course, this overall picture is not true, but so deep is the resentment of many Negroes to this overall picture that the technique of non-violent action is regarded by them as being an expression of cowardice. The problem, therefore, is to maintain in non-violent action an increment of courage that would be disassociated from the so called "hat in the hand" attitude. I am quite enthusiastic about any attempt on the part of interracial units to combine directly non-violent action and a program of constructive adjustment in group relations. Grave indeed, is my concern as I watch the mounting tension all over the country. I have traveled some thirteen or fourteen thousand miles since early June, and the picture is the same everywhere—sporadic outbursts of violence, meaness, murder, bloodshed, and a great paralysis in the presence of it all. It seems to me that one of the important solutions is to be found in the work of small groups in communities all over the United States demonstrating courageous, peaceful action, carefully planned and carefully executed.[6] I am listing below certain organizations and individuals with whom you may get in contact.

Walter White[7]	James H. Hubert[8]
N A A C P	National Urban League
69 Fifth Avenue	202 West 136th Street
New York City	New York City

A. Philip Randolph	Dr. Mary M. Bethune
March on Washington	National Council of Negro Women
	Committee
Hotel Theresa	1812 8th Street, N. W.
New York, New York	Washington, D.C.

It was very good to hear from you.
Sincerely yours,
[*signed*] Howard Thurman
Dean
Mr. Kay H. Beach
Larch Mountain C.P.S. Camp
Box 128, Route 1
Corbett, Oregon

TLS. HTC-MBU: Box 2.

1. The CPS camps were established in 1940 to provide an alternative to military service for conscientious objectors (COs). Most were located at former Civilian Conservation Corps camps, with the costs for upkeep shared between the U.S. government and the three "historic peace churches," the Quakers, the Mennonites, and the Church of the Brethren. The COs at CPS Camp 21, which had two sites, at Cascade Locks and Larch Mountain,

worked on conservation projects in the Mt. Hood National Forest. At about the time of Beach's letter to Thurman, CPS 21 was involved in an act of civil disobedience, successfully blocking the transfer of a Japanese CO to an internment camp. See Charles Davis and Jeffey Kovac, "Confrontation at the Lock: A Protest of Japanese Removal and Incarceration during World War II," *Oregon Historical Quarterly* 107 (Winter 2006): 486–509.

2. For more detail about the Odell Waller (1917–42) trial and protests, see Richard B. Sherman, *The Case of Odell Waller and Virginia Justice, 1940–1942* (Knoxville: University of Tennessee Press, 1992).

3. From Kay H. Beach, 28 July 1942, HTC-MBU: Box 2.

4. Kay Haines Beach (1907–89) was a Quaker who worked in China and India after World War II.

5. From Kay H. Beach, 29 July 1942, HTC-MBU: Box 2.

6. For early efforts to use Gandhian tactics in the struggle for racial equality, see Herbert Garfinkel, *When Negroes March: The March on Washington Movement in the Organizational Politics for FEPC* (Glencoe, Ill.: Free Press, 1959), and August Meier and Elliott Rudwick, *CORE: A Study in the Civil Rights Movement, 1942–1968* (New York: Oxford University Press, 1973).

7. During World War II, Walter Francis White (1893–1955), executive secretary of the NAACP from 1931 until his death, went to the European and Pacific theaters of war to investigate charges of discrimination against black soldiers and to advance the idea that an Allied victory should lead to the end of European colonialism around the world and the beginning of racial equality for African Americans.

8. James H. Hubert (1886–1970), a native of Georgia and a graduate of Morehouse College, was an official and executive director of the New York Urban League from 1919 to 1942. Hubert's autobiography, published posthumously, is *Profiles of Adventure; Transcripts of Negro Heritage* (New York: Vantage, 1970).

To Alain L. Locke
16 September 1942
Washington, D.C.

On 8 August 1942, the All India Congress Party sparked a crisis by issuing its "Quit India" declaration, which called for the immediate establishment of Indian independence and the withdrawal of all British troops. The declaration also called for a campaign of massive civil disobedience if the demands were not met. British authorities in India treated the proposition as an act of sedition in wartime; all of the Congress Party leaders, including Gandhi, were arrested the next day and remained incarcerated for much of the rest of the war, and thousands of acts of disobedience (both nonviolent and violent) spread across portions of India.

Many groups in the United States called on President Roosevelt to intercede with Britain to achieve an accommodation with the Indian independence movement, and African American organizations were in the forefront of this fight. Walter White of the NAACP wrote to Roosevelt suggesting that he back the establishment of an international board for the defense of India that would strictly limit British suzerainty,[1] *and a New York City rally on behalf of a free India sponsored by the Council of African Affairs attracted an audience of more than four thousand, with speakers including Paul Robeson, Max Yergan, Adam Clayton Powell Jr., and Channing Tobias.*[2]

Thurman also became involved in this campaign. He and four other Howard University educators ask their distinguished colleague philosophy professor Alain Locke to join them in signing a statement, printed below, that called on President Roosevelt to ameliorate the India crisis.

Dear Dr. Locke:

The present world crisis has raised the "Indian Question" to a new plane of significance for us all. At this particular period of history the solution of this problem is not only possible; it is imperative. Further, our own Government should take the lead in trying to break the present stalemate, and in effecting a solution of the problem within the framework of the United Nations.[3]

As Negro Americans, we have a special interest in the problem of Indian independence. Moreover, because of our relations to the present world conflict, together with that of other non-white peoples in the United Nations, this is a question upon which we can speak with assurance that we shall be "heard."

The five of us whose names appear below have drafted the enclosed statement to the President as an expression from a select group of Negro leaders. We invite you to join with us in signing and transmitting this statement.

Please sign and return the enclosed postal card, authorizing us to list you as one of the signers of the statement. <u>Do this at once</u>. We hope to forward the statement to the President on September 21.

Very truly yours,
[*signed*] Howard Thurman
Howard Thurman
Robert W. Brooks[4]
Rayford W. Logan[5]
William S. Nelson
Doxey A. Wilkerson[6]

1. "U.S. Mediation of Indian Crisis Sought by NAACP," *Chicago Defender*, 15 August 1942.

2. "Rally for Cause of Free India," *Chicago Defender*, 12 September 1942.

3. The "United Nations" refers to the war effort of the nations pledged to defeat the Axis powers, that is, the United States, Great Britain, the Soviet Union, and their allies, and not to the international organization formed in San Francisco in the summer of 1945 as the

successor to the League of Nations. There had been disagreements between Roosevelt and British Prime Minister Churchill for some time over the postwar status of the British Empire. The third clause of the Atlantic Charter, signed by Roosevelt and Churchill in August 1941, pledged that both nations would "respect the right of all peoples to choose the form of government under which they will live," though unlike Roosevelt, Churchill never accepted that this applied to British colonies. For an overview of American attitudes, see William Roger Louis, *Imperialism at Bay: The United States and the Decolonization of the British Empire, 1941–1945* (New York: Oxford University Press, 1978).

4. Robert Williams Brooks (1892–1952), born outside of Memphis, Tennessee, graduated from Fisk in 1919 and received degrees from the University of Chicago Divinity School in 1918 and 1919. He was minister of the Lincoln Congregational Temple in Washington, D.C., from 1924 to 1952 and taught in the Howard University School of Religion for seventeen years.

5. Rayford Whittingham Logan (1897–1982), a native of Washington, D.C., was a historian and author of many books on African American history. He graduated from Williams College and received a PhD in history from Harvard in 1936. After teaching at Virginia Union University and Atlanta University, Logan joined the faculty of Howard University in 1938 and was chairman of the history department from 1942 until his retirement in 1964.

6. Doxey Alphonso Wilkerson (1905–93) was born in Excelsior Springs, Kansas. He received a BA from the University of Kansas and a PhD in education from New York University. He taught at the Howard University School of Education from 1935 to 1942. After leaving Howard, Wilkerson became one of the most prominent African American leaders of the Communist Party, and he was a longtime leader of the Jefferson School of Social Science in New York City. He left the party in 1957, and from the early 1960s through 1973 he taught at Yeshiva University, where he became a leader in early childhood education. He authored numerous books, among them *Special Problems of Negro Education* (Washington, D.C.: U.S. Government Printing Office, 1939) and *The Negro People and the Communists* (New York: Workers Library, 1944).

[ENCLOSURE: DRAFT LETTER TO THE PRESIDENT]

NEGRO LEADERS APPEAL TO THE PRESIDENT REGARDING INDIA

21 SEPTEMBER 1942

White House

The President

Dear President Roosevelt:

In view of the failure of the British Government and the Indian people to resolve the problem of Indian independence, and in view of the resultant tragic consequences for a free world, especially during this period of crisis, we appeal to you for bold and decisive leadership in resolving this problem.

Mr. President, history and the destiny of world civilization impose upon you a tremendous responsibility in this crisis.

As the powerful leader of a disinterested ally of Britain, use your influence to help reopen negotiations between the Indian Nationalist Party[1] and the British Government.

Call for the creation of a commission from the United Nations to work out a constructive formula for the immediate establishment of a provisional war government of India within the framework of the British Commonwealth and the United Nations, pending a final implementation of Indian independence.[2]

In many crises of the past, you have shown a genius for swift and decisive action. The present emergency situation in India calls for precisely such action.

Brush aside the faint-hearted who counsel inaction and delay. Lead the world boldly to victory—and to the building of a society which befits the dignity of man.[3]

Respectfully yours,
[*unsigned*]

TLc. HTC-MBU: Box 12.

1. All India Congress Party.

2. The "provisional war government" envisioned by Thurman and his colleagues would have kept India on the side of the Allies fighting Germany and Japan. This is somewhat different from the stated aim of the All India Congress Party, which held that if the British withdrew then India would be less likely to be attacked by Japan and would henceforth maintain a careful neutrality between the two sides. But Roosevelt never would have supported a call for a neutral India, and the statement was no doubt drafted with an eye to political realities. Nonetheless this appeal to President Roosevelt to "lead the world boldly to victory" is one of the few times the pacifist Thurman appeared to publicly endorse American war aims during World War II.

3. Whether the statement was sent in this form (or sent at all) is unknown. Roosevelt did indicate after the Quit India movement that the U.S. government was willing to serve as an intermediary between the British government and the India independence movement to establish an international trusteeship for India, but Churchill decisively rejected American pressure.

From Marjorie Penney

22 October 1942
Philadelphia, Pa.

In 1936 Marjorie Penney[1] was a cofounder of one of the first efforts to create a regular interracial religious gathering in the United States, the Young People's Inter-racial Fellowship. Under the auspices of the Committee of Race Relations of the Society of Friends, it was not quite a church—it met only once a month and did not have full-time ministerial support—but it was an important experiment in interracialism. Thurman was one of the favored speakers at the Inter-racial Fellowship, appearing there regularly in the late 1930s and early 1940s. By 1940

Penney could write to Thurman that the monthly meetings have "taken a firm hold upon the imagination of many Philadelphians. This season the auditorium has been packed to capacity."[2] *The meetings had evidently also "taken a firm hold" on Thurman, who mentioned to Penney his possible interest in becoming pastor if the Philadelphia project ever became a full-time congregation. Thurman's good experiences with what was informally known as the "Fellowship Church" was no doubt on his mind when, a year later, A. J. Muste first told Thurman of a similar interracial project in San Francisco.*[3]

Dear Howard:

I hope, by now, that you are back in Washington, having gotten whatever theatrical gauze and other knick knacks you hoped to find in New York.

I think with the deepest satisfaction of what you did for us, Sunday last. While it is always gratifying to us who operate The Fellowship Church to entertain so popular a preacher, it is of infinitely more importance to us to be sure that what the preacher says expresses the Fellowship point of view.

Certainly the Congregation was deeply impressed with your words (I was, and I am not the kindest of critics). Believe me, if and when the Fellowship Church becomes more than a series of services, we shall be seriously thinking of what you said regarding your interest in it.

I am hoping your secretary reads your mail. In that event, I will receive, quite promptly, the sum of your expenses in coming to us.

Very gratefully,
[*signed*] Marjorie
Marjorie Penney
Director

ALS. HTC-MBU: Box 17.

1. Marjorie Penney (1908–83) established the first Fellowship House in Philadelphia in 1941 as an outgrowth of the Friends' Young People's Inter-Racial Fellowship Committee on Race Relations. The Fellowship House provided a setting for people of all races and backgrounds to meet and interact. Working almost entirely on a volunteer basis, Penney and the Fellowship House staff organized a number of social and educational programs at the local level while also pursuing a broader agenda of reform that sometimes extended to the national level, including efforts to fight lynching and anti-Semitism and attempts to bring open housing and integrated recreational facilities. Fellowship House/Farm Records, Temple University Urban Archives, Acc. 723, 1931–94.

2. From Marjorie Penney, 25 April 1940, HTC-MBU: Box 17.

3. Thurman had first heard of the Philadelphia "Fellowship Church" in early 1936, when he was traveling in India, and it was one of the inspirations of his epiphany at the Khyber Pass, where he determined, on his return to America, to create an interracial and interdenominational church. See HT, "The Historical Perspective," in The Fellowship Church of All Peoples (San Francisco, 1947), 3.

From William Worthy

24 October 1942
Philadelphia, Pa.

One of the many young people in Thurman's wide ambit in the early 1940s was William Worthy,[1] *the secretary of the Philadelphia Inter-racial Fellowship, a pacifist and conscientious objector during the war and later a distinguished and controversial journalist.*

Dear Dr. Thurman:

During our conversation at the Fellowship[2] service last Sunday I forgot to mention that you will be unable to write to Bill Sutherland[3] directly, but you can write to his family and have them include a message to him in one of their letters to him. I might say that Mrs. Sutherland especially is taking Bill's imprisonment very hard and that she will certainly appreciate your interest in him. It seems to me that she is quite sensitive to what other people are thinking and is comforted to learn that some admire Bill's stand.

In the Youth Committee we are trying to carry on what Bill bequeathed to us and to build an organization, which will unite young people around a program of "total democracy now." I worked with Bill at Bates in the Student Christian Movement and am sure that even within the walls of prison he is preaching the gospel of social and political action.

I do hope that you will publish a new edition of Olive Schreiner's works.[4] On Tuesday I secured "Dreams"[5] from the library and after a busy day stayed up late reading and re-reading those very imaginative allegories. As you said, she deserves far greater recognition.

Sincerely,
[*signed*] Bill Worthy
Bill Worthy
Philadelphia Secretary

TLS. HTC-MBU: Box 22.

1. William Worthy (1921–) launched his life of activism as a student at Bates College (1938–42). A conscientious objector during World War II, he served as secretary of the Philadelphia branch of the Youth Committee for Democracy in the 1940s. He went on to serve as the Russian correspondent for CBS News, the *New York Post*, and the *Baltimore*

Afro-American during the 1950s. In 1956 he traveled to China in defiance of a U.S. travel ban—he was the first American reporter to visit China after the 1949 revolution—and upon his return his passport was confiscated. After traveling to Cuba in 1961, he was convicted of passport violations, a sentence later overturned in federal appeals court. He thereafter worked as a journalist and professor of journalism. In 1982 Worthy, two fellow journalists, and the American Civil Liberties Union successfully sued the federal government for confiscating documents related to the CIA's monitoring of Iran. Worthy later taught as the Annenberg Distinguished Visiting Professor in the School of Communications at Howard University (1990–93).

2. Fellowship House in Philadelphia.

3. William "Bill" Sutherland (1919–2010) graduated from Bates College (where he had met Thurman) in 1940 and joined the American Friends Service Committee's student peace service. Sutherland explained to Thurman in 1941 that he was torn in trying to prioritize race relations, economics, and "peace," but he ultimately concluded that "the problem of war . . . overshadowed the rest," and he spent four years in jail during World War II for resisting the draft (From William Sutherland, 1 June 1941, HTC-MBU: Box 20). In the 1950s Sutherland was involved in antinuclear protests around the world. Along with Bayard Rustin and George Houser of CORE, Sutherland established Americans for South African Resistance in an effort to support the African National Congress's campaign. He moved to the Gold Coast in West Africa (now Ghana) in 1953 and worked with the government of Kwame Nkrumah. His book *Guns and Gandhi in Africa: Pan-African Insights on Nonviolence, Armed Struggle and Liberation in Africa* (Trenton, N.J.: Africa World, 2000), co-authored with Matt Mayer, examines from the point of view of those who led the liberation movements the strategies and tactics used in achieving an end to colonialism.

4. Thurman expended considerable efforts to assemble a Schreiner anthology in the early 1940s; see To Hedwig S. Kuhn, 30 April 1942, HTC-MBU: Box 11, and To Samuel Cronwright, 25 May 1942, HTC-MBU: Box 4. Three decades later this anthology was eventually published as *A Track to the Water's Edge: The Olive Schreiner Reader* (New York: Harper & Row, 1973).

5. Olive Schreiner's collection of stories, *Dreams* (London: Unwin, 1891).

To Charles Barton

29 December 1942
Washington, D.C.

Thurman took his responsibility as a molder of young men and women very seriously, and he combined encouragement with chastisement. Here Thurman criticizes his student worker for slacking off on his duties around the Thurman home.

My dear Barton:

Before I say what is on my mind, I want to wish you and your family a very happy Christmas season. I know your mother was pleased to have you back home for the holidays, particularly if you made her Christmas season full of joy as an intelligent son would.

Now to the point. What kind of man are you anyway? You left here unceremoniously. The floors were not waxed; the cookies were left piled up at the front door; the basket of fruit from Florida stayed in the middle of the floor in the downstairs hall and was left there. A thoughtful man would have found out if there was anything he could do to tide things over until he returned. He would have found out whether there were any special jobs incident to the Christmas holiday entertainment, or anything else. I am frank to say that your work has not turned out as I hoped that it would. You are a very thorough worker, but you have no initiative. You do what you are told and nothing more. You will recall that when I asked you about taking the job I told you that I would be busy and Mrs. Thurman would be very busy, and that we would expect you to take a personal interest in keeping things going. As it turned out you could only come occasionally in the forenoon and for a little while in the afternoon. There were so many other things that you had to do that more and more the house had to be neglected. This meant that it was necessary to hire someone extra to do any special thing that came up. With the kind of entertaining that we do, it is sometimes necessary to get in touch with the person who helps sometime in the evening for an emergency. You were never available because you were busy every night at the book store. This adds up to the fact that several times I have been forced to hire different people to do work which the university expects me to have done out of the tuition scholarship which they permit me to give from my budget. The amount of money for labor is exhausted and I must insist that you arrange your program so as to keep the house going. If you cannot do this, then I think that in all fairness you ought to give up the job.

I am speaking frankly with you as I always do. You know by this time how much I think of you as a person and how much confidence I have in you and in your future, but I am convinced that through poor planning on your part you have let me down terribly. All of this has a bearing on your future as an army officer. If you do not learn how to use your imagination, to see a job that needs to be done and do it, and exercise initiative with responsibility, you will always be a Second Lieutenant or be demoted to the ranks. If you are to be leader of men in the armed forces, you must be able to make quick accurate judgments and take full responsibility for them. I say this as a father would talk to you. You need not get sore because you are very sensitive and thin-skinned. You cannot make an impression on me by sulking. Take it on the chin because you deserve everything I am saying. Make up your mind about it all and let me know your decision when you get back.

Remember me to your mother even though I have not met her. Tell her that I am trying to build on the excellent foundation which she gave you. The family joins me in greetings to you.

Sincerely,
[*signed*] Howard Thurman
Dean

Mr. Charles Barton
109 Collins Street
Lynn, Massachusetts

TLS. HTC-MBU: Box 2.

FROM BERNICE FISHER

20 JANUARY 1943
CHICAGO, ILL.

Bernice Fisher,[1] who helped James Farmer organize the Chicago-based Committee of Racial Equality (CORE)—later Congress of Racial Equality—seeks Thurman's advice and insights on establishing a national network of organizations informed by the teachings of Gandhi. Thurman did not attend the subsequent gathering but did meet CORE leadership to discuss the content of such a conference.

Dear Dr. Thurman:

Your only possibility of remembering me would be as the Chicago friend of John and Madeline . . . although you met me through Martha Eells, you'll recall.

A few weeks ago James L. Horace[2] told me that he expected you in the Chicago area the first of February. That gives some promise of seeing you personally to discuss some of the problems of our action in CORE.

The Committee of Racial Equality has probably been mentioned to you by Jim Farmer. Here in Chicago we are venturing in action in the fields of Housing, Public Places, Education, and Hospitals and Schools. Attacking the basic issues with the technique of non-violent direct action presents the most meaningful program that I have yet met . . . and at the same time the definite problems of a young movement.

Our urgent need is for a meeting of all the similar groups around the country to think through the implications of the analysis and technique in terms of a national movement.[3] Certainly we should meet early this spring to take into consideration the possibilities of such a coordination of local groups.

Obviously, in addition to such possible local representatives as we now know, we must have the benefit of the point of view of men like yourself with the wider prospective and the deeper analysis. When do you expect to be in Chicago this spring? We must know as soon as possible; so that we can fix a tentative date for such a conference.

The Action Committee of CORE is anxious to discuss both {L}ocal and National problems with you immediately. Will you have an hour that you could give to us the first of February?

That means that we are depending on you to let us know the chances of meeting with the local Action Group the first of the month, and to give us a possible time that you will be available in this area to consult with the group on possibilities of a national coordination!

Do give my love to the Johnsons . . . and as usual remind them that they owe me a letter!

Cordially,
[*signed*] Bernice Fisher
Bernice Fisher
Dr. Howard Thurman
Howard University
Washington, D.C.

TLS. HTC-MBU: Box 2.

1. Bernice Fisher (1916–66), originally from Punxsutawney, Pennsylvania, was a labor organizer and a founder of CORE while a student at the University of Chicago.

2. James L. Horace was pastor of Monumental Baptist Church in Chicago from 1933 to 1952 and president of the Illinois Baptist General State Convention from 1939 to 1960.

3. The conference held on 15 June 1943 brought together about thirty activists of like mind from Seattle, Denver, New York, Philadelphia, Evanston, and Chicago. They formed the National Federation of Committees of Racial Equality. Farmer became its chairman and Fisher, secretary-treasurer. James Farmer, *Lay Bare the Heart: An Autobiography of the Civil Rights Movement* (New York: New American Library, 1985), 112.

"FELLOWSHIP WITH GOD AND PRAYER"
FEBRUARY 1943

In November 1942 and February 1943, Thurman published a pair of articles in the Intercollegian, *"Sources of Strength for Trying Days,"*[1] *and "Fellowship with God and Prayer," respectively. The purpose of the articles was, as he wrote in "Sources of Strength for Trying Days," to "examine the sources of strength available to the individual" when "the demands of the present moment are so exacting upon all of us." Both articles draw heavily on previous writings and publications, among them "The Significance of Jesus" series, "Sources of Power for Christian Action," and "Christian, Who Calls Me Christian?" all published in this volume.*

In "Sources of Strength for Trying Days" he argues that the only antidote to the "indirection, indecision, and inner confusion" which is the lot of the "average student at the average college" is "the concentration of life on some all-inclusive purpose." This sort of "loyalty to a great cause" releases "in the individual all of the psychological and spiritual resources needful for sustained achievement. It makes for freedom of mind, for a kind of orderly recklessness of action, it makes courage possible, and it robs man of his fear of death." When one does this, on the highest ethical level, one becomes "a fellow-worker with Jesus." And in doing so, one establishes a fellowship with other like-minded persons, so that he can have "the springs of his life fed by a fellowship of kindred spirits in which he can get refreshment and reorganization for the tasks to which he is committed."

But the necessary catalyst for this, he continues in "Fellowship with God and Prayer," is "fontal contact" with God, "the ultimate spiritual resource for human life." He briefly discusses how to achieve this contact, through the Quaker notion of "centering down," an unburdening and uncluttering of one's life through placing oneself under the divine scrutiny. In this way, "against the darkness of one's times or one's ways there can be seen clearly the illumined finger of God pointing in the direction which one must take."

God is the ultimate spiritual resource for human life. For many of the tasks to which our hands are set by the imperious demands of high moral adventure, it is sufficient for our need to get the inspiration and strength that come from singleness of purpose. For still others, we may find all needful resources from entering actively into fellowship with Jesus Christ. Again, it may be enough for our need to be in intimate communion with a group of like-minded seekers who surround us with a wide variety of insistent fellowship. But, fundamentally, in the task that calls for the faithful transformation of our individual lives and the redemption of man and society from evil, only an infinite energy can meet the exhaustive demand. To state it categorically, only an infinite resource can meet an infinite need. Anyone who has faced the abysmal churnings of evil in his own spirit out of which come in crimson stream deeds that fill the life with shame and the days with anguish, knows that only God is sufficient. When stripped to the literal substance of himself, with all pretenses peeled away, with all defenses and alibies seen for what they are, the naked self exposed to the steady gleam of the divine scrutiny—at long last man must make his peace with God. What is it that God desires of him? What is the meaning of his own desires? What is life's purpose and at what point may his life count most fully? Questions like these can no longer be escaped. Sometimes in austere solitariness, sometimes on the crest of a wave of tragedy or joy, sometimes in a circling series of activities far removed from the seemingly important functions of one's life—the moment comes, the man and God alone seem to exist in the entire universe.

The basis of fellowship with God is found in the realm of original fontal contact with Him. To keep fresh in one's mind and experience this contact, this sense of presence is at once the most important thing in life. For to such a man God is the conscious Guarantor of his deeds, the Corrective of his desires, so that he may *desire* to desire the right; the Source of power for days of great weariness and despair. This may not mean that one's problems are solved—not at all; but it does mean that the deep tensions about existence and the vicissitudes of life are relaxed.

Prayer as Behavior

Prayer and meditation then become *ways of behaving* profoundly and practically, by which the springs of the spiritual life are consistently renewed. How is this accomplished? In the first place prayer brings the mind to a point of focus on God. It is what some mystics call "centering down." Little by little things that clutter the mind and make awkward the purposes are pushed to the periphery of one's concern and *sometimes* they are even shrivelled at their roots. Here confessions of error and wrongdoing are trued for rightness and refocussing—a fresh commitment issues in the recharging of one's purposes. Again, the mind is given windows through which wider perspectives may be envisioned which in turn will be guides at moments when the trek is long and the way without light. Again, particular strength for particular need is yielded—one's silent potent fears and dreads are attacked—one's unuttered hurts are exposed for dressing and healing—one's uncanny temptations are called by their true name and their power is somehow weakened or undermined. In fine, all of this means that the waste places of one's life are restored in the warmth and glow of His presence. Against the darkness of one's times or one's ways there can be seen clearly the illumined finger of God pointing in the direction which he must take. For such a person, even death becomes a little thing, and naught of the vicissitudes of life can destroy the triumphant music of his heart. One's *will* to act the Kingdom of God and to make life everywhere yield its maximum weal for every man, takes on a new dynamic.

"Fellowship with God and Prayer," *Intercollegian* 60, no. 4 (1943): 86.

1. "Sources of Strength for Trying Days," *Intercollegian* 60, no. 2 (1942), 28–29.

From Thoburn T. Brumbaugh
3 February 1943
Detroit, Mich.

Thurman plans to travel to Detroit in March to preach at the annual Lenten services of the Detroit Council of Churches, making him the first African American to preach at the event. Thoburn T. Brumbaugh,[1] a white leader of the council, assures Thurman that a Detroit hotel will accept his reservation.

Dear Dr. Thurman:

Thanks for your letter of January 23rd.[2] The photograph and other material have not yet arrived and I am anxious to have them at the earliest possible moment.

We have arranged as heretofore that all of our Lenten speakers shall in turn be lodged at the Statler Hotel. When the management noted your name, they raised a question but we assured them you had stopped at the Statler and other Detroit hotels on previous occasion{s} and that we would naturally expect the same accommodations for you as for the others. We are sure you realized the delicateness of race relations in Detroit.[3] Our largest hotels are finding it increasingly difficult to observe even the practices of earlier days when there were fewer Negroes in the city. Accordingly the hotel people agreed to accept your reservation. We assured them of your fine Christian character and that we are confident all concerned will cooperate to prevent any misunderstanding or difficulty.

As to our constituency we have found a happy reaction to your coming and the prospect of hearing your messages throughout the week of March 22–26.

Ever sincerely yours,
[*signed*] T.T. Brumbaugh
Executive Secretary
TTB:M

TLS. HTC-MBU: Box 3.

1. Thoburn Taylor Brumbaugh (1896–1974) graduated from the Boston University School of Theology in 1924. In 1943 he was the executive director of the Detroit Council of Churches, and he later served as executive director of the Japan International Christian University Foundation (1946–58). Brumbaugh authored *Religious Values in Japanese Culture* (Tokyo: Kyo bun kwan, 1934) and *My Marks and Scars I Carry: The Story of Ernst Kisch* (New York: Friendship, 1969).

2. HT to T.T. Brumbaugh, 27 January 1943, HTC-MBU

3. Racial tensions ran high in Detroit during World War II as thousands of white and black workers migrated from the South and competed for jobs in war industries. In 1942, for example, residents of an all-white neighborhood used violence to try to prevent black families from moving into the Sojourner Truth Homes. Forty people were injured and one

hundred arrested before black residents finally moved in. This confrontation foreshadowed the Detroit race riot in June 1943, three months after Thurman spoke there. See Richard W. Thomas, *Life for Us Is What We Make It: Building Black Community in Detroit, 1915–1945* (Bloomington: Indiana University Press, 1992). See from A. J. Muste, 14 March, 1941, printed in this volume, and Richard W. Thomas, etc.

To James Farmer
11 March 1943
Washington, D.C.

On 30 December 1942, A. Philip Randolph announced that his March on Washington Movement would in their May conference "consider launching a broad national program based on non-violent civil disobedience and non-cooperation along the lines of the campaign of Mohandas K. Gandhi." This would require all African-Americans, except for those in the armed forces or at work, 'to disobey any law which violates their basic citizenship rights, such as Jim-Crow cars and all forms of discrimination."[1] *James Farmer, among others on the pacifist left, worried that without proper training in non-violent resistance this campaign could result in "shootouts in the South and bloody massacres . . . that would set back a non-violent movement in the United States for decades."*[2] *On 1943 February 1, Farmer, editor of the Newsbulletin of FOR's Non-Violent Action Committee, sent a questionnaire (printed as an enclosure below) to Thurman and others (such as Reinhold Niebuhr). After reading the responses published in the March and April issues of the Newsbulletin, Randolph decided indefinitely to postpone the civil disobedience campaign and to work closely with FOR and CORE.*

Dear Jimmie:

I am sorry that I am just getting around to reacting to the questionnaire which you sent out. I have decided that I shall make my days count as fully as possible, and when I have done that, I shall have no apologies for unfinished business. My general reaction to A. Philip Randolph's proposal is this. First, non-violent civil disobedience is a technique that presupposes very definite discipline. It is an act of the will arising out of a profound spiritual conviction, which by its very nature is devoid either of ill-will, contempt, or cowardice. I was very much interested in the fact that Mr. Gandhi told me that such civil disobedience broke down in India because the masses of the people were not able to sustain so lofty a creative idea over a time interval of sufficient duration to be practically effective. They were unable so to do, not because they were lacking in courage or in willingness, but rather in vitality. It occurs to me further, Jimmie, that civil disobedience more in wide spread now is the final gesture of the human spirit before martyrdom. It means that every means for social change as the exploited and this alone is left. As long as there is available due process before the courts there are some who would question civil disobedience as a wide spread technique. This second consideration I simply mention in passing. My fundamental reaction to the proposal is that it is a very good thing provided it is built upon definite disciplines so that the masses of the people will not be inspired by fear, revenge or hate. I am sorry that I am so late in getting this in.

Sincerely,
[*signed*] Howard Thurman
Dean

Mr. James Farmer
Fellowship of Reconciliation
2929 Broadway
New York, New York

1. The campaign was to be carried out through Randolph's March on Washington (MOW) movement, which in 1941 had pressured President Franklin Roosevelt into opening the defense industry to black workers. From James Farmer, 1 February 1943, HTC-MBU: Box 8 (enclosure printed below).

2. James Farmer, *Lay Bare the Heart: An Autobiography of the Civil Rights Movement* (New York: New American Library, 1985), 156.

[Enclosure: James Farmer to HT, 1 February 1943]

The Fellowship of Reconciliation
Non-Violent Direct Action NEWSBULLETIN
2929 Broadway
New York, New York

Symposium Questions: Is Civil Disobedience the Answer to Jim-Crow?

Should Negroes practice organized, non-violent civil disobedience to jim-crow, systematically disobeying laws and violating customs which manifest segregation and race discrimination? Why? If not, is there any other alternative to continued coöperation with jim-crow practices? What is it?

What consequences, good and/or bad, are likely to come to the Negro people as a result of such disobedience? Can those consequences be met and dealt with in such as way as to secure from the venture lasting gains and the least setbacks? If so, how?

What should be the relation of progressive and sympathetic whites to, or their role in, such a venture of civil disobedience? (If your answer to Question I was negative, then state here the role of progressive whites in the alternative which you recommended.)

What organizational framework would be required to execute such a program of civil disobedience? Does such a framework already exist? If so, where?

If not, is it now being developed? By whom? (If you answer to Question I was negative, then answer these questions in relation to the alternative which you recommended.)

Note: Though limitations of space in the NEWSBULLETIN require that the symposium answers be brief, please answer the questions as fully as necessary in order to make your points clear. If we have to condense some of your answers for inclusion in the NEWSBULLETIN, we shall make sure to do that without doing an injustice to your complete point of view as expressed.[1]

TLc. HTC-MBU: Box 8.

1. Farmer published the responses to his questionnaire as a symposium in the March and April issues of FOR's *News Bulletin,* which he edited. After reading the responses, Randolph decided to delay the launching of his civil disobedience campaign and pledged to work with Farmer and CORE on such efforts in the future.

To Virginia Scardigli
21 April 1943
Boston, Mass.

In a letter to friend Virginia Scardigli,[1] *Thurman provides glimpses of the strain of the war on some of his other acquaintances.*

Dear Virginia:

Not infrequently, a slight chuckle reaches my ear and I realize that it is your pet gargoyle communicating with me from my pocket. This is not a letter but merely a note to thank you for your nice letter. I am hoping that even though you may be in Valejo when I come out to California in June you will be present at the Institute at Mills[2] so that we may have some time to talk. My days and weeks are so full that I have not had time to work out any lecture subjects for the Institute, but I hope to do so before long.

I received a very warm letter from some Japanese friends in the Relocation Center in Amache, Colorado, urging me to stop by on my way to the coast. I shall try to do so for I would enjoy seeing them and having a chance to spend two or three days in fellowship and in talk. I am trying to go easy on extra commitments because I am coming to the end of the year very very worn and weary. I must combine my work this summer with enough recreation actually to make the work possible. Harold Chance[3] tells me that the indications are that there shall be a very fine attendance at Mills. Many changes are taking place down at Whittier[4] because according to the bulletin I saw the other day, President Mendenhall[5] and several members of the faculty have resigned because the trustees voted to accept an army training center on the campus. They felt that this was in violation of the Quaker college and testimony.

Last Wednesday we presented Carl Sandburg[6] in Chapel. Do you know him? He is a grand fellow, regular in every way with a great passion and a good sense of humor. He read some of his poetry, talked about democracy, and ended by playing his guitar and singing folk songs. It was one of the high points of the year for me.

Let me hear from you again.

Sincerely,

[*signed*] Howard Thurman

Dean of the Chapel

Miss Virginia Scardigli

36 Bernard Street

San Francisco, California

TLS. HTC-MBU: Box 20.

1. Virginia Caldwell Scardigli (1912–2007) graduated from the University of California at Berkeley and was part of the arts circle that included author John Steinbeck. From 1942 to 1946, she worked with the Quaker-led National Japanese American Student Relocation Council on the West Coast to help students interned in camps gain admission to colleges elsewhere to complete their education. She was an active member of the Fellowship Church and for a while served as its secretary. She helped type the manuscript for Thurman's book *Jesus and the Disinherited* (1949) and later taught English and journalism at the high school level in California.

2. Thurman was at the Institute of Interracial Relations at Mills College from 27 June to 7 July 1943. Mills College, a liberal arts institution, was founded in 1852 as the Young Ladies' Seminary in Benicia, California. In 1871 it relocated to its campus in Oakland. It is the largest women's college west of the Rockies and one of the oldest colleges for women in the country.

3. Harold Chance (1898–1975), was active in the American Friends Service Committee for many decades, and director of the Friends Peace Service after 1942.

4. Whittier College was established as Whittier Academy in 1887 and chartered by the state of California in 1901. Named for John Greenleaf Whittier, noted Quaker poet and abolitionist, the school maintained a commitment to social justice issues and traditional Quaker values.

5. William O. Mendenhall served as president of Whittier College from 1934 to 1943.

6. Carl Sandburg (1878–1967) was an internationally acclaimed poet, historian, and folklorist who won the Pulitzer Prize in 1940 for his biography *Abraham Lincoln: The War Years* (1939). In 1943 he published a book of essays titled *Home Front Memo*. At Howard, Sandburg may have sung selections from his volume of folk songs, *American Songbag* (1927).

To L. Maynard Catchings

29 April 1943
Washington, D.C.

Herbert King,[1] *Thurman's close friend, was national student secretary for the YMCA from 1936 to 1943, with special responsibilities for Negro colleges. In 1943, the leaders of the YMCA wished to combine the position with responsibility for visiting white southern colleges as well. King and many of his friends, including Thurman, thought that the changed position was an affront to King, to the needs of black colleges, and to the roles of blacks in the Student Christian Movement. In a personally wrenching decision, King resigned shortly before he would have been relieved of his position. Thurman writes to YMCA official Maynard Catchings to let him know that if Herbert is fired from his position as a national associate secretary at the Y's headquarters in New York City without being given a fair hearing, then Thurman and Frank Wilson will withdraw their support and cooperation from the Student Movement.*

Dear Catchings:[2]

It seems as if the thing has broken on Herb's head, and there is a well defined scheme underfoot to give him the ax. I cannot write you all the details at the present moment, but in due course you will get them. See what you can pick up from anyone around there. Herb, Frank and I are in constant consultation as to steps that are being taken. From my point of view, this is a very despicable piece of skullduggery because he has not been given any chance to answer Roland's[3] charges, or officially to know anything about them. I am sending this note, however, to say to you that we have agreed that if Herb is not given a fair, formal hearing, we shall no longer cooperate with the Student Movement, and shall spread this affirmation as fully through the Negro constituency as is possible. This is all for now, you will get more later.

Sincerely,
[*signed*] Howard Thurman
Dean of the Chapel
Mr. L. Maynard Catchings
Secretary, Southern Field Council
National Student YMCA's
706 Standard Building
Atlanta, Georgia

TLS. HTC-MBU: Box 4.

1. For Herbert King's position in the YMCA controversy, see "The Case for an Additional Negro Secretary to Work Under Auspices of the Student Division of the National Board of the YMCA," (c.1941), Howard Thurman Papers Project Subject Files.

2. Lincoln Maynard Catchings (1914–1984) served as the southern regional secretary of the National Student YMCA (1942–1944). He was born in Houston, Texas, and earned his BS Degree from Prairie View College (1935), BD degree from Howard University (1941) and MA degree from Howard (1942). He taught Mathematics at Jackson High School in Rosenburg, Texas, (1936–1938). After his stint with the YMCA, Catchings worked as a special consultant for Christian and Religious Organization in the Department of Race Relation of the American Missionary Association and was affiliated with the Fisk University Social Science Institute (1945–1947). In 1947 he was named pastor of Plymouth Congregational Church in Washington, D.C., a church previously pastored by Herbert King. Catchings served on the Montclair, New Jersey, school board in the early 1970s. He was also a member of the Montclair Town Commission from 1976 through 1980.

3. A. Roland Elliott was King's supervisor at the YMCA. For additional information about him, see volume 1.

To Mira B. Wilson
6 May 1943
Washington, D.C.

Thurman writes Mira Wilson,[1] principal of Northfield School, to inform her of his daughter Olive's decision to room with a Jewish student in the fall of 1943. Many elite white schools that admitted a few students from "minority communities" had a policy of enrolling an even number of students from minority groups in a given class so they could share rooms. Thurman recognizes that Olive's decision will create a logistical problem for Wilson, but he urges her to support Olive and her new Jewish roommate.

Dear Miss Wilson:

Mrs. Thurman and I discussed with Olive, when she was home for vacation, the entire question involved in her proposal to room with Naomi Goldberg. We gave her all of the pros and cons in the matter, leaving the decision for her own mind, with the assurance that we would approve {the}decision. She has decided to room with Naomi, and we are herewith giving our approval.

I am sure that you will agree with us that this matter is a rather delicate situation.

The two girls involved are from minority communities and have, therefore, more sensitivity in areas involving human relationships, than their years would indicate. A decision on the part of adults against their rooming together, other things being equal, may sustain an injury for them from which recovery may be difficult. We appreciate the problem that may be present next year in the matter of the rooming of the colored students, but we hope that a satisfactory adjustment can be made.

We do want you to know that we are very happy over the excellent development which has been made possible for Olive at Northfield. With every kind regard.

Sincerely,
[*signed*] Howard Thurman
Dean of the Chapel
Miss Mira B. Wilson
Principal
Northfield Seminary
East Northfield, Massachusetts

TLS. HTC-MBU: Box 22.

1. Mira Bigelow Wilson (1893–1953) earned an AB from Smith College (1914) and a BD from Boston University (1918). She was an assistant professor of religion and biblical literature at Smith until 1929, when she became headmistress of Northfield, a position she held for twenty-three years.

To Benjamin E. Mays
8 May 1943
Washington, D.C.

Thurman seeks Benjamin Mays's help in finding a job for Herbert King, reminding him of their racial obligation to take care of their own.

Dear Bennie:

I wish I could talk to you about what is happening to Herb in the Movement. It seems to me that it is of primary importance that we see to it that Herb is given a fair deal, and in addition, that we look around to see into what he can land. The white fellows always take care of their own when the ax begins to fall. We must do this for Herb; for even if he is vindicated in some kind of hearing his usefulness in the Movement is over as far as his own point of view is concerned. I don't suppose he will ever recover from the fact that the Executive Committee took drastic action against him without his even knowing it. If this is not handled well, it will be very difficult to take care of our students in the Student Christian Movement.

I hope all goes well with you.
Sincerely,
[*signed*] Howard Thurman
President B. E. Mays
Morehouse College
Atlanta, Georgia

TLS. HTC-MBU: Box 191.

To Herbert King

1 June 1943
Washington, D.C.

Thurman suggests to Herbert King that he resign from his current position as a strategy to focus attention on injustices in the YMCA Student Christian Movement.

Dear Herb:

I have read your letter with very profound satisfaction. You have put your hands on the core of the problem and stated your position unequivocally and with great clarity. I send you my warmest felicitations.

Last week my mind had arrived at such a state of deadness that I went up to Lincoln to spend a few days with Frank.[1] We mowed grass, weeded the garden, planted seed, wandered around the woods. It brought a new measure of peace to a troubled mind. On the last day we talked at length about our common problem. We both decided that it would be the wisest tactical move for you to resign, leaving the burden of proof on the shoulders of the committee. I am suggesting to Maynard Catchings, when he comes next week, that he too should resign. My reason for thinking that you ought to resign is {not}a very complicated one. It seems to me that if you stay in the Movement and fight your case all the way up to the highest tribunal, it will be interpreted as a man who is fighting for a job. I do not see how it is possible for you to maintain the fight within the Movement on the high ground which is implicit in your position. You are dealing with politicians and with men, who themselves, are not concerned fundamentally either about justice, or about the welfare of the Student Christian Movement, but who wish to exercise power and control as if for them the Student Movement was a vested interest. You may not agree with this position, and in the last analysis you{r} judgment must prevail. When the resignation should go in—what you would do afterwards, are questions that must be decided. If you resigned, then the meaning of all the letters that Frank sent out, and the subsequent correspondence in which he has engaged with other men all over the country, will bring the whole thing to a head. If you wait until the expiration of their dead-line, then technically, you will have been killed merely by the passing of a certain date. There would be no issue because the occasion for the issue would have passed. Think it through and let us pray it through. I need not say to you that whatever you decide to do I am sticking with you all the way. I put completely at your disposal anything that I have, including myself.

I shall be coming through Chicago on the 23rd of June enroute to the Pacific Coast. Could we meet in Chicago for a few hours on Wednesday afternoon, June 23rd? You will be at Geneva[2] and you may be able to run up to see me. Let me hear on this point.

Sue sends her love and urges you to keep your shirt on.

Sincerely,
[*signed*] Mr. Herbert King
Hollister, Missouri

TLS. HTC-MBU: Box 11.

1. Frank Wilson.
2. Lake Geneva, Wisconsin. The area is home to a number of Christian resorts and retreat centers and was one of the conference hubs used by the YMCA movement each summer.

To Henry P. Van Dusen
21 June 1943
Washington, D.C.

Thurman writes to Henry Van Dusen,[1] a member of the YMCA personnel committee responsible for Herbert King's firing. In an earlier letter Van Dusen had tried to reassure Thurman that the King situation was not a reflection of a change in the organization's interracial commitments but rather an example of a talented person whose skills did not match the needs of the position. Thus his termination was necessary. Here Thurman responds that even though the King situation may not be motivated by race, it would be difficult to convince African American students involved in the movement that race was not a factor. Further, he says, the mishandling of the entire situation will lead to disunity at a time when the movement cannot afford it.

Dear Pitt:

I am very sorry that I was tied up every afternoon at Dobbs Ferry so that it was impossible for me to come down the hill to Estabrook to see you. We had a good session with your group on Saturday afternoon.

I was exceedingly anxious to see you because I wanted to have a talk with you about the Herb King affair. It is needless to say that I am deeply troubled by the turn that the affair has taken. Whatever the justifications may be for the action of the Executive Committee, the fact that the action was taken without Herb's having the opportunity of statement gives to the whole transaction an unfortunate and tragic character. At a moment when all the ranks should be solidified, I fear that this unfortunate action will make profoundly for disunity. Although the issue seems not to be one of race, this fact can never be made clear to Negro students. There is little expectation that persons who are not concerned about being christian will be of the will to justice where Negroes are concerned. But, when the Student Christian Movement acts in a manner that exposes it to a judgment of unfairness the cause to which we are all dedicated suffers irreparable damage. Of course, I suppose the Executive Committee thought all of this through before it acted, but I wanted to go on record in this matter because the Student Christian Movement in America is more important even than its Executive Committee. If you have time, I would appreciate hearing from you.

With every kind regard, I am

Faithfully,

[*signed*] Howard Thurman

Dean of the Chapel

Dr. Henry P. Van Dusen

Union Theological Seminary

New York, New York

TLS. DHU-MS: Box 4046.

1. Henry Pitney Van Dusen, a Presbyterian minister, was at this time a professor of theology at Union Theological Seminary. For additional information about him, see the biographical footnote in volume 1.

"The Will to Segregation"

August 1943

In this article originally published in Fellowship, *Thurman explains how the war led to an increased sense of civic responsibility on the part of blacks and a heightened tendency toward segregation on the part of whites. Thurman suggests that a relaxation of the will to segregation can only be achieved through new paradigms of Christian love. This will not immediately lead to dissolution of all race-based organizations, including churches, but he insists that freedom of choice must be given to all.*

Any discussion of the relationship between Negro and white people in the year 1943 must examine certain important developments that exercise wide influence in this area.

The first and most important single fact is the war. Under ordinary circumstances the Negro is at most a citizen, second class. He pays taxes on property, participates in the franchise in some sections, and holds a few offices of public trust, but for the most part normal life for him is two or three steps removed from what may be regarded as normal life for other members of the community. At a time of national peril, much of this situation is altered. Even the least citizen begins to count in terms of specific assignments that are deemed essential for survival. Thus war has caused the average Negro to become aware of counting civically in a new way: he is encouraged to buy bonds and defense stamps, he participates in the leadership program, his manpower comes under the selected judgment of the National Selective Service Act, he is involved in Civilian Defense in many of its manifestations, he is taking special training courses for carrying increasing responsibility in defense industry and the farms, he is in the armed forces.

Civic character is possible only where men are permitted to carry civic responsibility. With this new sense of civil responsibility, a new kind of civic character is beginning to appear. This new character, although occasioned by the war, makes for the development of a more careful regard for the future not only of democracy but also the particular future of the Negro in labor, professions, politics, etc. In a sense it is like the coming of age when the first full bloom of manhood possesses the mind and the body. It is unfortunate that it took a global war with its concomitant effect upon our national life to give the Negro a fresh sense of significance and power.

The second significant development stems from the fact that it is no longer possible merely to define national aspirations in terms of "making the world safe for democracy"; it is necessary now to talk concretely in terms of the four freedoms, adding footnotes to make them more definite and less general than they would appear on the surface. The Axis nations have made clear their goals in terms of a thorough-going fascism, and thus defined their political, social and economic philosophy. The United Nations must be just as concrete and specific. Mere slogans are completely meaningless. High ranking government spokesmen in public utterances are defining democracy in language that the simplest man can understand.

Meanwhile, the diseases in the body politic become much more acute in the minds of less privileged persons such as Negroes. As these diseases are exposed to the searching diagnosis of the meaning of democracy, the gulf between the dream as uttered and the idea as practiced is wide, abysmal, and deep. The measure of the frustration of Negroes is in direct proportion to the degree to which the meaning of democracy is made clear and definite. We behold then the spectacle of the Negro with a new civic character growing out of a new sense of civic and social responsibility, yet caught in the grip of a deeper frustration and restlessness than he has ever known.

In the third place, the fact that we were attacked by Japan has aggravated greatly the tension between the races. I am not suggesting that the war between Japan and the United States is a race war, but certainly many people have thought of it in terms of a non-white race "daring" to attack a white race. This has given excellent justification for the expression of the prejudices against non-white peoples just under the surface of the American consciousness. There has been a relaxation of the mutual regard and respect between the races in many walks of life where these previously existed. This has made for definite reactions on the part of Negroes, often reactions in kind with increasing bitterness, intolerance, hatred.

And in the fourth place, the attitudes described above have been met by an increasing determination and grimness on the part of white Americans. It seems perfectly clear to them that Negroes everywhere are getting out of their place. The argument runs like this: "Negroes do not know what to do with their new sense of significance. They are flippant, arrogant, bigoted, overbearing. Therefore, they must be curbed, held in check so that when the war is over they may drop quickly back into their prewar secondary citizen status." With this kind of situation facing the two groups in America, what can be done?

"The Will to Segregation"

The most fundamentally important thing that must be done is to relax the "will to segregation" that through the years has become the American technique for the control of the Negro minority. This "will to segregation" has taken the form of policy in business, in the church, in the state, in the school, in living zones. Let us examine this "will to segregate."

It is important to realize that segregation can exist only between peoples who are relatively weak and relatively strong, respectively. The strong may separate themselves in certain ways from the weak, but because the initiative remains in their hands they are ever at liberty to shuttle back and forth between the proscribed areas. The weak can only be segregated because, lacking the initiative, they cannot move at will between the proscribed areas. A simple case in point may be observed on any Southern train carrying day coaches. Members of the train crew, who are white, often sit in the section of the coach designated for Negroes. They may sit, by custom, in either section. The train porter, who is a Negro, may sit only in the Negro coach. White passengers move at will from one section to the other, but the passengers in the Jim Crow car sometimes experience difficulty even in passing through the other coaches en route to the diner. Waiters in the diner must always use the toilet facilities in the Jim Crow coach, while white members of the train crew may use either facilities.

The psychological effect of segregation on both groups is the critical issue. For segregation dramatizes a stigma, and becomes a badge of inferiority. A group segregated systematically over many generations experiences a decisive undermining of self-respect. For the sensitive, it means a constant, persistent resentment that is apt so to disease the personality that mental health is critically attacked. It is easy to say that the sensitive should resist segregation without including in their resistance the persons who are directly responsible for the laws and the social patterns that uphold them, but there are many who regard such a position as mere romanticism.

For the less sensitive there is ever the possibility of the acceptance of segregation, with its concomitant conscious admission of inferiority, of humiliation, of despair. Men who are despised, or who are treated systematically as if they were despised, are apt eventually to despise themselves. There is a sense in which society is a mirror through which individuals and groups see themselves reflected. It requires the veriest kind of vigilance and wide awareness to resist the temptation to accept the judgment of society upon one's group. Society sets the mode or the frame of reference that is apt to determine judgment. It is in an effort to overcome this that minority groups seem inclined to develop tendencies towards chauvinism, racism and other manifestations of the "cult of segregation."

More than all of this there is at least one great fear growing out of segregation: the fear of violence. The fear of physical violence is characteristic of most human beings and other animals, but among the segregated the fear takes on a heightened significance because they are so circumscribed by society that exposure to direct violence is ever present and there are no particular types of behavior that may guarantee immunity. The basic fact is that when human beings are segregated they provide a "tethered goat" on whose innocent and unsuspecting head vengeance may be poured for deeds infinitely removed from anything for which they may have responsibility. The ghetto and the Negro section are always present and into them may be dumped releases from frustration and from social and economic blunders, and revenge for private wrongs that originate in a world into which the victims are not even permitted to enter. To the extent to which this is true the mere fact of being active provides a specific liability over and above the normal fate of the average man!

This fear of violence is not traceable merely to the fear of death. To accommodate oneself to the fact of death is one of the basic elements in a normal adjustment of life. Everyone knows that for him death is inevitable; "one by one the duties end; one by one the lights go out." But the fear of violence is a part of the fear that man has of dying out of his bed; dying under circumstances that degrade and debase; dying like a dog in an alley, or a rat in a gutter. Death by accident, or as a result of some freakish act of nature has some of the elements of horror that are present here, but such deaths have in them something that is clean, unconscious, whole. But to be killed by other men without benefit of purpose or great cause is to die ignobly and in shame. The last thread of dignity and worthfulness is stripped from personality and death under such circumstances is sordid, nasty, ghoulish.

The result of this fear makes for a definite alteration in the behavior pattern. Very early the tendency is to make the body commit to memory the ways of behavior that may reduce the exposure to immediate violence. This explains in large part why there is so little organized resistance against segregation. Each new generation of children is psychologically and socially conditioned in an effort to reduce the exposure to spasmodic, irresponsible, systematic, and calculating sadistic impulses. The injury to personality is far greater than can be adequately grasped even by the most sensitive. To be denied freedom of movement, freedom of participation in the common life, is to have the ground of personality value seriously shaken. When in moments of national crises the segregated are granted temporary citizenship, one of the first acts is to attack segregation. This is a sound instinct of self-preservation and it provides the opening for all people of good will to give concrete expression to their commitments.

The effect of segregation on the part of the white group is just as deadly. It gives them a false sense of superiority. What is in essence a superiority of advantage becomes rationalized into superiority based upon logical, physical and spiritual difference. It is impossible for a white child to grow up in an atmosphere in which normal impulses of friendliness must be constantly short-circuited so as to apply to his own kind, without there dawning upon him that the fact of this difference in attitude is not due to a difference in superior essence. The mind becomes a seed-bed of all kinds of fears and superstitions with reference to Negroes, and if there is nothing in the environment at home or abroad to counteract these fears they become facts on the basis of which the life is planned and years are fulfilled. All emphasis on brotherhood or love inherent in the Christian religion is doomed to recognize these "fear facts" as extenuating circumstances in which love and brotherhood are not supposed to be effective!

There, unless the "will to segregate" is relaxed there can be no sound basis of hope for the fulfillment of the dream of democracy in this life of ours.

The Church's Task

For the church this means a radical internal reorganization of policy and of structural change. I am realistic enough to know that this cannot be done overnight. My contention is that if the "will to segregate" is relaxed in the church then the resources of mind and spirit and power that are already in the church can begin working formally and informally on the radical changes that are necessary if the church is to become Christian. This of course, may not mean that there will be no congregations that are all Negro, or that are all white, but freedom of choice, which is basically a sense of alternatives, will be available to any persons without regard to the faithful perpetuation of the pattern of segregation upon which the Christian church in America is constructed.

How dare we undertake to teach reverence to children when we ourselves do not believe in reverence for life in general or life in particular as a valid concept in our kind of world? Shall we teach lies to children? How dare we proclaim sincerity and genuineness as essential qualities for healthy living if in our innermost selves we do not have confidence in the survival values of such ideals of living? Can we teach trust when we are bound by a vast network of impersonal social relations which create the kind of climate in which trust cannot possibly thrive? Or can we teach trust even as we confess how little of trust we have in each other, in our cause and in our God? I wonder. What do we mean when we teach the brotherhood of man, when over and over again we give the sanction of our religion and the weight of our practice to those subtle anti-christian practices expressed in segregated churches and even in segregated graveyards! Can we expect more of the state, of the body politic, of industry than we expect of the church? How can we teach love from behind the great high walls of separateness?[1]

A MAN'S TASK

But more personally, what must a man do who wishes to work effectively on this problem within the framework of Christian ethics?

In the first place I must see to it that what I condemn in society, I do not permit to grow and flower in me. The will to discriminate against other men must be rooted out of the springs of my own action.

But even if my heart is pure, my motives above reproach and my personal action unequivocal and positive, this is not enough. I must share the guilt of my age, my society, and my race. Therefore, I must exhaust all possible means that do not conflict with my ends for bringing about the kind of society in which it is possible for men to love in large groups without external limitations, to experience the good life. This means that for my second action I must put my creative mind to work in the devising of techniques, personal and group, for the achievement of these ends.

High among these techniques are those that belong in the general classification of moral suasion, attempts to make individual and social conscience articulate with reference to a specific sin. Moral suasion has only one serious limitation: the amount of moral atrophy that has taken place in the mind and character of the persons who are to be aroused. I must be patient. I must keep working and persuading and appealing on the assumption, of course, that all men are the children of God—the good and the bad. This means that the Christian will brood over the hearts of men as the living instrument of the Spirit of God until there is a stirring of consciousness both of sin and of sonship in their hearts.

The third type of personal action is even more difficult because a conflict of loyalties makes the decision of positive Christian action in a given situation very difficult to determine. There may be a conflict between my loyalty to the ideal brotherhood viewed with reference to the weak, and my kinship with them. The strong are my brothers as truly as the weak are my brothers. I am apt to be caught between the recognition of fundamental kinship with the strong, and the desperation of the weak. Or the conflict may arise from a completely ethical demand of my religion that I wash my hands of the doers of iniquity and leave them to go on their recklessly destructive way, feeling that there are some types of struggle in which even God does not demand that I participate. I may say this type of action is not for me and to all the pull of the needy who are on the receiving end of the violence of the wicked I may turn a deaf ear if I can.

But I may decide that I cannot wait for the thing to work itself out. There is too much agony, too much hunger, too much poverty and misery everywhere, too many flagrant denials of kinship and brotherhood all along the line. Something concrete must be done now. To wait for moral pressure to work its perfect work may be too late.

What do I do then? I may resort to the exercises of some form of shock, by organizing a boycott, or widespread non-cooperation, or the like. The function of these techniques is to tear men free from their alignments to the evil way, to free them so that they may be given an immediate sense of acute insecurity and out of the depths of their insecurity be forced to see their kinship with the weak and the insecure. Men do not voluntarily relinquish their hold on their place. It is not until something becomes movable in the situation that men are spiritually prepared to apply Christian idealism to un-ideal and un-christian situations. Examples of these techniques are being developed by FOR groups and others in different parts of the world even now.

Action of this kind requires great discipline of mind, emotions and body to the end that forces may not be released that will do complete violence both to one's ideals and one's purpose. All must be done with the full consciousness of the Divine Scrutiny.

Fellowship, August 1943, 144–46.

1. The same paragraph appeared in "Our Underlying Spiritual Unities," published in this volume.

"RELIGION IN A TIME OF CRISIS"

1 AUGUST 1943

Set against the backdrop of a world at war, Thurman gave the commencement address at the Garrett Biblical Institute in Evanston, Illinois, on 7 July 1943. The address was published as "Religion in a Time of Crisis" the following month in the Garrett Tower. *In this piece Thurman wrestles with whether or not the selflessness and social unity demonstrated by individuals and nations in wartime can ever be duplicated in times of peace.*

Curious indeed is the fact that at a time of crisis men must be constantly reminded that the crisis does not mark the end of all things. It is of the nature of crisis so to dominate the horizon of men's thoughts that everything that is not directly related to the crisis situation seems irrelevant and without significance. At such times men seem to accept the contradictions of experience as being in themselves ultimate. The crisis throws everything out of proportion, out of balance and the balance seems always superficially to be on the side of disaster, on the side of negation. At such moments right is seen as being "on the scaffold" and wrong as being "on the throne"—the human spirit is apt to cry all men have bowed their knees "to Baal and I, I only am left."[1] If the contradictions of experience are ultimate, then the conflict between right and wrong, good and evil, order and chaos can never be resolved and human life is caught eternally in the agonizing grip of a grim and eternal struggle between these two forces. But such a dualism has never been able to satisfy the deepest searchings of the mind and the heart of man. The human spirit at long last is not willing to accept the contradiction of life as being ultimate. There continues ever a margin on the side of the good—yes, the ultimate destiny of man is good—this affirmation becomes the ground of optimism and inspiration in the bitterest crisis when the times are "out of joint," when men have lost their reason and sitting in the "sepulchers of gloom watch their dreams go silently to dust."[2] It is the peculiar task of the preacher to recognize this deep urge within man and to call it to bear witness at all times, but particularly at such a moment as is our own, now that the whole round world is rolling in darkness.

If the ultimate destiny of man is good then he must find *in the present* a way of life that is worth living—he must maintain a faith that can be honestly and intelligently held—he must work for the kind of world in which even the weakest may find refuge and refreshment—in which the smoking flax will not be quenched; nor the bruised reed crushed.

A Way of Life that is Worth Living

We are all of us in quest of a way of life that is worth living. We want to feel that we are engaged in a total enterprise that is meaningful. There must be a sense of something at stake in the day's experience. If this is not true for us then life grows dingy on our sleeve and days are but days and nights are but treacherous interludes before the monotonous round begins anew. It is for this reason that war, despite its terror, wreckage and stark tragedy, makes so great an appeal to men, women and even children. It is not because there is no memory of what war has cost the human race, it is not because men are deceived into thinking that war is a lark, a holiday—men know that war is a cruel, evil, nasty business. But when war comes, something is at last at stake in the day's living.

Witness our own land at this moment. It is only for war that we permit all the details of our lives to be shifted, thrown out of normal balance, readjusted. Something is at stake. The ordinary individual now counts in a strange new way. His country cares about what he does—all secondary and tertiary citizens become citizens, first class. It becomes critically important what everybody does. No one is exempt. Everybody and everything counts. Something is in the air—things are happening, the deadly monotony of ordinary living is blasted out of the doldrums. Something is at stake! A new kind of civic character appears sired by new and awful responsibilities. My country needs me—I fly to the rescue. It is one of the most tragic commentaries on modern life that only in times of war is there seen to be something at stake that is so vitally dependent upon even the common man.

It is your peculiar task as preachers, my young friends, to call attention again and again to the fact that something more than one's country is at stake everyday, every moment of every day. God is at stake. God is at stake in everything that every man does. There is a sharp and pointed urgency in the living of every day. Each man, be he high or low, rich or poor, learned or unlearned, sick or well, every man lives directly under the Divine Scrutiny. There is no escape from God.

He sees all I do
He hears all I say
My Lord's writing all the time.[3]

Stripped bare of all pretense, of all shadowy seemings, God sees man *minutely.* Before Him all motives are clear for what they are, purposes stand naked before His gaze—there is no desire of the heart or stirring of the mind that escapes Him.

This truth must be proclaimed, clearly and unequivocally so that even the most humble person will know that he must live each day in the consciousness of the awareness of the all-encompassing mind of God. What I do, what you do, then is important. How I live is never merely my business. This is the meaning of that ancient truth of religion that men are children of God. This truth remains before, during, and after the crisis and is the logical corollary of the affirmation that the ultimate destiny of man is good.

A Faith that Can Be Honestly and Intelligently Held

In the second place you must declare a faith that can be honestly and intelligently held. Every man must make each day an act of faith towards himself. He must do this again and again. It is important to observe that only on the rarest occasions does a man relax his hold upon himself. As a rule he clings to himself as his basis for moving meaningfully out upon the world. Despite all the things that I know about myself, I cling to myself. I am not as good as my mother or my daughter thinks I am; I am not as bad as some other persons think I am, yet I refuse to give myself up. I cling to myself with an abiding enthusiasm; again and again I make an act of faith toward myself.

This act of faith towards myself arises out of a deeper fount of values that sustains and guarantees me. It is but a manifestation of a profound grounding in God the source of life. Someone long ago whose name I no longer recall expressed it—the statement "know thyself" has been taken more mystically from the statement, "thou hast seen thy brother, thou has seen thy God."[4]

I must make also an act of faith towards my fellowmen even though my fellowmen may be at the moment my national enemy. So much that is not good has flown from me towards my fellowmen that I have learned to look with compassion on much that flows from my fellowman to me. As preachers we must declare this truth. Religion insists upon this as the only antidote against developing a great hatred of men, particularly at a time of war. We must see clearly the function of teaching hate of fellowmen at such a time.

Hate is a powerful force. For weak people who are trapped and encircled by an enemy who has at his completest disposal all the powers of destruction it is easy to turn to hate as the last spasmodic convulsion of the human spirit before it goes down to destruction. I know from the inside the meaning of that. But for the strong, for the powerful, hate serves still another purpose. It becomes the cloak of moral justification for the doing of deeds which under normal circumstances would leave the individual or nation covered with shame and inner spiritual confusion. During times of war we teach men to hate the enemy because if we did not do this, it would be impossible for self-respecting persons to do the things to the enemy that the exigencies of war require. Let us not be mistaken. We must declare the truth that God requires of men that they make again and again an act of faith towards their fellowmen, towards all their fellowmen—black, white, brown, yellow—*all* their fellowmen. If this is not done, any discussion even of love is an empty echo among the barren hills of a desolate experience. Under such circumstances prayer for the kingdom of God is addressed to an empty sky and a deserted heaven.

A Social Order in Which Even the Weakest May Find Refuge and Refreshment

If men are to find a way of life that is worth living and make an act of faith towards themselves and their fellowmen, then it follows that they must work for a society in which the smoking flax will not be quenched, nor the bruised reed crushed.

Long ago it was Eugene Debs who said:

While there is a lower class I am in it
While there is a criminal element I am of it
While there is a man in jail I am not free.[5]

For better or for worse we are tied together in the world. I can never be what I ought to be until you are what you ought to be. The present global war is a tragic illustration of the modern version of this truth. Some years ago there was an invasion of Manchukuo[6]—some months later Mussolini, drunk with the dream of Empire, moved into Ethiopia—then Hitler, began swimming across Europe in seas of blood tying laurels on his brow with other people's lives and other people's heart strings—and now the whole round world is one battle ground where "ignorant armies clash by night."[7] We are all children of God and our destiny is a common destiny—and no one of us can go his way alone.

It matters not how far before him the turtle extends his two front feet: he cannot move his body until he brings up his hind legs. Into one of the larger welfare agencies in an Eastern city a man came to make formal request for an increase in his allowance. The justification was very simple—because of rapidly failing eyesight he could no longer see how to select the most edible portions from certain garbage pails out of which he had been securing his food for some time.Persons with better eyesight were eliminating him from competition. He needed more funds so as to purchase his food in the open market. This in the year 1942.

One important lesson at least we are learning from the records of the Selective Service Boards. Illiteracy and disease are the double scourge of our man power. It is Illinois' business that schools are poor in Mississippi, or that economic conditions are so wretched for the masses of the people that often simple precautions as to health and diet are not possible. If men cannot vote in Georgia the voters in every other state in the Union are threatened with disenfranchisement. We are one. If India cannot be given her freedom under the Atlantic Charter,[8] then freedom of men everywhere can be throttled and side-stepped if the time is not ripe or has become over-ripe.

Rufus Jones told me in a conversation that the one thing he wanted to do when the war was over was to send 3 million biddies[9] to Europe by airplane so as to provide chickens for those who must build their countryside anew.

We must proclaim the truth that all life is one and that we are all of us tied together. Therefore it is mandatory that we work for a society in which the least person can find refuge and refreshment. This even on behalf of our own fulfillment.

As prophets and priests of the most High God it is your divine assignment to announce that man lives his days under the persistent scrutiny of God—that God is at stake in man's day. How men treat each other, what they do to the environment in which little children must grow and develop, how they earn their living—all things in the making of which they play a significant part stand bare before the eyes of God. You must live and proclaim a faith that will make men affirm themselves and their fellowmen as children of God. You must lay your lives on the altar of social change so that wherever you are there the Kingdom of God is at hand!

Garrett Tower, August 1943, 1–3.

1. This is a loose paraphrase of 1 Kings 19:9–18. In this Old Testament story, Elijah exclaims to Yahweh that his fellow Israelites have abandoned the covenant and torn down the altar. "I am the only one left and now they want to kill me," Elijah declares. Yahweh tells Elijah to anoint Jehu king of Israel and to instruct the new leader to kill the worshipers of the idol Baal but to spare "all the knees that have not bent before Baal, all the mouths that have not kissed him."

2. From "Fraternity," in *Fugitive Papers of Russell Gordon Smith* (New York: Columbia University Press, 1930), 118.

3. From the Negro spiritual "My Lord's Writing All the Time."

4. Thurman is quoting Clement of Alexandria, a second century CE church father (ca 150–215), from his *Stromata* (Book II, Chapter XV), in the mid–nineteenth century translation of William Wilson, in Alexander Robert and James Donaldson, eds., *Ante-Nicene Christian Library* vol XII (Edinburgh: T & T Clark, 1860), 43.

5. In November 1931 Japan invaded the Manchurian city of Shenyang on Chinese soil. Within five months the Japanese had created out of the three historic Manchurian provinces a puppet state called Manchuko, which they occupied until 1945, when the long-contested area was conquered by the Soviet Union.

6. From the last stanza of Victorian poet Matthew Arnold's "Dover Beach" (1867).

7. British prime minister Winston Churchill and U.S. president Franklin D. Roosevelt issued the Atlantic Charter on 14 August 1941. It declared the two leaders' commitment to

territorial sovereignty and self-determination and to the principles of economic security and fair labor standards for all nations.

8. Biddies are chickens.

To Herrick B. Young

12 August 1943
Washington, D.C.

While Thurman was a supporter of historically black educational institutions, he speaks firmly here against the continued segregation of black students at Lincoln and Johnson C. Smith seminaries.[1]

Dear Dr. Young:[2]

You will please pardon my long delay in replying to your letter under date of July 20th.[3] Today is the first time since I have been back from the coast that I have been able to give the kind of thoughtful consideration to your letter that it demands.

With reference to the problem which you raised, I am making the following suggestions:

(1) I am opposed on general principle, and because of specific considerations which I need not outline, to any move that deepens the pattern of segregation in American life in general and in religious life in particular. I am convinced that segregation, whatever may be its apparent justification, is both, immoral and un-Christian. It is clear then to me that if the Presbyterian Church were to merge Johnson C. Smith and Lincoln Seminaries and locate them in a new place, making for a new Theological Seminary for Negroes, it would deepen the pattern of segregation in the church. I am unqualifiedly opposed to this.

(2) It is entirely possible, however that merging the two schools on one or the other of the campuses would mean in a sense perpetuating the work that is now being done. This would be a compromise but would not mean widening the pattern of segregation. If this were done then, it is my considered judgment that Lincoln is the place to do it rather than Johnson C. Smith. The reasons are simple: (1) Such a faculty could be interracial without having to deal with the social pattern of the South particularly or with state statutes; (2) The student body could be interracial thereby making of the seminary institution at Lincoln the Presbyterian Church's national experiment in genuine Christian education; (3) The location of Lincoln is ideal for the training of prophets because it combines isolation with proximity to large urban centers of Negro populations.

There is another suggestion that occurs to me to the effect that if the two schools for Negroes were closed and the funds used to assure an interracial faculty and an interracial student body in at least two of the predominately white seminaries of the Presbyterian Church a whole new dimension would obtain in the task of redeeming American life from the tragedy of racial friction and prejudice.

I shall not say more in reply to your letter, but covet the opportunity to confer with you on the whole problem in the fall sometime when I am in New York, or when you are in Washington.

Sincerely yours,
[*signed*] Howard Thurman
Dean of the Chapel
Dr. Herrick B. Young, Secretary
The Board of Foreign Missions of the Presbyterian Church
156 Fifth Avenue
New York, New York

TLS. HTC-MBU: Box 22.

1. The Biddle Memorial Institute in Charlotte, NC in 1867 was renamed the Johnson C. Smith Institute in 1923. It became an independent college affiliated with the Presbyterian Church of America in 1938. In 1969, it moved to Atlanta and became the Presbyterian component of the Interdenominational Theological Center (ITC). Lincoln University in Pennsylvania was founded as the Ashman Institute in 1854 and renamed Lincoln University in 1866. It closed its seminary in 1959. In 1943, the Lincoln seminary had sixteen students and the Johnson C. Smith seminary had seventeen.

2. Herrick B. Young (1904–1990) was the executive secretary of the Presbyterian Board of Foreign Missions from 1936–1950. Previously, he was a professor of English and Literature at Alborz College in Tehran, Iran. Young earned his A.B. degree in English from Indiana University in 1925, his M.S. in Indo-Iranian Studies from Columbia University in 1928 and a Ph.D. in Education Administration from the University of Pennsylvania in 1936.

3. From Herrick B. Young, 20 July 1943, HTC-MBU

Index

Page references in **bold** refer to photographs; page references in *italics* refer to biographical information contained in the notes.

www.ingramcontent.com/pod-product-compliance
Lightning Source LLC
Chambersburg PA
CBHW060817310726
48980CB00002B/321

* 9 7 8 1 6 1 1 1 7 0 4 3 6 *